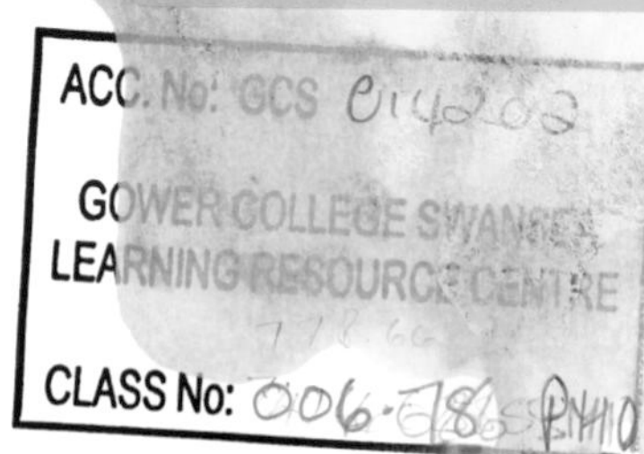

Adobe® Photoshop® CS5 **Digital Classroom**

Jennifer Smith and AGI Creative Team

Wiley Publishing, Inc.

Adobe Photoshop® CS5 Digital Classroom

Published by
Wiley Publishing, Inc.
10475 Crosspoint Boulevard
Indianapolis, IN 46256

Published by Wiley Publishing, Inc., Indianapolis, Indiana
Published simultaneously in Canada
ISBN: 978-0-470-60777-0
Manufactured in the United States of America
10987654321

For general information on our other products and services or to obtain technical support, please contact our Customer Care Department within the U.S. at (800) 762-2974, outside the U.S. at (317) 572-3993 or fax (317) 572-4002.

Please report any errors by sending a message to errata@agitraining.com

Library of Congress Control Number: 2010921240

Adobe® Photoshop® CS5 Digital Classroom

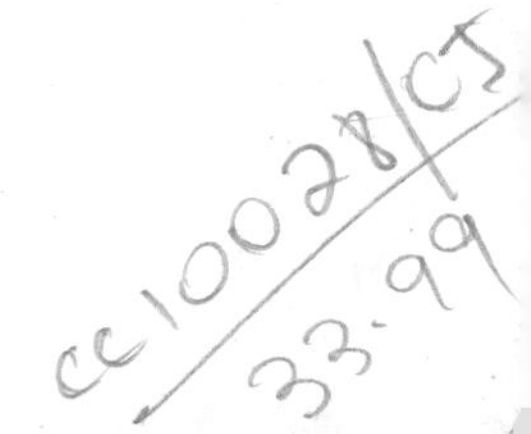

About the Authors

Jennifer Smith has more than two decades of design and electronic publishing experience. Jennifer delivers professional development education for companies around the world relating to effective ways to use creative technology to achieve design and user experience objectives. She is a founding member of American Graphics Institute (AGI) and serves as Vice President of AGI. Prior to founding AGI she worked in advertising as an art director and served as a principal in a Pennsylvania-based design firm. Jennifer is widely regarded as one of the foremost authorities in electronic publishing and design and is often requested as a speaker at seminars and conferences around the world. Jennifer is the author of more than ten books on electronic publishing, including ***Adobe Creative Suite 5 Design Premium for Dummies***, published by Wiley. She has also written several of the ***Classroom in a Book*** series for Adobe Press. Jennifer bridges the gap between technical and creative, working easily with both developers and designers. Her ability to translate technical skills to address business issues allows organizations to reach their objectives with effective design and creativity. She uses technology to achieve design objectives for use on-line or in print. A renaissance artist with technology, you'll find Jennifer integrating her Photoshop work in interactive projects using Flash or Silverlight, and finessing her creations using her skills with coding, creating 3-D renderings for product designers, or working with graphics professionals to achieve the highest quality and most accurate color.

AGI Creative Team is composed of Adobe Certified Experts and Adobe Certified Instructors from American Graphics Institute (AGI). The AGI Creative Team has authored many of Adobe's official training guides, and works with many of the world's most prominent companies, helping them to use creative software to communicate more effectively and creatively. They work with marketing, creative, and communications teams around the world, and teach regularly scheduled classes at AGI's locations. More information at ***agitraining.com***.

Acknowledgments

Thanks to our many friends at Adobe Systems, Inc. who made this book possible and assisted with questions and feedback during the writing process. To the many clients of AGI who have helped us better understand how they use Photoshop and provided us with many of the tips and suggestions found in this book. A special thanks to the instructional team at AGI for their input and assistance in the review process and for making this book such a team effort.

Thanks to iStockPhoto (***iStockPhoto.com***) for their permission to use exclusive photographers for images throughout the Adobe Photoshop CS5 Digital Classroom book.

Credits

Additional Writing
Jeremy Osborn, Christopher Smith

Series Editor
Christopher Smith

Executive Editor
Jody Lefevere

Technical Editors
Barbara Holbrook, Haziel Olivera

Editor
Marylouise Wiack

Editorial Director
Robyn Siesky

Business Manager
Amy Knies

Senior Marketing Manager
Sandy Smith

Vice President and Executive Group Publisher
Richard Swadley

Vice President and Executive Publisher
Barry Pruett

Senior Project Coordinator
Lynsey Stanford

Graphics and Production Specialist
Lauren Mickol

Media Development Project Supervisor
Jeremy Osborn

Proofreading
Jay Donahue

Indexing
Broccoli Information Management

Stock Photography
iStockPhoto.com

Contents

Starting Up

Lesson 1: Exploring Photoshop

Lesson 2:Getting to Know the Workspace

Lesson 3: Using Adobe Bridge

Lesson 4: The Basics of Working with Photoshop

Lesson 5: Making the Best Selections

Lesson 6: Painting and Retouching

Lesson 7: Creating a Good Image

Lesson 8: Getting to Know Layers

Lesson 9: Taking Layers to the Max

Lesson 10: Getting Smart in Photoshop

Lesson 11: Using Adobe Photoshop Filters

Lesson 12: Creating Images for Web and Video

Starting up

About Photoshop Digital Classroom

Adobe® Photoshop® CS5 is the industry's leading digital image editing software. It is the perfect creative tool for designing and manipulating images for print layouts, web publishing, multimedia, video, photography, and for visually expressing your creative ideas.

The *Adobe Photoshop CS5 Digital Classroom* helps you to understand the capabilities of Photoshop and get the most out of your software so you can get up-and-running right away. You can work through all the lessons in this book, or complete only specific lessons. Each lesson includes detailed, step-by-step instructions, along with lesson files, useful background information, and video tutorials.

Adobe Photoshop CS5 Digital Classroom is like having your own expert instructor guiding you through each lesson while you work at your own pace. This book includes 14 self-paced lessons that let you discover essential skills, explore new features, and understand capabilities that will save you time. You'll be productive right away with real-world exercises and simple explanations. Each lesson includes step-by-step instructions, lesson files, and video tutorials, all of which are available on the included DVD. The *Adobe Photoshop CS5 Digital Classroom* lessons are developed by the same team of Adobe Certified Instructors and Photoshop experts that have created many of the official training titles for Adobe Systems.

Prerequisites

Before you start the *Adobe Photoshop CS5 Digital Classroom* lessons, you should have a working knowledge of your computer and its operating system. You should know how to use the directory system of your computer so that you can navigate through folders. You also need to understand how to locate, save, and open files, and you should also know how to use your mouse to access menus and commands.

Before starting the lessons files in the *Adobe Photoshop CS5 Digital Classroom*, make sure that you have installed Adobe Photoshop CS5. The software is sold separately, and not included with this book. You may use the free 30-day trial version of Adobe Photoshop CS5 available at the *Adobe.com* web site, subject to the terms of its license agreement.

Adobe Photoshop CS5 versions

Photoshop CS5 comes in two versions: Adobe Photoshop CS5 and Adobe Photoshop CS5 Extended. The Extended version offers everything you find in Photoshop CS5, along with additional tools for editing video, motion-graphics, 3-D content, and performing image analysis. This book covers both versions of Photoshop CS5. Where appropriate, we have noted any features that are available only in the Extended version. Adobe Photoshop CS5 is used to refer to both versions of the software throughout the book.

System requirements

Before starting the lessons in the *Adobe Photoshop CS5 Digital Classroom*, make sure that your computer is equipped for running Adobe Photoshop CS5, which you must purchase separately. The minimum system requirements for your computer to effectively use the software are listed below.

Windows OS

- 1.8GHz or faster processor
- System: Microsoft® Windows® XP with Service Pack 2 (Service Pack 3 recommended) or Windows Vista® Home Premium, Business, Ultimate, or Enterprise with Service Pack 1 (certified for 32-bit Windows XP and 32-bit and 64-bit Windows Vista)
- RAM: 512MB of RAM (1GB recommended)
- Hard-disk: 1GB of available hard-disk space for installation; additional free space required during installation (cannot install on flash-based storage devices)
- Monitor: 1,024×768 display (1,280×800 recommended) with 16-bit video card
- Some GPU-accelerated features require graphics support for Shader Model 3.0 and OpenGL 2.0
- DVD-ROM drive: DVD-ROM Drive required
- Broadband Internet connection required for online services
- Browser: IE 6.0, Netscape 4.x, 6.1, 6.2 or 7.0, AOL 6.0 or 7.0, Opera 8.0+, Firefox 1.0.5+
- Multimedia: QuickTime 7.2 software required for multimedia features

Macintosh OS

- Processor: PowerPC® G5 or multicore Intel® processor
- System: Mac OS X v10.4.11–10.5.4
- RAM: 512MB of RAM (1GB recommended)
- Hard-disk: 2GB of available hard-disk space for installation; additional free space required during installation (cannot install on a volume that uses a case-sensitive file system or on flash-based storage devices)
- Monitor: 1,024×768 display (1,280×800 recommended) with 16-bit video card
- Some GPU-accelerated features require graphics support for Shader Model 3.0 and OpenGL 2.0
- DVD-ROM drive: DVD-ROM Drive required
- Broadband Internet connection required for online services
- Browser: IE 5.5+, Netscape 8.0+, AOL 5.0+, Safari 1.0+, Opera 8.0+, Firefox 1.0.5+
- Multimedia: QuickTime 7.2 software required for multimedia features

Starting Adobe Photoshop CS5

As with most software, Adobe Photoshop CS5 is launched by locating the application in your Programs folder (Windows) or Applications folder (Mac OS). If you are not familiar with starting the program, follow these steps to start the Adobe Photoshop CS5 application:

Windows

1 Choose Start > All Programs > Adobe Photoshop CS5. If you have a Creative Suite installed, you will navigate to that folder to locate the Photoshop CS5 folder.

2 Close the Welcome Screen when it appears.

Mac OS

1 Open the Applications folder, and then open the Adobe Photoshop CS5 folder. If you have a Creative Suite installed, you will open that folder to locate the Photoshop CS5 folder.

2 Double-click on the Adobe Photoshop CS5 application icon.

3 Close the Welcome Screen when it appears.

Menus and commands are identified throughout the book by using the greater-than symbol (>). For example, the command to print a document is identified as File > Print.

Resetting Adobe Photoshop CS5 preferences

When you start Adobe Photoshop, it remembers certain settings along with the configuration of the workspace from the last time you used the application. It is important that you start each lesson using the default settings so that you do not see unexpected results when working with the lessons in this book.

As you reset your preferences to the default settings, you may wish to keep your color settings. This is important if you have created specific color settings, or work in a color-calibrated environment.

Use the following steps to reset your Adobe Photoshop CS5 preferences and save your color settings. If you are confident that you do not need to save your color settings, you can skip to the section, "Resetting Adobe Photoshop CS5 preferences."

Saving Adobe Photoshop CS5 color settings

1 Launch Adobe Photoshop.

2 Choose Edit > Color Settings, and then press the Save button. The Save dialog box opens. Enter an appropriate name for your color settings, such as the date. Leave the destination and format unchanged, then press the Save button. The Color Settings Comment dialog box opens.

3 In the Color Settings Comment dialog box, enter a description for the color settings you are saving, then press OK. Press OK again in the Color Settings dialog box to close it. You have saved your color settings so they can be accessed again in the future.

4 Choose File > Quit, to exit Adobe Photoshop CS5.

Steps to reset Adobe Photoshop CS5 preferences

Press and hold the Ctrl+Alt+Shift keys (Windows) or Command+Option+Shift keys (Mac OS) simultaneously before launching Adobe Photoshop CS5. A dialog box appears verifying that you want to delete the Adobe Photoshop settings file. Release the keys, then press OK.

Restoring previous Adobe Photoshop CS5 color settings

1 Start Adobe Photoshop CS5. Choose Edit > Color Settings. The Color Settings dialog box appears.

2 From the Settings drop-down menu, choose your saved color settings file. Press OK. Your color settings are restored.

A note about color warnings

Depending upon how your Color Settings are configured, there may be times when you will receive a Missing Profile or Embedded Profile Mismatch warning. Understand that if you reset your preferences before each lesson (without restoring your color settings) you should not see these color warnings. This is because the default color setting of North America General Purpose 2 has all warning check boxes unchecked.

If you do receive Missing Profile and Embedded Profile Mismatch warnings, choose the Assign working option, or Convert document's colors to the working space. What is determined to be your working space is what you have assigned in the Color Settings dialog box. Color Settings are discussed in more detail in Lesson 6, "Painting and Retouching" and in Lesson 7, "Creating a Good Image."

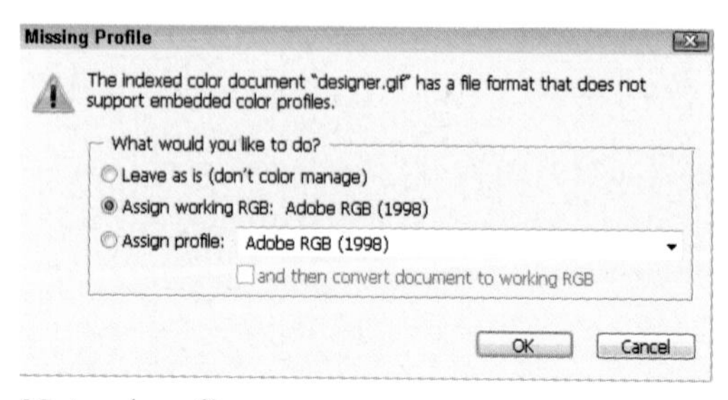

Missing color profile.

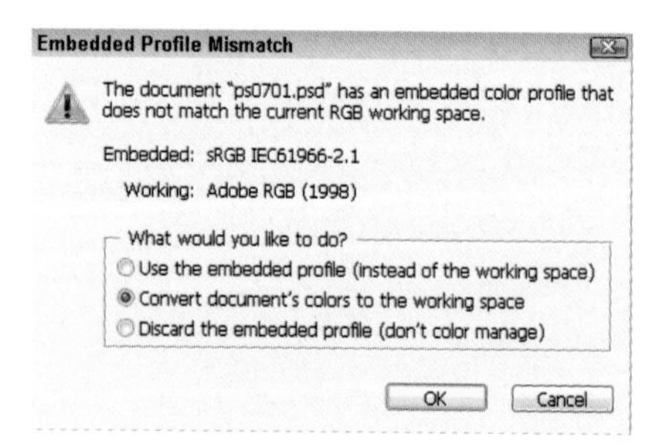

Mismatched color profile.

Loading lesson files

The *Photoshop CS5 Digital Classroom* DVD includes files that accompany the exercises for each of the lessons. You may copy the entire lessons folder from the supplied DVD to your hard drive, or copy only the lesson folders for the individual lessons you wish to complete.

For each lesson in the book, the files are referenced by the file name of each file. The exact location of each file on your computer is not used, as you may have placed the files in a unique location on your hard drive. We suggest placing the lesson files in the My Documents folder (Windows) or at the top level of your hard drive (Mac OS).

Copying the lesson files to your hard drive:

1 Insert the *Photoshop CS5 Digital Classroom* DVD supplied with this book.

2 On your computer desktop, navigate to the DVD and locate the folder named pslessons.

3 You can install all the files, or just specific lesson files. Do one of the following:

- Install all lesson files by dragging the pslessons folder to your hard drive.
- Install only some of the files by creating a new folder on your hard drive named pslessons. Open the pslessons folder on the supplied DVD, select the lesson you wish to complete, and drag the folder(s) to the pslessons folder you created on your hard drive.

Unlocking Mac OS files

Macintosh users may need to unlock the files after they are copied from the accompanying disc. This only applies to Mac OS computers and is because the Mac OS may view files that are copied from a DVD or CD as being locked for writing.

If you are a Mac OS user and have difficulty saving over the existing files in this book, you can use these instructions so that you can update the lesson files as you work on them and also add new files to the lessons folder

Note that you only need to follow these instructions if you are unable to save over the existing lesson files, or if you are unable to save files into the lesson folder.

1 After copying the files to your computer, click once to select the pslessons folder, then choose File > Get Info from within the Finder (not Photoshop).

2 In the pslessons info window, click the triangle to the left of Sharing and Permissions to reveal the details of this section.

3 In the Sharing and Permissions section, click the lock icon, if necessary, in the lower right corner so that you can make changes to the permissions.

4 Click to select a specific user or select everyone, then change the Privileges section to Read & Write.

5 Click the lock icon to prevent further changes, and then close the window.

Working with the video tutorials

Your *Photoshop CS5 Digital Classroom* DVD comes with video tutorials developed by the authors to help you understand the concepts explored in each lesson. Each tutorial is approximately five minutes long and demonstrates and explains the concepts and features covered in the lesson.

The videos are designed to supplement your understanding of the material in the chapter. We have selected exercises and examples that we feel will be most useful to you. You may want to view the entire video for each lesson before you begin that lesson. Additionally, at certain points in a lesson, you will encounter the DVD icon. The icon, with appropriate lesson number, indicates that an overview of the exercise being described can be found in the accompanying video.

DVD video icon.

Setting up for viewing the video tutorials

The DVD included with this book includes video tutorials for each lesson. Although you can view the lessons on your computer directly from the DVD, we recommend copying the folder labeled *Videos* from the *Photoshop CS5 Digital Classroom* DVD to your hard drive.

Copying the video tutorials to your hard drive:

1 Insert the *Photoshop CS5 Digital Classroom* DVD supplied with this book.

2 On your computer desktop, navigate to the DVD and locate the folder named Videos.

3 Drag the Videos folder to a location onto your hard drive.

Viewing the video tutorials with the Adobe Flash Player

The videos on the *Photoshop CS5 Digital Classroom* DVD are saved in the Flash projector format. A Flash projector file wraps the Digital Classroom video player and the Adobe Flash Player in an executable file (.exe for Windows or .app for Mac OS). However, please note that the extension (on both platforms) may not always be visible. Projector files allow the Flash content to be deployed on your system without the need for a browser or prior standalone player installation.

Playing the video tutorials:

1 On your computer, navigate to the Videos folder you copied to your hard drive from the DVD. Playing the videos directly from the DVD may result in poor quality playback.

2 Open the Videos folder and double-click the PSvideos_PC.exe (Windows) or PSvideos_Mac.app (Mac OS) to view the video tutorial.

3 Press the Play button to view the videos.

The Flash Player has a simple user interface that allows you to control the viewing experience, including stopping, pausing, playing, and restarting the video. You can also rewind or fast-forward, and adjust the playback volume.

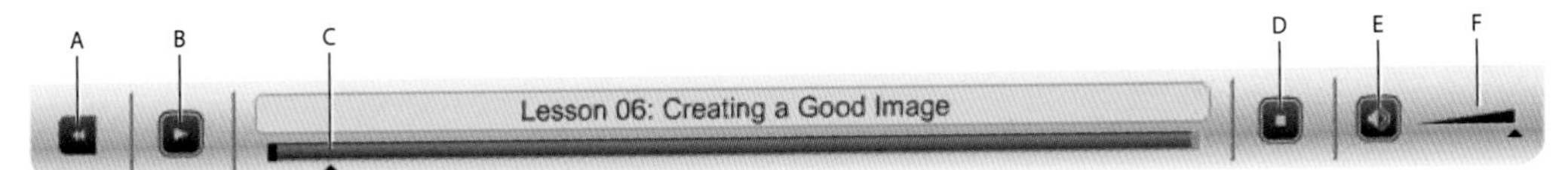

***A**. Go to beginning. **B**. Play/Pause. **C**. Fast-forward/rewind. **D**. Stop. **E**. Volume Off/On. **F**. Volume control.*

Playback volume is also affected by the settings in your operating system. Be certain to adjust the sound volume for your computer, in addition to the sound controls in the Player window.

Additional resources

The Digital Classroom series goes beyond the training books.You can continue your learning online, with training videos, at seminars and conferences, and in-person training events.

Book series

Expand your knowledge of creative software applications with the Digital Classroom training series. Learn more at *digitalclassroombooks.com*.

Seminars and conferences

The authors of the Digital Classroom seminar series frequently conduct in-person seminars and speak at conferences, including the annual CRE8 Conference. Learn more at *agitraining.com* and *CRE8summit.com*.

Resources for educators

Visit *digitalclassroombooks.com* to access resources for educators, including instructors' guides for incorporating Digital Classroom into your curriculum.

Lesson 1

What you'll learn in this lesson:

- How to work with multiple documents
- Creating a simple composition
- Masking features
- Introduction to the Puppet Warp feature

Exploring Photoshop

In this lesson, you are offered the opportunity to dive right into Adobe Photoshop CS5 and put together an exciting composition. This lesson was created to help current users (or fast learners) quickly discover some of the hottest new features in Photoshop CS5.

Starting up

Before starting, make sure that your tools and panels are consistent by resetting your preferences. See "Resetting Adobe Photoshop CS5 preferences" on page 3.

Note that users of all levels can follow this step-by-step exercise, but if you are a new user, it is recommended that you start with Lesson 2, "Getting to Know the Workspace," and return to this lesson when you have completed the remaining lessons.

You will work with several files from the ps01lessons folder in this lesson. Make sure that you have loaded the pslessons folder onto your hard drive from the supplied DVD. See "Loading lesson files" on page 5. Now, let's take a look at what's new in Photoshop CS5.

See Lesson 1 in action!

Use the accompanying video to gain a better understanding of how to use some of the features shown in this lesson. The video tutorial for this lesson can be found on the included DVD.

Taking a look at the final project

In this lesson, you'll create photocomposition that will come from several different sources, allowing you to use some of the new tools and features available in Adobe Photoshop CS5.

1 Choose File > Browse in Bridge, or click on the Launch Bridge (Br) in the Application bar. You will be using Adobe Bridge to locate your images for this lesson, but it can also help you to search for, organize, and manage your documents. Refer to Lesson 3, "Using Adobe Bridge," to find out more about Adobe Bridge.

2. In Bridge choose Window > Workspace > Essentials to see the entire workspace.

   If you are unfamiliar with Adobe Bridge, simply click on the Folders tab in the upper-left corner of the workspace to navigate from one folder to another. If you saved your lesson files on the desktop, use the slider and click on Desktop; all the folders on your desktop appear in the Content panel.

3 Navigate to the ps01lessons folder and double-click to open the file named ps0101_done.psd. An image of a wakeboarder appears. If you receive a warning dialog box about your video card, click OK.

The completed panoramic image.

In addition to some standard Photoshop features, some *need-to-know* new features have been integrated into this lesson, including some improved selection features and content-aware retouching.

4 Now that you have seen the final image, choose File > Close. If a Warning dialog box appears, click No (Windows) or Don't Save (Mac OS).

Creating a panorama from three images

In this part of the exercise, you will merge three images together into one using the Auto-Align feature in Photoshop.

1 Choose File > Browse in Bridge, or click on the Launch Bridge (Br) in the Application bar. Using the Favorites tab in the upper-right of the Bridge workspace, choose Desktop and locate the ps01lessons that you copied from your DVD to the Desktop.

2 Open the ps01lessons folder and double-click to open the ps0101.psd file. An image of an ocean appears.

3 Choose File > Save As, to open the Save As dialog box. Using the Save In drop-down menu, navigate to the ps01lessons folder. Type **ps0101_work** in the File Name text field and choose Photoshop from the Format drop-down menu. Then click Save. If the Photoshop Format Options dialog box appears, press OK.

   This ocean image file contains three layers that were shot separately, and then copied and pasted into one image. In the next part of this lesson, you will align these into one large panoramic image.

4 If your Layers panel is not visible choose Window > Layers to locate it now. You see the three layers; Layer 0, Layer 1, and Layer 2.

5 Select Layer 0 by clicking on it in the Layers panel, then hold down the Shift key and click on Layer 2. This selects all three of the layers.

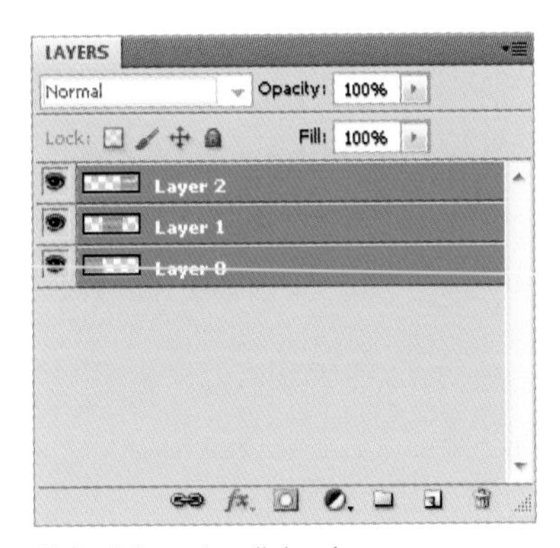

Shift+click to select all three layers.

6 Select your Move tool () and click on the Auto-Align layers button () on the Move tool Options bar. The Auto Align dialog box appears.

7 Select Auto and press OK. The images are automatically aligned into a panoramic image.

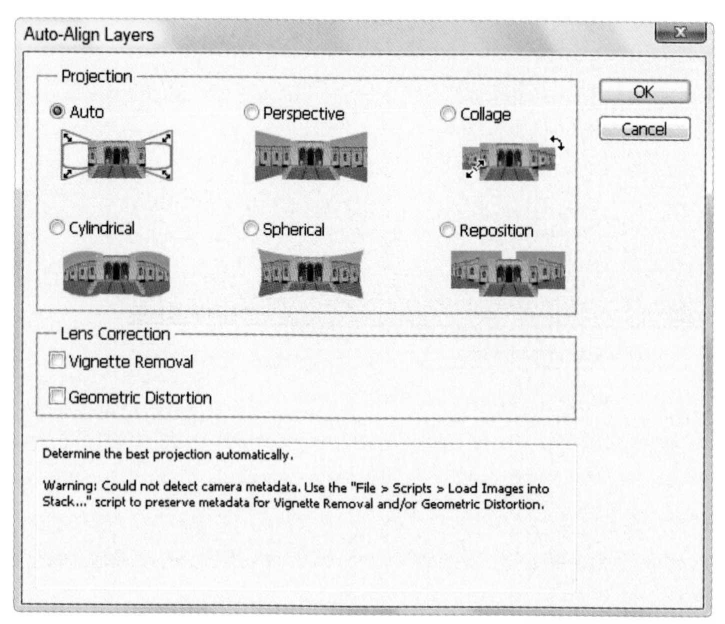

Use the Auto-Align feature to merge images together.

5 Choose File > Save, or use the keyboard shortcut Ctrl+S (Windows) or Command+A (Mac OS) to save the file. Keep it open so that you can crop it in the next part of this lesson.

Cropping your image

A fundamental task to creating a successful composition is having the ability to crop an image. In this part of the exercise, you will crop the image to even out the edges where the panoramic image doesn't perfectly fit.

1 Before you start it will be helpful to see the entire image. A helpful keyboard shortcut to know is Ctrl+0 (zero) (Windows) or Command+0 (zero) (Mac OS). You can also use the menu item View > Fit on screen. This allows you to see the entire image.

2 With the ps0101_work images still open, select the Crop tool (⌗) from the Tools panel. Click and drag from the upper-left corner to the lower-right corner. A crop preview area appears.

3 Choose View > Snap so that the Snap feature in Photoshop is deactivated. This makes it easier for you to control resize your crop area.

4 Using the handles on the corners, click and drag to reposition the crop area so that the transparent edges are eliminated.

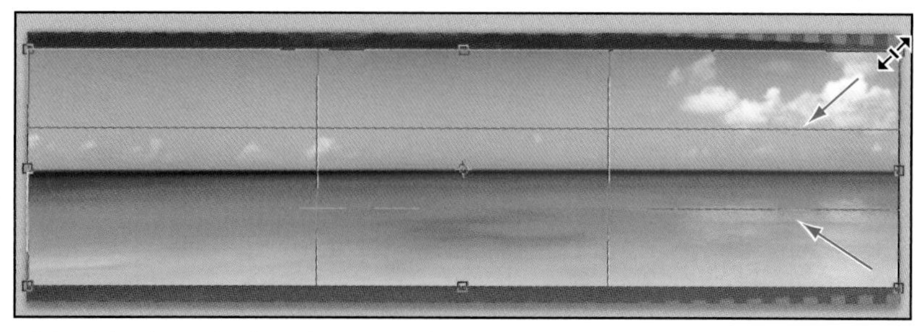

Click and drag the crop handles to determine the final crop area.

5 When you have the crop area positioned correctly, click on the Commit checkmark button (✓) in the far right of the Options bar, or press the Enter (Windows) or Return (Mac OS) key.

If you make a mistake and need to release the crop tool and start over, press the Esc key in the upper-left of your keyboard.

6 From the Layers panel menu (▾≡), choose Flatten image to combine the three layers into one.

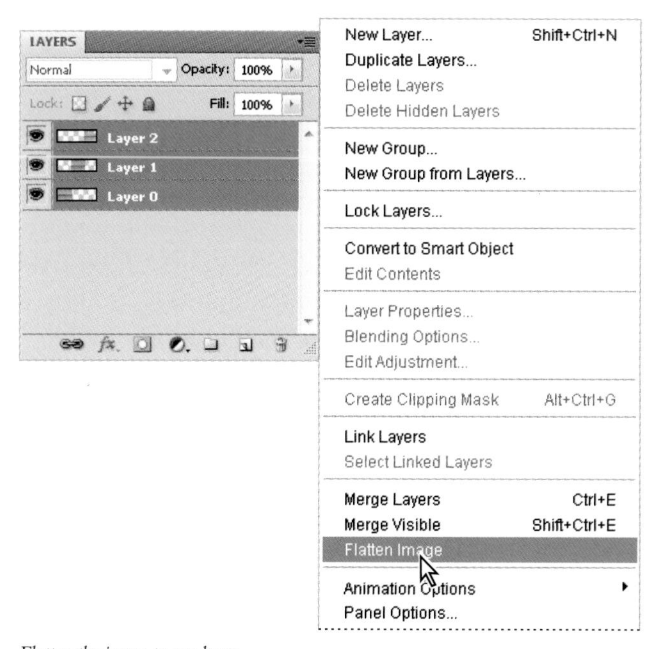

Flatten the image to one layer.

Adding a selection to your image

In this next section, you will move an image from one file into another. You will then take advantage of the new and improved selection features to create a mask.

1 Choose File > Browse in Bridge, and double-click on the image named ps0102.psd that is located inside the ps01lessons folder. An image of a surfer running on the beach appears.

   You now have two images open. In the default setting, multiple images appear as tabs across the top of the Photoshop work area. Because it is important to see both images at the same time, you will choose to tile your images.

2 Choose 2 Up from the Arrange Documents button (■) in the Application bar at the top of the Photoshop workspace. The images now appear side-by-side.

3 Select your Move tool (▸+) and click on the beach image and drag it on top of the panoramic image. Release your mouse when you see the cursor with the plus sign (↖⊞), or a border appear around the panoramic image. You have just added the beach image as a layer in your panoramic image.

Click and drag one image into the other.

4 Click on the tab for the ps0102.psd image and then choose File > Close. If you are asked to save changes, choose No (Windows) or Don't Save (Mac OS).

5 Using the Move tool, click and drag the newly added layer to align the water line in both of the images. A perfect match is not necessary.

Click and drag the beach layer to align the water lines.

6 Choose File > Save. Keep the file open for the next part of the lesson.

Fading one image into another

In this part of the lesson, you will create a layer mask to allow you to blend the beach image into the large panoramic image.

1 If your Layers panel is a not open, choose Window > Layers. Click on the topmost layer.

2 Click the Add layer mask button (◙) at the bottom of the Layers panel. A mask, that specifically applies to the selected layer appears to the right of the Layer thumbnail in the Layers panel.

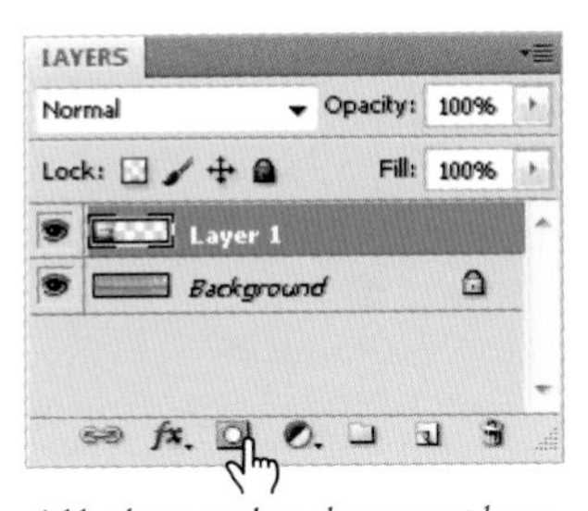

Add a layer mask to the topmost layer.

Since you did not have an active selection, nothing visually changes in this image. A layer mask offers you the opportunity to paint a mask. In this example, you will use a gradient so that you can fade the transition from one image another. The lines on the corners of the layer mask indicate that the layer mask is selected and ready for you to edit. If you deselect a layer mask, you can click back on the thumbnail to reactivate it.

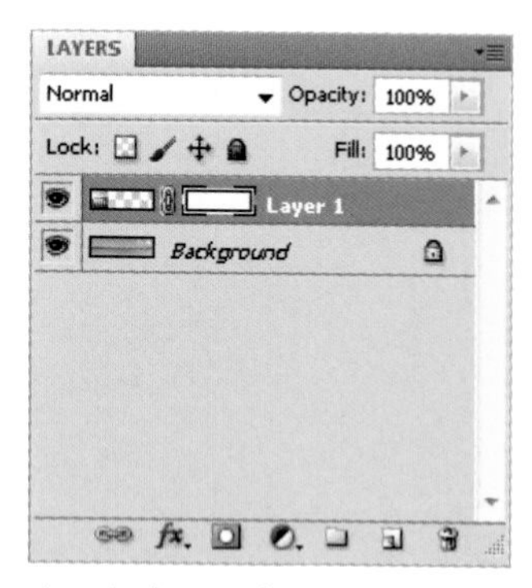

An active layer mask is positioned off to the right of the selected layer.

3 Select the Gradient tool (■) from the Tools panel, and press the keyboard shortcut, **D**. This assures that you are at the default foreground and background colors of Black and White.

4 Click and drag a small distance from the left to the right in the beach image. The length and angle determine the gradient's result. If you want a large fade from one image to another, click and drag further. If you want a short transition, click and drag a shorter distance.

Click and drag to create a gradient on the layer mask.

If you want to keep the gradient straight, hold down the Shift key as you drag with the Gradient tool.

When you release the Gradient tool, you see that you have created the gradient on the mask, not the actual image. The gradient functions as a mask, masking out any area that is black, and exposing any area in white.

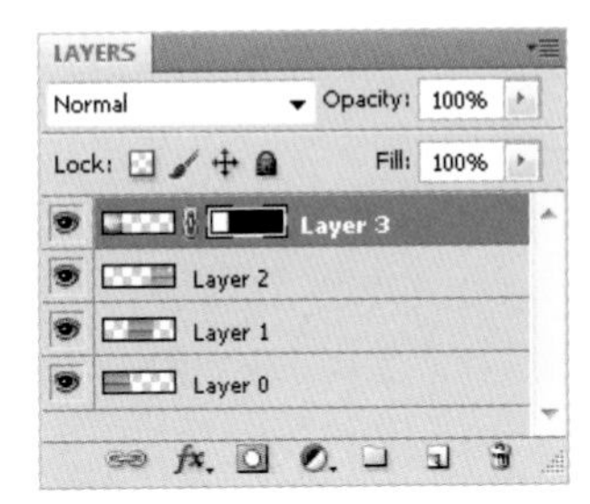

The Gradient is on the layer mask.

5 Choose File > Save. Keep the file open for the next part of this lesson.

Using the new Content-Aware feature

In the next part of the lesson, you will remove the surfer from the beach image using the new content aware option in the Spot Healing Brush tool.

1 Select the Spot Healing Brush tool ( ) from the Tools panel.

2 With the Spot Healing Brush tool selected, note that the Options bar offers the opportunity to turn on the Content-Aware feature. Click on the Content-Aware option.

3 Since you are no longer working on the layer mask, and want to retouch the actual image, click once on the Layer thumbnail for Layer 1 in the layers panel.

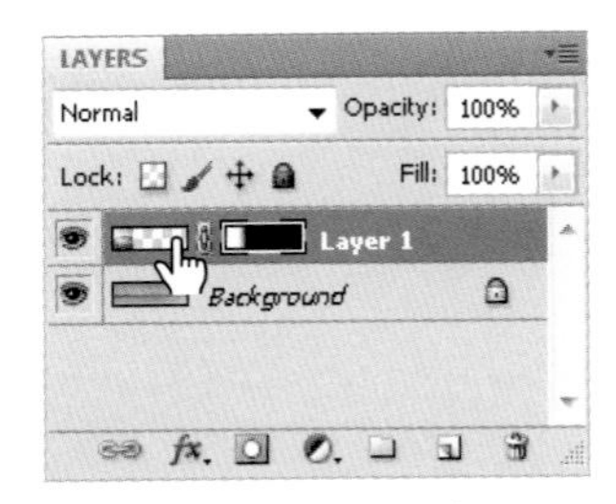

Click on the Layer thumbnail to activate the image instead of the mask.

5 With the Spot Healing Brush tool selected paint over the head of the surfer and then release. Notice that Photoshop tries to match and replace the head with the surrounding content.

Now continue and paint over the rest of the body, including the reflection. The initial result may not be perfect, but you can return to the problem areas and paint over them again until you have a better result.

Paint over the part of the image you want to replace.

The initial result, which you can improve with additional painting.

6 Choose File > Save and keep this file open for the next part of this lesson.

Using the improved selection features

In this section, you have the opportunity to take advantage of the new and improved Refine Edge feature. The improvements make it easier for you to make difficult selections like fur and hair.

1 Choose File > Browse in Bridge and locate the image named ps0103.psd, which is located in the ps01lessons folder. Double-click to open the file in Adobe Photoshop. Again, you will position the images so that you can easily drag one image file to the other.

2 Choose 2 Up from the Arrange Documents button (▦) in the Application bar at the top of the Photoshop workspace. The images now appear side-by-side.

3 Make sure that Layer 1 is the active layer in the Layers panel. This assures that the new layer lands on top of the stacking order.

4 Select the Move tool (▸+) and click and drag the image of the wakeboarder on top of the large panoramic image. Release when you see the cursor with the plus sign (▸⊞). You do not have to put the wakeboarder in any specific location, just make sure that you can see the entire boarder's body, as you will be masking that part of the image.

Drag and drop the image.

5 Click back on the ps0103.psd image and choose File > Close to close the file. If asked, do not save the file.

6 Select the Quick Selection tool from the Tools panel and paint over the wakeboarder's body. Notice that Photoshop automatically builds a selection based upon the image area you are painting.

When you release your mouse and then continue painting the selection is added to. You can delete from the selection by holding down the Alt (Windows) or Option (Mac OS) key while painting the selection. Find out more about selections in Lesson 5, "Making the Best Selection."

7 If necessary, hold down the Alt (Windows) of Option (Mac OS) to delete the inside section of the boarder.

Hold down the Alt/Option key to deselect the selection.

Refining your selection

In this next section, you will refine you initial selection by using the new and improved Refine Edge feature.

1 With your selection still active, click on the Refine Edge button in the Options bar. The Refine Edge dialog box appears.

2 Using the View drop-down menu select the On White preview.

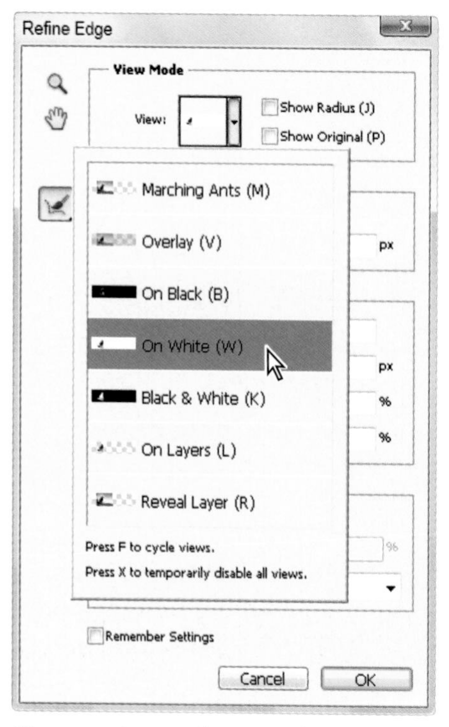

Choose to preview your selection on a white background.

3 Press Ctrl++(Plus sign) (Windows) or Command++(Plus sign) (Mac OS) to zoom into the present selection of the water skier. You can hold down the space bar and click and drag to reposition the view. As you can see, the selection, especially around the hair, leaves a lot to be desired. You will fix this selection by taking advantage of the newly added Edge detection feature.

4 Click and drag the Radius slider (in the Edge Detection section) to the right until you reach a value around 8.You can already see a refinement in the selection.

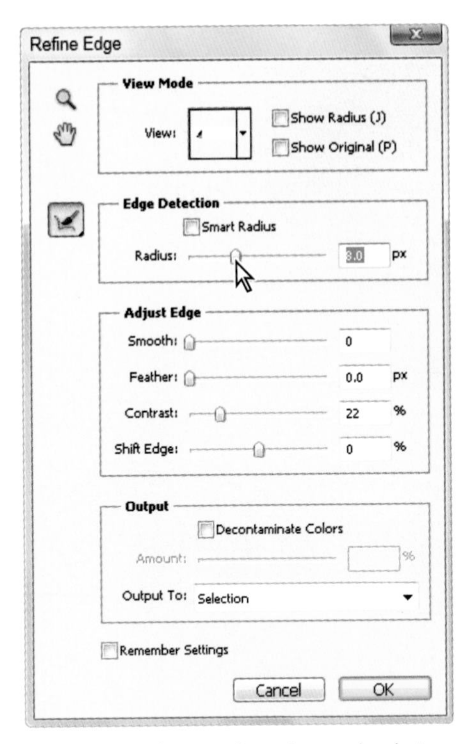

Increase the edge detection radius to improve the selection.

5 Select the Refine Radius tool (), located to the left of the Edge Detection section of the Refine Edge dialog box. Click in the area of the hair to refine the selection around the hair.

Refine the selection using the Refine Radius tool.

When you feel the selection is complete, choose Layer Mask from the Output To drop-down menu in the Output section of the Refine Edge dialog box. Press OK.

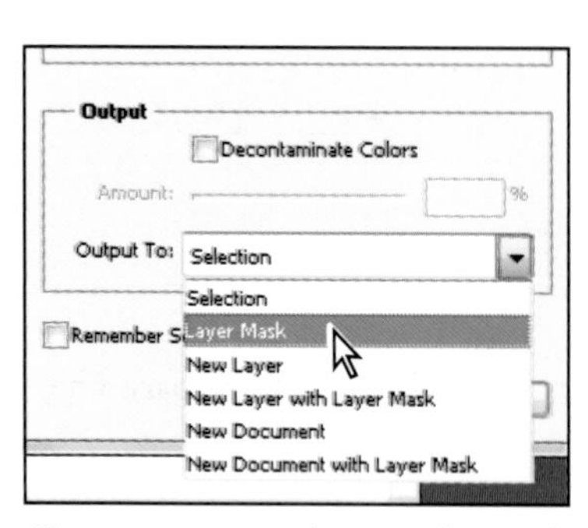

Choose to output your selection as a layer mask.

Result.

6 Using the Move tool (▸+), reposition the boarder to the right side of your image.

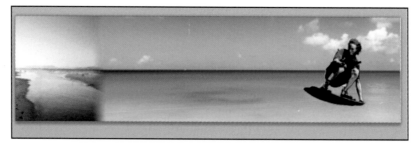

The image after the mask is complete.

If your mask did not eliminate the entire background area, you might see it as you reposition your water skier image. If this is the case, you can simply click on the layer mask for the water skier image, and then press "X" to bring black forward as your foreground color. Take your Brush tool and paint over those areas, essentially masking them out.

Refine your layer mask with the Brush tool.

Adding a Type layer

You will now add a text layer to this document.

1 Select the Type tool (T) from the Tools panel and click on the left side of the image. A cursor appears, and the Options bar reflects properties for your text.

2 In the Set the font family drop-down menu, type **Myri** to enter the Myriad Pro typeface. If you would prefer, you can select the drop-down menu and scroll to the Myriad Pro typeface.

3 In the Set the font style drop-down menu, select Bold.

4 In the Set the font size dialog box, enter **130**.

5 Click once on the Set the text color box (on the right side of the Options bar). The Color picker appears. Select white, or a light color. Press OK

6 Type **SUMMER** in all caps.

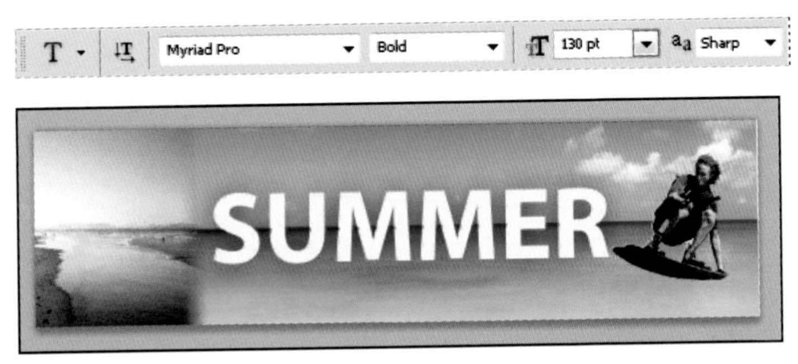

Set the font family, size and color.

7 Press the Commit check button (✓) in the upper right of the Options bar.

8 Press **3** to set the opacity of the type layer to 30%. If you would prefer, you can drag the Opacity slider (in the Layers panel) to 30%.

Adding the Vertical text

You will now add the text for the year, and then rotate and position it on the left side of the image.

1 Press the letter **D**, as this sets the foreground and background color back to the default of black and white.

2 Select the Type tool (T) from the Tools panel and click anywhere on the artboard.

3 When the cursor appears, type **2010**, or whatever year you prefer.

4 To confirm your text and exit the type editing tool, you can press Ctrl+Enter (Windows) or Command+Return (Mac OS). You can click on the confirmation checkbox (✓) in the upper-right of the Type tool Options bar.

5 Once you exit the type editing mode, press **3** to set the opacity of this new text layer to 30% as well.

Create a separate type layer for the year and change the opacity to 30%.

6 Choose Edit > Free Transform, or press Ctrl+T (Windows) or Command+T (Mac OS) to turn on the Free Transform bounding box. Note that the Options bar now offers resources that allow you to resize and rotate this layer.

7 Type **-90** into the Rotate text field and press the Enter /Return key.

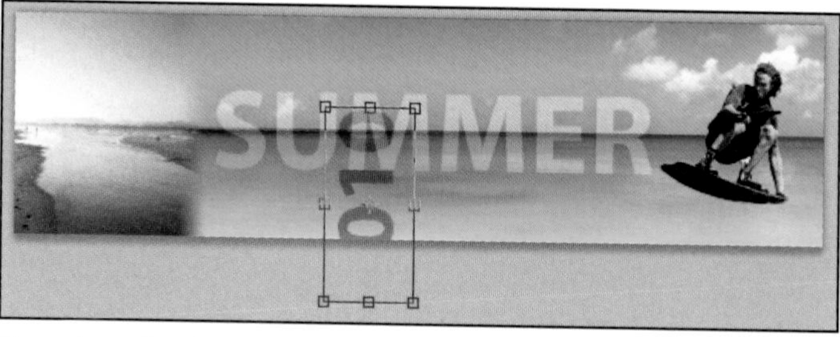

Rotate the text layer by -90 degrees.

8 Select the Move tool (▸₊) and reposition the new text layer on the left side of the image.

Making some waves using the Puppet Warp feature

In this last part of the lesson you take advantage of the new Puppet Warp feature. Before you start you will create a copy of the bottom Background layer.

1 With the Move tool select the Background layer and hold down the Alt (Windows) or Option (Mac OS) and drag it to the Create new layer button in the Layers panel. By holding down the Alt/Option key you have the opportunity to name this layer before it is duplicated. Name this layer **Warp**.

2 Choose Edit > Puppet Warp. In this example, you create your own wave design using the Puppet Warp feature,

3 Click once on the far right of the image, at about the water line, then click below, then again at the water line and again below, and so on, creating a zigzag pattern with the pins.

Continue clicking to create a zigzag pattern with the Puppet Warp pins.

4 Click on one of the top pins and then Shift+click on the remaining pins positioned at the top.

5 Release the Shift key and click and drag up into the sky. The exact amount is not important.

6 Click once on one of the bottom pins, then Shift+click to select the remaining bottom pins. Click and drag downwards; again, the exact amount is not important.

7 To see the result you can uncheck the Show Mesh checkbox in the Options bar. When you are finished, select the Confirmation checkbox in the upper-right corner of the Options bar.

Create waves using the new Puppet Warp feature.

8 Choose File > Save and File Close.

Congratulations! You have finished Lesson 1, "Exploring Photoshop."

Getting to Know the Workspace

What you'll learn in this lesson:

- Opening a file using Adobe Bridge
- Using Photoshop tools
- Navigating in your image area
- Using panels

In this lesson, you'll learn how to best use the Adobe Photoshop CS5 work area. You will also discover how to open a document using Adobe Bridge, how to use the Tools panel, and how to easily navigate images.

Starting up

Adobe Photoshop is an image-editing program that can open an image captured by a scanner or digital camera, or downloaded from the Web. It can also open captured video images and vector illustrations. In addition, you can create new documents in Photoshop, including vector graphics, which are scalable image files (for example, the images can be enlarged or reduced in size with no loss of clarity).

Before starting, make sure that your tools and panels are consistent by resetting your preferences. See "Resetting Adobe Photoshop CS5 preferences" on page 3.

You will work with several files from the ps02lessons folder in this lesson. Make sure that you have loaded the pslessons folder onto your hard drive from the supplied DVD. See "Loading lesson files" on page 5.

See Lesson 2 in action!

Use the accompanying video to gain a better understanding of how to use some of the features shown in this lesson. The video tutorial for this lesson can be found on the included DVD.

Opening an existing document in Adobe Bridge Mini Bridge

As mentioned previously, Adobe Mini Bridge works like the stand-alone Adobe Bridge application, but resides in Photoshop. You can be access Mini Bridge by using the File menu, or by using the Launch Mini Bridge button (Mb) that is found on the Application bar in Photoshop CS5.

1 Launch Adobe Photoshop CS5. If the Welcome menu appears, choose Close.

2 Choose File > Browse in Mini Bridge; Mini Bridge appears.

3 If Desktop is not visible in the Navigation Pod, click on Browse. Desktop appears in the list to the right.

4 Click on Desktop. Locate and double-click on the pslessons folder that you dragged to the Desktop and then open the ps02lessons folder contained within it.

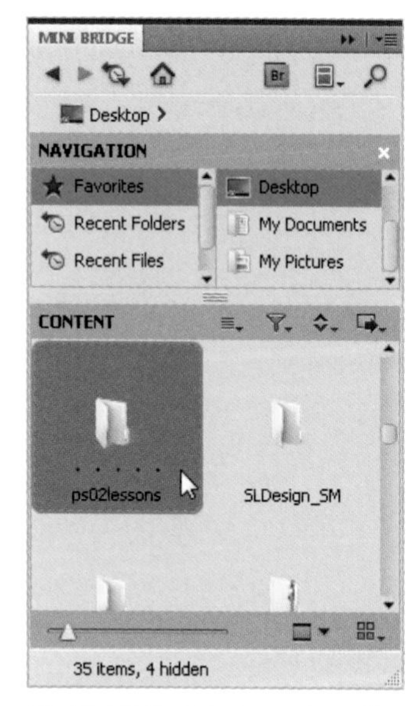

Use Mini Bridge to locate your lesson files.

5 Locate and double-click to open the file named ps0201_done.psd. An image of a woman biking with a child appears.

As you practice with the files throughout this book, you will find that you are instructed to save a work file immediately after opening the original file.

6 Choose File > Save As to save a copy of this document to your ps02lessons folder.

7 Navigate to the ps02lessons folder. In the File name text field, type **ps0201_work**, and choose Photoshop from the Format drop-down menu. Click Save.

Discovering the Tools panel

When you start Photoshop, the Tools panel appears docked on the left side of the screen—it is not a floating Tools panel, as it was in earlier versions of Photoshop. There are four main groups of tools, separated by functionality on the Tools panel: selection, cropping, and measuring; retouching and painting; drawing and type; and 3D and navigation.

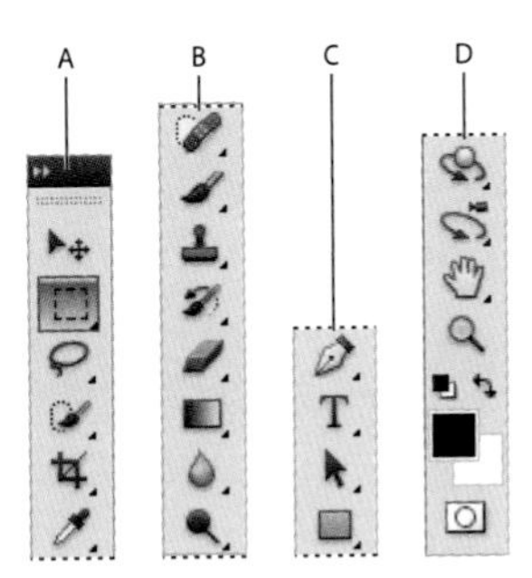

A. Selection, cropping, and measuring tools.
B. Retouching and painting tools.
C. Drawing and type tools.
D. 3D and navigation tools.

Selection, Cropping, and Measuring Tools

ICON	TOOL NAME	USE	WHERE IT'S COVERED
	Move (V)	Moves selections or layers.	Lesson 5
	Marquee (M)	Makes rectangular, elliptical, single row, and single column selections.	Lesson 5
	Lasso (L)	Makes freehand, polygonal (straight-edged), and magnetic selections.	Lesson 5
	Quick Selection (W)	Paints selections.	Lesson 5
	Crop (C)	Crops an image.	Lesson 3
	Eyedropper (I)	Samples pixels.	Lesson 6

Retouching and Painting Tools

ICON	TOOL NAME	USE	WHERE IT'S COVERED
	Spot Healing (J)	Removes imperfections.	Lesson 6
	Brush (B)	Paints the foreground color.	Lesson 6
	Clone Stamp (S)	Paints with a sample of the image.	Lesson 6
	History Brush (Y)	Paints a duplicate of the selected state or snapshot.	Lesson 6
	Eraser (E)	Erases pixels—or reverts to a saved history state.	Lesson 6
	Gradient (G)	Creates a gradient.	Lesson 6
	Blur (no shortcut)	Blurs pixels.	Lesson 12
	Dodge (O)	Lightens pixels in an image.	Lesson 5

You can create a floating Tools panel by clicking on the gray title bar at the top of the Tools panel and then dragging it to a new location. You can dock it again by dragging it back to the left side of the workspace; release when you see the vertical bar appear.

Drawing and Type Tools

ICON	TOOL NAME	USE	WHERE IT'S COVERED
	Pen (P)	Draws a vector path.	Lesson 5
T	Horizontal Type (T)	Creates a type layer.	Lesson 4
	Path Selection (A)	Allows you to manipulate a path.	Lesson 7
	Rectangle (U)	Draws vector shapes.	Lesson 2, 10

3D and Navigation Tools

ICON	TOOL NAME	USE	WHERE IT'S COVERED
	Object Rotate (K)	Rotates 3D objects.	Lesson 13
	Rotate Camera (N)	Changes the view of 3D objects.	Lesson 13
	Hand (H)	Navigates the page.	Lesson 2
	Zoom (Z)	Increases and decreases the relative size of the view.	Lesson 2

Can't tell the tools apart? You can view tooltips that reveal a tool's name and keyboard shortcut by positioning your cursor over the tool.

The Tools panel is in a space-saving, one-column format. Click on double arrows in the gray title bar area above the Tools panel to bring the Tools panel into the two-column view. Click on the double arrows again to bring the Tools panel back to the default, single-column view. Keep the Tools panel set to whichever format works best for you.

Accessing tools and their options

With the selection of most tools comes the opportunity to change options. In this exercise, you will have the opportunity to use the new and improved Spot Healing Brush tool and change its options to become even more powerful.

1 With the ps0201_work.psd image open, select the Spot Healing Brush tool (). Look in the Options bar to see a variety of options you can change.

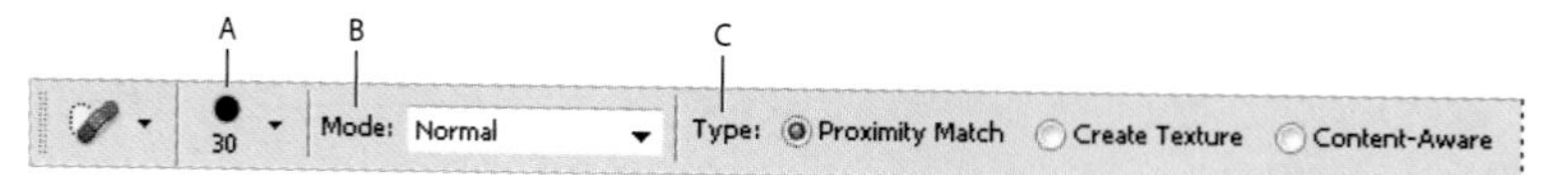

A. Brush Preset Picker. B. Painting Mode. C. Type of Spot Healing tool.

Most tools have additional options available in the Options bar (at the top of the workspace.)

2 Click on the Content-Aware radio button.

Content-Aware retouching is new to Photoshop CS5. With the Content-Aware option selected, you can paint over an image area and automatically fill-in with pixels from the surrounding area. You will use this feature to remove parts of the large bike in the foreground of the photo.

3 With the Spot Healing Brush selected, start painting on the blue water bottle top that appears in the bottom center of the image. Photoshop automatically starts filling in the painted area with the surrounding pixels.

Paint over the top of the water bottle.

The water bottle is replaced with the surrounding pixels.

Hidden tools

Some of the tools in the Tools panel display a small triangle at the bottom-right corner; this indicates that there are additional tools hidden under the tool.

1 Click and hold (or right click on) the Brush tool to see the hidden Pencil, Color Replacement and Mixer Brush tools.

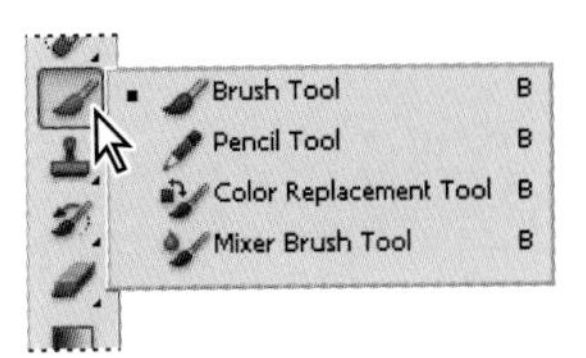

Selecting a hidden tool.

2 Drag to the Color Replacement tool () and release. The Color Replacement tool is now the visible tool.

You will now change the foreground color by selecting Set the foreground color in the Tools panel.

3 Click once on the foreground color at the bottom of the Tools panel; the Color Picker appears.

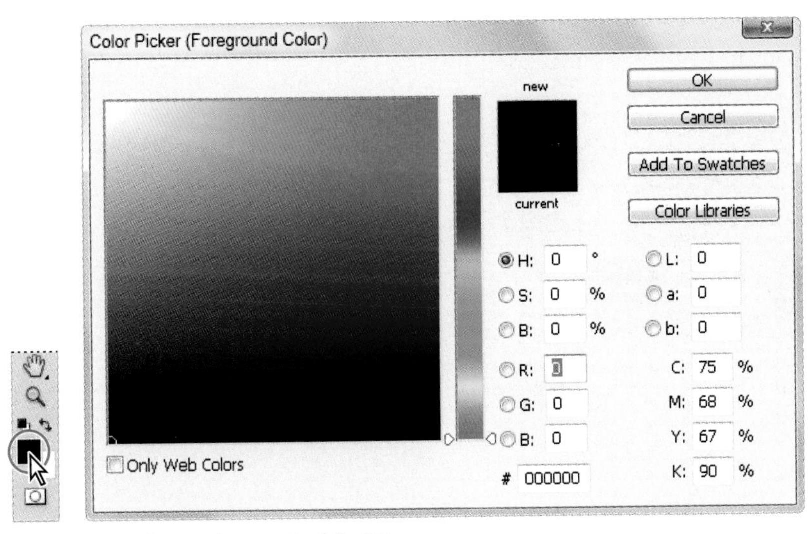

Click once on Set foreground to open the Color Picker.

4 Position your cursor on the color (Hue slider) to the right of the color pane and click and drag it up until yellow appears in the color pane.

5 Click once in the color pane to select a yellow color. Any yellow color will do for this exercise, but you can also type a value into the text fields for a more accurate selection. In our example we choose a color with the RGB value of R: **241**, G: **231**, B: **66**. You will find out more about color in Lesson 6, "Painting and Retouching." Click OK.

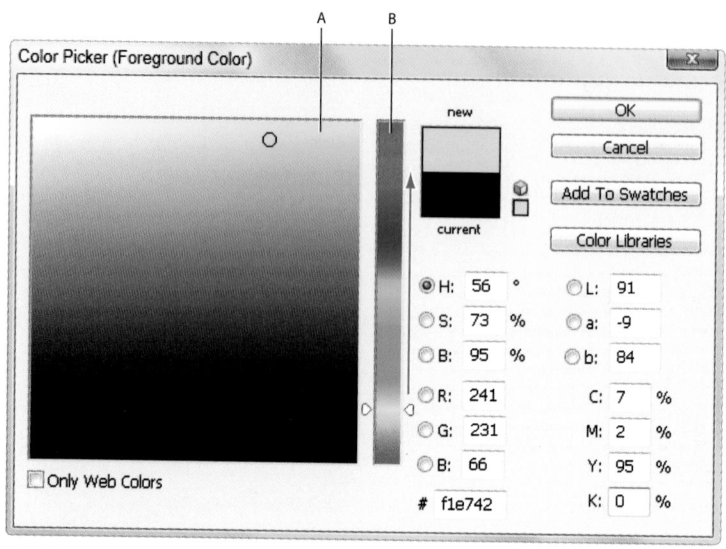

A. Color pane. B. Hue slider.

6 Click on the Brush Preset picker button in the Options bar and set the following attributes for the Color Replacement tool.

Mode: Color

Size: **400 px** (This indicates the size of the brush, in this example a very large brush is indicated)

Hardness: **20%** (A value of 100% would be a hard edged brush)

Leave all other settings at their defaults.

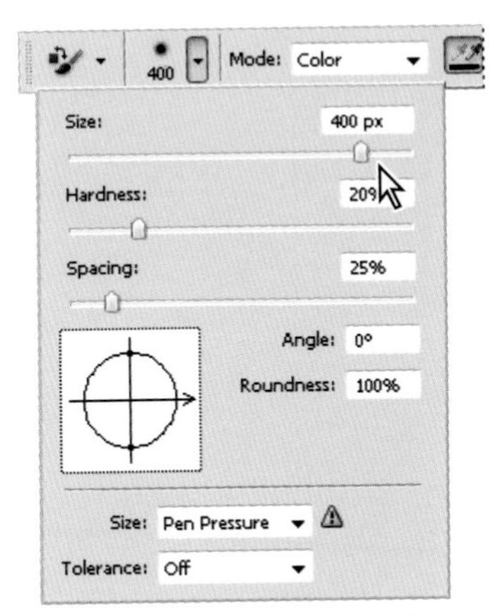

Changing the Color Replacement tool's brush.

7 Click on the Limits drop-down menu in the Color Replacement tools Options bar and select Discontiguous. This indicates that you want to replace the colors directly under the pointer as you paint, whereas Contiguous would direct the tool to paint over only the colors that are touching the area underneath the pointer.

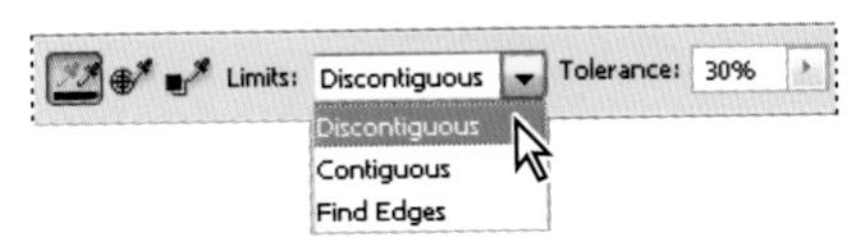

Change the Limits selection to Discontiguous to paint all the pixels underneath the pointer.

8 Press Ctrl+0 (zero) (Windows) or Command+0 (zero) (Mac OS.) This is the keyboard shortcut for Fit on Screen, and it assures that you see the entire image area.

9 With the Color Replacement tool selected, click and drag from the lower-right to the lower-left of your image area in one large brush stroke. If you make a mistake, press Ctrl+Z (Windows) or Command+Z (Mac OS) to revert to the previous image and try again.

A Yellow tint replaces the colors across the painted area in the bottom of the image area.

10 Choose File > Save, or use the keyboard shortcut Ctrl+S (Windows), or Command+S (Mac OS) to save your file.

Navigating the image area

To work most efficiently in Photoshop, you'll want to know how to zoom (magnify) in and out of your image. Changing the zoom level allows you to select and paint accurately and helps you see details that you might otherwise have overlooked. The zoom function has a range from a single pixel up to a 3200 percent enlargement, which gives you a lot of flexibility in terms of viewing your images.

You'll start by using the View menu to reduce and enlarge the document view, and end by fitting the entire document on your screen.

1 Choose View > Zoom In to enlarge the display of ps0201_work.psd.

2 Press Ctrl+plus sign (Windows) or Command+plus sign (Mac OS) to zoom in again. This is the keyboard shortcut for the Zoom In command that you accessed previously from the View menu.

3 Press Ctrl+minus sign (Windows) or Command+minus sign (Mac OS) to zoom out. This is the keyboard shortcut for View > Zoom Out.

Now you will fit the entire image on the screen.

4 Choose View > Fit on Screen, or use the keyboard shortcut Ctrl+0 (zero) (Windows) or Command+0 (zero) (Mac OS), to fit the document to the screen.

5 You can also display artwork at the size it will print by choosing View > Print Size.

Using the Zoom tool

When you use the Zoom tool (🔍), each click increases the view size to the next preset percentage, and centers the display of the image around the location in the image that you clicked on. By holding the Alt (Windows) or Option (Mac OS) key down (with the Zoom tool selected), you can zoom out of an image, decreasing the percentage and making the image view smaller. The magnifying glass cursor is empty when the image has reached either its maximum magnification level of 3200 percent or the minimum size of one pixel.

1 Choose View > Fit on Screen.

2 Select the Zoom tool, and click two times on the child to zoom in. You can also use key modifiers to change the behavior of the Zoom tool.

3 Press Alt (Windows) or Option (Mac OS) while clicking with the Zoom tool to zoom out.

You can accurately zoom into the exact region of an image by clicking and dragging a marquee around that area in your image. To do this you must disable a new Zoom tool option.

4 Uncheck the Scrubby Zoom checkbox in the Zoom tool's Option bar to disable this feature. The Scrubby Zoom feature is new to Photoshop CS5 and allows you to click and drag to zoom immediately. In this example, you need a more predictable zoom area.

Disable the Scrubby Zoom in the Zoom tool's Option bar.

5 With the Zoom tool still selected, hold down the mouse and click and drag from the top left of the child to the bottom right of the child. You are creating a rectangular marquee selection around the child. Once you release the mouse, the area that was included in the marquee is now enlarged to fill the document window.

Dragging a marquee over the child.

6 Double-click the Zoom tool in the Tools panel to return to a 100 percent view.

Because the Zoom tool is used so often, it would be tiresome to continually have to change from the Zoom tool back to the tool you were using. Read on to see how you can activate the Zoom tool at any time without deselecting your current tool.

7 Select the Move tool (▸+) at the very top of the Tools panel.

8 Hold down Ctrl+spacebar (Windows) or Command+spacebar (Mac OS). Note that on the Mac OS you must hold down spacebar before the Command key, otherwise you trigger Spotlight; the Move tool is temporarily converted into the Zoom In tool. While still holding down Ctrl/Command+spacebar, click and drag over the child again, then release. Note that although you have changed the zoom level, the Move tool is still active.

You can zoom out by holding down Alt+spacebar (Windows) or Option+spacebar (Mac OS).

9 Choose View > Fit on Screen.

Using the Hand tool

The Hand tool allows you to move or pan the document. It is a lot like pushing a piece of paper around on your desk.

1 Select the Zoom tool (🔍), then click and drag on an area surrounding the child.

2 Select the Hand tool (✋), then click and drag to the right to push the picture to the right. Notice that when the Hand tool is active, four view buttons appear in the Options bar (at the top of the work area) that allow you to change your current view to Actual Pixels, Fit Screen, Fill Screen, and Print Size.

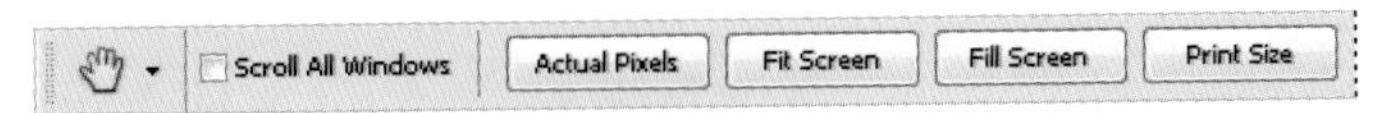

View options are available in the Options panel.

3 Select the Zoom tool and hold the spacebar. Notice that the cursor turns into the Hand tool. Click and drag left to view the child again. By holding down the spacebar, you can access the Hand tool without deselecting the current tool.

4 Double-click the Hand tool in the Tools panel to fit the entire image on your screen. This is the same as using Ctrl+0 (zero) (Windows) or Command+0 (zero) (Mac OS).

NAVIGATION SHORTCUTS	WINDOWS	MAC OS
Zoom In	Ctrl+plus sign Ctrl+spacebar	Command+plus sign Command+spacebar
Zoom Out	Ctrl+minus sign Alt+spacebar	Command+minus sign Option+spacebar
Turn Zoom In tool into Zoom Out tool	Alt	Option
Fit on Screen	Ctrl+0 (zero) or double-click the Hand tool	Command+0 (zero) or double-click the Hand tool
Hand tool (except when Type tool is selected)	Press spacebar	Press spacebar

Tabbed windows

In Photoshop CS5, you have control over how your windows appear in the workspace. You can work with floating image windows, or choose to tab your windows across the top of the workspace. If you are working on the Windows OS tabbed windows are the default. In this section, you find out how to use the new tabbed workspace.

1 If you are a Macintosh user and want to experiment with tabbed windows choose Window > Application Frame.

2 If the Mini Bridge is not visible, choose File > Browse in Mini Bridge. In the Navigation pod, double-click on the image named ps0202.psd to open it in Photoshop.

3 The image is displayed as a separate tab within Photoshop, allowing you to click on the tab to switch between active images.

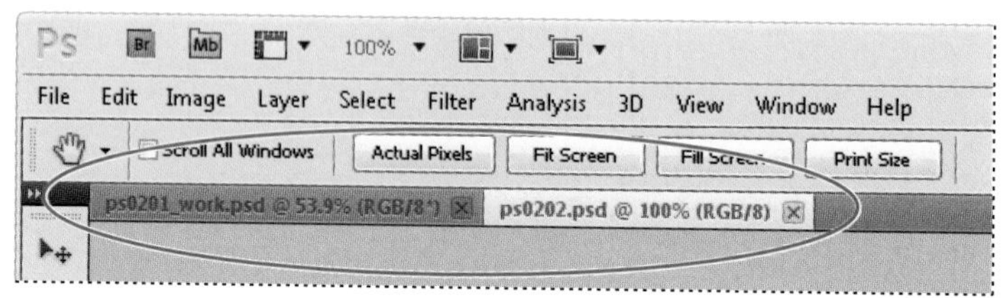

Multiple open images appear as tabs at the top of the screen.

4 Click on the ps0202.psd tab and then click and drag the tab away from its tabbed position and release the mouse button. The image window is now floating.

5 Click the title bar of the floating window and drag upwards until your cursor is next to the tab of the other image. When you see a blue bar appear, release the mouse button. The image is now back to a tabbed window. Keep in mind that you can stop a window from tabbing accidently by holding down the Ctrl (Windows) or Command (Mac OS) key while dragging the floating window.

If you would prefer not to take advantage of the tabbed window feature, you can choose Edit > Preferences (Windows) or Photoshop > Preferences (Mac OS), then choose Interface. In the Panels & Documents section, uncheck Open Documents as Tabs and press OK.

To quickly move all floating windows back to tabbed windows, choose Window > Arrange > Consolidate All to Tabs.

Maximizing productivity with screen modes

Now that you can zoom in and out of your document, as well as reposition it in your image window, it's time to learn how to take advantage of screen modes. You have a choice of three screen modes in which to work. Most users start and stay in the default—Standard Screen mode—until they accidentally end up in another. Screen modes control how much space your current image occupies on your screen, and whether you can see other Photoshop documents as well. The Standard Screen mode is the default screen mode when you open Photoshop for the first time. It displays an image on a neutral gray background for easy and accurate viewing of color without distractions, and also provides a flexible work area for dealing with panels. Note that Macintosh users will only see this neutral gray background if they have the Application Frame (discussed in the earlier in this section) active.

1 Click on the tab of the ps0201_work.psd image to make that image active.

2 Position your cursor on the vertical line that runs down the left side of the panel docking area. Click on the line and drag to the left. Notice that this not only expands the panel docking area, but it also dynamically changes the image window when you release the mouse. The document window is resized when dock widths change.

The image area dynamically changes as the panel docking area is resized.

3 Press the Tab key; the Tools panel and other panels disappear, creating much more workspace. Press the Tab key again to bring the Tools panel and other panels back.

4 Press Shift+Tab to hide the panel docking area while keeping the rest of the panels visible. Press Shift+Tab to bring the hidden panels back. Both the Tools panel and the panel docking area should now be visible.

As you position your cursor over various tools, you see a letter to the right of the tool name in the tooltip. This letter is the keyboard shortcut that you can use to access that tool. You could, in fact, work with the Tools panel closed and still have access to all the tools via your keyboard.

You will hide the panels once more so that you can take advantage of a hidden feature in Photoshop CS5.

Press the Tab key to hide the panels. Then position your cursor over the thin gray strip where the Tools panel had been, and pause. The Tools panel reappears. Note that the Tools panel appears only while your cursor is in the Tools panel area, and it disappears if you move your cursor out of that area. Try this with the panel docking area to the right of the screen, and watch as that also appears and disappears as your cursor moves over it.

By changing the screen modes, you can locate over-extended anchor points and select more accurately up to the edge of your image. Changing modes can also help you present your image to clients in a clean workspace.

5 Press the Tab key again to display all the panels.

6 Press **F** to cycle to the next screen mode, which is Full Screen Mode With Menu Bar. This view surrounds the image out to the edge of the work area with a neutral gray (even behind the docking area) and displays only one image at a time, without tabs and centered within the work area. You can access additional open images by choosing the image name from the bottom of the Window menu.

You can also change your screen mode by clicking and holding on the Change Screen Mode button in the Application bar and selecting Full Screen Mode With Menu Bar.

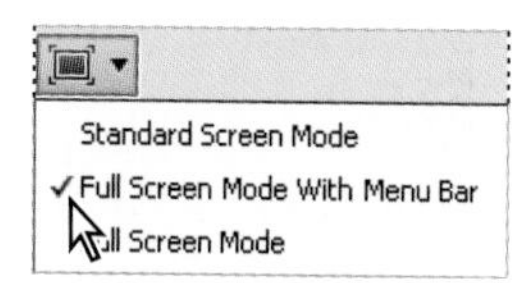

The Change Screen Mode button accessed in the Application bar.

7 Notice that the gray background area (pasteboard) now extends to fill your entire screen, and your image is centered within that area. One of the benefits of working in this mode is that it provides more area when working on images.

The Full Screen mode with Menu bar.

8 Press **F** on the keyboard again to see the last screen mode, Full Screen Mode. You may receive a warning dialog box in this screen mode, indicating that you can exit the screen mode by pressing the F or Esc key because all the interface elements are hidden.

Full Screen mode.

This is Full Screen mode. A favorite with multimedia folks, it allows you to show others your document full-screen with no distracting screen elements. All menus and panels are hidden automatically in this mode; however, they are still accessible by hovering the cursor over the area where the panels normally reside. The panels temporarily reappear for easy access. If you'd like to see the panels while in this mode, simply press the Tab key to display and hide them.

9 Press the **F** key once to cycle back into Standard Screen mode, or click and hold on the Screen Mode button in the Application bar at the top of your screen and select Standard Screen Mode. Stay in this mode throughout this lesson.

Using panels

Much of the functionality in Photoshop resides in the panels, so you will want to know how to navigate them, and find the ones you need quickly and easily. In this section, you will learn how to resize, expand, and convert panels to icons and then back to panels again. You will also learn how to save your favorite workspaces so that you don't have to set them up every time you work on a new project.

The default panel locations.

Putting the panel system to use

Photoshop has a default setting for all the panels, it's what you see when you initially launch Photoshop. There are many panels, and not all of them are needed for all projects. That is why Photoshop has defined workspaces which can help you streamline your workflow. There are many prebuilt workspaces available under the Show more workspaces and options button. This button is to the right of the three main workspaces that are already listed in the Application bar.

Find workspaces on the right side of the Application bar.

1 Click on the Design button on the right side of the Application bar. Notice that the panels are changed to expose panels that might help you if you are a designer. Instead of the Color panel, you see the Swatches panel, and Adjustments panel is exchanged with the Character panel. Of course, you can still customize and save your own your workspace. You will do this later in this exercise.

To open panels that are not visible choose the Window menu. If there is a check mark to the left of the panel listed; it is already open. Photoshop CS5 is smart enough to know if a panel is hidden behind another and will not indicate that it is open, making it easy for you to select it in the Window menu and have it brought forward.

2 Select the Brush tool (✓) (the last paint tool that you used was the Color Replacement tool, so you will have to click and hold down on that tool to select the Brush tool.)

3 Click on the color named Pure Cyan Blue in the Swatches panel. Notice that when you cross over a color a Tooltip appears. You can also make it easy on yourself by selecting Small List from the Swatches panel menu (▾≡) in the upper right corner.

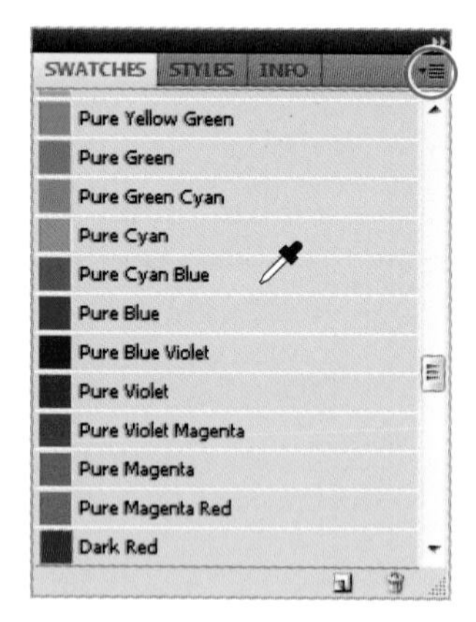

Choose to view the Swatches panel as a list.

4 In the Brushes Options bar, Click on the Brush Preset picker and change the brush size to **300 px**, and make sure the Hardness is set to **0%**. This makes a large soft brush for you to paint with.

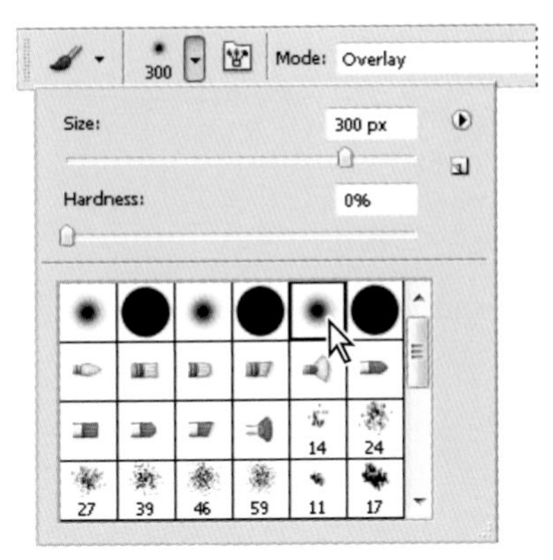

Change the Brush Size and Hardness in the Options bar.

5 Still in the Brush tool options, click on the drop-down menu to the right of Mode and select Overlay. This will paint an overlay of blue over the top of the image.

6 With the Brush tool selected, click and drag an arch of color across the top of the image. The sky turns a deeper blue where you paint. If you want to undo and try again, press Ctrl+Z (Windows) or Command+Z (Mac OS).

Paint the overlay of blue across the top of the image.

Choosing other panels

You will now select another panel, the History panel. The History panel allows you to undo and redo steps, as well as save versions of your image while you work. In this exercise, you will use the History panel to undo and redo steps. In Lesson 6, "Painting and Retouching," you spend more time in the History panel.

1 Click on the History panel icon (⌛) that is visible in the Design workspace. If you cannot locate it, choose Window > History.

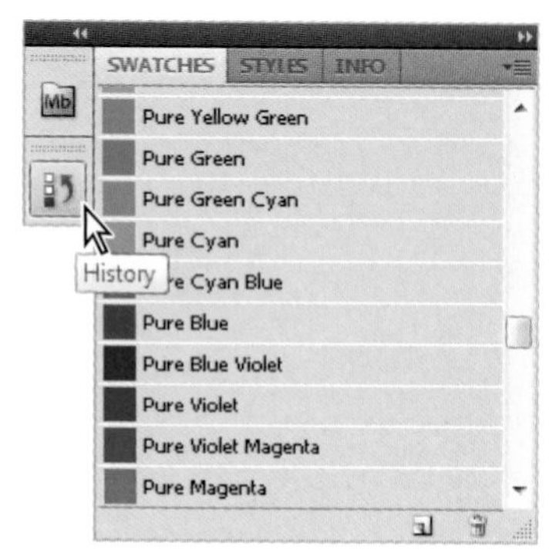

Selecting the History panel.

Each row in the History panel represent a history state (or step). You can click back on earlier states to undo steps that you have taken, or redo by clicking on the grayed out history state. Keep in mind that (with the default settings) if you step back in history and then complete a new step that all the states after (grayed out) disappear.

2 Click back on the various history states to see how your steps are undone, click forward again to see your steps redone.

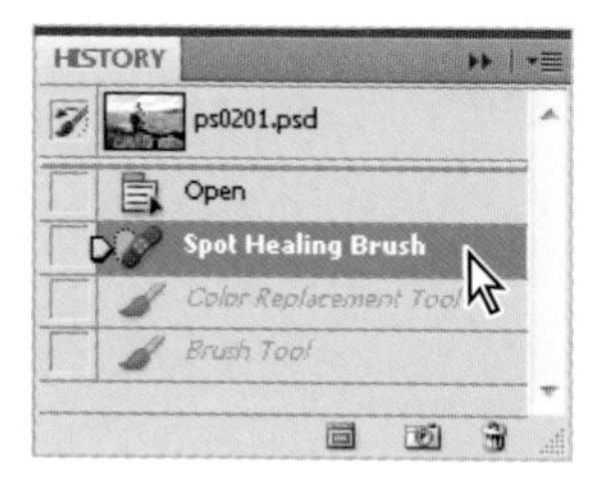

Undoing a step in the History panel.

Expanding your panels

If you do not like deciphering what the panel icons represent, you can expand your panels. You can do this automatically with a preconfigured workspace, or you can choose to expand only the panels you want to see.

1 Click and hold on the Workspace button on the Application bar, select Essentials. The Essentials workspace is the default workspace in Photoshop and provides a workspace with all the panels expanded.

2 You may find that you need to reset your workspace to bring it back to its original configuration. If this is necessary choose Window > Workspace > Reset Essentials.

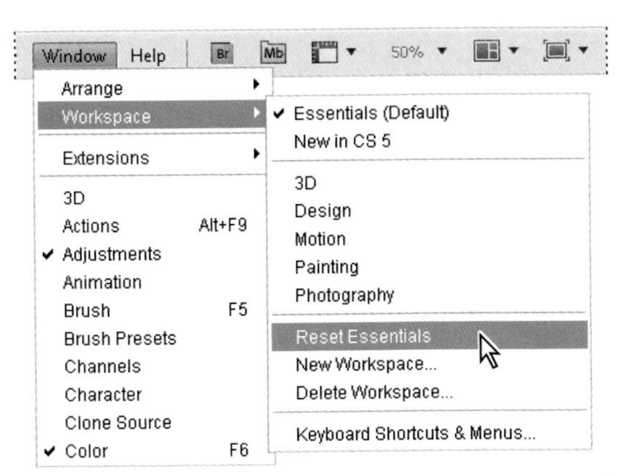

You may need to reset your workspace to put it back into its original configuration.

3 Collapse panels by double-clicking on the dark gray bar (title bar) at the top of the panel docking area. Double-click on the dark gray bar again to expand them.

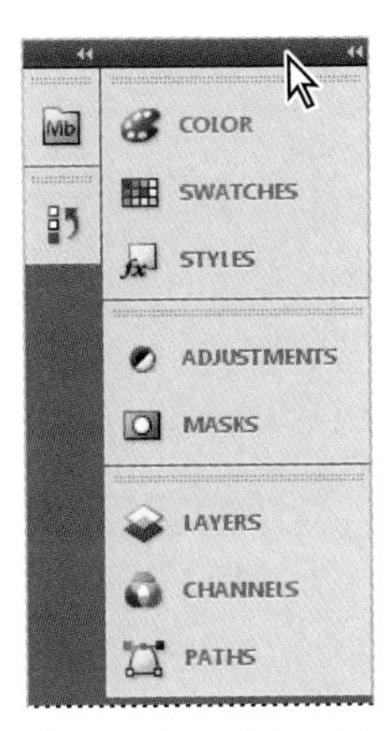

Collapse the panel by clicking on the title bar.

In addition, you can collapse specific panel groups by double clicking on the gray bar above each panel group to collapse and expand them.

Customizing your panels

A panel group is made up of two or more panels that are stacked on top of each other. To view the other panels in a group, select the name on the tab of the panel. You will now learn how to organize your panels the way that you want.

1 Select the tab that reads Swatches; the Swatches tab is brought forward.

2 Now, select the Color tab to return the Color panel to the front of the panel group.

3 Click on the tab of the Color panel, and drag it away from the panel group and into the image area. The panel looks slightly transparent as you drag it away from the group. Release it—you have just removed a panel from a panel group and the docking area. Rearranging panels can help you keep frequently used panels together in one area.

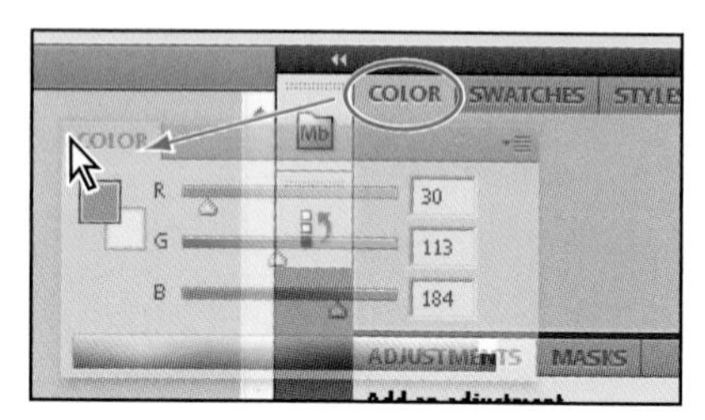

The Color panel as it is dragged away from a panel group.

4 Click the title bar area at the top of the Swatches panel and drag it over the Color panel. It appears slightly transparent as you drag. As soon as you see an outline around the Color panel, release the mouse. You have now made a panel group.

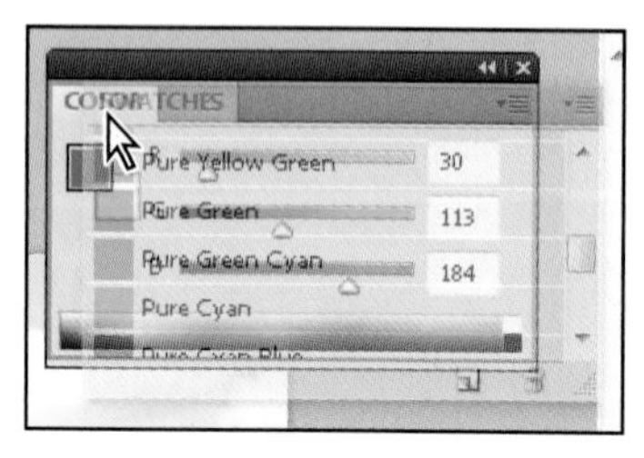

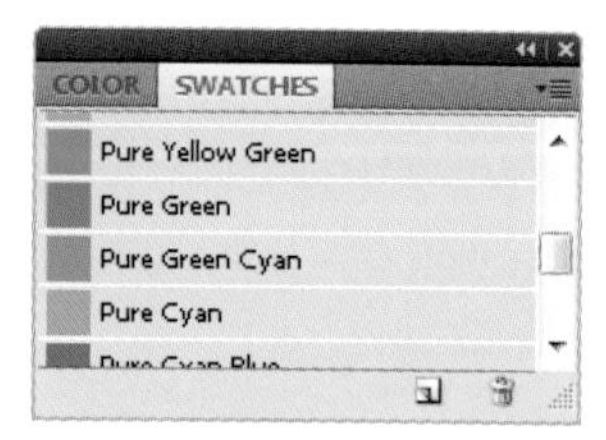

The Actions panel dragged over the History panel.

You'll now save a custom workspace. Saving a workspace is a good idea if you have production processes that often use the same panels. Saving workspaces is also helpful if you are in a situation where multiple users are sharing Photoshop on one computer.

5 Click on the double arrows at the far-right side of the Application bar and choose New Workspace.

6 In the Save Workspace dialog box, type **1st Workspace**.

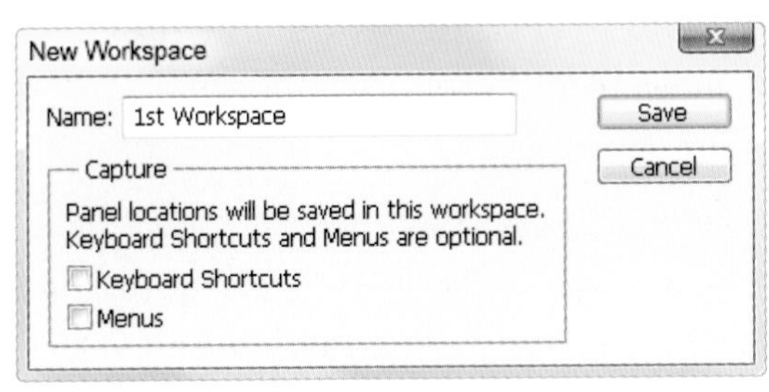

The Actions panel dragged over the History panel.

7 Whenever you want to reload a workspace, whether it's one that you created or one that comes standard with Photoshop, simply click the Workspace button in the Application bar and select the desired workspace from the list.

You have completed the "Getting to Know the Workspace" lesson. You can choose File > Save and then File > Close to close this file, or keep it open while you continue through the Self study and Review sections.

Self study

Choose File > Browse to access a practice file in your ps02lessons folder. You can double-click on ps0202.psd to explore workspaces further.

1 The Application bar contains several buttons that provide quick access to commonly used features inside Photoshop. One of those buttons, called Arrange Documents, allows you to arrange several open document windows in different ways. Explore the different views that Photoshop provides by choosing various icons found under the Arrange Documents button.

2 Using the new Content-Aware Spot Healing Brush remove the tree to the right of the railroad tracks.

3 Click on the tabs of various panels and practice clicking and dragging panels from one group to another. You can put your panels back in order when you are finished experimenting by clicking on the Workspace button in the Application bar and choosing Essentials.

4 Use the Window menu to open the Info, Histogram, and Layers panels, and then save a new workspace called color correction. These panels are covered in Lesson 7, "Creating a Good Image."

5 Take a look at some of the pre-built workspaces Photoshop has already made for you. They will change the panel locations, and some will highlight things in the menu that are relevant to each workspace. For instance, by selecting New in CS5, you see the new panels and new features highlighted in the menus.

Review

Questions

1 What is the Full Screen mode?

2 Name two ways to fit your image to the screen.

3 What happens in the Essentials workspace when you exit one panel and select another?

4 How do you save a workspace?

5 Can you delete a workspace?

Answers

1 The Full Screen mode displays a document window on a black background and hides all interface elements from view.

2 You can fit your image to the screen by using the View menu, or by double-clicking the Hand tool, right-clicking while you have the Zoom or Hand tool selected, or by pressing Ctrl+0 (zero) (Windows) or Command+0 (zero) (Mac OS).

3 When you leave one panel to select another, the initial panel returns to its original location in the docking area.

4 You can save your own workspace by clicking on the double arrows in the Application bar and choosing New Workspace.

5 Yes, you can delete a workspace by clicking on the double arrows in the Application bar and choosing Delete Workspace. Note that you cannot delete any of the default workspaces.

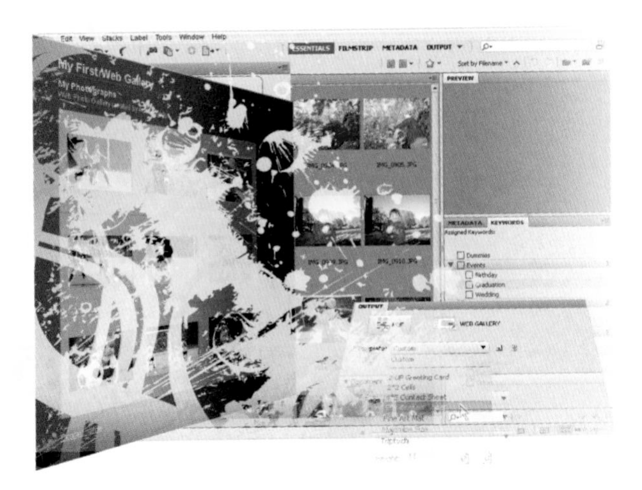

What you'll learn in this lesson:

- Navigating Adobe Bridge
- Using folders in Bridge
- Making a Favorite
- Creating metadata
- Using automated tools

Using Adobe Bridge

Adobe Bridge is the command center of the Creative Suite. In Adobe Bridge, you can manage and organize your files, utilize and modify XMP metadata for faster searches, and quickly preview files before opening them.

Starting up

Before starting, make sure that your tools and panels are consistent by resetting your preferences. See "Resetting Adobe Photoshop CS5 preferences" on page 3.

You will work with several files from the ps03lessons folder in this lesson. Make sure that you have loaded the pslessons folder onto your hard drive from the supplied DVD. See "Loading lesson files" on page 5.

See Lesson 3 in action!

Use the accompanying video to gain a better understanding of how to use some of the features shown in this lesson. The video tutorial for this lesson can be found on the included DVD.

What is Adobe Bridge?

Adobe Bridge is an application included with Adobe Photoshop and the other Adobe Creative Suite 5 components. Adobe Bridge helps you locate, organize, and browse the documents you need to create print, web, video, and audio content. If you have Photoshop or any one of the Creative Suite applications, you can start Adobe Bridge using the File menu, or you can select the Launch Bridge button (Br).

This lesson covers the functionality of the complete Bridge application, not the Mini Bridge that is available as a panel in your Photoshop workspace.

You can use Bridge to access documents such as images, text files, and even non-Adobe documents, such as Microsoft Word or Excel files. Using Adobe Bridge, you can also organize and manage images, videos, and audio files, as well as preview, search, and sort your files without opening them in their native applications.

Once you discover the capabilities of Adobe Bridge, you'll want to make it the control center for your Photoshop projects. With Bridge, you can easily locate files using the Filters panel and import images from your digital camera right into a viewing area that allows you to quickly rename and preview your files. This is why the recommended workflow throughout this book includes opening and saving files in Adobe Bridge. Reading through this lesson will help you to feel more comfortable with Adobe Bridge, and will also make you aware of some of the more advanced features that are available to you for your own projects.

Adobe Bridge contains more features when installed as part of one of the Creative Suites. The tools and features demonstrated in this lesson are available in both the single product install and the Suite install, unless otherwise noted.

Navigating through Bridge

In order to utilize Adobe Bridge effectively, you'll want to know the available tools and how to access them. Let's start navigating!

1 Choose File > Browse in Bridge to launch the Adobe Bridge application. If you receive a dialog box asking if you want Adobe Bridge to launch at start-up select Yes.

2 Click on the Folders panel to make sure it is forward. Click on Desktop (listed in the Folders panel). You see the ps03lessons folder that you downloaded to your hard drive. Double-click on the ps03lessons folder and notice that the contents of that folder are displayed in the Content panel, in the center of the Adobe Bridge window. You can also navigate by clicking on folders listed in the Path bar that is located in the upper-left corner of the content window.

You can view folder contents by double-clicking on a folder, or by selecting the folder in the Path bar.

You can navigate through your navigation history by clicking on the Go back and Go forward arrows in the upper-left corner of the window. Use the handy Reveal recent file or go to Recent folder drop-down menu (⟲) to find folders and files that you recently opened.

3 Click on the Go back arrow to return to the desktop view.

A. Go back. B. Go forward. C. Go to parent or Favorites. D. Reveal recent file or go to recent folder. E. Path bar.

4 Click on the Go forward arrow to return to the last view, which is the ps03lessons folder.

Using folders in Adobe Bridge

Adobe Bridge is used for more than just navigating your file system. Bridge is also used to manage and organize folders and files.

1 Click on the tab of the Folders panel in the upper-left corner of the Bridge window to make sure it is still forward. Then click on the arrow to the left of Desktop so that it turns downward and reveals its contents.

2 Click on Computer to reveal its contents in the center pane of the Bridge window. Continue to double-click on items, or click on the arrows to the left of the folder names in the Folder panel, to reveal their contents.

You can use Adobe Bridge to navigate your entire system, much like you would by using your computer's directory system.

Managing folders

Adobe Bridge is a great tool for organizing folders and files. It is a simple matter of dragging and dropping to reorder items on your computer. You can create folders, move folders, move files from one folder to another, and copy files and folders to other locations; any organizing task that can be performed on the computer can also be performed in Adobe Bridge. This is a great way to help keep volumes of images organized for easy accessibility, as well as easy searching. The advantage of using Adobe Bridge for these tasks is that you have bigger and better previews of images, PDF files, and movies, with much more information about those files at your fingertips.

3 Click on Desktop in the Folder panel to reveal its contents again.

4 Click on ps03lessons to view its contents. You'll now add a new folder into that lessons folder.

5 Click on the Create a new folder icon (📁) in the upper-right corner of the Bridge window to create a new untitled folder inside the ps03lessons folder. Type the name **Apple Picking**.

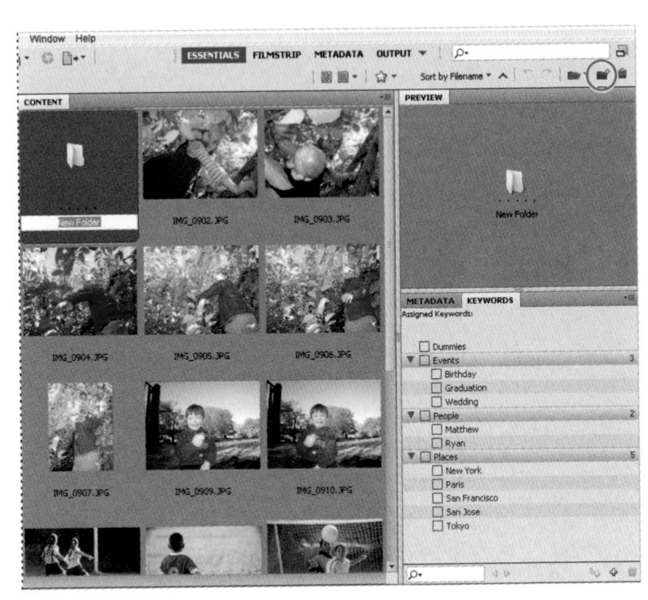

Creating a new folder in Bridge.

You can use Adobe Bridge to organize images. Since you are able to see a preview of each file, you can more easily rename them, as well as relocate them to more appropriate locations in your directory system. In the next step, you will move files from one folder to the new Apple Picking folder you have just created.

6 Click once on the image named IMG_0902.JPG, then hold down the Shift key and select image IMG_0910.JPG. All the images in between are selected.

You can easily reduce and enlarge the size of your thumbnails by pressing Ctrl+plus sign or Ctrl+minus sign in Windows or Command+plus sign or Command+minus sign in Mac OS.

7 Click and drag the selected images to the Apple Picking folder. When the folder becomes highlighted, release the mouse. The files have now been moved into that folder.

You can select multiple images and organize folders directly in Adobe Bridge.

8 Double-click on the Apple Picking folder to view its contents. You see the two images that you moved.

9 Click on ps03lessons in the Path bar to return to the ps03lessons folder content.

Making a Favorite

As you work in Photoshop, you will find that you frequently access the same folders. One of the many great features in Bridge is that you can designate a frequently used folder as a Favorite, allowing you to quickly and easily access it from the Favorites panel. This is extremely helpful, especially if the folders that you are frequently accessing are stored deep in your file hierarchy.

1 Select the Favorites panel in the upper-left corner of the Bridge window to bring it to the front. In the list of Favorites, click on Desktop. Double-click on the ps03lessons folder to see the Apple Picking images. Since the Apple Picking folder is going to be frequently accessed in this lesson, you'll make it a Favorite.

2 Place your cursor over the Apple Picking folder in the center pane (Content), and click and drag the Apple Picking folder until you see a horizontal line appear in the Favorites panel. Be careful not to drag this folder into a folder (highlighted with a blue box) in the Favorites panel. When a cursor with a plus sign (+) appears, release the mouse. The folder is now listed as a Favorite.

Drag a folder to the bottom of the Favorites panel to make it easier to locate.

3 Click on the Apple Picking folder shown in the Favorites panel to view its contents. Note that creating a Favorite simply creates a shortcut for quick access to a folder; it does not copy the folder and its contents.

If your Favorite is created from a folder on an external hard drive or server, you will need to have the hard drive or server mounted in order to access it.

Creating and locating metadata

Metadata is information that can be stored with images. This information travels with the file, and makes it easy to search for and identify the file. In this section, you are going to find out how to locate and create metadata.

1 Make sure that you are viewing the contents of the Apple Picking folder in the center pane of Adobe Bridge. If not, navigate to that folder now, or click on the Apple Picking folder in the Favorites panel.

2 Choose Window > Workspace > Reset Standard Workspaces. This ensures that you are in the Essentials view and that all the default panels for Adobe Bridge are visible. Alternatively, you can click Essentials in the Application bar at the top-right of the Bridge workspace. You may need to maximize your Bridge window after you reset the workspace.

Note that if you click and hold on the arrow to the right of the workspace presets, you can choose other workspaces, and even save your own custom workspace.

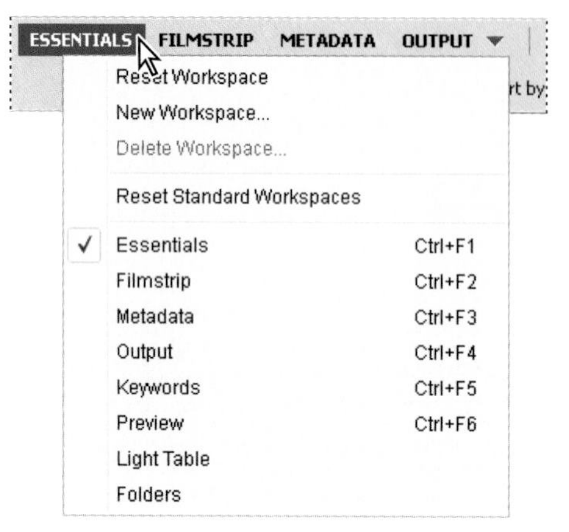

Resetting the workspace using the Workspace drop-down menu.

3 Click once on IMG_0902.JPG, and look for the Metadata and Keywords panels in the lower-right area of the Adobe Bridge workspace.

4 If the Metadata panel is not visible, click on the Metadata panel tab. In this panel, you see the image data that is stored with the file. Take a few moments to scroll through the data and view the information that was imported from the digital camera that was used to take the photo.

Click and drag the bar to the left of the Metadata panel farther to the left if you need to open up the window.

5 Select the arrow to the left of IPTC Core to reveal its contents. IPTC Core is the schema for XMP that provides a smooth and explicit transfer of metadata. Adobe's Extensible Metadata Platform (XMP) is a labeling technology that allows you to embed data about a file, known as metadata, into the file itself. With XMP, desktop applications and back-end publishing systems gain a common method for capturing and sharing, valuable metadata.

6 On the right side of this list, notice a series of pencils. The pencils indicate that you can enter information in these fields.

If you are not able to edit or add metadata information to a file, it may be locked. Make sure that you are not working directly off the Lesson DVD, and then right-click on the file (in Adobe Bridge) and choose Reveal in Explorer (Windows) or Reveal in Finder (Mac OS). In Windows, right-click on the file, choose Properties, and uncheck Read-only; in Mac OS, right-click on the file, choose Get Info, then change the Ownership and Permissions to Read and Write.

7 Scroll down until you can see Description Writer, and click on the pencil next to it. All editable fields are highlighted, and a cursor appears in the Description Writer field.

8 Type your name, or type **Student**.

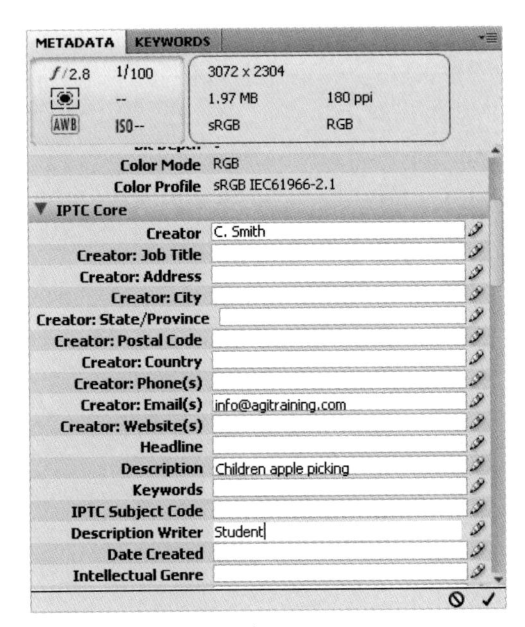

Reveal the IPTC contents and enter metadata information.

9 Scroll up to locate the Creator: City text field. Click on the pencil icon to the right of the Creator City text field, type the name of your city, and then press the Tab key. The cursor is now in the State text field. Enter your state information.

10 Check the Apply button (✓), located in the bottom-right corner of the Metadata panel, to apply your changes. You have now edited metadata that is attached to the image, information that will appear whenever someone opens your image in Bridge or views the image information in Adobe Photoshop, using File > File Info.

Using keywords

Keywords can reduce the amount of time it takes to find an image on a computer, by using logical words to help users locate images more quickly.

1 Click on the Keywords tab, which appears behind the Metadata panel. A list of commonly used keywords appears.

2 Click on the New Keyword button (✚) at the bottom of the Keywords panel. Type **Apple** into the active text field, and then press Enter (Windows) or Return (Mac OS).

3 Check the empty checkbox to the left of the apple keyword. This adds the Apple keyword to the selected image.

4 With the Apple keyword still selected, click on the New Sub Keyword button (✚). Type **Picking** into the active text field, then press Enter (Windows) or Return (Mac OS).

5 Check the empty checkbox to the left of the picking keyword. You have now assigned a keyword and a sub keyword to the IMG_0902.JPG image.

   Notice that the keywords you added appear at the top, under Assigned Keywords.

6 Select the Apple keyword, and then click on the New Keyword button (✚) at the bottom of the Keywords panel; a blank text field appears. Type **New England** and press Enter (Windows) or Return (Mac OS). Then check the checkbox next to New England to assign the keyword to this image.

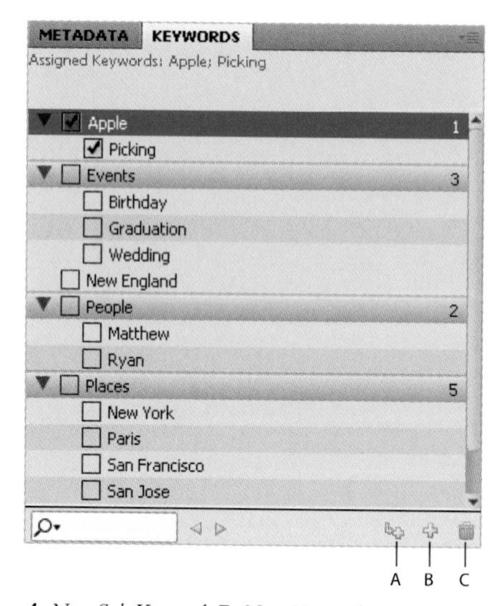

A. New Sub Keyword. B. New Keyword. C. Delete Keyword.

7 Right-click (Windows) or Ctrl+click (Mac OS) on the New England keyword, and choose the option Rename. When the text field becomes highlighted, type **Fall**, press Enter (Windows) or Return (Mac OS).

You can also enter information directly into the image by opening the image in Adobe Photoshop, and then choosing File > File Info. The categories that appear on the top include Description, Camera Data, IPTC, and IPTC Extension, among others. Once it is entered in the File Info dialog box, the information is visible in Adobe Bridge.

Creating a Metadata Template

Once you have added metadata to an image, you can easily apply it to more by creating a metadata template. In this exercise, you apply the metadata template from the IMG_0902.JPG image to some others in the same folder.

1 Make sure that IMG_0902.JPG is selected in Adobe Bridge.

2 Choose Tools > Create Metadata Template. The Create Metadata Template window appears.

3 In the Template Name text field (at the top), type **Fall Apple Picking**.

In the Create Metadata Template window, you can choose the information that you want to build into a template. In this exercise, we will choose information that already exists in the selected file, but if you wanted to, you could add or edit information at this point.

4 Check the Checkboxes to the left of the following categories; Creator, Creator Email(s), Description, Keywords, and Description Writer, then press Save.

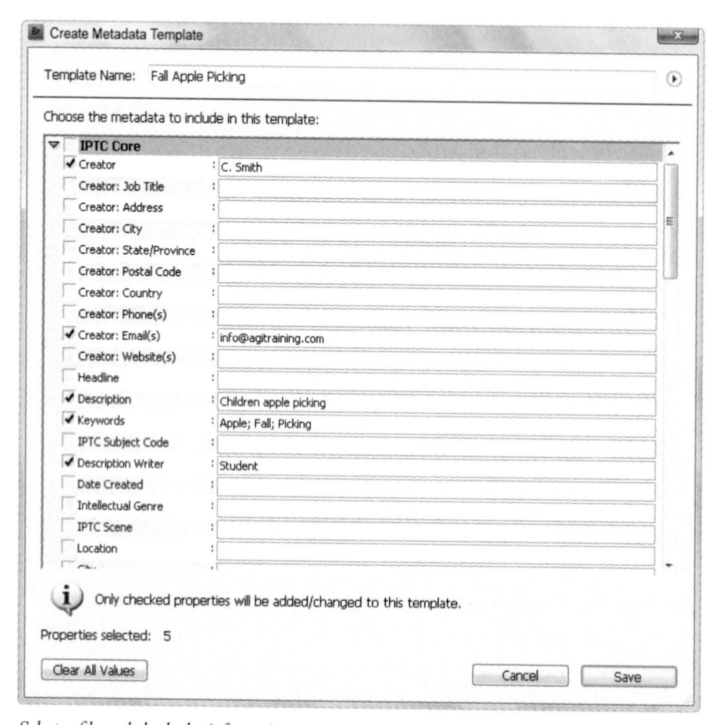

Select a file and check the information you want to save into a metadata template.

You have just saved a template. Next, you will apply it to several other images in this folder.

7 Select the IMG_0903.JPG image, and then hold down your Shift key and select the IMG_0907.JPG image. All the images in between are now selected.

8 Choose Tools > Replace Metadata and select Fall Apple Picking. Note that you can also choose Append Metadata if you are adding metadata to files that already have existing metadata. The same metadata has now been applied to all the images at once.

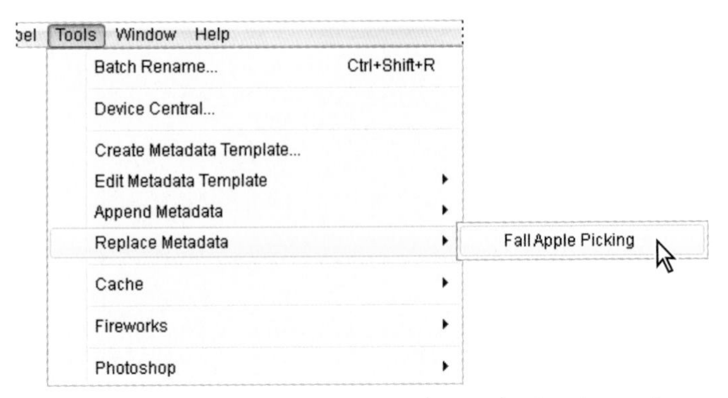

Choose the metadata template you want to use to replace metadata in an image or images.

Opening a file from Adobe Bridge

Opening files from Adobe Bridge is a great way to begin the work process in Adobe Photoshop. Not only is it very visual, but important data stored with the files also makes it easier to locate the correct file.

1 In the Favorites panel, click on the Apple Picking folder, and then double-click on image IMG_0910.JPG to open the file in Adobe Photoshop.

Sometimes you will find that double-clicking on a file opens it in a different application than expected. This can happen if you are working in generic file formats such as JPEG and GIF. To avoid this problem, you can right-click (Windows) or Ctrl+click (Mac OS) on the image, and choose Open With to select the appropriate application.

2 Choose File > Close and Go to Bridge to close the file in Photoshop and return to Adobe Bridge.

3 You can also click once to select an image and then choose File > Open, or use the keyboard shortcut Ctrl+O (Windows) or Command+O (Mac OS).

Searching for files using Adobe Bridge

Find the files that you want quickly and easily by using the Search tools built directly into Adobe Bridge, and taking advantage of the Filter panel.

In this example, you have a limited number of files to search within, but you will have the opportunity to see how helpful these search features can be.

Searching by name or keyword

What's the benefit of adding all this metadata if you can't use it to find your files later? Using the Find dialog box in Adobe Bridge, you can narrow your criteria down to make it easy to find your files when needed.

1 Click on ps03lessons in the Path bar to return to the ps03lessons folder content.

2 Choose Edit > Find, or use the keyboard shortcut, Ctrl+F (Windows) or Command+F (Mac OS). The Find dialog box appears.

3 Select Keywords from the Criteria drop-down menu, and type **apple** into the third text field (replacing Enter Text.) Then press Enter (Windows) or Return (Mac OS). Because you are looking within the active folder only, you get a result immediately. The image files, IMG_0902.JPG through IMG_0907.JPG appear.

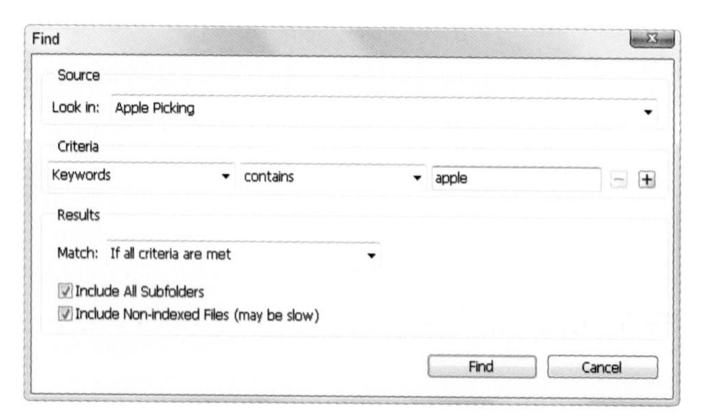

Search your folders using the tools built right into Adobe Bridge.

Using the Filter panel

If you have ever been in the position where you knew you put a file into a folder, but just couldn't seem to find it, you will love the Filter panel.

Using the Filter panel, you can look at attributes such as file type, keywords, and date created or modified, in order to narrow down the files that appear in the content window of Adobe Bridge.

1 Select the Apple Picking folder from the Favorites tab. This is the favorite that you added earlier in this lesson. Notice that the Filter panel collects the information from the active folder, indicating the keywords that are being used, as well as modification dates and more.

2 Click to turn down the arrow next to Keywords in the Filter panel, and select Apple from the list to see that only the image with the Apple keyword applied is visible. Click on Apple again to deselect it and view all the images.

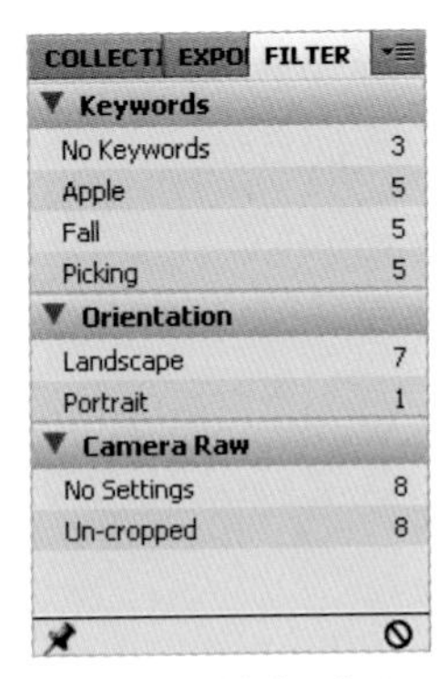

Find files quickly by selecting different criteria in the Filters panel.

3 Press the Clear filter button (⦸) in the lower-right of the Filter panel to turn off any filters.

Saving a Collection

If you like using Favorites, you'll love using Collections. A Collection allows you to take images from multiple locations and access them in one central location. Understand that Adobe Bridge essentially creates a shortcut (or alias) to your files and does not physically relocate them or copy them to a different location.

1 If your Collections tab is not visible, Choose Window > Collections or click on the tab next to Filter. The Collections panel comes forward.

2 Click on the New Collection button in the lower right of the Collections panel and type **Fall Images** into the new collection text field.

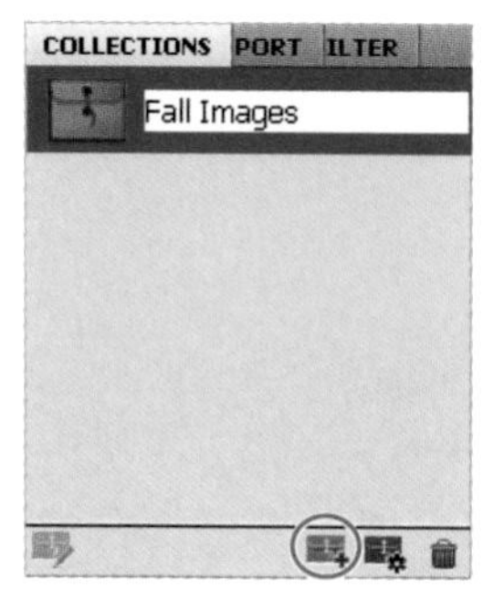

Create a new collection and rename it Fall Images.

3 Click on Apple Picking in the Favorites tab and drag two images (it does not matter which ones) to the newly created Fall Images collection.

4 Using the navigation features at the top of Adobe Bridge, click back on ps03lessons, to return to that folder.

Navigate back to the ps03lessons folder.

5 Take two random soccer images and drag them to the Fall Images collection as well.

6 Click on the Fall Images collection folder to see that even though you selected images from two different folders, you can easily access them at once in this collection. The files also remain intact in their original location.

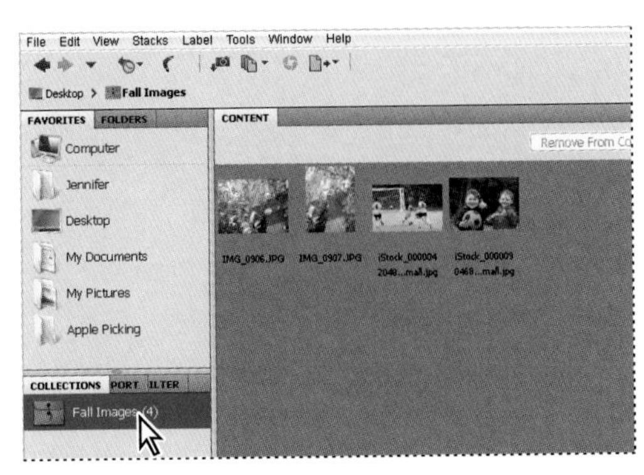

A collection can help you to organize files without actually moving them to new locations.

Automation tools in Adobe Bridge

Adobe Bridge provides many tools to help you automate tasks. In this section, you will learn how to access and take advantage of some of these features.

Batch renaming your files

You may have noticed that in the ps03lessons file there are many files that contain iStock in the filename. These images were downloaded from *iStockphoto.com*, and instead of changing the names immediately we have opted to change them simultaneously using the batch rename feature in Adobe Bridge.

1 Press the Go back arrow in the upper-left of the Adobe Bridge window to go back to the ps03lessons folder.

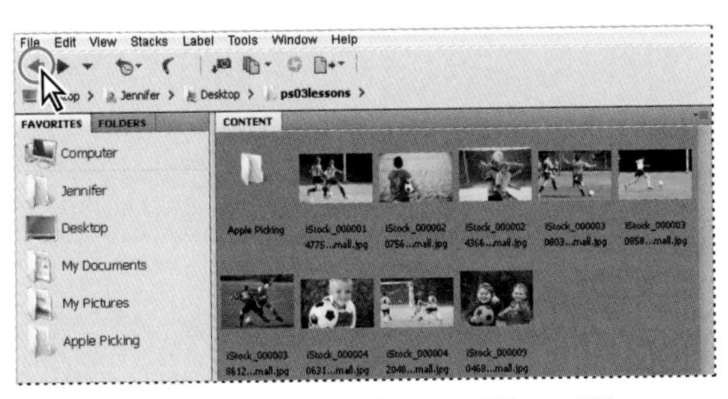

Click on the Go back arrow to go back to the ps03lessons folder.

2 Choose Edit > Select All, or press Ctrl+A (Windows) or Command+A (Mac OS.) All the images are selected.

3 Choose Tools > Batch Rename. The Batch Rename dialog box appears.

In this instance we want a simple uncomplicated name. If you look in the Preview section at the bottom of the Batch Rename dialog box you can see that the Current filename and New filename are pretty long strings of text and numbers. You will simplify this by eliminating some of text from the filenames.

4 In the New Filenames section, type **Soccer** in the text field to the right of default criteria of Text.

5 For the next two criteria, click on the Minus sign button (⊟) (Remove this text from the file names) to remove them. The New filename in the Preview section becomes significantly shorter.

6 In the Sequence Number row, change Four Digits to Two Digits. The New filename is a very simple Soccer01.jpg now. Press the Rename button. All the selected files automatically have their name changed.

Automated tools for Photoshop: Web Photo Gallery

If you want to share images online, you can use the Web Photo Gallery, which creates a web site that features a home page with thumbnail images and gallery pages with full-size images. You select the images you want to include in the site and Adobe Bridge does the rest, from automatically creating navigation images, like arrows, links, and buttons, to creating Flash files. This is a fun feature that you can take advantage of quickly, even if you have no coding experience. If you have coding experience, or if you want to edit the pages further, you can open the pages in Adobe Dreamweaver or any other HTML editor to customize them.

1 Make sure that you are viewing the contents of the ps03lessons folder, and press Ctrl+A (Windows) or Command+A (Mac OS) to select all the images.

2 Hold down the Ctrl (Windows) or Command (Mac OS) and click on the Apple Picking folder to deselect it. If it is easier, you can leave the folder selected, you will receive a warning that some of the selected files are not supported image files, but it will not cause any errors.

3 Click and hold down on the Output drop-down menu in the Application bar, and choose Output; the workspace changes to reveal an Output panel on the right.

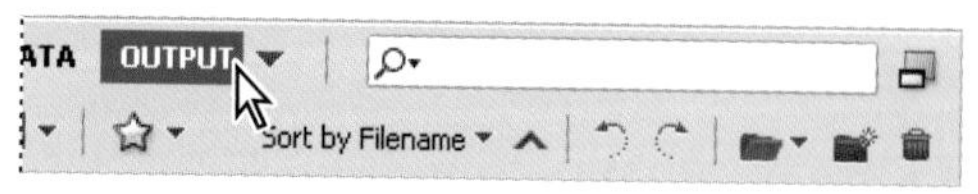

Select multiple images and then select Output.

If you cannot see all the options in the Output panel, click and drag the vertical bar to the left of the panel to increase its size.

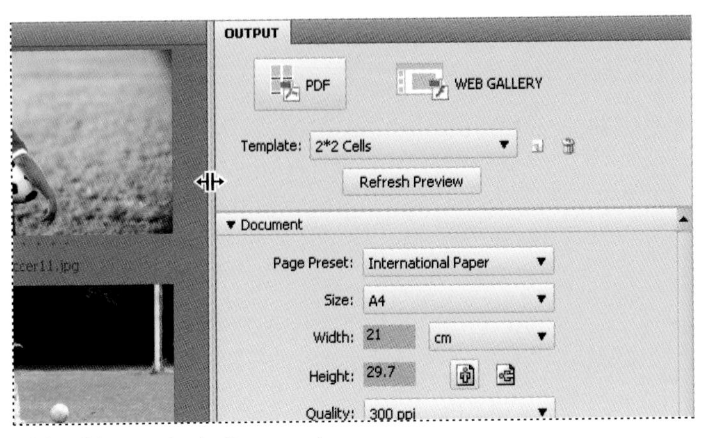

Click and drag to resize the Output panel.

4 Press the Web Gallery button at the top of the Output panel.

5 Click and hold on the Templates drop-down menu, and choose HTML Gallery. As you can see, there are a lot of options to choose from, including Lightroom Flash Galleries. In this example, you will keep it simple.

6 From the Styles drop-down menu, if it's not already visible, choose Lightroom.

7 In the Site Info section of the Output panel, type a title in the Gallery Title text field; for this example, you can type **My First Web Gallery**.

8 You can also add photograph captions if you like, as well as text in the About This Gallery text field, to include more information. In this example, those are left at their defaults.

9 Using the scroll bar to the right of the Style Info section, click and drag to scroll down through the rest of the options. Note that you can add additional contact information, and define colors that you want to use for different objects on the page, including text.

10 Press the Preview in Browser button that is located in the upper half of the Output panel; your web site is automatically created.

Note that if you had your Apple Picking folder selected, you will get a warning that some of the files are not support image types, Press OK.

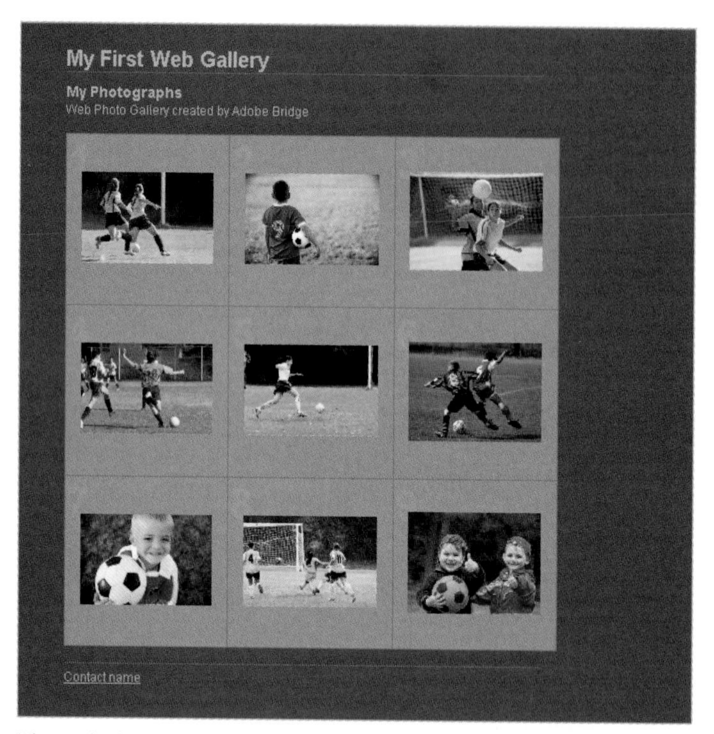

The completed web site, using Web Gallery.

11 Note that the preview is in a browser window. You will want to close that window before you move to the next part of this lesson.

Saving or uploading your Web Gallery

So now you have an incredible Web Gallery, but what do you do with it? The Web Photo Gallery feature creates an index page, individual gallery pages, and images, and so you need someplace to put them. You have a couple of options available if you click the scroll bar to the right of Site Info and drag down until you see the option under Create Gallery for Gallery Name. Note that you can choose to save your Gallery to a location on your hard drive, or input the FTP login information directly in Adobe Bridge to upload your file directly to a server. In this example, you will save the Web Gallery to in your ps03lessons folder.

1 Scroll down in the Output panel until you see the Create Gallery section. Click the Browse button to the right of Save Location. Navigate to the ps03lessons folder on your desktop, and click Open.

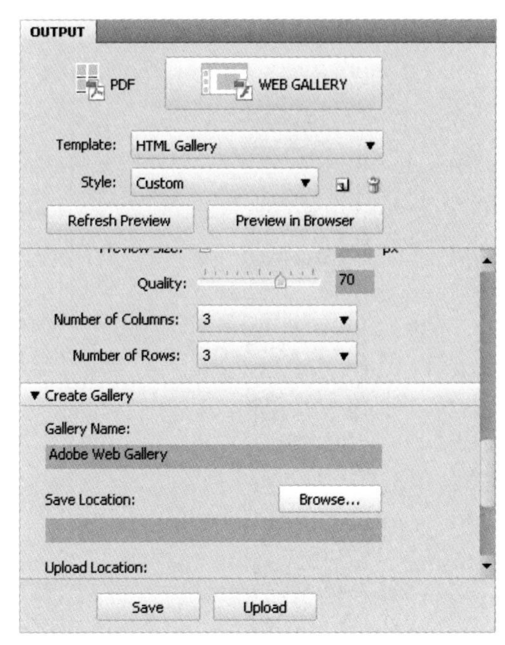

Choose to Save your web gallery.

2 Click on the Save button at the bottom of the Output panel. A dialog box appears, indicating that you have successfully created a Gallery; press OK.

You have successfully saved your Web Gallery. Use Adobe Bridge to navigate and open the contents of this folder to see that a folder named My First Web Gallery is inside your Adobe Web Gallery folder. Open the contents to see that your components are neatly organized so that you can open them in your web editor and customize them, or send them to your web site administrator for uploading.

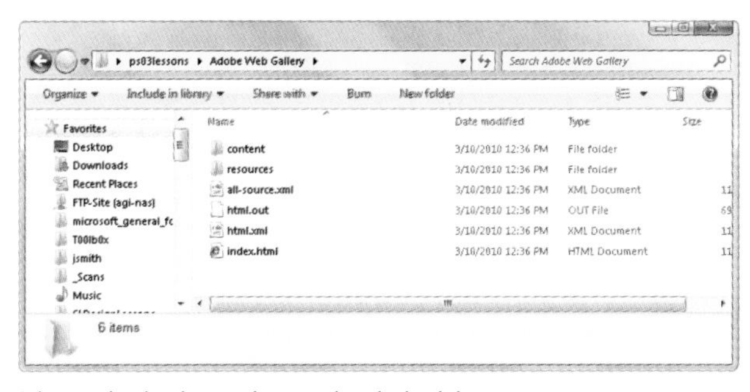

The completed web site, when saved to the hard drive.

Automated tools for Photoshop: PDF contact sheet

By creating a PDF contact sheet, you can assemble a series of images into one file for such purposes as client approval and summaries of folders.

1 To make it easy to select just the images you want, click on Essentials to change the Adobe Bridge workspace back to the defaults. If you do not see the contents of the ps03lessons folder in the content window in Bridge, choose the Favorites panel and click on Desktop. Double-click on the ps03lessons folder. If you stored the lesson files elsewhere, use the navigation tools in Bridge to locate your lesson files.

2 Click on the first soccer image you see and then Shift+click on the last, selecting all the soccer images, but neither of the folders inside the ps03lessons folder.

3 Select Output from the upper-right of the Adobe Bridge workspace.

4 In the Output panel, click on the PDF button, then from the Template drop-down menu, choose 5*8 Contact Sheet.

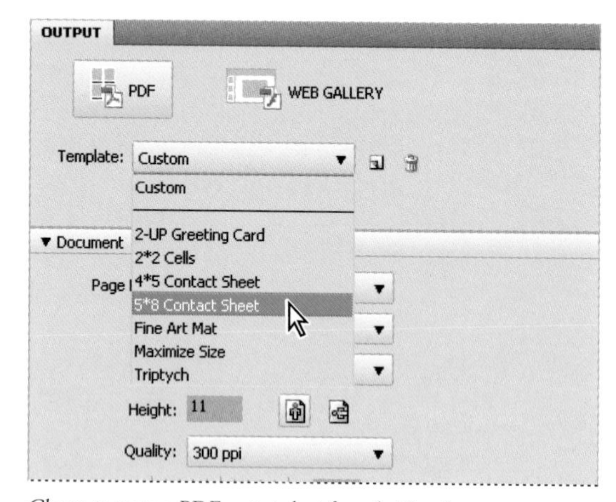

Choose to create a PDF contact sheet from the Template drop-down menu.

5 In the Document section of the Output panel, choose U.S. Paper from the Page Preset drop-down menu.

Scroll down and notice that you have options for final size, document quality, and even security in the Output panel. You will leave these items at the default and scroll down to the Playback section of this panel.

6 At the bottom of the Output panel check the checkbox to View PDF After Save; then press the Save button. The Save As dialog box appears.

7 In the Save As dialog box, type **contact**, and then browse to save the file in your ps03lessons folder; press Save.

   A dialog box appears, indicating that you have successfully created a PDF contact sheet; press OK. The contact.pdf file is saved in your ps03lessons folder and your contact sheet is launched in Adobe Acrobat for you to view.

8 After examining your contact sheet in Adobe Acrobat, choose File > Close to close the contact.pdf file, and return to Adobe Bridge.

The completed PDF contact sheet.

Changing the view

You can work the way you like by adjusting the look and feel of Adobe Bridge. Changing the view can help you focus on what is important to see in the Content section of the Bridge workspace. Whether you need to focus on content or thumbnails, there is a view that can help you.

1 Before experimenting with the views, make sure that you are in the Essentials workspace by selecting the Essentials button located in the upper-right in the Bridge workspace.

2 Click on the Click to Lock to Thumbnail Grid button (▦) in the lower-right corner of the Bridge workspace. The images are organized into a grid.

3 Now click on the View Content as Details button (▬≡) to see a thumbnail and details about creation date, last modified date, and file size.

Changing the view of Adobe Bridge.

4 Choose the View Content as List button (:═) to see the contents consolidated into a neat list, which you can easily scroll through.

5 Click on the View Content as Thumbnails button (∷∷) to return to the default thumbnail view.

6 Experiment with changing the size of the thumbnails in the Content panel by using the slider to the left of the preview buttons. Don't forget, you can also change the thumbnail size by pressing Ctrl++ (plus sign) or Ctrl+- (minus sign) (Windows) or Command++ (plus sign) or Command+- (minus sign) (Mac OS).

Self study

As you work with Bridge, create some new Favorites of folders that you frequently use. You might also want to practice removing Favorites: highlight the Favorite and choose File > Remove from Favorites. Also, explore creating a PDF slide show when in the Adobe Media Gallery workspace. By turning on the Playback options in the Output panel, you can create a full-screen presentation of the images in the Content panel of Adobe Bridge.

Review

Questions

1 How do you access Photoshop automation features from within Adobe Bridge?

2 Where do you find the metadata for an image, and how do you know if the metadata is editable?

3 Which panel in Adobe Bridge enables you to organize your files on your computer?

4 Which panel allows you to create Web Galleries, PDF presentations, and contact sheets?

Answers

1 You can access automated tools for Adobe Photoshop by choosing Tools > Photoshop.

2 You find metadata information in the Metadata and Keywords panels in the lower-right corner of the Bridge workspace. Metadata is editable if it has the pencil icon next to it.

3 You can use the Folders panel to organize your files.

4 You must be in the Output panel to create Web Galleries, PDF presentations, and contact sheets.

What you'll learn in this lesson:

- Combining images
- Understanding document settings
- Removing backgrounds
- Saving files

The Basics of Working with Photoshop

In this lesson, you'll learn how to combine images while gaining an understanding of image resolution and file size. You'll also learn about file formats and options for saving your files for use on the Web or in print.

Starting up

Before starting, make sure that your tools and panels are consistent by resetting your preferences. See "Resetting Adobe Photoshop CS5 preferences" on page 3.

You will work with several files from the ps04lessons folder in this lesson. Make sure that you have loaded the pslessons folder onto your hard drive from the supplied DVD. See "Loading lesson files" on page 5.

In this lesson, you'll use multiple images to create a composite image that you will then save for both print and online use. While this lesson covers some basic information about working with files for online distribution, you can learn even more about saving files for the web in Lesson 12, "Creating Images for Web and Video."

See Lesson 4 in action!

Use the accompanying video to gain a better understanding of how to use some of the features shown in this lesson. The video tutorial for this lesson can be found on the included DVD.

A look at the finished project

In this lesson, you will develop a composite using several images, while addressing issues such as resolution, resizing, and choosing the right file format.

To see the finished document:

1 Choose File > Browse in Bridge to open Adobe Bridge, or click the Launch Bridge (Br) or the Mini Bridge button (Mb) in the Application bar. Using Adobe Bridge, navigate to the pslessons folder on your hard drive and open the ps04lessons folder.

2 Double-click on the ps04_done.psd file, and the completed image is displayed in Photoshop.

The completed lesson file.

3 Make sure that the Layers panel is active by choosing Window > Layers.

4 Click on the visibility icon (👁) to the left of the cow layer to hide the layer. Click the box where the visibility icon used to be to make the layer visible again.

Layers allow you to combine different elements into a single file while retaining the ability to move and modify each layer independently of the others. In this chapter, you'll be creating multiple layers in Photoshop just like the ones in this finished file.

5 You can keep this file open for reference, or choose File > Close to close the file. If a Photoshop warning box appears, choose Don't Save.

Opening an existing document

Now you will assemble all the images that are part of the final combined image.

1 Return to Adobe Bridge by choosing File > Browse in Bridge or selecting the Launch Bridge or Mini Bridge button in the Options bar.

2 Navigate to the pslessons folder you copied onto your system, and open the ps04lessons folder.

3 From the ps04lessons folder, select the file named ps0401.psd. Hold down the Ctrl key (Windows) or Command key (Mac OS), and also select the ps0402.psd and ps0403.psd files. Choose File > Open or double-click any one of the selected files. All the selected images open in Adobe Photoshop.

If you receive an Embedded Profile Mismatch warning when opening the images, you may have forgotten to reset your preferences using the instructions on page 3. If you receive the warning, choose the Use Embedded Profile option, and then click OK.

Understanding document settings

In this section, you will move images from one file to another to create your mock-up. Before you combine the images, you need to be familiar with each document's unique attributes, such as size, resolution, and color mode. Moving layers between documents that have different resolutions may create unexpected results, such as causing the images to appear out of proportion.

Viewing an image's size and resolution

1 Click on the tab of the image of the barn, ps0401.psd, to make it active. Press Alt (Windows) or Option (Mac OS) and click the file information area in the status bar, located in the lower-left corner of the document window. The dimensions of the barn image is displayed as 885 pixels wide by 542 pixels tall and the Resolution is 72 Pixels/inch.

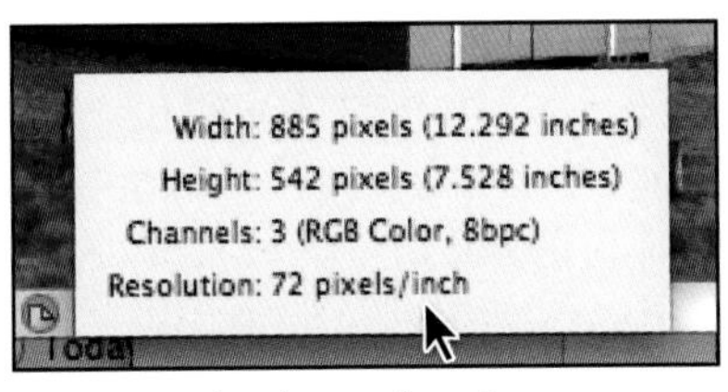

Image size and resolution information.

2 If the picture of the rooster, ps0402.psd, is not visible, choose Window > ps0402.psd or click on the tab for that image at the top of the screen to make it the active window. After confirming that this is the active document, select Image > Image Size to open the Image Size dialog box.

The Image Size dialog box appears.

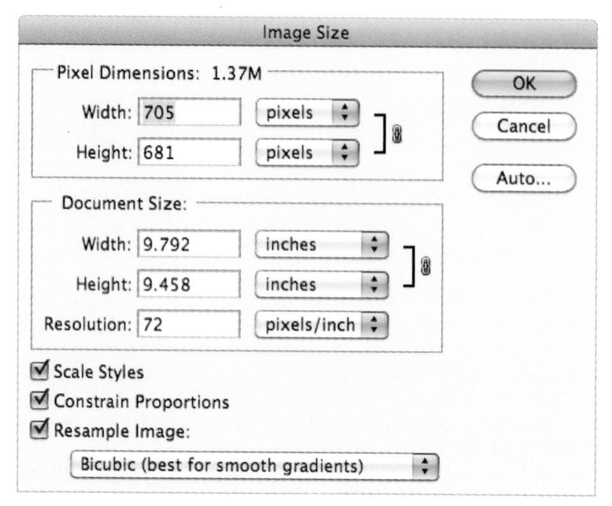

Image size plays an important role when combining images.

The Image Size dialog box is divided into two main areas: Pixel Dimensions and Document Size. Pixel Dimensions shows the number of pixels that make up the image. For web graphics, the pixel dimensions are more relevant than the document's actual printing size. Document Size shows the resolution information, as well as the actual physical size of the image.

The most important factors for size and resolution of web images are the pixel dimensions and the pixels per inch (ppi). If you are designing content for the Web, you should reference the top (Pixel Dimensions) section of the Image Size dialog box. As a print designer, you should reference the bottom (Document Size) section of the Image Size dialog box.

3 The image size of the rooster is 705 pixels by 681 pixels. At this size, the rooster is taller than the barn, which would be apparent when you combine the two files. While this might work for an *Attack of the Roosters* horror movie, you're interested in making the rooster smaller.

4 Make sure that the Resample Image and Constrain Proportions checkboxes are both selected. In the Image Size dialog box, type **200** pixels for height in the Pixel Dimensions portion at the top half of the dialog box. Press OK to apply the transformation and close the Image Size dialog box.

5 The rooster is now an appropriate size to combine with the barn image.

Combining the images

For this project, you'll use several methods to combine the images.

Using Copy and Paste

1 If necessary, click the tab of the rooster image, ps0402.psd, to make it active.

You can have many documents open at once in Photoshop, but only one of them is active at any given time.

2 Choose Select > All to select the entire image. This creates a selection marquee around the outside edge of the image. You can learn more about selections in Lesson 5, "Making the Best Selections."

3 Choose Edit > Copy to copy the selected image area. The image is now in your computer's clipboard, ready to be pasted into another document.

4 Select the tab of the barn picture, ps0401.psd, to make it the active document. Choose Edit > Paste to place the image of the rooster into the picture of the barn.

The rooster appears on top of the barn, and the background surrounding the rooster blocks part of the image. Both these items will be addressed in future steps in this lesson.

The image of the rooster is now in the middle of the barn.

5 Select the tab of the rooster image, ps0402.psd, and choose File > Close to close the file. Do not save any changes.

Dragging and dropping to copy an image

In this section, you'll drag and drop one image into another.

1 Click on the Arrange Documents button (▦), in the Application bar, and choose 2 Up from the drop-down menu to view both the cow (ps0403.psd) and the barn (ps0401.psd) pictures at the same time. The Arrange commands allow you to determine how windows are displayed on your monitor; the Tile command allows you to see all the open images.

2 Select the Move tool (▸+), and then select the picture of the cow, which is the ps0403.psd image. Click and drag the cow image over to the barn image. When your cursor is positioned over the picture of the barn, release your mouse. The cow picture is placed into the barn picture on a new layer.

Like using the Copy and Paste command, you can use the Move tool to copy images from one document to another.

Click and drag the cow image into the picture of the barn.

3 Select the tab of ps0403.psd and choose File > Close to close the file containing the picture of the cow. Do not save any changes to the file.

4 With the composite image of the barn, rooster, and cow active, choose View > Fit on Screen, or use the keyboard shortcut Ctrl+0 (zero) (Windows) or Command+0 (zero) (Mac OS). This fits the entire image into your document window.

The barn picture combined with the other images.

5 Choose File > Save As to save this file. When the Save As dialog box appears, navigate to the ps04lessons folder and type **ps0401_work** in the Name text field. Choose Photoshop from the format drop-down menu and press Save. If the Photoshop format options dialog box appears, press OK.

Transforming and editing combined images

Although you have combined three images together, they still require some work. The background remains in the two imported images, and the picture of the cow is out of proportion when compared with the barn.

In order to use the transform options, the affected area must reside on a layer. Layers act as clear overlays on your image and can be used in many ways. Find out more about layers in Lesson 8, "Getting to Know Layers," and Lesson 9, "Taking Layers to the Max."

In this section, you will do the following:

- View the stacking order of the layers that were automatically created when you combined the images;
- Remove the background from the copied images;
- Refine the edges of the combined images;
- Name the layers to organize them.

Changing the size of a placed image

While you could have adjusted the image size prior to dragging and dropping it into the barn picture, you can also make adjustments to layers and the objects that reside on the layers. Here you will adjust the size and position of the placed images.

1 Make sure the Layers panel is visible. If you do not see the Layers panel, choose Window > Layers.

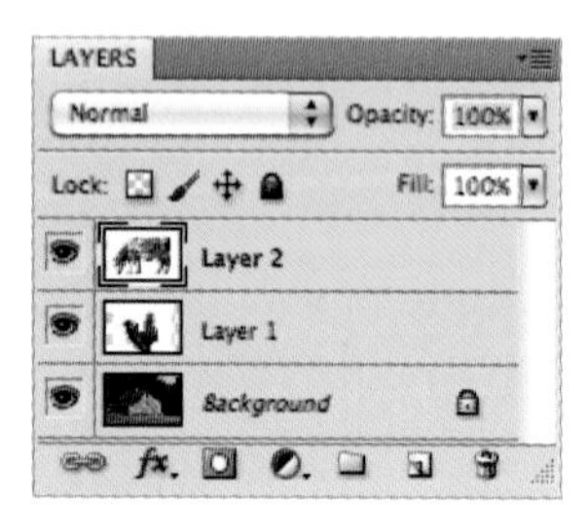

The Layers panel, with the layers that are part of the combined file.

2 Double-click on the words Layer 1, to the right of the image thumbnail of the rooster in the Layers panel. When the text field becomes highlighted, type **rooster**, and then press Enter (Windows) or Return (Mac OS) to accept the change. Repeat this process to rename Layer 2, typing the name **cow**.

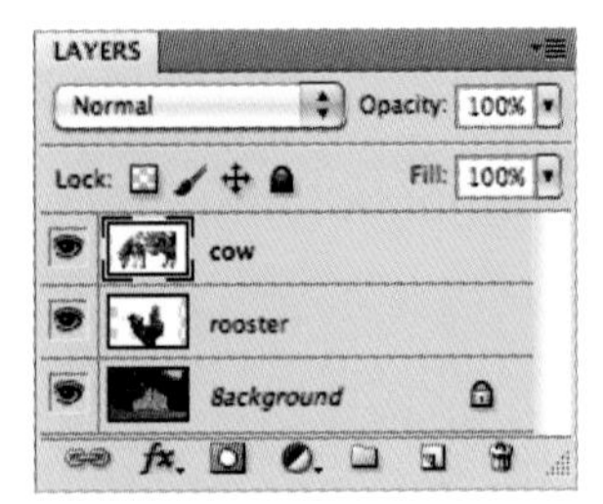

The layers renamed.

3 With the cow layer selected in the Layers panel, choose Edit > Free Transform, or use the keyboard shortcut Ctrl+T (Windows) or Command+T (Mac OS). Handles appear around the edges of the cow. Keep the cow selected. If you do not see handles press Ctrl+0 (zero) (Windows) or Command+0 (zero) (Mac OS) to fit the image into the window.

4 Press and hold Alt+Shift (Windows) or Option+Shift (Mac OS), and then click and drag any one of the handles on the outside corner edges of the cow toward the center. The image size is reduced.

Notice that the scale percentages in the Options bar change as you scale the image. Reduce the size of the cow image to approximately 50 percent of its original size. Holding the Shift key maintains the proportions as you scale, while the Alt or Option key scales the image toward its center.

5 In the Options bar, click the Commit Transform button (✓), or press Enter (Windows) or Return (Mac OS), to accept the changes.

6 If you do not see the Rooster image, use the Move tool to reposition the cow to reveal it. In the Layers panel, click to activate the rooster layer, and then choose Edit > Free Transform.

7 Press and hold Alt+Shift (Windows) or Option+Shift (Mac OS) and reduce the size of the rooster to approximately 60 percent, using the Options bar as a guide to the scaling you are performing. Click the Commit Transform button, or press Enter (Windows) or Return (Mac OS), to accept the changes.

The cow layer being reduced in size, using the Free Transform command.

Removing a background

Photoshop CS5 makes it easy to remove the background of an image. Here you'll use a method that works well with solid backgrounds, such as the white behind the cow and rooster.

1 Select the cow layer in the Layers panel.

2 In the Tools panel, click to select the Magic Eraser tool (). You may need to click and hold on the Eraser tool to access the Magic Eraser tool.

3 Position the Magic Eraser tool over the white area behind the cow, and click once to remove the white background.

Use the Magic Eraser tool to remove the background behind the cow.

4 In the Layers panel, click to activate the rooster layer.

5 Position the cursor over the white area adjacent to the rooster, and click once to remove the white background.

Understanding the stacking order of layers

Layers are much like pieces of clear film that you could place on a table. The layers themselves are clear, but anything placed on one of the layers will be positioned on top of the layers that are located beneath it.

1 Confirm that the rooster layer remains selected. Click to select the Move tool (✥) from the Tools panel.

2 Position the Move tool over the rooster image in the document window, and drag the rooster so your cursor is positioned over the head of the cow. Notice that the rooster image is positioned under the cow. This is because the cow layer is on top of the rooster layer in the Layers panel.

3 In the Layers panel, click and hold the rooster layer. Drag the layer up so it is positioned on top of the cow layer. Notice in the document window how the stacking order of the layers affects the stacking order of the objects in the image.

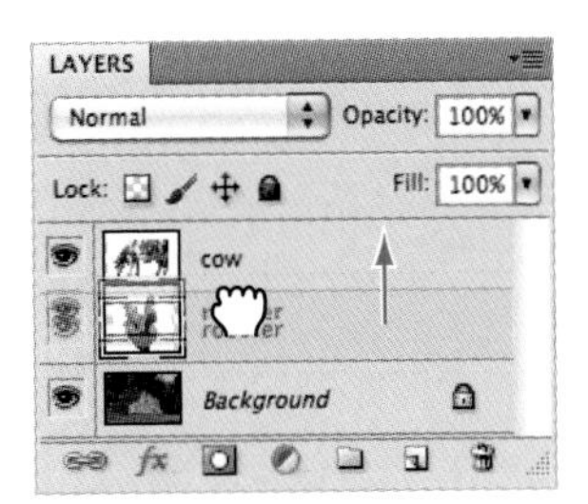

Click and drag the rooster layer up to place it on top of the cow layer.

4 Using the Move tool, click and drag the rooster to position it in the lower-left corner of the image, in front of the fence and along the side of the barn. If your image seems to *jump* when you are trying to position the image, choose View > Snap to prevent the edge of the image from snapping to the edge of the document.

5 Click to activate the cow layer, and then, continuing to use the Move tool, click and drag the cow to position it in the lower-right corner of the image. Position the cow so it appears to be grazing on the grass without hanging outside the image area.

6 Choose File > Save. Keep the file open for the next part of this lesson.

Refining the edges of copied images

When the images were copied, they maintained very hard edges, making it very clear where the picture of the cow or rooster stops and the original image starts. This hard edge makes the images look contrived. You will blend the images so they look more natural together.

1 Click to select the cow layer in the Layers panel. Choose the Zoom tool (🔍) from the Tools panel, then click and drag to create a zoom area around the entire cow. The cow is magnified to fill the entire display area.

2 Choose Layer > Matting > Defringe. The Defringe dialog box opens.

3 In the Defringe dialog box, maintain the default setting of 1 pixel, then click OK. The Defringe command blends the edges of the layer into the background, making it appear more natural.

The cow before it is defringed.

The cow after it is defringed.

4 Press **H** on the keyboard to choose the Hand tool (✋). Using the Hand tool, click and drag the window to the right to reveal the content positioned on the left side of the image. Stop dragging when the rooster is visible.

5 In the Layers panel, click to activate the rooster layer, then choose Layer > Matting > Defringe. The Defringe dialog box opens.

6 In the Defringe dialog box, once again maintain the default setting of 1 pixel, and then click OK. The Defringe command affects only the selected layer.

Notice that both the rooster and the cow now look more naturally blended into the background.

7 Press Ctrl+Z (Windows) or Command+Z (Mac OS) to undo the application of the Defringe command. Notice the hard edge around the perimeter of the rooster. Press Ctrl+Z or Command+Z again to re-apply the Defringe command.

8 Double-click the Hand tool in the Tools panel to fit the entire image in the document window. This can be easier than choosing View > Fit on Screen, yet it achieves the same result.

9 Choose File > Save.

Adding text

You will now add text to the image.

1 With the ps0401_work file still open, click to select the rooster layer in the Layers panel.

2 In the Tools panel, click to select the Type tool (T) and click in the upper-left corner of the image, just above the roof of the barn. Notice that a layer appears on top of the rooster layer in the Layers panel.

3 In the Options bar, select the following:

- From the font family drop-down menu, choose Myriad Pro. If you do not have this font, you can choose another.
- From the font style drop-down menu, choose Bold Italic.
- From the font size drop-down menu, choose 72.

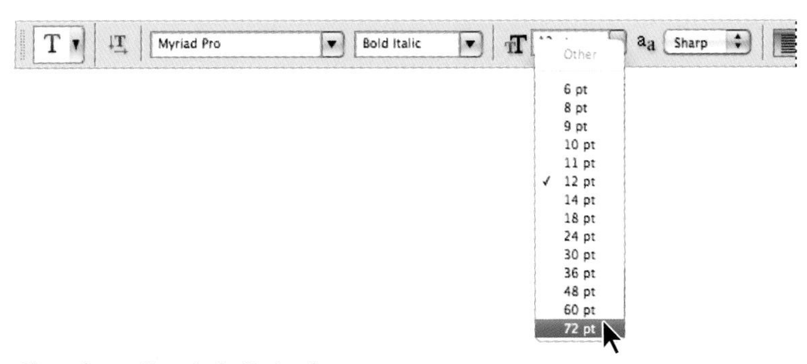

Choose font attributes in the Options bar.

4 Click once on the Set Text Color box (■) in the Options bar. The text Color Picker appears. Click on white or any light color that appears in the upper-left corner of the color pane, then press OK to close the Color Picker window.

5 Type **Big Red Barn**; the text appears above the roof of the barn. When you are finished typing, click on the Commit checkbox (✓) in the Options bar to confirm the text.

6 With the text layer still active, click the Add a Layer Style button (*fx*) at the bottom of the Layers panel, and choose Stroke. The Layer Style dialog box opens, with the Stroke options visible; click on the color box and choose a red color. Press OK to accept the color, and then click OK again to apply the stroke. A stroke is added to the border of the text.

7 Choose File > Save. Keep the file open for the next part of this lesson.

Saving files

Adobe Photoshop allows you to save your files in a variety of file formats, which makes it possible to use your images in many different ways. You can save images to allow for additional editing of things such as layers and effects you have applied in Photoshop, or save images for sharing with users who need only the finished file for use on the Web or for printing. In all, Photoshop allows you to save your file in more than a dozen unique file formats.

As you work on images, it is best to save them using the default Photoshop format, which uses the .PSD extension at the end of the filename. This is the native Photoshop file format, and retains the most usable data without a loss in image quality. Because the Photoshop format is developed by Adobe, many non-Adobe software applications do not recognize the PSD format.

Additionally, the PSD format may contain more information than you need, and may be a larger file size than is appropriate for sharing through e-mail or posting on a web site. While you may create copies of images for sharing, it is a good idea to keep an original version in the PSD format as a master file that you can access if necessary. This is especially important because some file formats are considered to be *lossy* formats, which means that they remove image data in order to reduce the size of the file.

Understanding file formats

While Photoshop can be used to create files for all sorts of media, the three most common uses for image files are web, print, and video production. Following is a list of the most common formats and how they are used.

WEB PRODUCTION FORMATS	
JPEG (Joint Photographic Experts Group)	This is a common format for digital camera photographs and the primary format for full-color images shared on the web. JPEG images use lossy compression, which degrades the quality of images and discards color and pixel data. Once the image data is lost, it cannot be recovered.
GIF (Graphic Interchange Format)	GIF files are used to display limited (indexed) color graphics on the Web. It is a compressed format that reduces the file size of images, but it only supports a limited number of colors and is thus more appropriate for logos and artwork than photographs. GIF files support transparency.
PNG (Portable Network Graphics)	PNG was developed as an alternative to GIF for displaying images on the Web. It uses lossless compression and supports transparency.

PRINT PRODUCTION FORMATS	
PSD (Photoshop document)	The Photoshop format (PSD) is the default file format and the only format, besides the Large Document Format (PSB), that supports most Photoshop features. Files saved as PSD can be used in other Adobe applications, such as Adobe Illustrator, Adobe InDesign, Adobe Premiere, and others. The programs can directly import PSD files and access many Photoshop features, such as layers.
TIFF or TIF (Tagged Image File Format)	TIFF is a common bitmap image format. Most image-editing software and page-layout applications support TIFF images up to 2GB in file size. TIFF supports most color modes and can save images with alpha channels. While Photoshop can also include layers in a TIFF file, most other applications cannot use these extended features and see only the combined (flattened) image.
EPS (Encapsulated PostScript)	EPS files may contain both vector and bitmap data. Because it is a common file format used in print production, most graphics software programs support the EPS format for importing or placing images. EPS is a subset of the PostScript format. Some software applications cannot preview the high-resolution information contained within an EPS file, so Photoshop allows you to save a special preview file for use with these programs, using either the EPS TIFF or EPS PICT option. EPS supports most color modes, as well as clipping paths, which are commonly used to silhouette images and remove backgrounds.
Photoshop PDF	Photoshop PDF files are extremely versatile, as they may contain bitmap and vector data. Images saved in the Photoshop PDF format can maintain the editing capabilities of most Photoshop features, such as vector objects, text, and layers, and most color spaces are supported. Photoshop PDF files can also be shared with other graphics applications, as most of the current versions of graphics software are able to import or manipulate PDF files. Photoshop PDF files can even be opened by users with the free Adobe Reader software.

VIDEO PRODUCTION FORMATS	
TIFF or TIF	*See Print Production Formats, above.*
TARGA (Truevision Advanced Raster Graphics Adapter)	This legacy file format is used for video production. The TARGA format supports millions of colors, along with alpha channels.

Choosing a file format

In this section, you will save your file to share online and for printing. You will use two common formats, JPEG and Photoshop PDF.

Saving a JPEG file

To save a copy of your image for sharing online, whether on a web site or to send through e-mail, you will save it using the JPEG file format. In this lesson, you will use the Save menu, but in Lesson 12, "Creating Images for Web and Video," you will discover additional features when saving files for use online, including how to use the Save for Web & Devices feature in Photoshop.

1 Choose File > Save As.

2 In the Save As dialog box, type **farm** in the File name text field. From the Format drop-down menu, choose JPEG. If necessary, navigate to the ps04lessons folder so the file is saved in this location, then press the Save button. The JPEG Options dialog box appears.

3 In the JPEG Options dialog box, confirm the quality is set to maximum, and leave the format options set to their defaults. Press OK. This completes the Save process for your file.

4 Choose File > Close to close the file.

Because JPEG is supported by web browsers, you can check your file by opening it using any web browser, such as Firefox, Internet Explorer, or Safari. Open the browser and choose File > Open, which may appear as Open File or Open Location, depending upon the application. Navigate to the ps04lessons folder and double-click to open the file you saved.

Saving for print

In this part of the lesson, you will change the color settings to choose a color profile more suitable for print to help you preview and prepare your file for printing. You will change the resolution of the image before saving it.

Changing the color settings

You will now change the color settings to get a more accurate view of how the file will print.

1 If ps0401 is not open choose File > Open Recent > ps0401_work.psd. You can use the Open Recent command to easily locate the most recently opened files. The file opens.

2 Choose Edit > Color Settings. The Color Settings dialog box appears.

3 From the Color Settings drop-down menu, choose North America Prepress 2. This provides you with a color profile based upon typical printing environments in North America. Press OK to close the Color Settings dialog box.

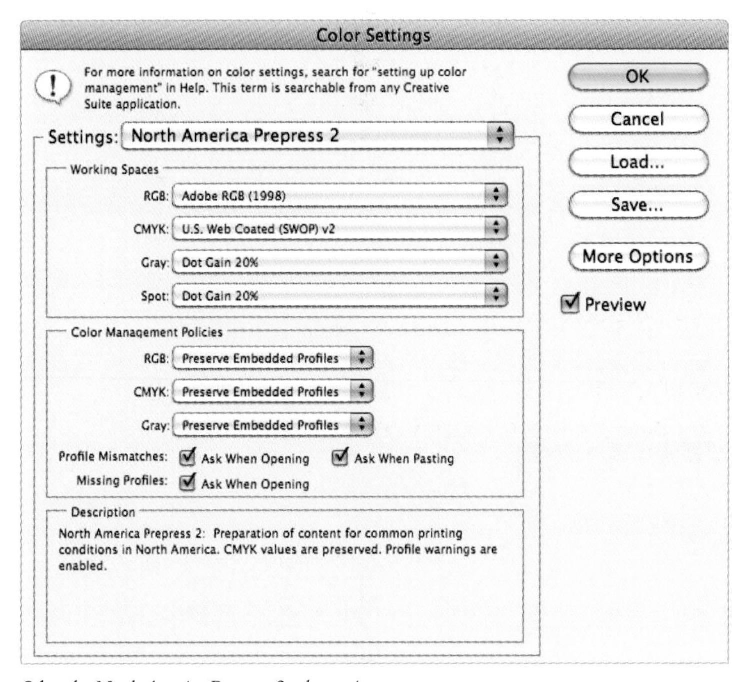

Select the North America Prepress 2 color setting.

4 Choose the Zoom tool (🔍) from the Tools panel, and then click and drag to create a zoom area around the text at the top of the image. The text is magnified to fill the entire display area.

5 Choose View > Proof Colors. Notice a slight change in the color of the red stroke around the text, as the colors appear more subdued. The Proof Colors command allows you to work in the RGB format while approximating how your image will look when converted to CMYK, the color space used for printing. While you will work on images in the RGB mode, they generally must be converted to CMYK before they are printed.

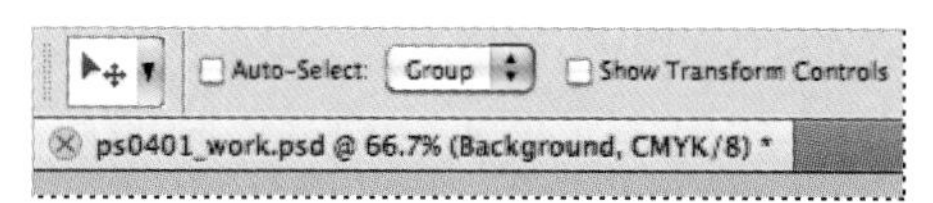

The title bar reflects that you are previewing the image in CMYK.

Adjusting image size

Next you will adjust the image size for printing. When printing an image, you generally want a resolution of at least 150 pixels per inch. For higher-quality images, you will want a resolution of at least 300 pixels per inch. While this image was saved at 72 pixels per inch, it is larger than needed. By reducing the physical dimensions of the image, the resolution (number of pixels per inch) can be increased.

1 Choose Image > Image Size; the Image Size dialog box appears. The image currently has a resolution of 72 pixels per inch.

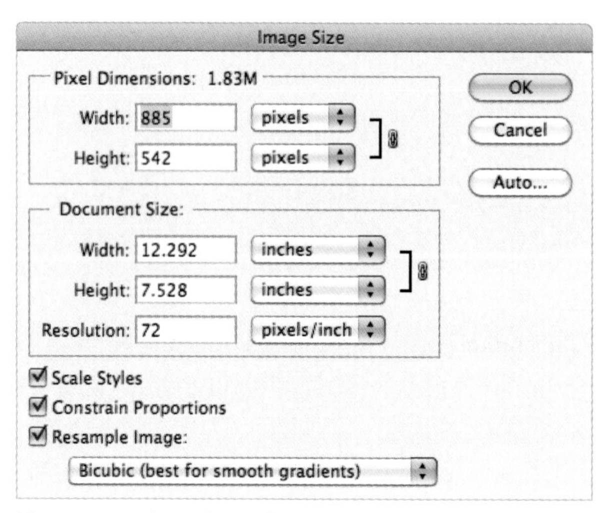

The image is at a low resolution of 72 pixels per inch.

This low resolution affects the image quality, and should be increased to print the best image possible. For this to occur, the dimensions of the image will need to be reduced so the image will be of a higher resolution, but will be smaller in size.

Resampling changes the amount of image data. When you resample up, you increase the number of pixels. New pixels are added, based upon the interpolation method you select. While resampling adds pixels, it can reduce image quality if it is not used carefully.

2 In the Image Size dialog box, uncheck Resample Image. By unchecking the Resample Image checkbox, you can increase the resolution without decreasing image quality.

You can use this method when resizing large image files, like those from digital cameras that tend to have large dimensions but low resolution.

3 Type **300** in the Resolution field. The size is reduced in the Width and Height text boxes to accommodate the new increased resolution but the Pixel Dimensions remain the same. For quality printing at the highest resolution, this image should be printed no larger than approximately 2.9 inches by 1.8 inches. Press OK.

In this image, you are not adding pixels, you are simply reducing the dimensions of the image to create a higher resolution.

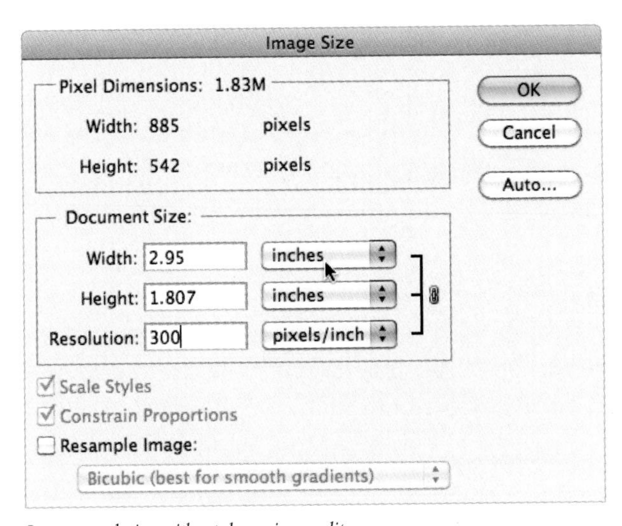

Increase resolution without decreasing quality.

4 Choose File > Save. Keep this file open for the next part of this lesson.

Saving a Photoshop PDF file

Images containing text or vector shapes may appear fine in low resolution when viewed on a computer display, even if the vector information is rasterized. When the same images are used for print projects, they should retain the resolution-independent vector elements. This keeps the text and other vector graphics looking sharp, so you do not need to worry about the jagged edges that occur when text and shapes are rasterized. To keep the vector information, you need to save the file using a format that retains both vector and bitmap data.

1 With the ps0401_work.psd image still open, choose File > Save As. The Save As dialog box appears.

2 In the Save In menu, navigate to the ps04lessons folder. In the Name text field, type **farm print version**. From the Format drop-down menu, choose Photoshop PDF, then press Save. Click OK to close any warning dialog box that may appear. The Save Adobe PDF dialog box appears.

3 In the Save Adobe PDF dialog box, choose Press Quality from the Adobe PDF Preset drop-down menu, then click Save PDF. If a warning appears indicating that older versions of Photoshop may not be able to edit the PDF file, click Yes to continue.

4 Your file has been saved in the Adobe PDF format, ready to be used in other applications such as Adobe InDesign, or shared for proofing with a reviewer who may have Adobe Acrobat or Adobe Reader.

Congratulations! You have finished the lesson.

Self study

1 Using the farm image, try adjusting the stacking order of the layers in the composite image.

2 Scale and move the layers to place the cow and rooster in different positions.

3 Add your own images to the composition, adjusting their position and scaling.

4 Save the images as PDF and JPEG files using the different compression options and presets to determine the impact these have on quality and file size.

Review

Questions

1 Describe two ways to combine one image with another.

2 What is created in the destination image when you cut and paste or drag and drop another image file into it?

3 What are the best formats (for print) in which to save a file that contains text or other vector objects?

Answers

1 **Copy and Paste:** Select the content from your source document and choose Edit > Copy. Then select your destination document and choose Edit > Paste to paste the artwork into it.

Drag and Drop: Make sure both your source and destination documents are visible. With the Move tool selected, click and drag the image from the source file to the destination file.

2 When you cut and paste, or drag and drop, one image into another, a new layer containing the image data is created in the destination file.

3 If your file contains text or vector objects, it is best to save the file in one of these three formats: Photoshop (PSD), Photoshop (EPS), or Photoshop (PDF).

What you'll learn in this lesson:

- Using the selection tools
- Refining your selections
- Transforming selections
- Using the Pen tool
- Saving selections

Making the Best Selections

Creating a good selection in Photoshop is a critical skill. Selections allow you to isolate areas in an image for retouching, painting, copying, or pasting. If done correctly, selections are inconspicuous to the viewer; if not, images can look contrived, or over-manipulated. In this lesson, you will discover the fundamentals of making good selections.

Starting up

Before starting, make sure that your tools and panels are consistent by resetting your preferences. See "Resetting Adobe Photoshop CS5 preferences" on page 3.

You will work with several files from the ps05lessons folder in this lesson. Make sure that you have loaded the pslessons folder onto your hard drive from the supplied DVD. See "Loading lesson files" on page 5.

See Lesson 5 in action!

Use the accompanying video to gain a better understanding of how to use some of the features shown in this lesson. The video tutorial for this lesson can be found on the included DVD.

The importance of a good selection

"You have to select it to affect it" is an old saying in the image-editing industry. To make changes to specific regions in your images, you must activate only those areas. To do this, you can use selection tools such as the Marquee, Lasso, and Quick Selection tools, or you can create a selection by painting a mask. For precise selections, you can use the Pen tool. In this lesson, you'll learn how to select pixels in an image with both pixel and pen (vector) selection techniques.

You'll start with some simple selection methods and then progress into more difficult selection techniques. Note that even if you are an experienced Photoshop user, you will want to follow the entire lesson; there are tips and tricks included that will help all levels of users achieve the best selections possible.

Using the Marquee tools

The first selection tools you'll use are the Marquee tools, which include Rectangular, Elliptical, Single Row, and Single Column tools. Some of the many uses for the Rectangular and Elliptical Marquee tools are to isolate an area for cropping, to create a border around an image, or simply to use that area in the image for corrective or creative image adjustment.

1 In Photoshop, choose File > Browse in Bridge or select the Launch Bridge button (Br), or use the Mini Bridge button (Mb) in the Application bar. Navigate to the ps05lessons folder and double-click on ps0501_done.psd to open the image. The completed image file appears. You can leave the file open for reference, or choose File > Close to close it.

The completed selection file.

2 Return to Adobe Bridge by choosing File > Browse in Bridge or selecting the Go to Bridge button or Mini Bridge button in the Options bar. Navigate to the ps05lessons folder and double-click on ps0501.psd to open the image. An image of a car appears.

3 Choose File > Save As. When the Save As dialog box appears, navigate to the ps05lessons folder. In the Name text field, type **ps0501_work**. Choose Photoshop from the Format drop-down menu and press Save. If the Photoshop format options dialog box appears, press OK.

4 Select the Rectangular Marquee tool (⬚), near the top of the Tools panel.

5 Make sure that Snap is checked by choosing View > Snap. If it is checked, it is already active.

6 Position your cursor in the upper-left side of the guide in the car image, and drag a rectangular selection down toward the lower-right corner of the guide. A rectangular selection appears as you drag, and it stays active when you release the mouse.

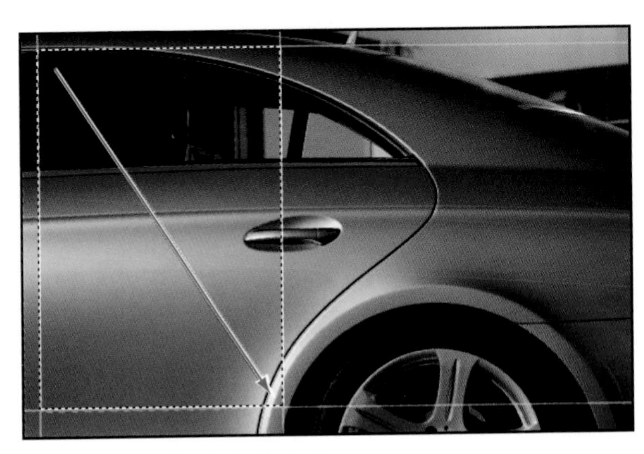

Creating a rectangular selection in the image.

You'll now apply an adjustment layer to lighten just the selected area of the image. You are lightening this region so that a text overlay can be placed over that part of the image.

7 If the Adjustments panel is not visible, choose Window > Adjustments and click on the Curves; the Curves Adjustments panel appears.

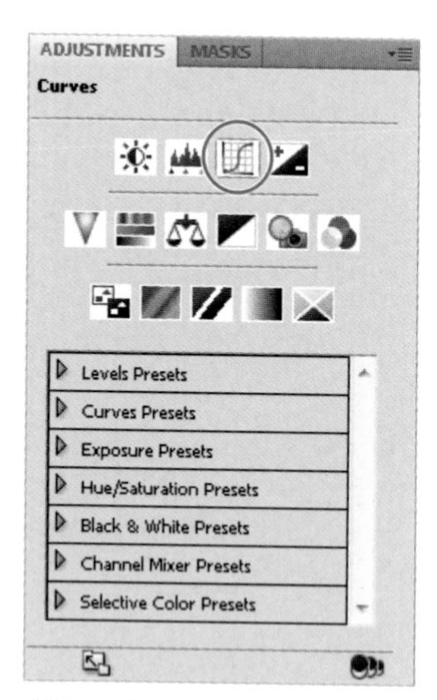

Click on the Curves button to create a new Curves adjustment layer.

8 To ensure consistent results, first click the panel menu (▾≡) in the upper-right corner of the Adjustments panel and choose Curves Display Options. In the Show Amount of: section, select Pigment/Ink%. Choosing Pigment for corrections makes the curves adjustment more representative of ink on paper. Click OK to close the Curves Display Options dialog box.

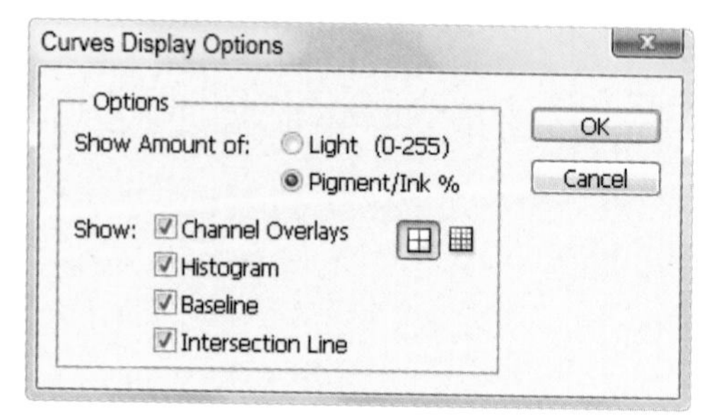

Select Pigment/Ink % in the Curve Display options.

9 Click and drag the upper-right anchor point (shadow) straight down, keeping it flush with the right side of the curve window, until the Output text field reads approximately 20, or type **20** into the Output text field. The rectangular selection in the image is lightened to about 20% of its original value.

Because you used an adjustment layer, you can double-click on the Curves thumbnail in the Layers panel to re-open the Curves panel as often as you like, to readjust the lightness in the rectangular selection.

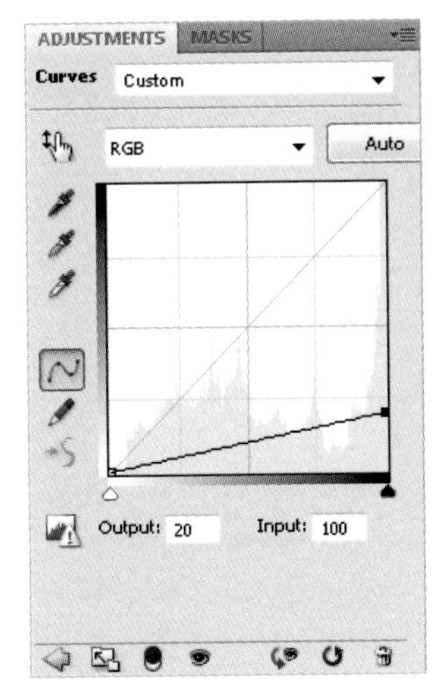

Make a curve adjustment to the selection.

The result.

10 Now go back to the Layers panel, click the box to the left of the text layer named poster text; the visibility icon (👁) appears, and the layer is now visible. The text appears over the lightened area.

11 Choose File > Save to save this file. Keep the file open for the next part of this exercise.

Creating a square selection

In this section, you'll learn how to create a square selection using the Rectangular Marquee tool.

1 Click on the Background thumbnail in the Layers panel to select it.

2 Select the Rectangular Marquee tool (⬚) and position your cursor over the taillight of the car. Click and drag while holding the Shift key. Note that your selection is constrained, creating a square selection. When you have created a square (size doesn't matter), first release the mouse and then the Shift key.

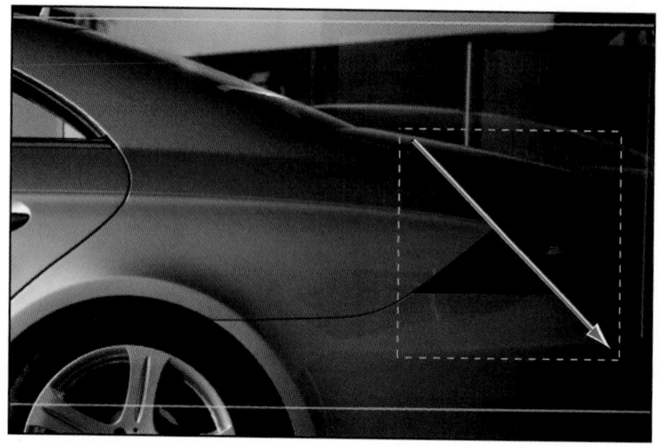

Click and drag while holding the Shift key.

3 With the square selection still active, position your cursor over the selected region of the image. Notice that an arrow with a dashed box appears (⬚). This indicates that the selection shape can be moved without moving any of the pixel information in the image.

4 Click and drag the selection to another location. Only the selection moves. Reposition the selection over the taillight.

5 Select the Move tool (▸+) and position the cursor over the selected region. Notice that an icon with an arrow and scissors appears (▸✂). This indicates that if you move the selection, you will cut, or move, the pixels with the selection.

6 Click and drag the selection; the selected region of the image moves with the selection.

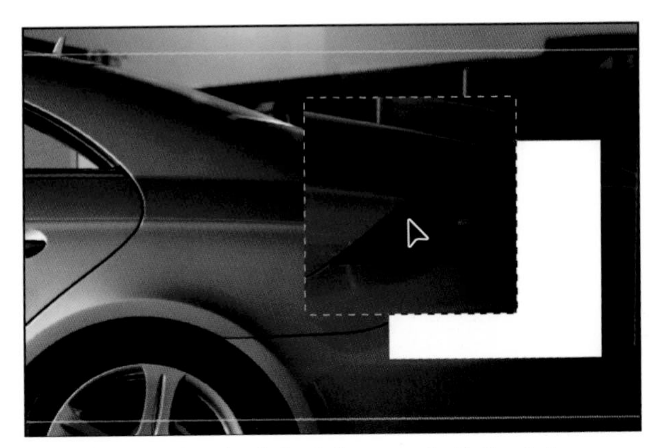

When the Move tool is selected, the pixels are moved with the selection.

7 Select Edit > Undo Move, or use the keyboard shortcut Ctrl+Z (Windows) or Command+Z (Mac OS) to undo your last step.

8 You'll now alter that section of the image. Note that in this example you edit a region of an image without creating a layer; you are affecting the pixels of the image and cannot easily undo your edits after the image has been saved, closed, and reopened. You will discover more ways to take advantage of the Adjustments panel later in this lesson.

9 Choose Image > Adjustments > Hue/Saturation.

You will now adjust the hue, or color, of this region. Click and drag the Hue slider to change the color of the selected region. Select any color that you like. In this example, the Hue slider is moved to -150. Click OK.

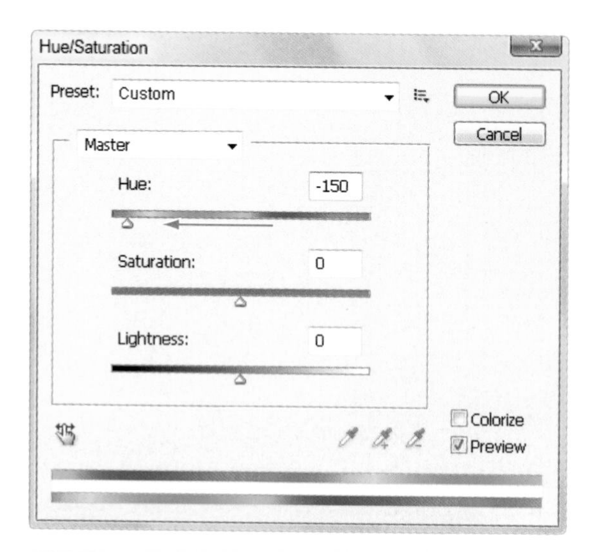

Changing the hue of the selected region.

10 The new hue is applied to the taillight region as an adjustment layer.

11 Choose File > Save; keep the image open for the next part of this lesson.

Creating a selection from a center point

1 Select the Background layer in the Layers panel, then click and hold on the Rectangular Marquee tool (⬚) and select the hidden Elliptical Marquee tool (◯).

Limber up your fingers, because this selection technique requires you to hold down two modifier keys as you drag.

2 You'll now draw a circle selection from the center of the image. Place your cursor in the approximate center of the tire, and then hold down the Alt (Windows) or Option (Mac OS) key and the Shift key. Click and drag to pull a circular selection from the center origin point. Release the mouse (before the modifier keys) when you have created a selection that is surrounding the tire. If necessary, you can click and drag the selection while you still have the Elliptical Marquee tool selected.

Hold down Alt/Option when dragging, to create a selection from the center.

While holding down the Alt (Windows) or Option (Mac OS) key and the Shift key, you can also add the space bar to reposition the selection as you are dragging with the Marquee tool. Release the space bar to continue sizing the selection.

3 Whether you need to adjust your selection or not, choose Select > Transform Selection. A bounding box with anchor points appears around your selection. Use the bounding box's anchor points to adjust the size and proportions of the selection. Note that you can scale proportionally by holding down the Shift key when you transform the selection.

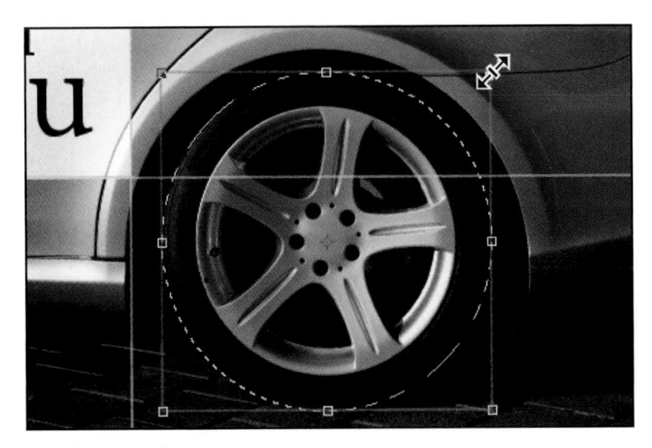

Transform your selection.

4 When you are finished with the transformation, press the check mark (✓) in the upper-right corner of the Options bar, or press the Enter (Windows) or Return (Mac OS) key to confirm your transformation change, or press the Esc key in the upper-left corner of your keyboard to cancel the selection transformation.

5 Choose File > Save. Keep this file open for the next part of this lesson.

Changing a selection into a layer

You will now move your selection up to a new layer. By moving a selection to its own independent layer, you can have more control over the selected region while leaving the original image data intact. You'll learn more about layers in Lesson 8, "Getting to Know Layers."

1 With the tire still selected, click on the Background layer to make it active. Press Ctrl+J (Windows) or Command+J (Mac OS). Think of this as the *Jump my selection to a new layer* keyboard shortcut. Alternatively, to create a new layer for your selection, you can select Layer > New > Layer via Copy. The selection marquee disappears and the selected region is moved and copied to a new layer, named Layer 1.

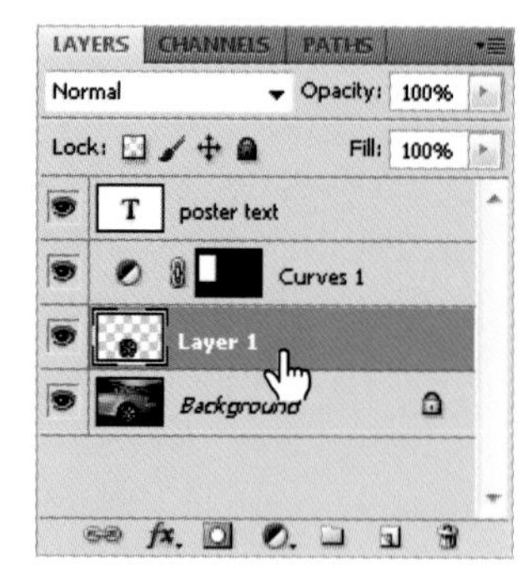

A new layer created from the selection.

2 Now you will apply a filter to this new layer. Choose Filter > Blur > Motion Blur. The Motion Blur dialog box appears.

3 In the Motion Blur dialog box, type **0** (zero) in the Angle text field and **45** in the Distance text field; then press OK. A motion blur is applied to the tire.

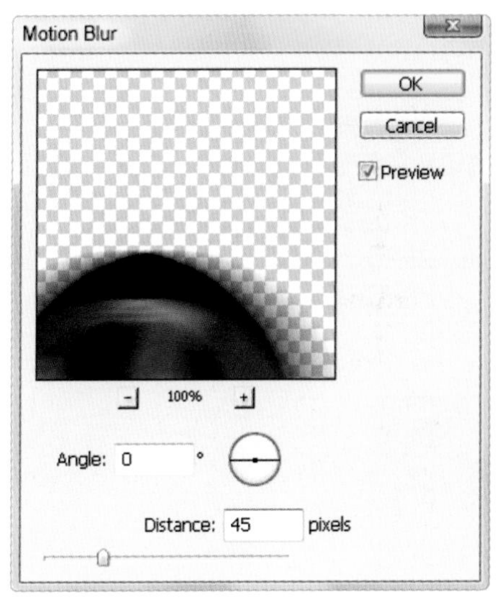

Applying the motion blur.

The result.

4 Select the Move tool (✣), move the tire slightly to the right, and press **5**. By pressing 5, you have changed the opacity of this layer to 50 percent.

5 Congratulations! You have finished the marquee selection part of this lesson. Choose File > Save, and then File > Close.

Working with the Magic Wand tool

The Magic Wand makes selections based on tonal similarities; it lets you select a consistently colored area (for example, a blue sky) without having to trace its outline. You control the range it automatically selects by adjusting the tolerance.

1 Choose File > Browse in Bridge or select the Launch Bridge button (Br) or the Mini Bridge button (MB) in the Application bar to launch Adobe Bridge. Then navigate to the ps05lessons folder and open the image ps0502.psd. An image of a kite appears.

2 Choose File > Save As; the Save As dialog box appears. Navigate to the ps05lessons folder and type **ps0502_work** into the Name text field. Make sure that Photoshop is selected from the Format drop-down menu, and press Save.

3 Select and hold on the Quick Selection tool ( ) to locate and select the hidden Magic Wand tool ( ).

4 In the Options bar, make sure the tolerance is set to **32**.

5 Position your cursor over the red portion of the kite and click once. Notice that similar tonal areas that are contiguous (touching) are selected. Place your cursor over different parts of the kite and click to see the different selections that are created. The selections pick up only similar tonal areas that are contiguous, which in this case is generally not the most effective way to make a selection.

6 Choose Select > Deselect, or use the keyboard shortcut Ctrl+D (Windows) or Command+D (Mac OS).

7 Click once in the sky at the top center of the image. The sky becomes selected. Don't worry if the sky is not entirely selected, it is because those areas are outside of the tolerance range of the area that you selected with the Magic Wand tool.

Image with the background selected.

To see what is included in a selection, position any selection tool over the image. If the icon appears as a hollow arrow with a dotted box next to it, it is over an active selection. If the icon of the tool or crosshair appears, then that area is not part of the active selection.

8 Press Ctrl+0 (zero) (Windows) or Command+0 (zero) (Mac OS) to fit the picture to the screen. Then hold down the Shift key and click the area of sky that was left unselected. Those areas are added to the selection of the sky.

9 Choose Select > Inverse. Now the selection has been turned inside out, selecting the kite. Inversing a selection is a helpful technique when solid colors are part of an image, as you can make quick selections instead of focusing on the more diversely colored areas of an image.

If you have control over the environment when you capture your images, it can be helpful to take a picture of an object against a solid background. That way, you can create quick selections using tools like Quick Selection and the Magic Wand.

10 Don't worry if you accidentally deselect a region, as Photoshop remembers your last selection. With the selection of the kite still active, choose Select > Deselect, and the selection is deselected; then choose Select > Reselect to reselect the kite.

11 Now you will sharpen the kite without affecting the sky. Choose Filter > Sharpen > Unsharp Mask. The Unsharp Mask dialog box appears.

12 Drag the Amount slider to the right to about 150, or type **150** into the Amount text field. Leave the Radius text field at 1. Change the Threshold slider to about 10, or type **10** into the Threshold text field. There are reasons that you have entered these settings, they are just not addressed in this selection lesson. Read more about unsharp mask in Lesson 7, "Creating a Good Image."

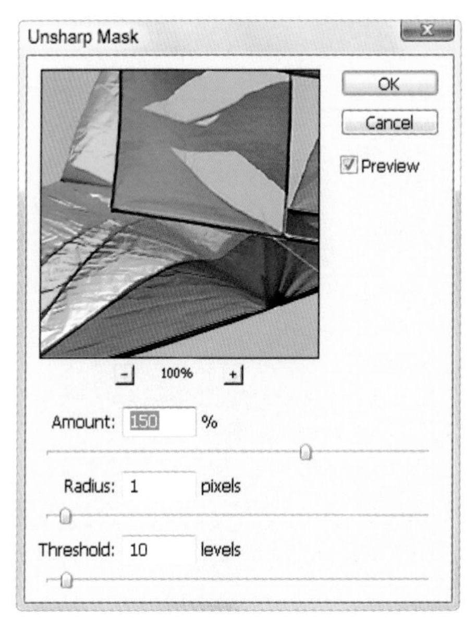

Sharpening the selection only.

13 Click and drag in the preview pane to bring the kite into view. Notice that in the preview pane of the Unsharp Mask dialog box, only the kite is sharpened. Position your cursor over the kite in the preview pane, and then click and hold. This temporarily turns the preview off. Release the mouse to see the Unsharp Mask filter effect applied. Press OK.

14 Choose File > Save. Then choose File > Close to close this file.

The Lasso tool

The Lasso tool is a freeform selection tool. It is great for creating an initial rough selection, and even better for cleaning up an existing selection. The selection that you create is as accurate as your hand on the mouse or trackpad allows it to be, which is why it lends itself to general cleaning up of selections. The best advice when using this tool is not to worry about being too precise; you can modify the selection, as you will see later in this section.

1 Choose File > Browse in Bridge, or select the Launch Bridge button (Br) or Mini Bridge button (Mb) in the Application bar, to open Adobe Bridge. Navigate to the ps05lessons folder inside the pslessons folder you copied to your computer. Double-click on ps0503.psd to open the image. An image of a building appears.

2 Choose File > Save As. When the Save As dialog box appears, navigate to the ps05lessons folder. In the Name text field, type **ps0503_work**. Choose Photoshop from the Format drop-down menu and click Save.

   You will now create an initial selection using the Magic Wand tool similar to the previous exercise, and then clean up that selection using the Lasso tool.

3 Select the Magic Wand tool in the Tools panel.

4 Click on the right side of the building in the background of the image to make an initial selection.

Clicking with the Magic Wand tool to create an initial selection.

Adding to and subtracting from selections

The Magic Wand tool has created a selection that encompasses a good portion of the building in the background, but it did not select the windows. You'll now use the Lasso tool to refine that selection to include the areas that the Magic Wand tool missed.

1 Select the Lasso tool (ᑭ) in the Tools panel.

2 Position your cursor over the building in the background. Hold down the Shift key and click and drag around areas that are currently not selected. This makes a new path that overlaps the active selection. As you just discovered, holding down the Shift key adds to the existing selection.

3 Continue circling areas using the Lasso tool while holding down the Shift key to continue adding areas to the existing selection. The goal here is to isolate the background from the building in the foreground.

The original selection.

Adding to the selection.

There may be some areas of the image where the initial selection went too far and selected part of the foreground building, which is undesirable. If your selection didn't extend into the building, you can go to the next section, "Using the Quick Selection tool." Otherwise, continue to step 4.

4 To subtract from your selection, hold down the Alt (Windows) or Option (Mac OS) key. This time, you see the Lasso tool with a minus sign next to it.

5 Click and drag from outside the selected area and into the active selection. Release the mouse when you have circled back to your original starting point. The new Lasso selection you made is deleted from the existing selection.

Using the Shift key to add to a selection, and the Alt (Windows) Option (Mac OS) key to delete from a selection, you can edit selections created with any of the selection tools.

6 Keep this image open for the next part of this lesson.

Using the Quick Selection tool

The Quick Selection tool allows you to paint your selection on an image. As you drag, the selection expands outward and finds defined edges of contrast to use as boundaries for the selection.

1 Make sure that ps0503_work.psd is open and that there is no active selection. If you have a selection active, deselect it by choosing Select > Deselect, or pressing Ctrl+D (Windows) or Command+D (Mac OS).

2 Choose View > Fit on Screen to see the entire image in your document window.

3 Choose the Quick Selection tool ( ) in the Tools panel.

4 Position your cursor over the foreground building. You see a circle with a small crosshair in the center ( ).

The circle and crosshair will not appear if you have the Caps Lock key depressed.

5 Now, click and drag to paint over the edge of the building in the foreground, making sure that the edge of your brush does not extend into the background building. You can release the mouse and continue painting as the new regions are added to the existing selection. Note that when you paint over the upper-left part of the building in the foreground, the selection may extend into the background; you will fix this later.

Initial selection with the Quick Selection tool.

6 Now you'll delete some of the selection of the background building in the upper-left. If it helps, zoom into the top of the foreground building. Press and hold the Alt (Windows) or Option (Mac OS) key, and paint around the ornate decoration at the top. Note that by holding down the Alt/Option key, you are deleting from the existing selection.

7 If it helps, adjust the Quick Selection brush size by pressing the [(left bracket) repeatedly to reduce the selection size, or the] (right bracket) to increase the selection size.

8 Keep the selection active for the next section.

Understanding the Refine Selection Edge feature

The Refine Selection Edge feature in Adobe Photoshop CS5 allows you to alter the edge of a selection using a choice of selection previews, making it easier to view your edits. In this section, you'll experiment with the varying results of this new feature.

1 With the ps0503_work.psd image still open and the building selection still active, select the Refine Edge button on the Options bar at the top of your screen. The Refine Edge dialog box appears.

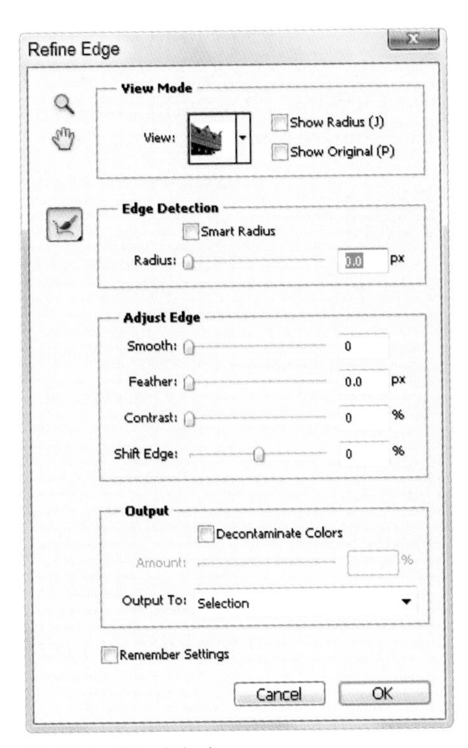

The Refine Edge dialog box.

2 The selected area of the image appears, previewed on a white background. Press the letter **F** on your keyboard to toggle through the different previews. At the top of the dialog box, you see the View Mode drop down menu as you toggle through them.

Refine Edge with white background.

Next, you will experiment with the new Edge Detection section. Using Edge Detection you can fine tune your selection, right in the Refine Edge dialog box.

3 While you still have the Refine Edge dialog box open, press Ctrl++(plus sign) (Windows) or Command++(plus sign) (Mac OS) to zoom in closer to the image.

You might notice that the edges are not crisp in some areas. You will use the edge detection feature to produce a harder, more accurate, selection

4 Increase the Edge Detection Radius to 1 by using the slider, or type **1** into the Radius text field. You should already see a difference in the selection edges.

5 Using the Contrast slider in the Adjust Edge section increase the contrast to approximately 10%.

6 To avoid any unexpected color entering into the edges of the border, you can check the Decontaminate color checkbox in the Output section.

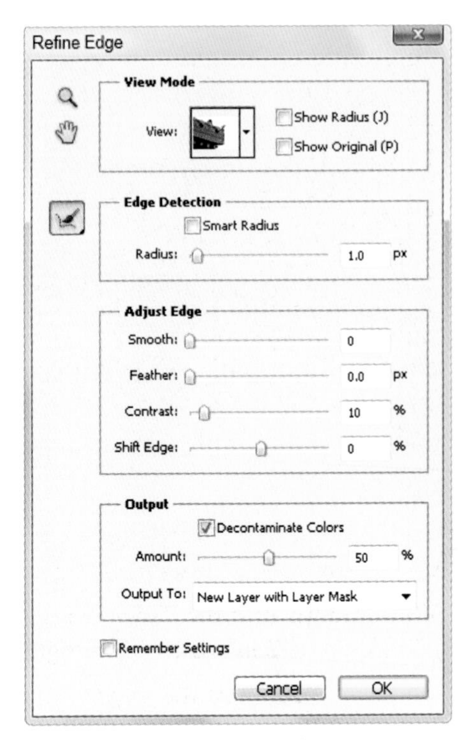

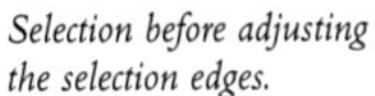

Selection before adjusting the selection edges.

Fine-tuning the edge selection.

Selection after fine-tuning the edge selection.

Notice a big improvement in the Refine Edge dialog box, is the option to Output to a separate layer with a mask. This default selection is extremely helpful, as it enables you to paint on the mask to make selection improvements.

Press OK to see that your selection is improved and created as a layer mask in the Layers panel.

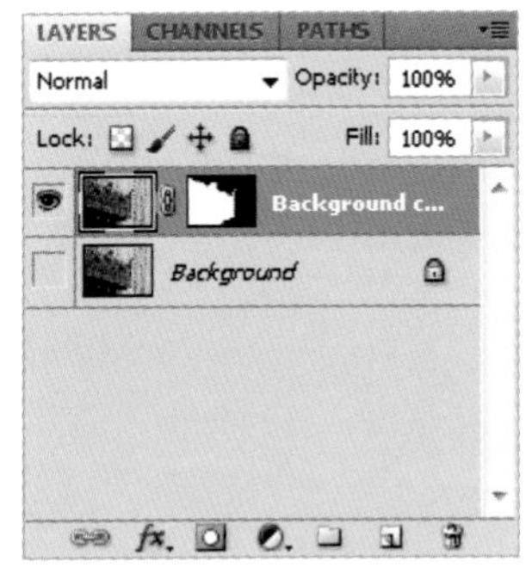

Using the Refine Edge feature you can output your selection as a layer mask.

7 Choose File > Save, and then File > Close to close the file.

Making difficult selections with the Refine Edge feature

Using the Refine Edge feature you can also improve your selection of difficult items such as fur and hair. There is still no *magic pill* for making a perfect selection, but the Refine Edge improvements certainly help.

1 Choose File > Browse in Bridge and open the image named ps0504.psd. Choose File > Save As. When the Save As dialog box appears, navigate to the ps05lessons folder. In the File name text field, type **ps0504_work**. Choose Photoshop from the Format drop-down menu and press Save. If the Photoshop Format Options dialog box appears, press OK.

2 Using the Magic Wand tool select the white area off to the right of the woman, then choose Select > Inverse to invert the selection. The woman is now selected.

3 Click on the Refine Edge button in the Control panel, the Refine Edge dialog box appears.

4 To get a better view of the hair selection, choose the Black & White option from the View drop-down menu.

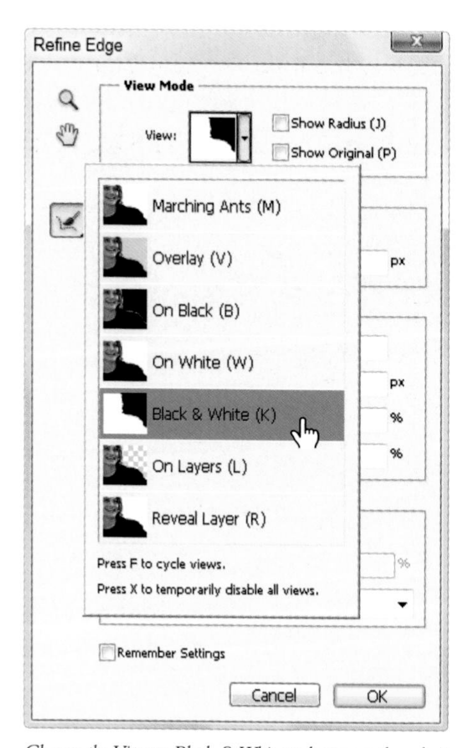

Change the View to Black & White to better see the selection edges.

5 Using the Radius slider in the Edge Detection, change the Radius value to **170**. This may seem like a rather drastic radius selection, but you can see that this masked the hair fairly well.

The issue you now have is that by increasing the radius to get a better selection of hair, you also degraded the edge selection of the shoulder, beneath the hair. You will use the Erase Refinements tool to help you clean up your selection.

6 Click and hold down on the Refine Radius tool and select the Erase Refinements tool.

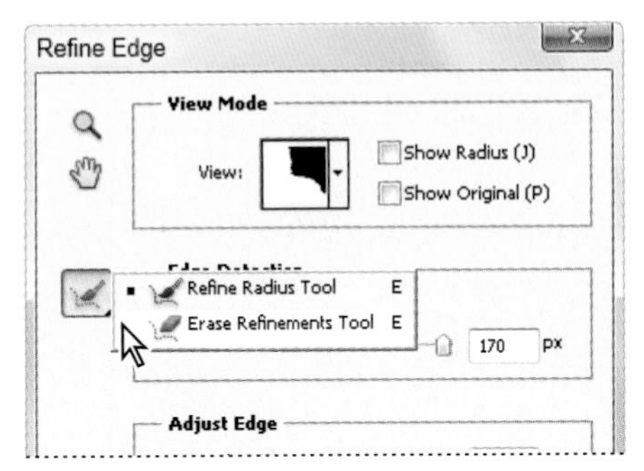

Clean up your selection using the Erase Refinements tool.

7 Position your cursor over an area in your image where you would like to clean up the selection. Note that you can increase or decrease your brush size by pressing the [(left bracket) or] (right bracket) keys.

8 Start painting over the areas that you do not want the refinements to take place, In this example, this is in the suit area.

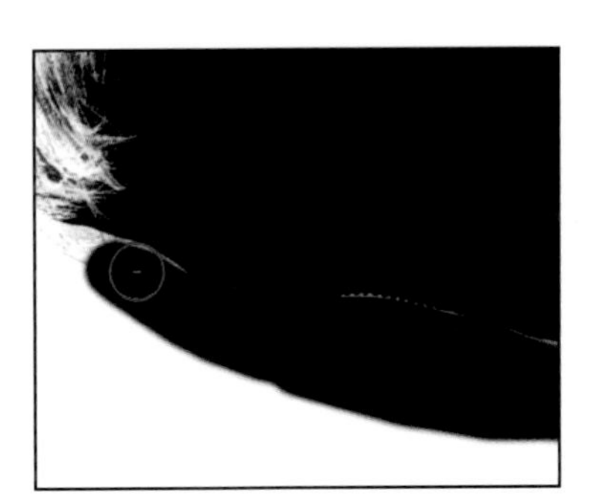
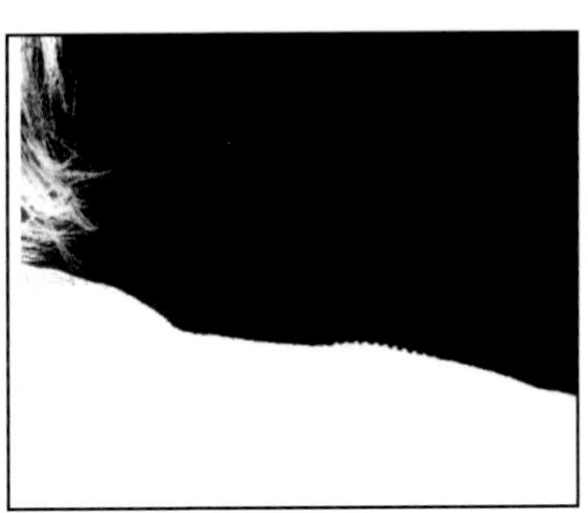

The selection before and after cleaning up the refinements.

9 Select Layer Mask from the Output drop-down menu and press OK. Since you have applied a layer mask, your results are shown as a transparent selection. Save and close the file.

The completed selection.

Using Quick Mask

Earlier in this lesson, you learned how to add to and subtract from selections. Another method for modifying selections is to use Quick Mask. Rather than using selection tools to modify the selection, you'll use the Paint Brush tool in the Quick Mask mode and paint to modify your selection. This is a type of art therapy for those who are selection-tool-challenged. Note that when creating a mask, by default it is the inverse of a selection; it covers the unselected part of the image and protects it from any editing or manipulations you apply.

In this lesson, you will create a mask using the Quick Mask feature, save the selection, and then copy and paste the selection into another image.

1 To see the file in its completed stage, choose File > Browse in Bridge and navigate to the ps05lessons folder. Locate the file named ps0505_done.psd and double-click to open it in Photoshop. A picture with a duck and penguins appears. You can keep the file open for reference or choose File > Close now.

The completed exercise.

2 Choose File > Browse in Bridge, or select the Launch Bridge button () or the Mini Bridge button () in the Application bar, to launch Adobe Bridge. Then navigate to the ps05lessons folder and open the image named ps0505.psd; an image of a duck appears.

Choose File > Save As. When the Save As dialog box appears, navigate to the ps05lessons folder. In the File name text field, type **ps0505_work**. Choose Photoshop from the Format drop-down menu and press Save. If the Photoshop Format Options dialog box appears, press OK.

3 Select the Lasso tool () and make a quick (and rough) selection around the duck. Make sure that as you click and drag, creating a selection that encompasses the duck, the Lasso tool finishes where it started, creating a closed selection around the duck. Don't worry about the accuracy of this selection, as you are going to paint the rest of the selection using Photoshop's painting tools in the Quick Mask mode.

4 Select the Quick Mask Mode button () at the bottom of the Tools panel, or use the keyboard shortcut **Q**. Your image is now displayed with a red area (representing the mask) over areas of the image that are not part of the selection.

5 Now you will use the painting tools to refine this selection. Select the Brush tool () in the Tools panel.

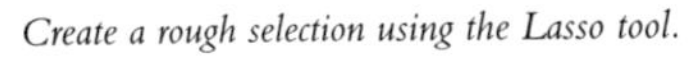

Create a rough selection using the Lasso tool.

The selection in the Quick Mask mode.

6 Click the Default Foreground and Background Colors button at the bottom of the Tools panel (), or press **D** on your keyboard, to return to the default foreground and background colors of black and white. Painting with black adds to the mask, essentially blocking that area of the image from any changes. Painting with white subtracts from the mask, essentially making that area of the image active and ready for changes.

These tips will help you to make more accurate corrections on the mask:

BRUSH FUNCTION	BRUSH KEYBOARD SHORTCUTS
Make brush size larger	] (right bracket)
Make brush size smaller	[(left bracket)
Make brush harder	Shift+] (right bracket)
Make brush softer	Shift+[(left bracket)
Return to default black and white colors	D
Switch foreground and background colors	X

7 Choose View > Actual Pixels to view the image at 100 percent. Zoom in further if necessary.

8 With black as your foreground color, start painting close to the duck, where there might be some green grass that you inadvertently included in the selection. Keep in mind that the areas where the red mask appears will not be part of the selection.

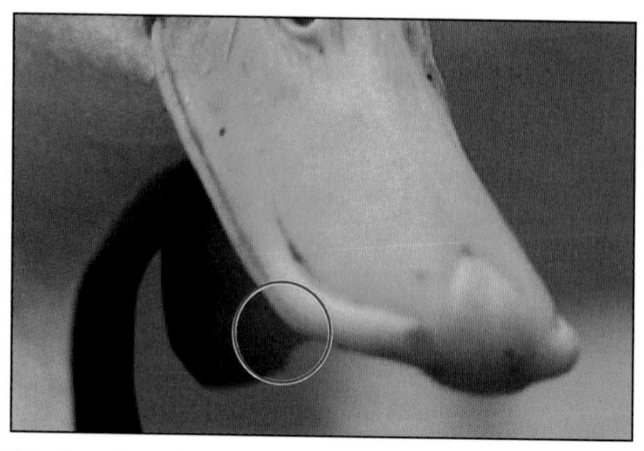

Paint the mask to make a more accurate selection.

9 If you accidentally paint into or select some of the duck, press **X** on your keyboard to swap the foreground and background colors, putting white in the foreground. Start painting with white, and you will see that this eliminates the mask, thereby making the regions that you paint with white part of the selection.

10 Continue painting until the selection is more accurate. When you are satisfied with your work, view the selection by clicking on the Quick Mask Mode button, at the bottom of the Tools panel, again or pressing **Q** on your keyboard. This exits the Quick Mask mode and displays the selection that you have created as a marquee. You can press **Q** to re-enter the Quick Mask mode to fine-tune the selection even further, if necessary. Keep the selection active for the next section.

Saving selections

You spent quite some time editing the selection in the last part of this lesson. It would be a shame to lose that selection by closing your file or clicking somewhere else on your image. In this part of the lesson, you'll learn how to save a selection so that you can close the file, reopen it, and retrieve the selection whenever you like.

1 With your duck selection active, choose Select > Save Selection.

2 Type **duck** in the Name text field and press OK.

3 If you can not see the Channels panel, choose Window > Channels to see that you have a saved channel (or selection) named duck. Selections that are saved with an image are known as alpha channels. Channels are not supported by all file formats. Only Photoshop, PDF, PICT, Pixar, TIFF, PSD, and Raw formats save alpha channels with the file.

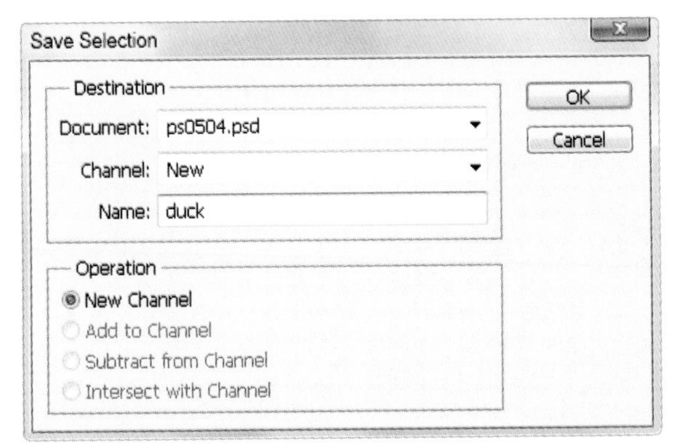

Name your saved selection.

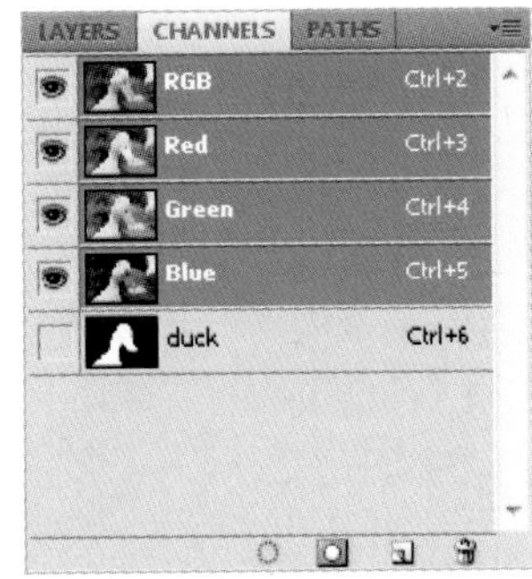

The Channels panel.

4 Choose Select > Deselect, or press Ctrl+D (Windows) or Command+D (Mac OS), to deselect the active selection.

5 Once a selection is saved, you can easily reselect it by choosing Select > Load Selection, or by Ctrl-clicking (Windows) or Command-clicking (Mac OS) on the channel in the Channels panel Select duck and click OK. The duck selection is reactivated.

You can save multiple selections in an image, but take note: your file size will increase each time you save a new selection. When multiple selections are saved, you will need to click on the Channel drop-down menu and choose which saved selection to display.

Copying and pasting a selection

There are many different methods for moving a selection from one image to another. In this lesson, you will simply copy a selection and paste it into another image.

1 Choose Edit > Copy, or use the keyboard shortcut Ctrl+C (Windows) or Command+C (Mac OS).

2 Choose File > Browse in Bridge, or press the Launch Bridge or Mini bridge button in the Options bar, and navigate to the ps05lessons folder. Double-click the file named ps0506.psd to open it in Photoshop. A photograph of penguins appears.

3 Choose File >Save As. In the Save As dialog box, navigate to the ps05lessons folder and type **ps0506_work** in the Name text field. Leave the format set to Photoshop and click Save.

4 With the image of the penguins in front, select Edit > Paste, or use the keyboard shortcut Ctrl+V (Windows) or Command+V (Mac OS). The duck selection is placed in the penguin image on its own independent layer, making it easy to reposition.

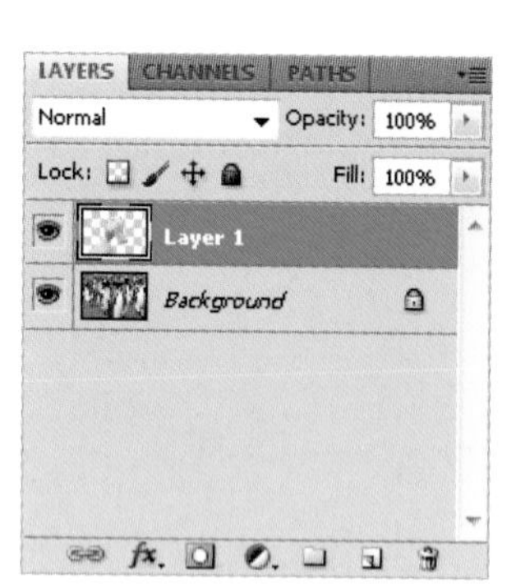

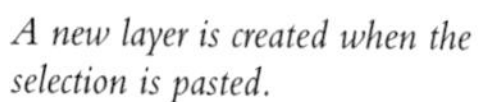
A new layer is created when the selection is pasted.

The result.

5 Select the Move Tool (▸+) and reposition the duck so that it is flush with the bottom of the image.

6 Choose File > Save, then choose File > Close to close the file. Close any other open files without saving.

Using the Pen tool for selections

The Pen tool (✒) is the most accurate of all the selection tools in Photoshop. The selection that it creates is referred to as a path. A path utilizes points and segments to define a border. Paths are not only more accurate than other selection methods, but they are also more economical, as they do not increase file size, unlike saved channel selections. This is because paths don't contain image data; they are simply outlines. In this section, you will learn how to make a basic path, and then use it to make a selection that you can use for adjusting an image's tonal values.

Pen tool terminology

Bézier curve: Originally developed by Pierre Bézier in the 1970s for CAD/CAM operations, the Bézier curve became the underpinning of the entire Adobe PostScript drawing model. The depth and size of a Bézier curve is controlled by fixed points and direction lines.

Anchor points: Anchor points are used to control the shape of a path or object. They are automatically created by the shape tools. You can manually create anchor points by clicking from point to point with the Pen tool.

Direction lines: These are essentially the handles that you use on anchor points to adjust the depth and angle of curved paths.

Closed shape: When a path is created, it becomes a closed shape when the starting point joins the endpoint.

Simple path: A path consists of one or more straight or curved segments. Anchor points mark the endpoints of the path segments. In the next section, you will learn how to control the anchor points.

1. Choose File > Browse in Bridge or click the Launch Bridge button (Br) or the Mini Bridge button (Mb) in the Options bar to launch Adobe Bridge. Then navigate to the ps05lessons folder and open image ps0507.psd.
2. Choose File > Save As. When the Save As dialog box appears, navigate to the ps05lessons folder. In the File name text field, type **ps0507_work**. Choose Photoshop from the Format drop-down menu and press Save. If the Photoshop Format Options dialog box appears, press OK.

   This part of the exercise will guide you through the basics of using the Pen tool.
3. Select the Pen tool (✒) from the Tools panel.

4 Position the cursor over the image, and notice that an X appears in the lower-right corner of the tool. This signifies that you are beginning a new path.

5 When the Pen tool is selected, the Options bar displays three path buttons: Shape layers, Paths, and Fill pixels. Click the second icon for Paths.

Select Paths in the Pen tool options.

6 Increase the zoom level by pressing the Ctrl+plus sign (Windows) or Command+plus sign (Mac OS), so that you can view the exercise file in the image window as large as possible. If you zoom too far in, zoom out by using the minus sign with the Ctrl or Command key.

7 Place the pen tip at the first box in Example A, and click once to create the first anchor point of the path. Don't worry if it's not exactly on the corner, as you can adjust the path later.

8 Place the pen tip at the second box on Example A and click once. Another anchor point is created, with a line connecting the first anchor point to the second.

9 Continue clicking on each box in the exercise until you reach the last box on the path. If you're having difficulties seeing the line segments between the points on your path, you can temporarily hide the Exercise layer by clicking on the visibility icon next to that layer.

10 Hold down the Ctrl (Windows) or Command (Mac OS) key, and click on the white background to deactivate the path that was just drawn to prepare for the next path.

In Example A, only straight line segments were used to draw a path; now you'll use curved line segments.

11 Reposition the document in the window so that Example B is visible.

12 With the Pen tool selected, click and hold on the small square (the first anchor point in the path) and drag upwards to create directional handles. Directional handles control where the following path will go. Note that when you create directional handles, you should drag until the length is the same or slightly beyond the arch that you are creating.

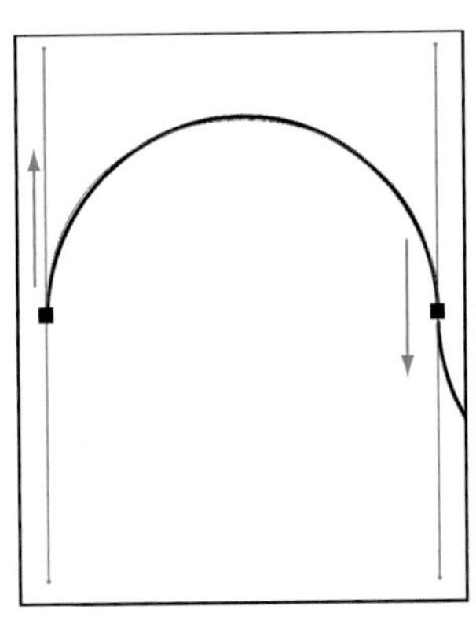

Click and drag with the Pen tool to create directional handles.

13 Click and hold on the second box in Example B, and drag the directional handle downward. Keep dragging until the path closely matches the curve of Example B. Don't worry if it's not exact for this part of the lesson.

14 Click on the third box in Example B, and drag upward to create the next line segment. Continue this process to the end of the Example B diagram.

15 To edit the position of the points on the path, you'll use the Direct Selection tool (). Click and hold on the Selection tool () and select the hidden Direct Selection tool.

16 Position the Direct Selection tool over a path segment (the area between two anchor points) and click once; the directional handles that control that line segment are displayed. Click and drag on any of the directional handles to fine-tune your line segments. You can also click directly on each anchor point to reposition them if necessary.

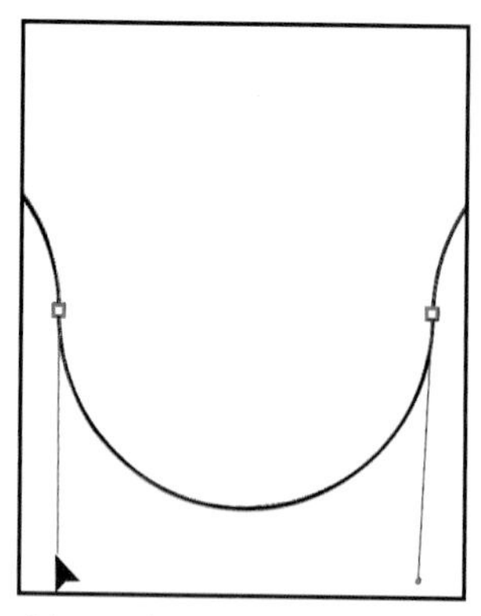

Adjusting the directional handles using the Direct Selection tool.

17 Choose File > Save, then choose File > Close to close the file.

Using the Pen tool to select an area of an image

1 Choose File > Browse in Bridge or click the Launch Bridge (Br) or Mini Bridge button (Mb) in the Application bar to launch Adobe Bridge. Then navigate to the ps05lessons folder and open image ps0508.psd.

2 Choose File > Save As. When the Save As dialog box appears, navigate to the ps05lessons folder. In the Name text field, type **ps0508_work**. Choose Photoshop PSD from the Format drop-down menu and press Save. If the Photoshop Format Options dialog box appears, press OK.

3 On the keyboard, hold down the Ctrl (Windows) or Command (Mac OS) key; then press the plus sign (+) once to zoom in at 200 percent, until your zoom percentage is at 200 percent. You'll see the zoom % in the lower-left corner of your workspace. Position the apple on the left side of the image that is in focus so that you can see the entire apple in the document window.

4 Select the Pen tool (✒), and begin drawing a path around the apple using the skills you learned in the previous exercise by clicking and dragging at the top edge of the apple and dragging a handle to the right.

5 Move the pen tool further along the apple, and click and drag again, dragging out directional handles each time, creating curved line segments that match the shape of the apple.

6 When you get back to the area where you began the path, the Pen tool has a circle next to it, indicating that when you click back on that first anchor point, it will close the path.

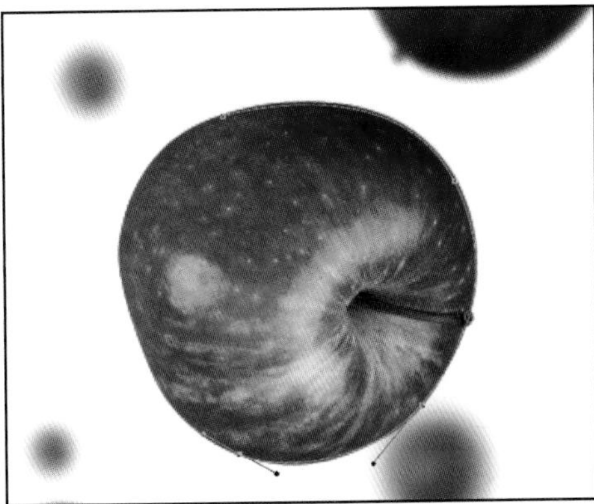

Creating a path around the edge of the apple.

7 Select the Paths panel. This is where path information is stored. You see one path in the panel, named Work Path.

8 Double-click on the name Work Path in the Paths panel. The Save Path dialog box appears. Type **Apple** in the Name text field and press OK.

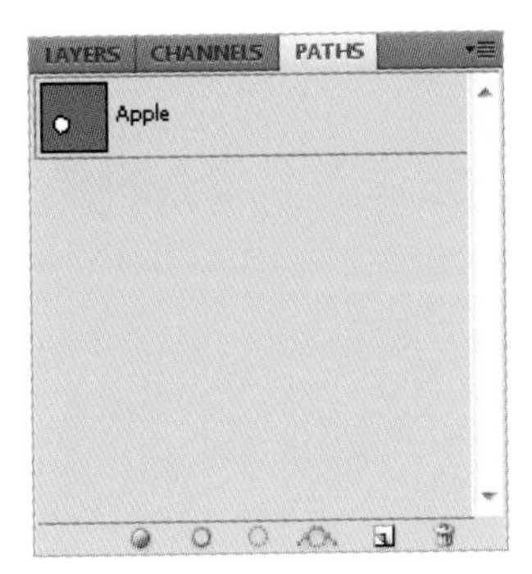

The Paths panel with the renamed path.

9 In the Paths panel, click below the name of the path to deselect the path. To reselect the path, simply click on the path name.

10 Now you'll apply an adjustment to this path selection. If the Layers panel is not visible, choose Window > Layers.

11 Click and hold on the Create New Fill or Adjustment Layer button (◐) at the bottom of the Layers panel and select Hue/Saturation. The Adjustments panel becomes active and the Hue/Saturation adjustment is displayed.

12 Drag the Hue slider to +116 or type the value into the Hue text field. You should see only the apple turn green.

13 A new adjustment layer is created, named Hue/Saturation 1. The pen path you created is visible to the right of the Hue/Saturation adjustment layer thumbnail and acts as a mask, blocking the adjustment from occurring outside of the path.

The Hue/Saturation adjustment layer.

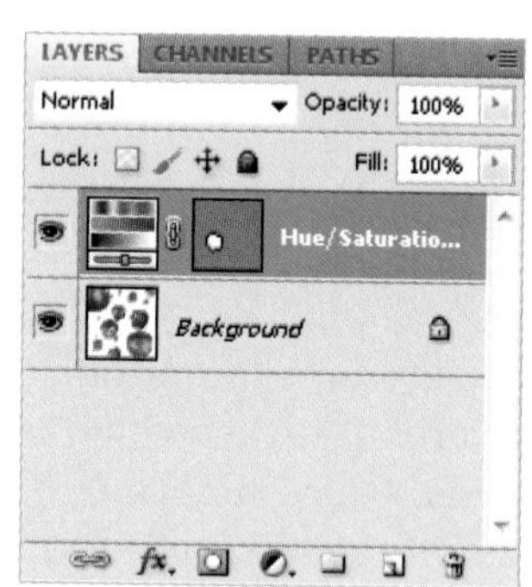

Adjustment layer with a vector mask.

The result.

If you want to have multiple paths in the Paths panel, deselect any active path before you begin drawing a new path. If you don't deselect, the new path you create will be added to, and become part of, the currently active path.

14 Choose File > Save, then choose File > Close to close the file.

More Pen tool selection techniques

In the last exercise, you created a curved path. Now you'll create a path with a combination of straight lines and curves.

1 Choose File > Browse in Bridge or select the Launch Bridge button (Br) or Mini Bridge button (Mb) in the Options bar to launch Adobe Bridge. Then navigate to the ps05lessons folder and open image ps0509.psd.

Choose File > Save As. When the Save As dialog box appears, navigate to the ps05lessons folder. In the Name text field, type **ps0509_work**. Choose Photoshop PSD from the Format drop-down menu and press Save. If the Photoshop Format Options dialog box appears, press OK.

2 Choose View > Fit on Screen, or use the keyboard shortcut Ctrl+0 (zero) (Windows) or Command+0 (zero) (Mac OS).

3 With the Pen tool (✒), create the first anchor point at the bottom-left side of the door by clicking once.

4 Staying on the left side of the door, click again at the location that is aligned with the top of the door frame's crossbar.

The second path point.

5 Now, to set up the path for a curve segment around the arc of the door window, place the pen over the last anchor point. When you see a right slash next to the pen cursor, click and drag to pull a Bézier directional handle. Drag until the directional handle is even with the top horizontal bar inside the door window. The purpose of this handle is to set the direction of the curve segment that follows.

The Bézier handle.

6 To form the first curve segment, place the pen cursor at the top of the arc of the door window, and then click, hold, and drag to the right until the curve forms around the left side of the window's arc; then release the mouse button.

The curve and its anchor point.

7 To finish off the curve, place your cursor at the right side of the door, aligned with the top of the door frame's crossbar. Click and drag straight down to form the remainder of the curve.

The completed curve.

8 Because the next segment is going to be a straight line and not a curve, you'll need to remove the last handle. Position the cursor over the last anchor point; a left slash appears next to the Pen cursor. This indicates that you are positioned over an active anchor point. Click with the Alt (Windows) or Option (Mac OS) key depressed; the handle disappears.

9 Click on the bottom-right side of the door to create a straight line segment.

10 To finish the path, continue to click straight line segments along the bottom of the door. If you need some help, look at the example.

The completed, closed path, selected with the Direct Selection tool.

11 Editing paths requires a different strategy when working with curve segments. With the Direct Selection tool (↖), select the path in the image to activate it, and then select the anchor point at the top of the door. Two direction handles appear next to the selected anchor point. You also see handles at the bottom of each respective curve segment to the left and the right. These are used for adjusting the curve.

12 Select the end of one of the handles and drag it up and down to see how it affects the curve. Also drag the handle in toward and away from the anchor point. If you need to adjust any part of your path to make it more accurate, take the time to do so now.

13 Double-click on the name Work Path in the Paths panel, and in the Name text field, type **door**. Keep the image open for the next section.

Converting a path to a selection

Paths don't contain image data, so if you want to copy the contents of a path, you need to convert it to a selection.

1 Make sure that the file from the last exercise is still open.

2 Click on the path named Door in the Paths panel to make the path active.

3 At the bottom of the Paths panel, there are five path icons next to the panel trash can:

- **Fill path with foreground color** ( ) fills the selected path with the current foreground color.
- **Stroke path with brush** ( ) is better used if you first Alt/Option+click on the icon and choose the tool from the drop-down menu that includes the brush you want to stroke with.
- **Load path as a selection** ( ) makes a selection from the active path.
- **Make work path from selection** ( ) creates a path from an active selection.
- **Create new path** ( ) is used to start a new blank path when you want to create multiple paths in an image.

4 Choose Load path as a selection to create a selection from the door path.

5 Choose Select > Deselect, or use the keyboard shortcut Ctrl+D (Windows) or Command+D (Mac OS), to deselect the selection.

6 Choose File > Close, without saving the document.

Self study

Take some time to work with the images in this lesson to strengthen your selection skills. For instance, you used ps0503.psd with the Lasso and Quick Selection tools. Try making different selections in the image as well as using the key commands to add and subtract from the selection border. Also experiment with Quick Mask.

Review

Questions

1 Which selection tool is best used when an image has areas of similar color?

2 Which key should you hold down when adding to a selection?

3 What can you do to select the image data inside a path?

4 Which dialog box allows you to edit your selection using different masking options?

Answers

1 The Magic Wand is a good tool to use when you have areas of an image with similar colors. The Magic Wand tool selects similar colors based on the Tolerance setting in the Options bar.

2 Hold down the Shift key to add to a selection. This works with any of the selection tools.

3 To select the pixel data inside of a path, you can activate the path by Ctrl+clicking (Windows) or Command+clicking (Mac OS) on the path in the Paths panel or by clicking the Load Path as Selection button at the bottom of the Paths panel.

4 The Refine Selection dialog box allows you to select the best masking technique and to preview edge selection changes that you are making.

What you'll learn in this lesson:

- Selecting color
- Using the Brush tool
- Applying transparency
- Using the blend modes
- Retouching images

Painting and Retouching

In this lesson, you get a quick primer in color and color models, and then you will have an opportunity to practice using Photoshop's painting tools, such as the painting, cloning, and healing tools.

Starting up

Before starting, make sure that your tools and panels are consistent by resetting your preferences. See "Resetting the Photoshop workspace" on page 3.

You will work with several files from the ps06lessons folder in this lesson. Make sure that you have loaded the pslessons folder onto your hard drive from the supplied DVD. See "Loading lesson files" on page 5.

See Lesson 6 in action!

Use the accompanying video to gain a better understanding of how to use some of the features shown in this lesson. The video tutorial for this lesson can be found on the included DVD.

Setting up your color settings

Before you begin selecting random colors for painting, you should have an understanding of color modes and Photoshop's color settings. Let's start with a basic introductory overview of the two main color modes that you will use in this lesson, RGB and CMYK.

Color primer

This lesson is about painting, adding colors, and changing and retouching images. It is important to understand that what you see on the screen is not necessarily what your final viewers will see (print or web). Bright colors tend to become duller when output to a printer, and some colors can't even be reproduced on the monitor or on paper. This is due to the fact that each device—whether it's a monitor, printer, or TV screen—has a different color gamut.

Understanding color gamut

The gamut represents the number of colors that can be represented, detected, or reproduced on a specific device. Although you may not realize it, you have experience with different gamuts already; your eyes can see many more colors than your monitor or a printing press can reproduce.

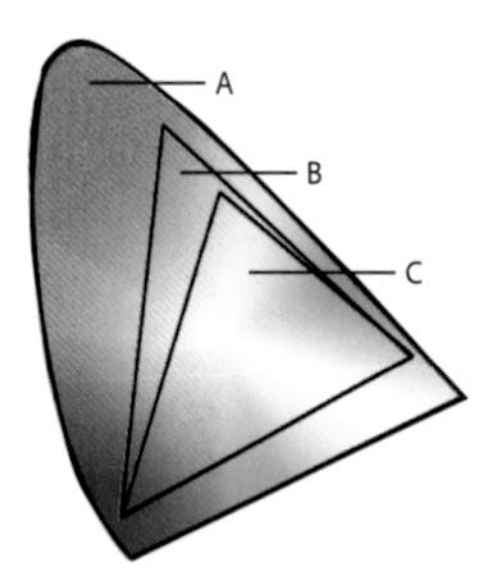

A. Colors that your eye recognizes. B. Colors that your monitor recognizes. C. Colors that your printer reproduces.

In this lesson, you will learn how you can address some of the color limitations that are inherent to working with color that is displayed or output by different devices. A quick introduction to the RGB and CMYK color models will help you to get a better grasp on what you can achieve. Understand that there are entire books on this subject, but you will at least gain enough information to be dangerous after reading this section.

If you receive a Missing Profile warning dialog box on any images used in this lesson, press OK to accept the default setting.

The RGB color model

The RGB (Red, Green, Blue) color model is an additive model in which red, green, and blue are combined in various ways to create other colors.

1 Choose File > Open, and navigate to the ps06lessons folder. Open the file named ps06rgb.psd. An image with red, green, and blue circles appears. Try to imagine the three color circles as light beams from three flashlights with red, green, and blue colored gels.

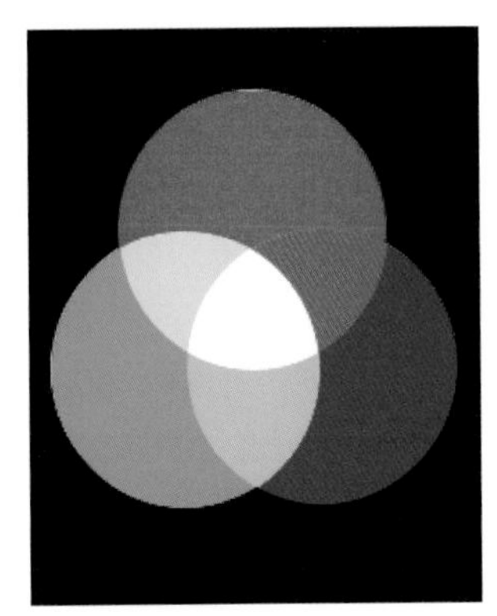

Red, green, blue.

2 Select the Move tool (▸+), and then check the Auto-Select checkbox in the Options bar. By checking Auto-Select, you can automatically activate a layer by selecting pixel information on that layer. One at a time, click and drag the red, green, and blue circles around on the image.

   Notice that white light is generated where the three colors intersect.

3 Now, turn off the visibility of the layers by selecting the visibility icon (👁) to the left of each layer name, with the exception of the black layer. It is just like turning off a flashlight; when there is no light, there is no color.

4 Choose File > Close. Choose to not save changes.

The CMYK color model

CMYK (Cyan, Magenta, Yellow, and Black [or Key]—black was once referred to as the *Key* color) is a subtractive color model, meaning that as ink is applied to a piece of paper, these colors absorb light. This color model is based on mixing the CMYK pigments to create other colors.

Ideally, by combining CMY inks together, the color black should result. In reality, the combination of those three pigments creates a dark, muddy color, and so black is added to create a panel with true blacks. CMYK works through light absorption. The colors that are seen are the portion of visible light that is reflected, not absorbed, by the objects on which the light falls.

In CMYK, magenta plus yellow creates red, magenta plus cyan creates purple, and cyan plus yellow creates green.

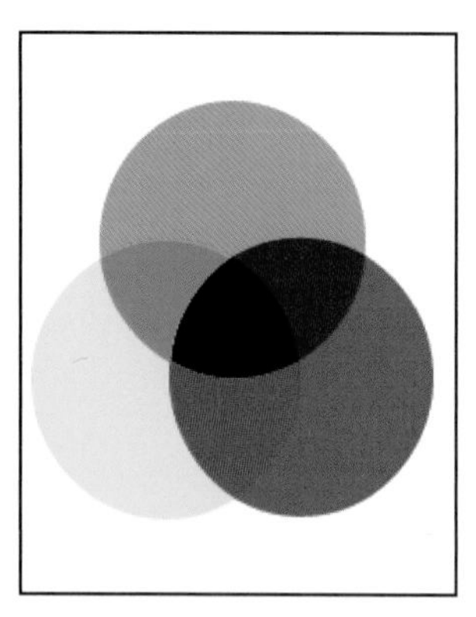

Cyan, magenta, yellow, and black.

1 Choose File > Open, and navigate to the ps06lessons folder. Open the file named ps06cmyk. An image with cyan, magenta, and yellow circles appears. Think of the colors in this file as being created in ink printed onto paper.

2 With the Move tool (▸+) selected, and the Auto-Select checkbox checked, individually click and drag the cyan, magenta, and yellow circles around on the image to see the color combinations that are created with ink pigments of these three colors. Notice that black appears at the intersection of all three, but, as mentioned earlier, it would never reproduce that purely on a printing press.

3 Choose File > Close to close the ps06cmyk image. Do not save your changes.

4 Uncheck the Auto-Select checkbox in the Options bar.

Working in the RGB mode

Unless you use an advanced color management system, you should do much of your creative work in the RGB mode. The CMYK mode is limited in its capabilities (fewer menu selections), and if you work in this mode, you have already made some decisions about your final image output that may not be accurate. Follow this short color primer to help you achieve the results that you expect.

In this lesson, you'll use generic profiles for your monitor and output devices. If you want to create a custom monitor profile, follow the instructions in the Photoshop Help menu, under the heading, "Calibrate and profile your monitor."

1 Choose File > Open, or select the Launch Bridge icon (Br) or Mini Bridge button (Mb) in the upper-right corner of the Application bar.

2 Navigate to the ps06lessons folder and open the image ps0601.psd. A very colorful image of a woman appears.

A colorful RGB image.

3 Press Ctrl+Y (Windows) or Command+Y (Mac OS); some of the colors become duller. By pressing Ctrl+Y/Command+Y, you have turned on the CMYK Preview. This is a toggle keyboard shortcut, which means you can press Ctrl+Y/Command+Y again to turn the preview off. Note that the text in your title bar indicates whether this preview is active or not. Keep the file open for the next part of this lesson.

Essentially, the preview is visually attempting to simulate what colors would look like if you were to print this image to a printer. Understanding the color settings is important, as the settings you choose affect the colors you use and how they appear in their final destination, whether that is the web, print, or video.

Editing color settings

For this lesson, you will adjust the color settings for Photoshop as if the final destination for this image is in print. Note that if you have any version of Creative Suite 5 installed, you can adjust your color settings suite-wide, using Adobe Bridge. Applying color settings through Adobe Bridge saves you the time and trouble of making sure that all the colors are consistent throughout your production process. If you have a suite installed, follow the steps that are indicated for suite users; if you have Adobe Photoshop installed independently, follow the steps for adjusting Photoshop color settings only.

1 Choose File > Browse in Bridge, or select the Launch Bridge button (Br) in the upper-right corner of the Application bar. If you do not have the entire Creative Suite 5 installed, leave Adobe Bridge open and skip to step 3.

2 Choose Edit > Creative Suite Color Settings and select North America Prepress 2, if it is not already selected. Press the Apply button. The new color settings are applied throughout the suite applications. Note that the setting you selected is a generic setting created for a printing process that is typical in North America.

3 In Photoshop, choose Edit > Color Settings, even if you have already set them in Adobe Bridge.

4 If North America Prepress 2 is not selected in the Settings drop-down menu, choose it now. Leave the Colors Settings dialog box open.

5 While still in the Color Settings dialog box, press Ctrl+Y (Windows) or Command+Y (Mac OS) to use the toggle shortcut for the CMYK preview. You can tell if you are in the CMYK preview by looking at the title bar of the image window. Notice that CMYK appears in parentheses at the end of the title.

ps0601.psd @ 66.7% (COLOR, RGB/8/CMYK) ×

The title bar indicates that this image is in the CMYK preview mode.

It is good to get this sneak peak into what your CMYK image will look like, but there is still the issue of having many different kinds of CMYK output devices. You might have one printer that produces excellent results and another that can hardly hold a color. In the next section, you will learn about the different CMYK settings and how they can affect your image.

6 Make sure that the CMYK preview is still on. If not, press Ctrl+Y (Windows) or Command+Y (Mac OS) again. From the CMYK drop-down menu in the Working Spaces section of the Color Settings dialog box, choose U.S. Sheetfed Uncoated v2.

Notice the color change in the image. Photoshop is now displaying the characteristics of the color space for images printed on a sheetfed press. This would be the generic setting you might choose if you were sending this image to a printing press that printed on individual sheets of paper.

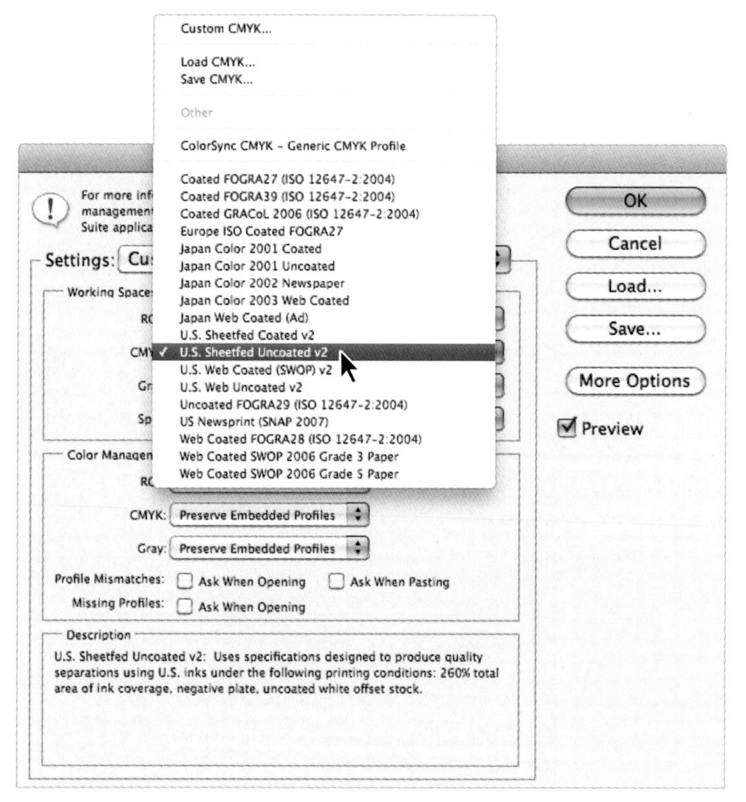

Choose various CMYK specifications from the CMYK drop-down menu.

7 From the CMYK drop-down menu, choose Japan Web Coated (Ad). Notice that the color preview changes again. You might use this selection if you were sending this image overseas to be printed on a large catalog or book press. A web press is a high-volume, high-speed printing press that uses rolls of paper rather than individual sheets.

You do not want to pick a CMYK setting just because it looks good on your screen; you want to choose one based upon a recommendation from a printer, or else you should use the generic settings that Adobe provides. The purpose of selecting an accurate setting is not only to keep your expectations realistic; it also helps you accurately adjust an image to produce the best and most accurate results.

8 From the Settings drop-down menu, choose the North America Prepress 2 setting again, and press OK. Keep the file open for the next part of this lesson.

Keep in mind that if you are using your images for web only, then you can also use the preview feature to view your image on different platforms. To make this change, you would choose View > Proof Setup and choose either Macintosh RGB or Windows RGB from the menu.

Selecting colors

There are many methods that you can use to select colors to paint with in Photoshop. Most methods end up using the Color Picker dialog box. In this section, you will review how to use the Color Picker to choose accurate colors.

1 Select the Set foreground color box at the bottom of the Tools panel. The Color Picker appears. It is tough to represent a 3D color space in 2D, but Photoshop does a pretty good job of interpreting colors in the Color Picker. Using the Color Picker, you can enter values on the right, or use the Hue slider and color field on the left to create a custom color.

2 Now, with the Color Picker open, click and drag the color slider to change the hue of your selected color. The active color is represented as a circle in the color field.

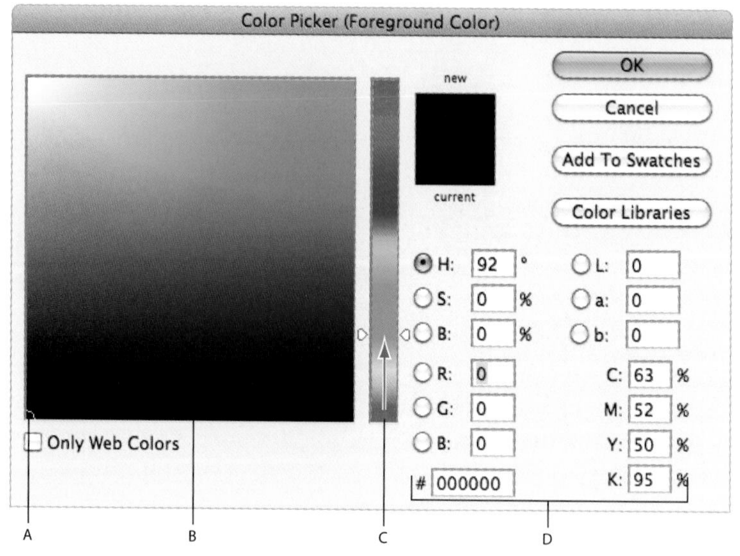

A. Selected color. B. Color field. C. Color slider. D. Color values.

3 Now, click in the color field, and then click and drag your selected color toward the upper-right corner of the color field, making it a brighter, more saturated color. To choose a lighter color, click and drag the selected color to the upper-left corner of the color field. Even though you can select virtually any color using this method, you may not achieve the best results.

4 Press Ctrl+Shift+Y (Windows) or Command+Shift+Y (Mac OS) to see how the CMYK preview affects the colors in the Color Picker. Notice that colors that will not print well in CMYK show up with in gray (gamut warning). Press Ctrl+Shift+Y/ Command+Shift+Y again to turn off the CMYK preview.

Perhaps you are creating images for the Web and you want to work with web-safe colors only. This is very restrictive, but you can limit your color choices by checking the Only Web Colors checkbox in the Color Picker.

5 Check and uncheck the Only Web Colors checkbox to see the difference in selectable colors in the color field.

There are also warning icons in the Color Picker to help you choose the best colors for print and the Web.

6 Click in the lower-left corner of the color field and drag up toward the upper-right corner. Note that at some point, when you enter into the brighter colors, an Out of gamut for printing warning icon (▲) appears. This indicates that although you may have selected a very nice color, it is never going to print, based upon your present color settings. Select the Out of gamut warning icon, and Photoshop redirects you to the closest color you can achieve.

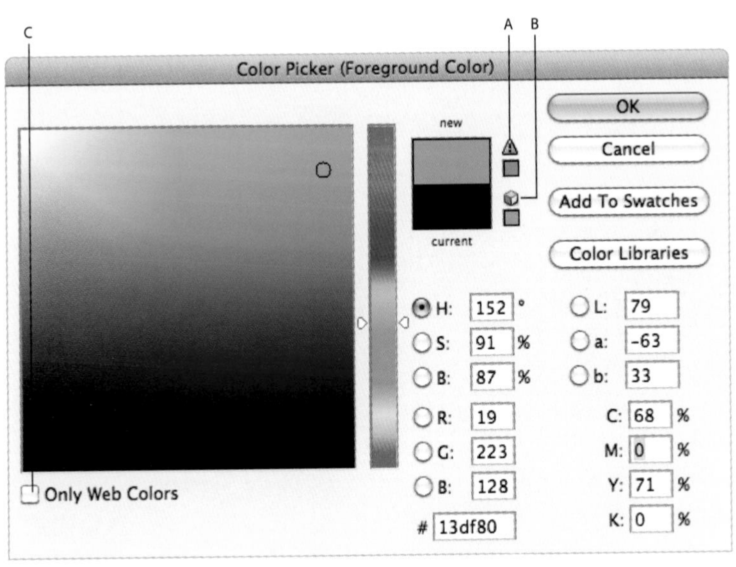

A. Out of gamut warning. B. Not a web safe color warning. C. Only Web Colors.

7 Click and drag your selected color in the color field until you see the Not a web safe color alert icon (⊛) appear. Click on the Not a web safe color icon to be redirected to the closest web-safe color.

8 Position the Color Picker so that you can see part of the ps0601.psd image, then position the cursor over any part of the image. Notice that the cursor turns into the Eyedropper tool (✒). Click to select any color from the image.

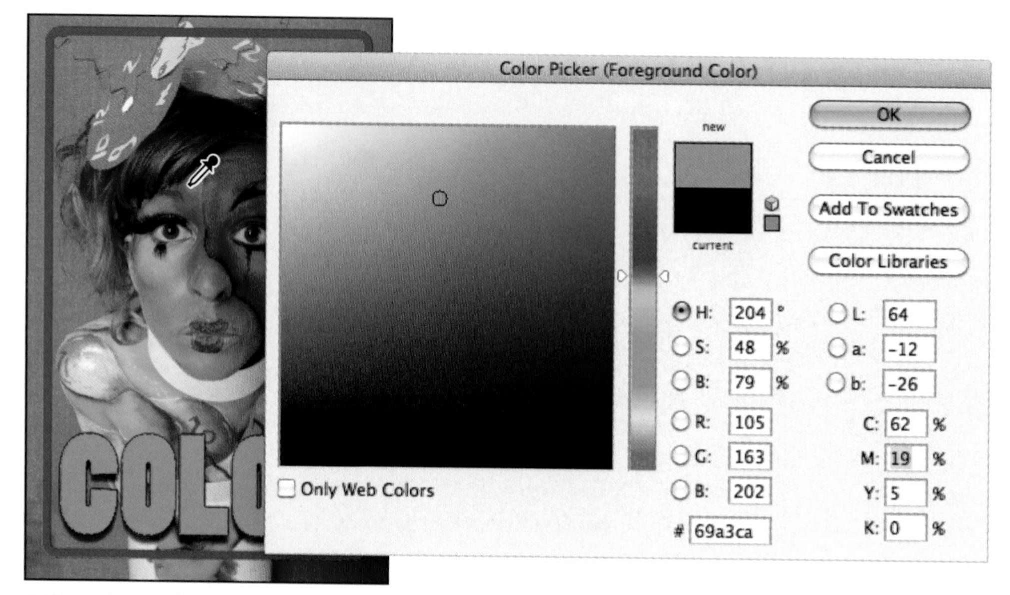

Click outside the Color Picker to sample a color from your image.

9 Press OK in the Color Picker dialog box.

10 Choose File > Close. If asked to save changes, select No.

Starting to paint

Now that you know a little more about color, and finding it in Photoshop, you will start to do some painting. You will work on a new blank document to begin with, but once you have the basics of the painting tools down, you'll put your knowledge to work on actual image files.

1 Under the File menu, choose New. The New dialog box appears.

2 Type **painting** in the Name text field. From the preset drop-down menu, choose Default Photoshop Size. Leave all other settings at their defaults and press OK. A new blank document is created; keep it open for the next part of this lesson.

Using the Color panel

Another way to select color is to use the Color panel.

1 If the Color panel is not visible, choose Window > Color.

Place your cursor over the color ramp at the bottom of the panel, then click and drag across the displayed color spectrum. Notice that the RGB sliders adjust to indicate the color combinations creating the active color. If you have a specific color in mind, you can individually drag the sliders or key in numeric values.

Note that the last color you activated appears in the Set Foreground Color box, located in the Color panel, as well as near the bottom of the Tools panel.

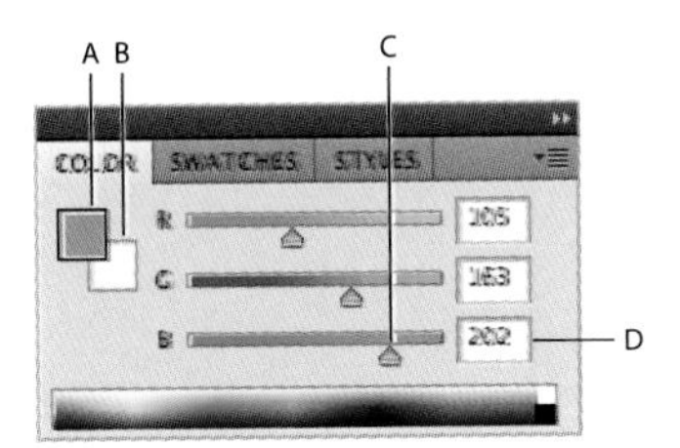

A. Set foreground color. ***B****. Set background color.*
C*. Slider.* ***D****. Color ramp.*

2 Click once on the Set Foreground Color box to open the Color Picker. Type the following values in the RGB text fields on the right side of the Color Picker dialog box: R: **74** G: **150** B: **190**. Press OK.

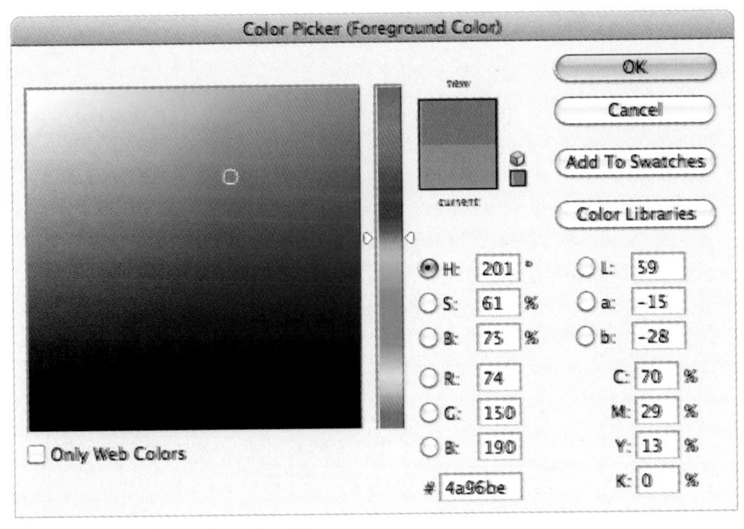

Manually enter values in the Color Picker.

Using the Brush tool

The Brush tool paints using the foreground color. You can control the brush type, size, softness, mode, and opacity with the Brush tool Options.

1 Select the Brush tool (🖌) in the Tools panel.

2 Press the arrow next to the brush size in the Options bar to open the Brush Preset picker.

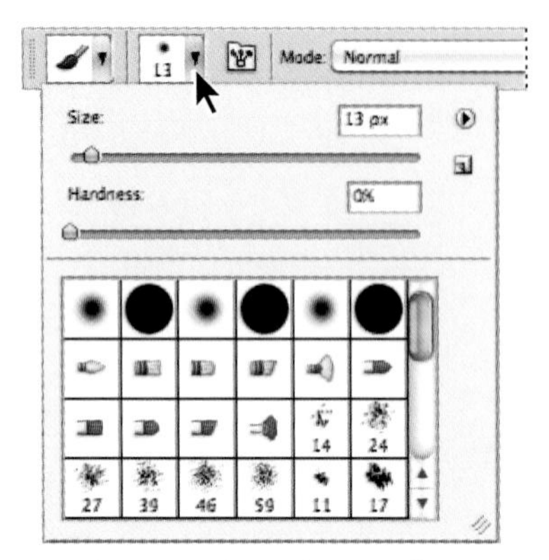

Press the arrow in the Brush Options bar to open the presets.

3 If you are not in the default panel view, click and hold on the panel menu in the upper-right corner of the Brush Preset picker and choose Small Thumbnail View.

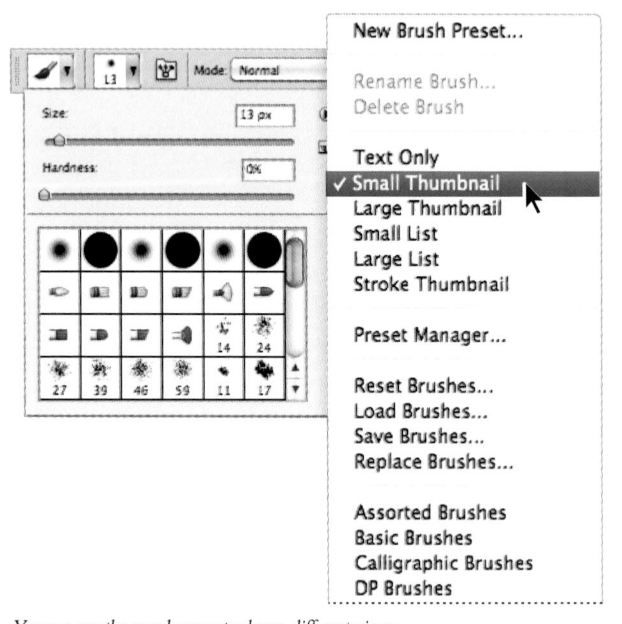

You can use the panel menu to choose different views.

4 Position your cursor over any of the brushes to see a tooltip appear. The tooltip provides a description of the brush, such as soft, airbrush, hard, or chalk, as well as its size in pixels.

5 Locate the brush with the description Soft Round Pressure Size pixels, toward the top of the panel, and click on it.

6 Use the size slider or enter **45** into the Size text field to change the diameter of the brush to 45 pixels, and press the Enter (Windows) or Return (Mac OS) key. The brush is selected and the Brushes Preset picker is closed.

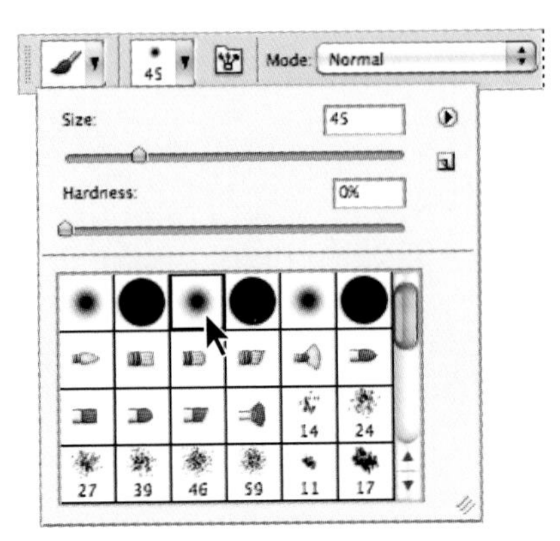

The Brush Preset picker and the Soft Round 45 pixel brush.

7 Position your cursor on the left side of the image window, then click and drag to paint a curved line similar to the example below.

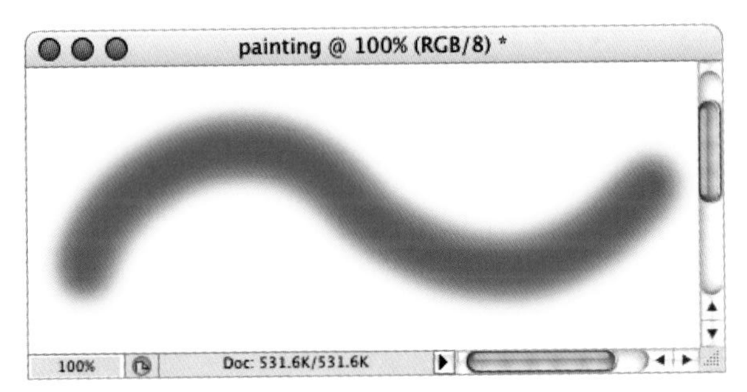

Painted brush stroke.

8 Using the Color panel, click on a different color from the color ramp (no specific color is necessary for this exercise). Then paint another brush stroke that crosses over, or intersects, with the first brush stroke.

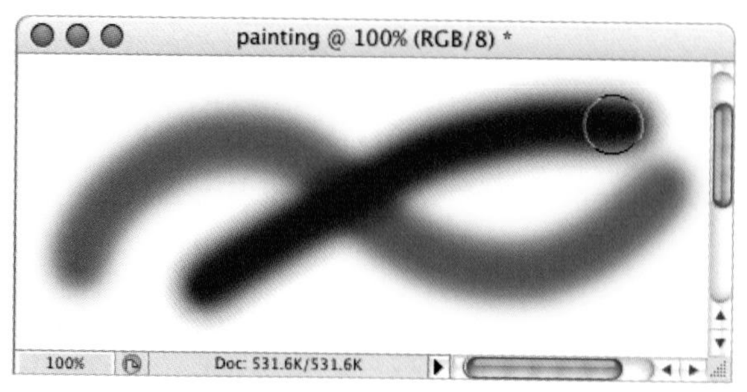

Painting a second brush stroke.

Note that when you paint, the Brush tool cursor displays the diameter of the brush that is selected. To resize the brush, you can return to the Brush Preset picker in the Options bar, but it is more intuitive to resize your brush dynamically, using a keyboard shortcut.

If you have the Caps Lock key selected, your Brush tool cursor appears as a crosshair.

9 Press the] (right bracket) key to increase the brush size. Now press the [(left bracket) key to decrease the size of the brush. As this blank document is for experimentation only, you can paint after resizing to see the size difference.

10 Choose File > Save to save the file. Keep the file open for the next part of this lesson.

Changing opacity

Changing the level of opacity affects how transparent your brush strokes look over other image information. In this section, you will experiment with different percentages of opacity.

1 If the Swatches panel is not visible choose Window > Swatches. The Swatches panel appears, with predetermined colors ready for you to use.

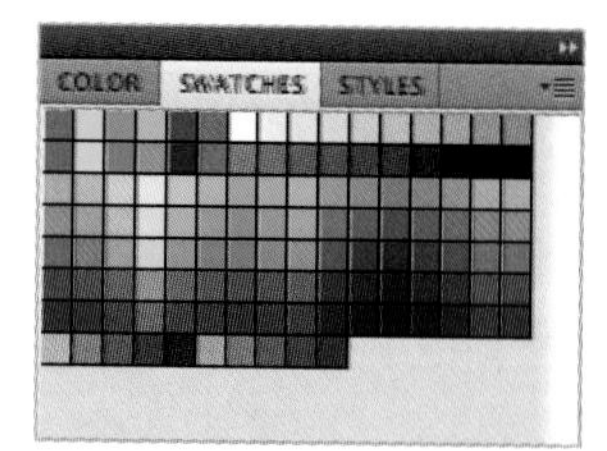

The Swatches panel.

2 Position your cursor over any swatch color and you'll see an eyedropper, along with a tooltip indicating the name of the color. Click on any one of the swatches; it becomes your current foreground color.

3 Now, to change its opacity, go to the Options bar at the top and click on the arrow next to 100%. A slider appears. Drag the slider to the left to lower the opacity to about 50 percent, and then click on the arrow to collapse the slider. Alternatively, you can type **50** into the opacity text field, if you prefer. Understand that changing the opacity of a color does not affect any of the painting that you have already completed, but it will affect future painting.

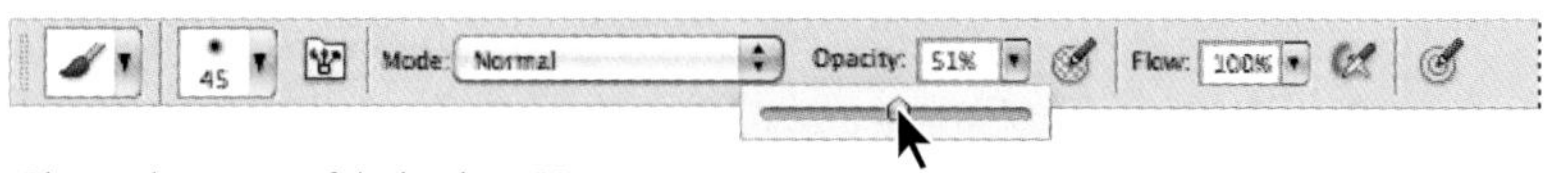

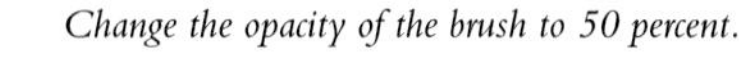

Change the opacity of the brush to 50 percent.

You can also change the opacity in Photoshop by hovering over the word Opacity in the Options bar. A double-arrow appears (), allowing you to slide the opacity down or up without revealing the slider.

4 Click and drag with the Brush tool to paint over the canvas. Make sure to overlap existing colors to see how one color interacts with another. Take some time here to experiment with different colors, opacity settings, and brush sizes.

5 Choose File > Save and then File > Close to close the file.

Save time—learn the shortcuts

There are many keyboard shortcuts to help you when painting in Photoshop, most of which are integrated into the exercises in this lesson. Here is a list that will help you save time and work more efficiently:

BRUSH FUNCTION	BRUSH KEYBOARD SHORTCUTS
Open the Brush Preset picker	Right-click (Windows) Ctrl+click (Mac OS)
Increase Brush size	] (right bracket)
Decrease Brush Size	[(left bracket)
Make Brush Harder	Shift+] (right bracket)
Make Brush Softer	Shift+[(left bracket)
Change Opacity	Type a value, such as 55 for 55 percent or 4 for 40 percent.
100% Opacity	Type **0** (zero)

Using the New Brushes

In Photoshop CS5 you will find more realistic brushes than ever, as well as new features, such as the context-sensitive Brush panel (and in the Options bar), that have been added to make painting easier than ever before. In this section, you find out how to take advantage of some of the new realistic brushes that have been added to Photoshop CS5.

1 Choose File > Browse in Bridge, or select the Launch Bridge (Br) in the Application bar, to launch or bring forward Adobe Bridge. Then navigate to the ps06lessons folder and open image ps0602.psd. An image of a woman playing a guitar appears.

The file before you apply new brush strokes.

2 Choose File > Save As. In the Save As dialog box, name the file **ps0602_work**. Navigate to your ps06lessons folder and store the image there. Press Save.

3 Select the Brush tool ( ) and then select the Toggle the Brush panel button ( ) in the Options bar. The Brush panel appears.

   You could spend hours reviewing all the options in the Brush panel, but for this example you will experiment with a few of the new bristle brushes that have been added to Photoshop CS5.

4 Select the Brush Presets tab to bring it forward and then select Small List from the panel menu. This will make it easier for you to identify the brushes by name.

5 Click on the Round Curve Low Bristle Percent.

6 Using the Size slider click and drag the size of the brush to approximately 205 px.

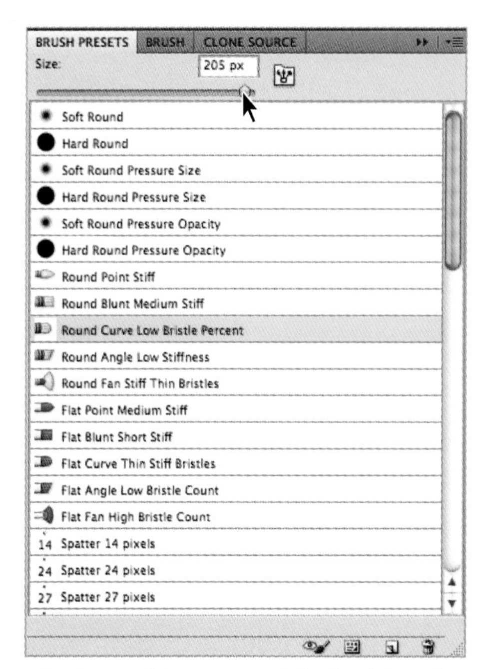

Select the Round Curve Low Bristle brush and change the size to 205 px.

7 With the Brush tool still selected, hold down the Alt (Windows) or Option (Mac OS) key and sample a color of the woman's skin color. Choose a darker shade if possible.

8 In the Options bar, click on the Mode drop-down menu and select Multiply.

9 Using large wide brush strokes paint over the woman playing the guitar. Since you are using a blending mode with a light color, the image is still visible. If you want to erase and try again, simply press Ctrl+Z (Windows) or Command+Z (Mac OS)

Note that as you paint a preview of your brush appears, and even shows the movement of the bristles as you paint.

The image after you apply the brush stroke.

You can store your brushes for future use by taking advantage of the Brush preset feature.

10 Click on the Create new brush (□) button in the lower right of the Brush Presets panel. The Brush Name dialog box appears. Type the name **My Large Rounded Brush**, and press OK. This brush now appears in the Brush Preset panel for future use.

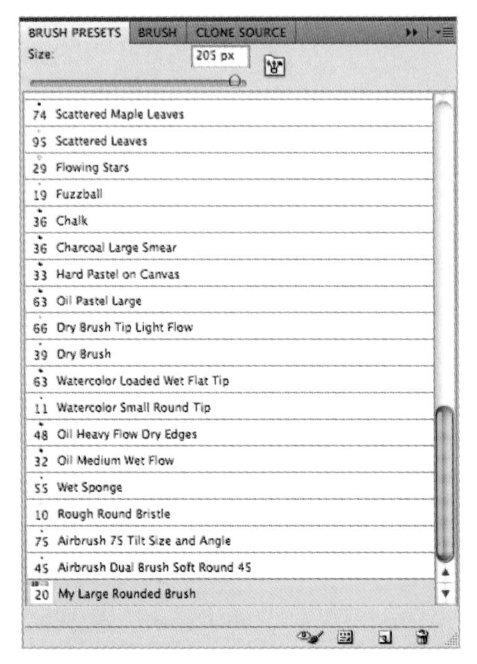

Store your brush for future use.

Using the Airbrush feature

In this section you discover how to change the brushes characteristics to act more like an airbrush. Using the airbrush option allows your paint to spread, much like the effect you would have using a true (non-digital) airbrush.

1 Select Round Fan StiffThin Bristles from the Brush Preset panel. Make sure the size is still close to 205 px. If not, use the slider to change it to that value now.

2 Press **D** to return to the Photoshop default colors of Black and white.

3 If the Mode (In the Options bar) is not set to Normal, set that now.

4 Click and hold (hold still) the brush anywhere on the image to essentially stamp a brush stroke onto the image. Do this a couple more times.You can press the [(left bracket) or] (right bracket) keys to change the size of the stamped brush.

Stamp the brush stroke to produce the effect of dabbing the brush onto the image.

5 Now, Select the Enable Airbrush Mode button in the Options bar. Notice that you can change the flow, or pressure, of the paint coming out of the airbrush using the Flow control to the left. In this example, this is set to 50%.

6 Using the same brush preset, click and hold on your image to notice that the paint spreads, as you hold.

With the Enable airbrush option the paint spreads as you hold down on the brush.

Experiment with different flows and sizes to see the effects that you have created.

Creating a Border using the Bristle brushes

In this next section, you use a bristle brush to create an artistic border around the edge of the image.

1 Select the Round Blunt Medium Stiff bristle brush from the Brush Presets panel.

2 Choose any color that you want to use for the border you are about to create. In this example we use the default black.

2 Click in the upper-left corner of the image. This is the top-left corner for your border.

Hold down the Shift key and click in the lower left corner. By Shift+clicking you have instructed Photoshop that you want a stroke to connect from the initial click to the next.

4 Shift+click in the lower-right corner, and then continue this process until you return to your original stroke origin in the upper-left corner.

The completed border.

5 Press Ctrl+S (Windows) or Command+S (Mac OS) to save this image, then choose File > Close.

Applying color to an image

You can color anything realistically in Photoshop by using different opacity levels and blending modes. In this part of the lesson, you'll take a grayscale image and tint it with color. Understand that you can also paint color images to change the color of an object, like clothing for a catalog, or just to add interesting tints for mood and effect.

1 Choose File > Browse in Bridge, or select the Launch Bridge (Br) in the Application bar, to launch or bring forward Adobe Bridge. Then navigate to the ps06lessons folder and open image ps0603.psd.

2 Double-click on the Zoom tool (🔍) in the Tools panel to change the view to 100 percent. You may need to resize the image window to view more of the image.

Resize your window automatically by checking the Resize Windows To Fit *checkbox in the Options bar at the top of the Photoshop workspace.*

3 Choose Image > Mode > RGB Color. In order to colorize a grayscale image, it needs to be in a mode that supports color channels.

4 Choose File > Save As; the Save As dialog box appears. Navigate to the ps06lessons folder and type **ps0603_work** into the Name text field. Choose Photoshop from the Format drop-down menu and Press Save.

5 If you do not see the Swatches panel, choose Window > Swatches.

6 Select the Brush tool and Right-click (Windows) or Ctrl+click (Mac OS) on the canvas to open the contextual Brush Preset picker. Select the Soft Round brush (this is the first brush.) Slide the Size slider to 17 and the Hardness slider to 0. Press Enter (Windows) or Return (Mac OS) to exit.

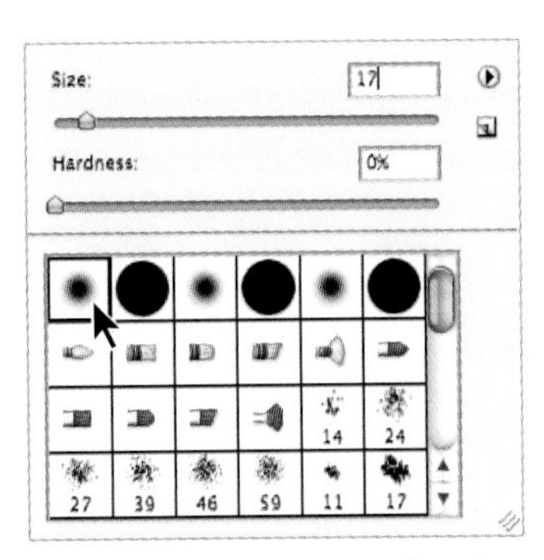

Change the brush size to 17 pixels, and make the brush softer.

7 Using the Opacity slider in the Options bar, change the opacity of the brush to 85 percent, or type **85** into the Opacity text field.

8 Position your cursor over an orange color in the Swatches panel until the tooltip indicates the color is *Pure Yellow Orange*, and then click to select the color.

9 Using the Brush tool, paint over the ceramic vessels at the bottom of the image. Notice that at 85 percent, the color is slightly transparent but still contains some of the image information underneath. You'll now paint these vases more realistically.

Painted vases at 85 percent opacity.

10 Choose File > Revert to return the image to the last saved version. Leave the file open.

Changing blending modes

Opacity is one way to alter the appearance or strength of a brush stroke. Another method is to change the blending mode of the painting tool you are using. The blending mode controls how pixels in the image are affected by painting. There are many modes to select from, and each creates a different result. This is because each blending mode is unique, but also because the blending result is based upon the color you are painting with and the color of the underlying image. In this section, you will colorize the photo by leaving the opacity at 100 percent and changing the blending mode.

1 Make sure that ps0602_work.psd is still open and double-click on the Zoom tool (🔍) in the Tools panel to change your view to 100 percent.

Make sure the Swatches panel is forward and the Brush tool (🖌) is selected for this part of the lesson.

2 Right-click (Windows) or Ctrl+click (Mac OS) anywhere in the document window. This opens the contextual Brush Preset picker.

3 Click on the panel menu of the Brush Preset picker in the upper-right corner and select Small List. When you release the mouse, the brushes appear as a descriptive list.

4 If it is not still active, double-click to select the Soft Round brush from the list of preset brushes. Leave the size and Hardness at the same settings.

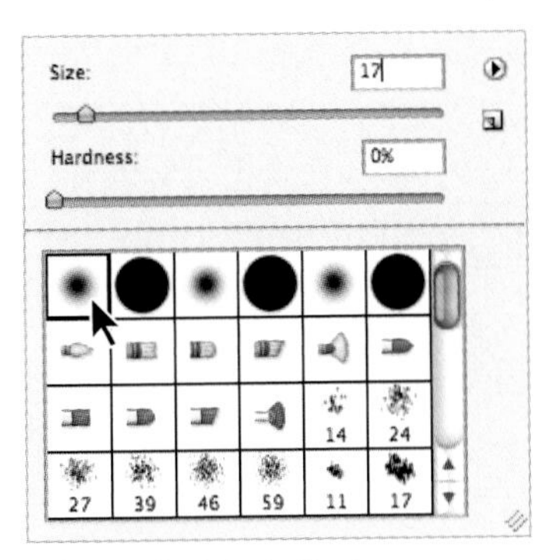

Selecting a brush in the list view.

5 Make sure that you still have the Pure Yellow Orange color selected from your Swatches panel; if not, select it now.

6 In the Options bar, change the opacity to 100 percent, or type **0** (zero). Typing zero when any painting or retouching tool is active is the keyboard shortcut to return to 100 percent opacity.

7 Select Color from the Mode drop-down list. This is where you select various blending modes for your painting tools. Color is close to the bottom of this drop-down menu, so you may have to scroll to see it.

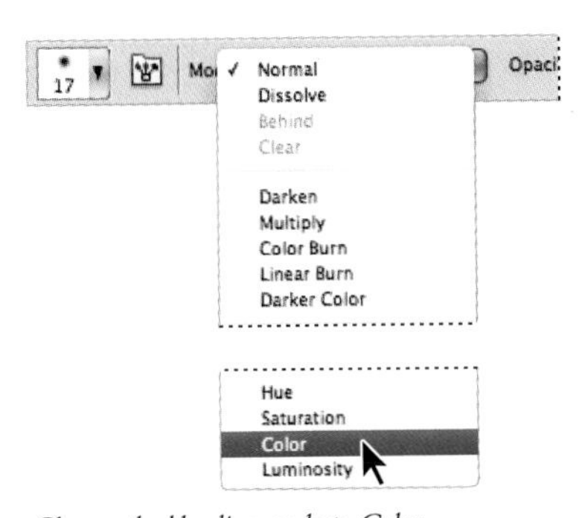

Change the blending mode to Color.

8 Using the Brush tool, paint over the ceramic vessels at the bottom of the image. Notice that the strength or opacity of the color varies according to the tonality of the painted area. This is because using the color blending mode you selected (Color) retains the grayscale information in the image. Where the image is lighter, the application of the orange color is lighter, and where the image is darker, the application of the orange color is darker.

Experiment with different colors to colorize the photo, but avoid painting the stone. Also try using different modes with the same color to see how differently each mode affects the colorization. Some modes may have no effect at all. Experiment all you want with painting at this point. You can choose Ctrl+Z (Windows) or Command+Z (Mac OS) to undo a brush stroke that you do not like, or use Ctrl+Alt+Z (Windows) or Command+Option+Z (Mac OS) to undo again and again.

You are changing actual pixels in the image; you will find out how to make non-destructive changes in Lessons 9 and 10 of this book.

Ceramic vases painted in the Color mode.

Don't like what you have done in just one area of the image? Select the Eraser tool and hold down Alt (Windows) or Option (Mac OS); then click and drag to erase to the last version saved. You can also change the brush size, opacity, and hardness of the Eraser tool, using the Options bar.

9 Choose File > Save, and leave the file open for the next section.

The Eyedropper tool

The Eyedropper tool is used for sampling color from an image. This color can then be used for painting, or for use with text color. In this section, you will sample a color from another image to colorize the stone building in ps0603.psd.

1 Make sure that ps0603_work.psd is still open, and choose File > Browse in Bridge, or select the Launch Bridge button (Br) or Mini Bridge button (Mb) in the Application bar. Navigate to the ps06lessons folder and open the file named ps0604.psd.

2 Click on the Arrange Documents button (▦), in the Application bar, and choose 2 Up from the drop-down menu.

3 Click on the title bar for the ps0604.psd image to bring that image forward.

Images tiled vertically.

4 Choose the Eyedropper tool (✐) and position it over the yellow building in the color image. Click once. The color is selected as the foreground color in the Tools panel.

5 Select the Brush tool, then using the Options bar at the top, make sure that Color is selected from the Mode drop-down menu and that the Opacity slider is set at 100 percent.

6 With the Brush tool (✐) selected, paint the stone wall with the color you just sampled. You can experiment at this point and sample other colors for painting. Don't forget that you can always undo what you don't like.

Colorizing the stone wall with the Brush tool.

7 Choose File > Save, then File > Close All to close both the ps0603_work.psd and the ps0604.psd files.

Retouching images

There are many techniques you can use to clean up an original image, from using any of the healing tools to that old standby, the Clone tool. In this lesson, you will retouch an image.

1 To view the final image, choose File > Browse in Bridge or select the Launch Bridge button (Br) in the Application bar to launch Adobe Bridge. Navigate to the ps06lessons folder and open image ps0605_done.psd.

The image after using the retouching tools.

2 You can choose File > Close after viewing this file, or leave it open for reference.

Using the Clone Stamp tool

One of the problems with old photographs is that they most likely contain a large number of defects. These defects can include watermarks, tears, fold marks, and so forth. There are many different ways to fix these defects; one of the most useful is the Clone Stamp tool. The Clone Stamp tool lets you replace pixels in one area of the image by sampling from another area. In this part of the lesson, you'll use the Clone Stamp tool, and you will also have an opportunity to explore the new Clone Source panel.

1 Choose File > Browse or select the Launch Bridge button (Br) or Mini Bridge button (Mb) in the Application bar to launch Adobe Bridge. Navigate to the ps06lessons folder and open image ps0605.psd.

2 Choose File > Save As; the Save As dialog box appears. Navigate to the ps06lessons folder and type **ps0605_work** into the Name text field. Choose Photoshop from the Format drop-down menu and press Save.

   You'll first experiment with the Clone Stamp tool. Don't worry about what you do to the image at this stage, as you will revert to saved when done.

3 Position your cursor over the nose of the girl in the image and hold down the Alt (Windows) or Option (Mac OS) key. Your cursor turns into a precision crosshair. When you see this crosshair, click with your mouse. You have just defined the source image area for the Clone Stamp tool.

4 Now position the cursor to the right of the girl's face, then click and drag to start painting with the Clone Stamp tool. The source area that you defined is recreated where you are painting. Watch carefully, as you will see a coinciding crosshair indicating the area of the source that you are copying.

The clone source and results.

5 Press the] (right bracket) key to enlarge the Clone Stamp brush. All the keyboard commands you reviewed for the Brush tool work with other painting tools as well.

6 Type **5**. By typing a numeric value when a painting tool is active, you can dynamically change the opacity. Start painting with the Clone Stamp tool again and notice that it is now cloning at a 50 percent opacity.

7 Type **0** (zero) to return to 100 percent opacity.

8 You have completed the experimental exercise using the Clone Stamp tool.

Choose File > Revert to go back to the original image.

Repairing fold lines

You will now repair the fold lines in the upper-right corner of the image.

1 Select the Zoom tool from the Tools panel, and if it is not already selected, check the Resize Windows To Fit checkbox in the Options bar. By checking this box, the window will automatically resize when you zoom.

2 Click approximately three times in the upper-right corner of the image. There you see fold marks that you will repair using the Clone Stamp tool.

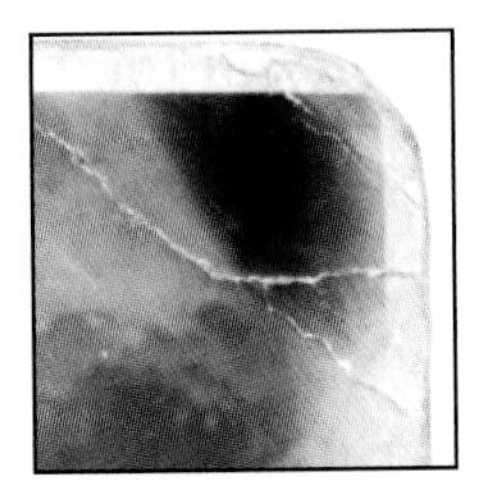

Fold marks that you will repair.

3 Select the Clone Stamp tool () from the Tools panel.

4 Right-click (Windows) or Ctrl+click (Mac OS) on the image area to open the Brush Preset picker. Click on the Soft Round brush and change the Size to 13 pixels. Press Enter or the Return key.

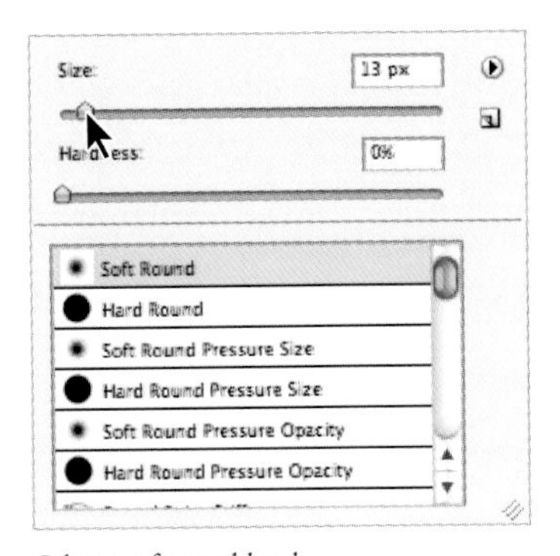

Select a soft round brush.

5 Position your cursor to the left of the fold mark, approximately in the center of the fold. Hold down Alt (Windows) or Option (Mac OS), and click to define that area as the source.

6 Position the Clone Stamp tool over the middle of the fold line itself, and click and release. Depending upon what you are cloning, it is usually wise to apply a clone source in small applications, rather than painting with long brush strokes.

7 Press Shift+[(left bracket) several times to make your brush softer. This way, you can better disguise the edges of your cloning.

8 Continue painting over the fold lines in the upper-left corner. As you paint, you will see crosshairs representing the sampled area. Keep an eye on the crosshairs; you don't want to introduce unwanted areas into the image.

It is not unusual to have to redefine the clone source over and over again. You may have to Alt/Option+click in the areas outside of the fold line repeatedly to find better-matched sources for cloning. You may even find that you Alt/Option+click and then paint, and then Alt/Option+click and paint again, until you conceal the fold mark.

Don't forget some of the selection techniques that you learned in Lesson 5, "Making the Best Selections." You can activate the edge of the area to be retouched so that you can keep your clone stamping inside the image area and not cross into the white border.

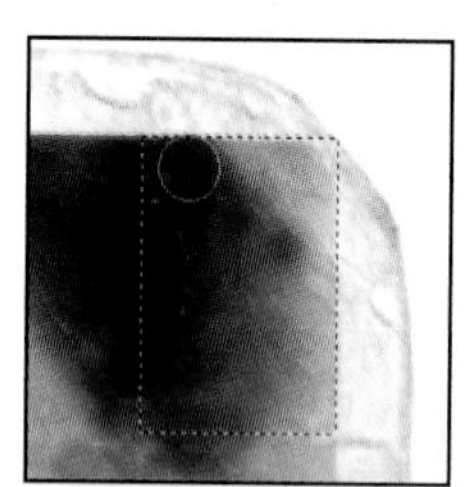

Create selections to help you control the cloning.

With the Clone Stamp tool, it is important to sample tonal areas that are similar to the tonal area you are covering. Otherwise, the retouching will look very obvious.

9 Choose File > Save. Keep this image open for the next part of this lesson.

The History panel

You can use the History panel to jump to previous states in an image. This is an important aid when retouching photos. In this section, you will explore the History panel as it relates to the previous section, and then continue to utilize it as you work forward in Photoshop.

1 Make sure that ps0605_work.psd is still open from the last section.

2 Choose Window > History. The History panel appears. Grab the lower-right corner of the panel and pull it down to expand the panel and reveal all the previous states in History.

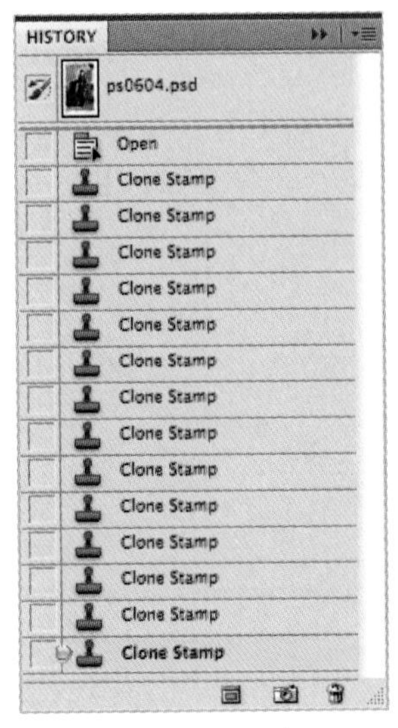

Resizing the History panel.

3 You see many Clone Stamp states, or a listing of any function that you performed while the image was open. As you click on each state, you reveal the image at that point in your work history. You can click back one state at a time, or you can jump to any state in the panel, including the top state, always the name of the file, which is the state of the original image when it was first opened. You can utilize this as a strategy for redoing work that does not meet with your satisfaction.

4 If you need to redo some of the cloning that you did in the previous section, click on a state in the History panel for your starting point, and redo some of your work.

All states in the History panel are deleted when the file is closed.

5 Choose File > Save. Keep this file open for the next part of the lesson.

The Spot Healing Brush

The Spot Healing Brush tool paints with sampled pixels from an image and matches the texture, lighting, transparency, and shading of the pixels that are sampled to the pixels being retouched, or healed. Note that unlike the Clone Stamp tool, the Spot Healing Brush automatically samples from around the retouched area.

1 With the ps0605_work.psd file still open, select View > Fit on Screen, or use the keyboard shortcut Ctrl+0 (zero) (Windows) or Command+0 (zero) (Mac OS).

2 Select the Zoom tool (🔍), then click and drag the lower-right section of the image to zoom into the lower-right corner.

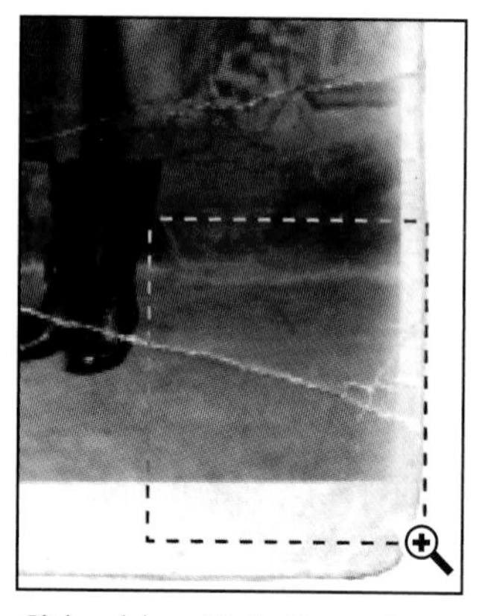

Click and drag with the Zoom tool.

Because you do not have to define a source with the Spot Healing tool, it can be easier to retouch. It is not the absolute answer to every retouching need, but it works well when retouching sections of an image that are not defined and detailed, like blemishes on skin or backgrounds.

3 Select the Spot Healing Brush tool (🖌), and then click and release repeatedly over the fold marks in the lower-right corner of the image. The tool initially creates a dark region, indicating the area that is to be retouched, but don't panic, it will blend well when you release the mouse. Now, using the Spot Healing Brush, repair the fold lines. Use the History panel to undo steps, if necessary.

4 Choose File > Save. Keep this file open for the next part of this lesson.

The Healing Brush

The Healing Brush tool also lets you correct imperfections. Like the Clone Stamp tool, you use the Healing Brush tool to paint with pixels you sample from the image, but the Healing Brush tool also matches the texture, lighting, transparency, and shading of the sampled pixels. In this section, you will remove some defects in the girl's dress.

1 Make sure that ps0605_work.psd is still open from the last section, and choose View > Fit on Screen.

2 Select the Zoom tool, then click and drag over the bottom area of the girl's dress.

Click and drag to zoom into the dress.

3 Click and hold on the Spot Healing Brush ( ) in the Tools panel to select the hidden tool, the Healing Brush ( ).

4 Position your cursor over an area near to, but outside, the fold line in the skirt, as you are going to define this area as your source. Hold down Alt (Windows) or Option (Mac OS), and click to define the source for your Healing Brush tool.

5 Now, paint over the fold line that is closest to the source area you defined.

6 Repeat this process; Alt/Option+click in appropriate source areas near the folds across the dress, then paint over the fold lines, using the Healing Brush tool. Don't forget to change the size using the left and right brackets, if necessary.

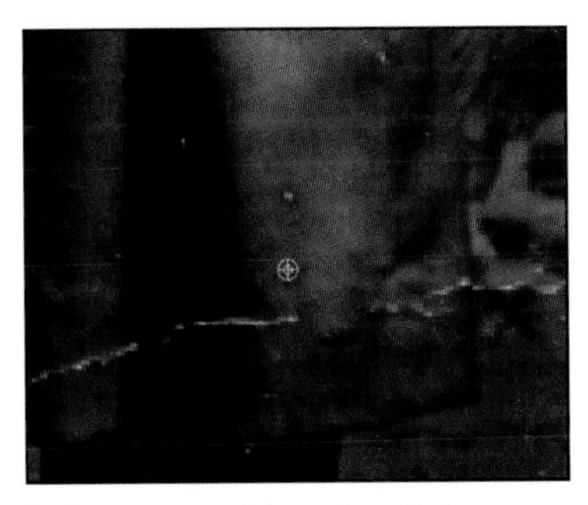

Define a source and then paint with the Healing Brush tool.

7 Choose File > Save, and leave this file open for the next part of this lesson.

Using the Patch tool

You may find that there are large areas of scratches or dust marks that need to be retouched. You can use the Patch tool to replace large amounts of an image with image data that you sample as your source. In this section, you will fix the large dusty area in the upper-left part of the image.

1 With the ps0605_work.psd file still open, choose View Fit on Screen, or use the keyboard shortcut Ctrl+0 (zero) (Windows) or Command+0 (zero) (Mac OS).

2 Select the Zoom tool (🔍), and then click and drag to zoom into the upper-left area of the image.

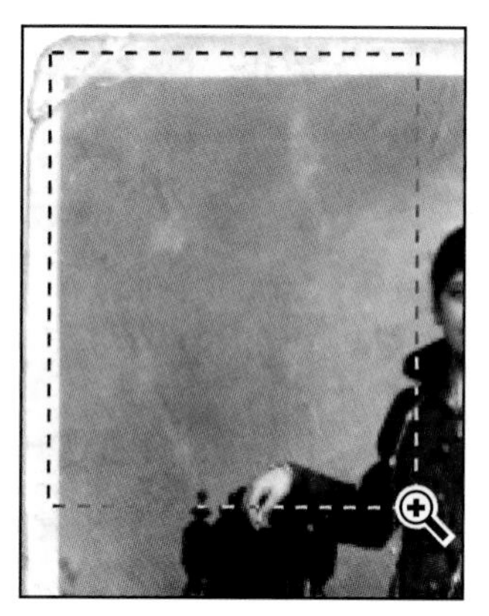

Click and drag to zoom into the upper-left corner.

3 Hold down on the Healing Brush tool (✎) and select the hidden Patch tool (⚙).

4 Click and drag a selection to select a small area with defects. Then click and drag that selection over an area of the image with fewer defects, to use as a source.

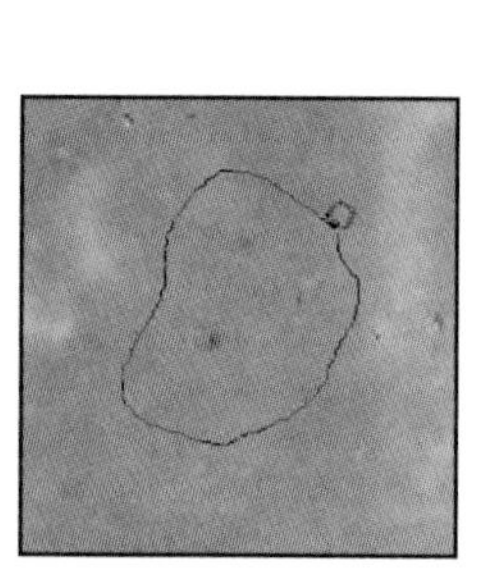

The original.

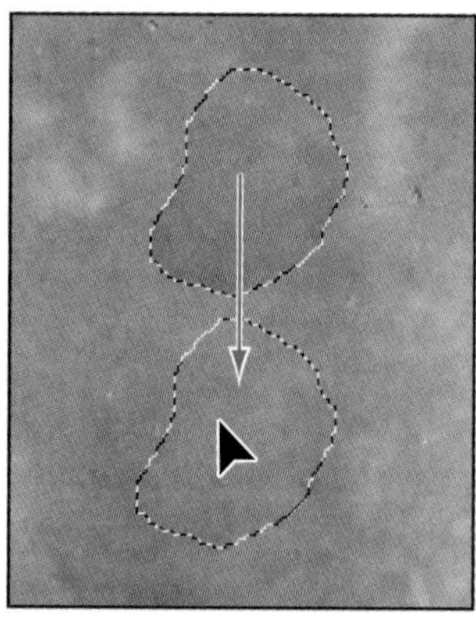

Drag with the Patch tool.

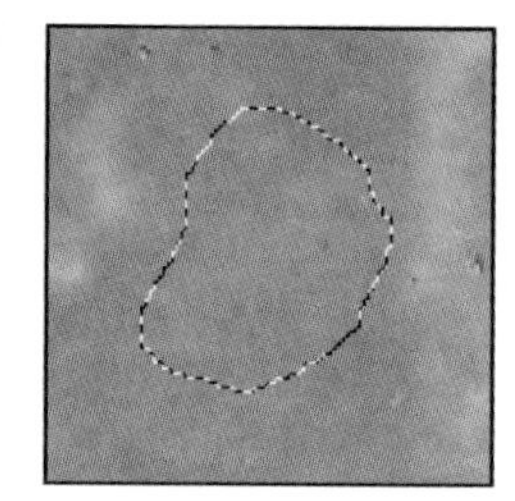

The result.

5 Continue to make selections and patch with the Patch tool to clean up most of the dust marks in the upper-left corner of the image.

6 Choose File > Save. Keep the file open for the next part of this lesson.

Using the Clone Source panel

When using the Clone Source panel, you can set up to five clone sources for the Clone Stamp or Healing Brush tools to use. The sources can be from the same image you are working on or from other open images. Using the Clone Source panel, you can even preview the clone source before painting, and rotate and scale the source. In this section, you will clone the upper-left corner of the ps0605_work.psd image and rotate it to repair the upper-right corner of the image. You will also define a second clone source to add an art deco border around the edge of the image.

1 Make sure that ps0605_work.psd is still open, and choose View > Fit on Screen.

2 Choose Window > Clone Source to open the Clone Source panel. If it helps, press Ctrl+plus sign (Windows) or Command+plus sign (Mac OS) on the upper-left corner.

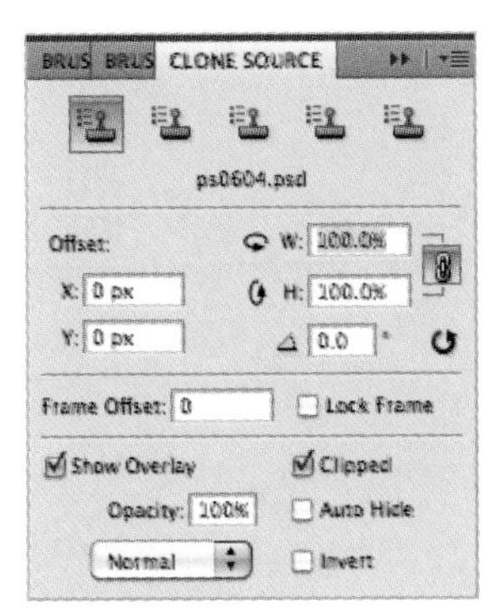

The Clone Source panel.

The Clone Source panel displays five icons, each representing a sampled source. You will start out using the first clone source.

3 Choose the Clone Stamp tool (![]). Verify in the Options bar that the Mode is Normal and Opacity is 100 percent.

4 Click on the first Clone Source icon in the Clone Source panel and position your cursor over the top-left corner of the image. Hold down the Alt (Windows) or Option (Mac OS) key and click to define this corner as the first clone source.

You will now use this corner to replace the damaged corner in the upper right.

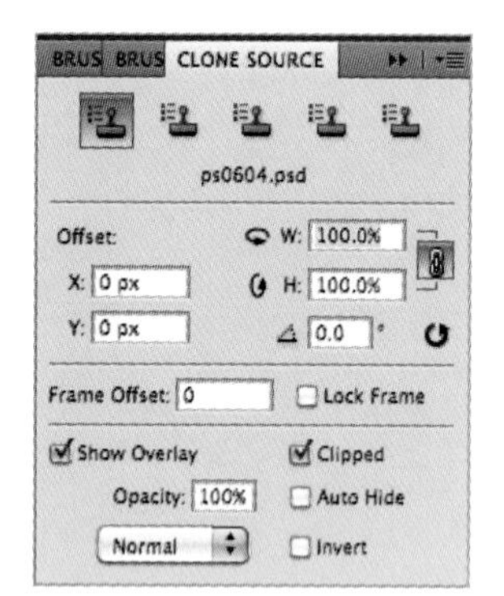

Select the first Clone Source icon.

Alt/Option+click on the upper-left corner.

5 If you zoomed into the upper-left corner, hold down the spacebar to turn your cursor into the Hand tool (✋), then click and drag to the left. Think of the image as being a piece of paper that you are pushing to the left to see the upper-right corner of the image.

6 When you are positioned over the right corner, check the Show Overlay checkbox (if it is unchecked) in the Clone Source panel. A ghosted image of your clone source is displayed. If necessary, hover over Opacity in the Clone Source panel and drag it to a lower level.

Note that you can uncheck the Clipped checkbox to see the entire clone source.

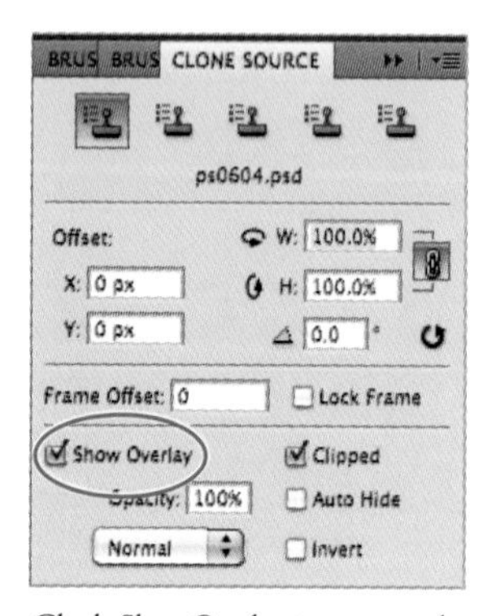

Check Show Overlay to see your clone source before cloning.

7 Now, type **90** in the Rotate text field in the Clone Source panel. The corner is rotated so that you can fit it in as a new corner in the upper-right area of the image.

Use the Clone Source panel to rotate your source.

8 Verify that your brush size is approximately the width of the white border. You can preview the brush size by positioning your cursor over the white border. If you do not see the brush size preview, you may have your Caps Lock key selected. If necessary, make your brush smaller using the [(left bracket), or larger using the] (right bracket) keys repeatedly.

9 Make sure the corner is aligned with the outside of the underlying image (original upper-right corner). Don't worry about aligning with the original inside border.

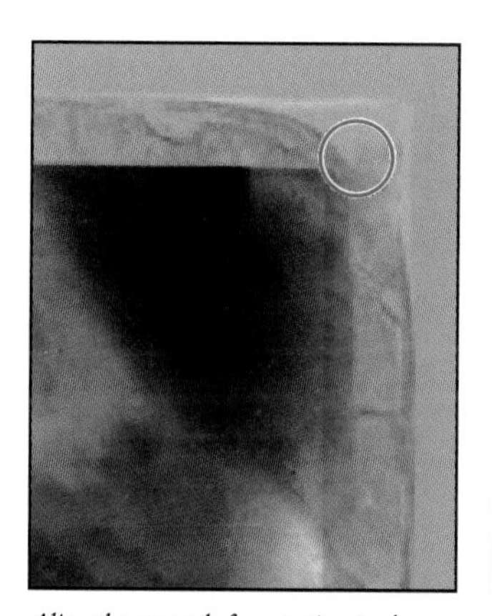
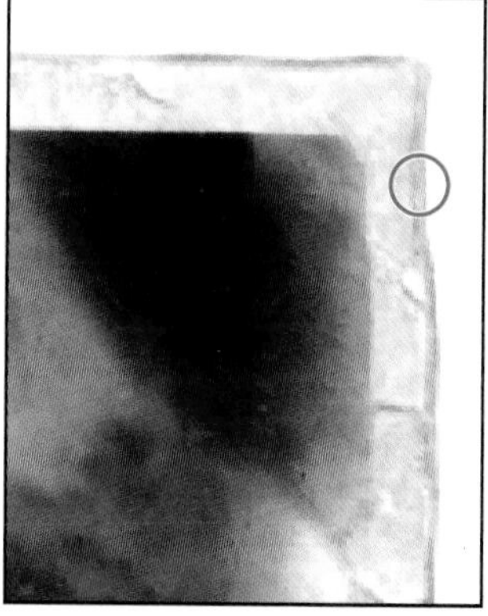

Align the corner before starting to clone.

10 Start painting only the corner with the Clone Stamp tool. Now the corner has been added to the image. Uncheck the Show Overlay checkbox to better see your results.

11 Choose File > Save and keep this file open for the next part of this lesson.

Cloning from another source

In this section, you will open an image to clone a decoration, and then apply it to the ps0605_work image.

1 Choose File > Browse in Bridge, or select the Launch Bridge button (Br) in the Application bar. When Adobe Bridge appears, navigate to the ps06lessons folder and double-click on the image named ps0606.psd. An image with a decorative border appears.

2 If the Clone Source panel is not visible, choose Window > Clone Source. Make sure that the Show Overlay checkbox is unchecked.

3 Select the Clone Stamp tool (⊥) and then click on the second Clone Source icon.

4 Position your cursor over the upper-left corner of the decorative border, and then hold down the Alt (Windows) or Option (Mac OS) key and click to define this area of the image as your second clone source.

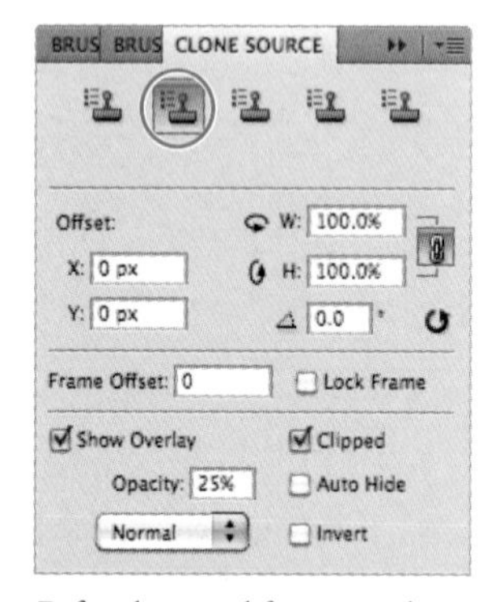

Define the upper-left corner as the second clone source.

5 Select the third Clone Source icon in the Clone Source panel.

6 Position your cursor over the upper-right corner of the decorative border, then hold down the Alt (Windows) or Option (Mac OS) key and click to define this area of the image as your third clone source.

7 Choose Window > ps0605_work.psd to bring that image to the front.

8 If you cannot see your entire ps0605_work.psd image, choose View > Fit on Screen, or use the keyboard shortcut Ctrl+0 (zero) (Windows) or Command+0 (zero) (Mac OS).

9 To make the clone of the decorative border appear *antique*, you will make some modifications to the Clone Stamp tool options. With the Clone Stamp tool selected, go to the Options bar and select Luminosity from the Mode drop-down menu. Type **50** into the Opacity text field.

10 Select the second Clone Source icon, then check the Show Overlay checkbox in the Clone Source panel.

11 Position your cursor in the upper-left corner of the ps0605_work.psd image, and you see the preview of the decorative border. When you have the decorative corner positioned roughly in the upper-left corner, start painting. Try to follow the swirls of the design as best you can, but don't worry about being exact. The blending mode and opacity that you set in the Options bar helps to blend this into the original image. Keep in mind that when you paint with a lighter opacity, additional painting adds to the initial opacity. If it helps to see the results, turn off the Show Overlay checkbox. Check it back on for the remainder of this lesson.

Paint with the Clone tool.

The result.

Now you will clone the third source to the upper-right corner of the image. This time, you can experiment with the position of the decoration on the image.

12 Navigate to the upper-right side of the ps0605_work image and select the third Clone Source icon from the Clone Source panel. You will now use the Clone Source panel to reposition the upper-right corner clone source.

13 Hold down Alt+Shift (Windows) or Option+Shift (Mac OS) and press the left, right, up, or down arrow key on your keyboard to nudge the overlay into a better position. No specific position is required for this lesson; simply find a location that you feel works well.

14 Once you have the clone source in position, start painting. Lightly paint the decoration into the upper-right corner. If you feel your brush is too hard-edged, press Shift+[(left bracket) to make it softer.

15 Choose File > Save. Keep the ps0605_work.psd file open for the next part of this lesson. Choose Window > ps0606.psd to bring that image forward. Then choose File > Close. If asked to save changes, select Don't Save.

Self study

Return to the ps0605_work.psd image and use a variety of retouching tools, such the Clone Stamp, Spot Healing, and Healing Brush tools, to fix the rest of the damaged areas in the image. Also use the retouching tools to remove dust.

Use the Clone Source panel to repair the lower-left and lower-right corners of the ps0605_work.psd image.

Review

Questions

1 If you have an image in the grayscale mode and you want to colorize it, what must you do first?

2 What blending mode preserves the underlying grayscale of an image and applies a hue of the selected color? Hint: it is typically used for tinting images.

3 What is the main difference between the way the Clone Stamp and Healing Brush replace information in an image?

4 How many clone sources can be set in the Clone Source panel?

Answers

1 In order to use color, you must choose a color mode that supports color, such as RGB or CMYK. You can change the color mode by selecting the Image > Mode menu.

2 The Color blending mode is used for tinting images.

3 The Clone Stamp makes an exact copy of the sampled area, whereas the Healing Brush makes a copy of the sampled area and matches the texture, lighting, transparency, and shading of the sampled pixels.

4 You can set up to five clone sources in the Clone Source panel.

What you'll learn in this lesson:

- Choosing color settings
- Using the histogram
- Discovering a neutral
- Using curves
- Unsharp masking
- Using Camera Raw

Creating a Good Image

You can create interesting imagery in Photoshop, including compositions, filter effects, and even 3D imagery when using Photoshop CS5 Extended; but it is important to have a great-looking image to serve as the foundation of your work.

Starting up

There are simple steps that you can take to create a brighter, cleaner, more accurate image. In this lesson, you'll learn how to use the Curves controls and how to sharpen your images. You'll learn what a neutral is and how to use it to color correct your images. You'll also have the opportunity to work with a Camera Raw image, using the improved Camera Raw plug-in.

Although the steps may at first seem time-consuming, they go quickly when not accompanied by the "whys and hows" included in this lesson. In fact, the process works almost like magic; a few steps and your image looks great!

Before starting, make sure that your tools and panels are consistent by resetting your preferences. See "Resetting Adobe Photoshop CS5 preferences" on page 3. You will work with several files from the ps07lessons folder in this lesson. Make sure that you have loaded the pslessons folder onto your hard drive from the supplied DVD. See "Loading lesson files" on page 5.

See Lesson 7 in action!

Use the accompanying video to gain a better understanding of how to use some of the features shown in this lesson. The video tutorial for this lesson can be found on the included DVD.

Choosing your color settings

What many Photoshop users do not understand is the importance of knowing where an image is going to be published; whether for print, the web, or even a digital device like a cell phone. You read a little about color settings in Lesson 6, "Painting and Retouching," where you discovered some of Photoshop's pre-defined settings. These help adapt the colors and values of an image for different uses. If not set properly, your images may appear very dark, especially in the shadow areas. For this lesson, you will use generic color settings that work well for a typical print image. You are also introduced to settings for other types of output, including the Web.

1 Choose Edit > Color Settings in Photoshop CS5. The Color Settings dialog box appears.

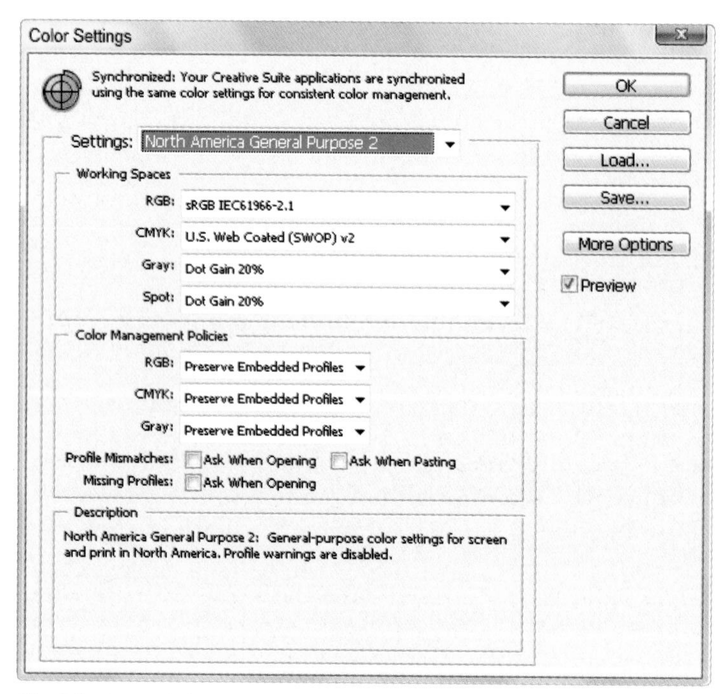

The Color Settings dialog box at its default settings.

2 As a default, North America General Purpose 2 is selected. This setting is good for images that are to be printed on coated paper stock. Coated paper has a coating that allows the paper to be printed without significant ink absorption. If you plan on printing on an uncoated stock, which, due to ink absorption, tends to produce a darker image, choose U.S. Sheetfed Uncoated v2 from the CMYK drop-down menu.

When you see U.S. Web Coated in the CMYK drop-down menu, it is not referring to the Web, as in Internet. A web press is used for printing books, catalogs, newspapers, and magazines. It is a high-run, high-speed, printing press that uses rolls of paper rather than individual sheets.

3 For this example, make sure that the default settings of North America General Purpose 2 are selected. Press OK to exit the Color Settings dialog box.

Opening the file

1 Choose File > Browse in Bridge. When Adobe Bridge is forward, navigate to the ps07lessons folder that you copied onto your hard drive.

2 Locate the image named ps0701.psd and double-click on it to open it in Photoshop. You can also choose to right-click (Windows) or Ctrl+click (Mac OS) and select Open with Adobe Photoshop CS5. An image of a boy appears; because this is not a professional photograph, it offers many issues that need to be addressed.

Note the comparison of images: the one on the left is uncorrected, and the one on the right is corrected. You'll correct the image on the left in the next few steps.

The image before correction.

The image after correction.

3 Choose File > Save As. The Save As dialog box appears. Navigate to the ps07lessons folder on your hard drive. In the Name text field, type **ps0701_work**, choose Photoshop from the Format drop-down menu, and press Save. Leave the image open.

Why you should work in RGB

In this lesson, you start and stay in the RGB (Red, Green, Blue) color mode. There are two reasons for this: you will that find more tools are available in this mode, and changes to color values in RGB degrade your image less than if you are working in CMYK. If you were sending this image to a commercial printer, you would make sure your color settings were accurate, and then convert your image to CMYK by choosing Image > Mode > CMYK Color.

If you want to see the CMYK preview while working in RGB, press Ctrl+Y (Windows) or Command+Y (Mac OS). This way, you can work in the RGB mode while you see the CMYK preview on your screen. This is a toggle keyboard shortcut, meaning that if you press Ctrl+Y or Command+Y again, the preview is turned off. You may not see a difference in the image, depending upon the range of colors, but the title tab indicates that you are in CMYK preview mode by displaying /CMYK after the title of the image.

Reading a histogram

Understanding image histograms is probably the single most important concept to become familiar with when working with images in Photoshop. A histogram can tell you whether your image has been properly exposed, whether the lighting is correct, and what adjustments will work best to improve your image. You will reference the Histogram panel throughout this lesson.

1 If your Histogram panel is not visible, choose Window > Histogram. The Histogram panel appears.

A histogram shows the tonal values that range from the lightest to the darkest in an image. Histograms can vary in appearance, but typically you want to see a full, rich, mountainous area representing tonal values. See the figures for examples of a histogram with many values, one with very few values, and the images relating to each.

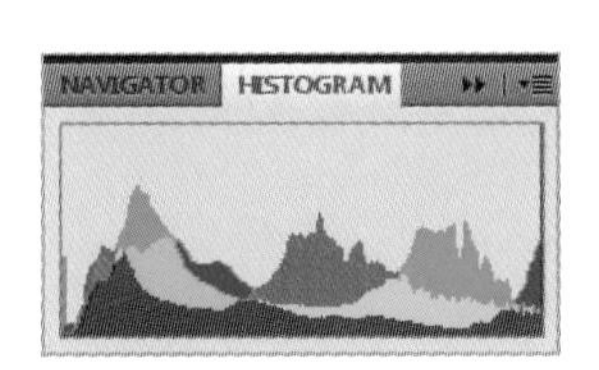

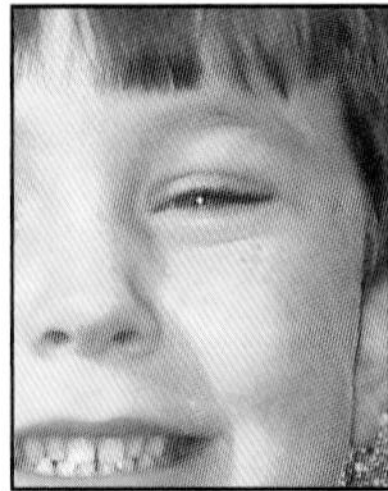

A good histogram and its related image.

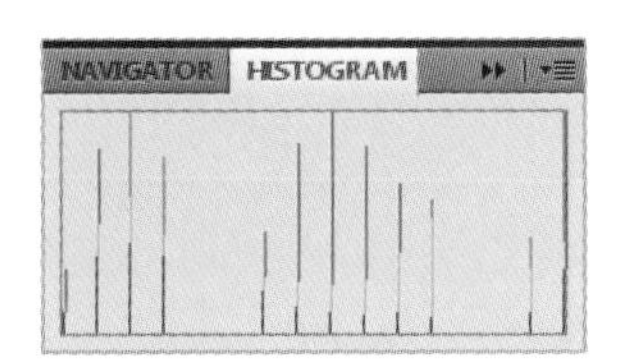

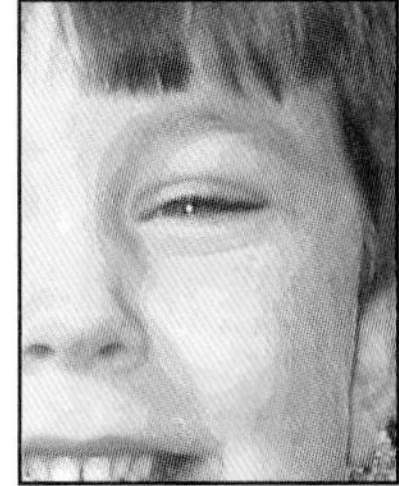

A poor histogram and its related image.

Keep an eye on your Histogram panel. Simply doing normal corrections to an image can break up a histogram, giving you an image that starts to look posterized (when a region of an image with a continuous gradation of tone is replaced with several regions of fewer tones.) Avoid breaking up the histogram by learning to use multi-function tools, like the Curves panel, and making changes using adjustment layers, which don't change your original image data.

2 To make sure that the values you read in Photoshop are accurate, select the Eyedropper tool (). Notice that the Options bar (across the top of the document window) changes to offer options specific to the Eyedropper tool. Click and hold on the Sample Size drop-down menu and choose 3 by 3 Average. This ensures a representative sample of an area, rather than the value of a single screen pixel.

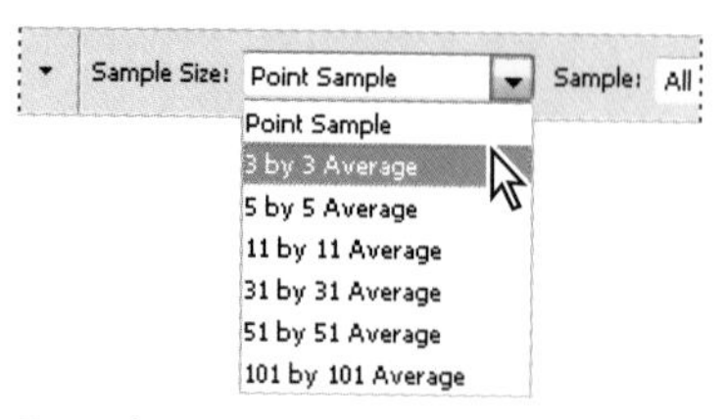

Set up the Eyedropper tool to sample more pixel information.

Making the Curve adjustment

You will now address the tonal values of this image. To do this, you will take advantage of the Curves Adjustments panel. Adjustment layers can be created by using the Adjustments panel, or in the Layers panel. To help you see the relationship between Adjustment layers and other layers, you will create one using the Layers panel.

1 If the Layers panel is not visible, choose Window > Layers. Click and hold on the Create New Fill or Adjustment Layer button () at the bottom of the Layers panel, select Curves, and release the mouse. The Curves Adjustment panel appears.

2 Click on the Switch Panel to Expanded View button (icon) in the lower-left corner of the Adjustments panel.

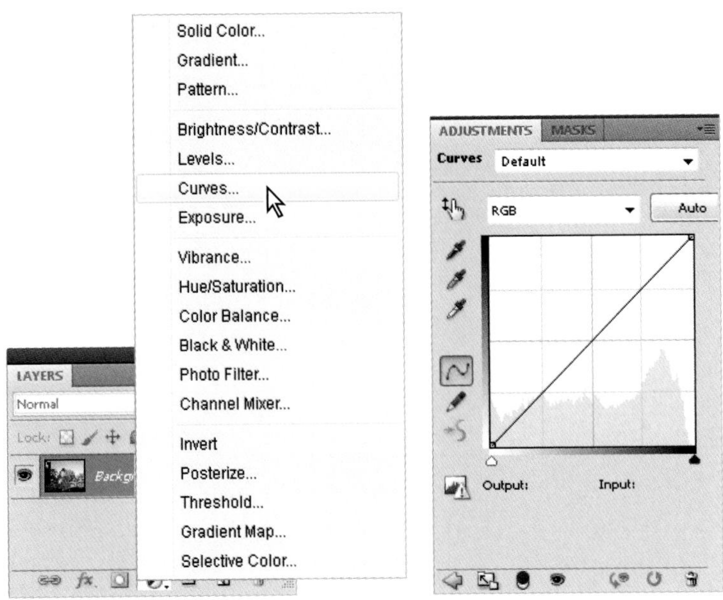

Select the Curves Adjustment.

The Curves dialog box appears.

By using adjustments, you can make changes to an image's tonal values without destroying the original image data. See Chapter 9, "Taking Layers to the Max," for more information about how to use the Adjustments panel. Leave the Curves Adjustments panel open for the next section.

Keep in mind that adjustments work very differently than in previous versions of Photoshop and could possibly be confusing to both new and existing Photoshop users. Read these tips before you proceed any further, and refer back to them if you have any problems following future adjustment steps.

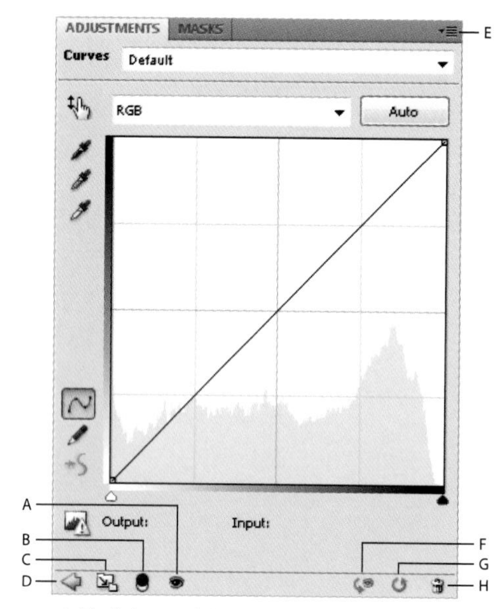

A. Toggle layer visibility. ***B****. Clip to layer below.* ***C****. Switch panel view.* ***D****. Return to adjustment list.* ***E****. Panel menu.* ***F****. View previous state.* ***G****. Reset to defaults.* ***H****. Delete adjustment layer.*

Once you choose to create an adjustment layer, it appears in the Adjustments panel; an example is the Curves adjustment panel that you just revealed. If you accidently leave the curves adjustment, by selecting another adjustment, or by pressing the Return to Adjustment List button (◀), at the bottom of the Adjustments panel, you see a panel with links to the other adjustments that you can make. If you want to return to the current adjustment, press the Return to Controls for Current Adjustment Layer button (▶).

If you make an error, you can undo one step by pressing Ctrl+Z (Windows) or Command+Z (Mac OS). If you want to return to the defaults for this adjustment, choose the Reset to Adjustment Defaults button (↻) in the lower-right corner of the Adjustments panel.

If you want to eliminate the adjustment layer, choose the Delete this Adjustment Layer button (🗑).

If you exit the Adjustments panel and want to edit an existing adjustment, select the adjustment layer from the Layers panel. When you click on the adjustment layer, the adjustment appears ready to edit in the Adjustments panel.

Defining the highlight and shadow

In this section, you'll set the highlight and shadow to predetermined values using the Set White Point and Set Black Point tools available in Curves Adjustments panel. Before you do this, you'll determine what those values should be. This is a critical part of the process, as the default for the white point is 0, meaning that the lightest part of the image will have no value when printed, and any detail in this area will be lost.

Some images can get away with not having tonal values in very bright areas. Typically, reflections from metal, fire, and extremely sunlit areas, as well as reflections off other shiny objects like jewelry, do not have value in those reflective areas.

These are referred to as specular highlights. By leaving them without any value, it helps the rest of the image look balanced, and allows the shine to pop out of the image. See the figure below for an example.

This image has specular highlights, which should be left with a value of zero.

Locating the White and Black Point

Back before digital imagery became so accessible, highly skilled scanner operators used large drum scanners to scan and color correct images. Back then, color experts followed many of the same steps that you will learn in this lesson. The most important step would be defining the tone curve based on what the operator thought should be defined as the lightest part of a tone curve, and the darkest.

There are many factors that can determine what appears to be a simple task. To produce the best image, you need to know where the image will be used; shiny coated paper, newsprint, or on screen only.

Before you get started, you will change a simple preference to make it easier for you to interpret the Curves panel.

1 With the Curves Adjustment panel open, click on the panel menu in the upper-right, and select Curves Display Options. The Curves Display Options dialog box appears.

2 Choose Show Amount of: Pigment/Ink%.

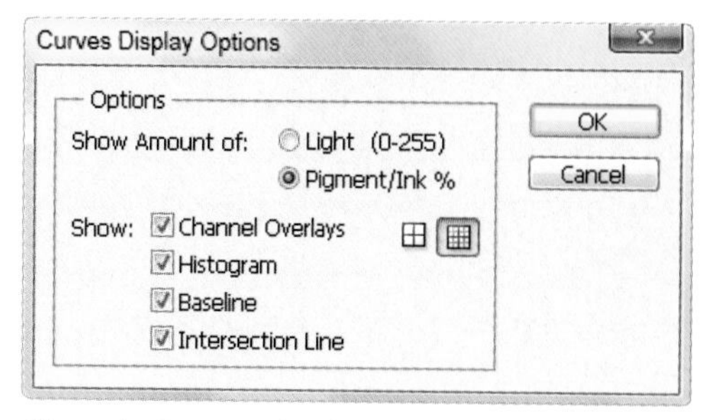

Change the Curves panel to display curve as if it was based upon ink.

Whether you work on print or web images it can be helpful to visually interpret the curves panel based upon ink, as this puts the lightest colors of the curve in the lower left and the darkest part of the image in the upper-right.

Inputting the white and black point values

The process of defining values for the lightest and darkest points in your image is not difficult, but it helps if you know where the image is going to be used. If you have a good relationship with a printer, they can tell you what values work best for their presses, or you can just use the generic values suggested in this book. The values shown in this example are good for typical printing setups and for web display.

1 Double-click on the Set White Point button (✐) found in the Curves Adjustments panel; the Select Target Highlight Color dialog box appears. Even though you are in RGB, you can set values in any of the color environments displayed in this window. In this example, you'll use CMYK values.

2 Type **5** in the C (Cyan) text field, **3** in the M (Magenta) text field, and **3** in the Y (Yellow) text field. Leave K (Black) at 0, and press OK. A warning dialog box appears, asking if you would like to save the target values, press Yes.

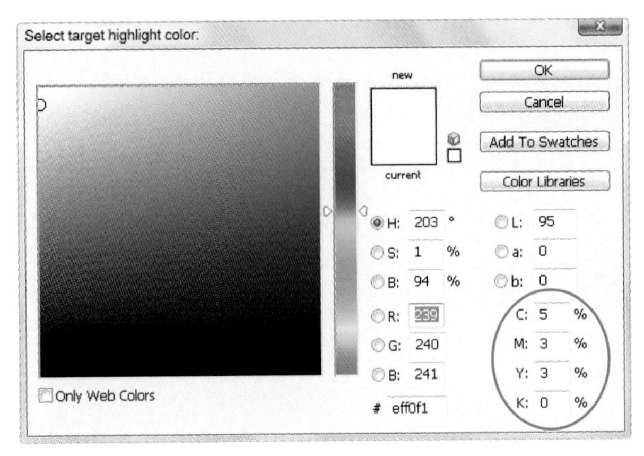

Setting the target highlight color.

3 Now, double-click on the Set Black Point button (✒). The Select Target Shadow Color dialog box appears.

If you have properly defined ink and paper in your Color Settings dialog box, you do not need to change the Black Point values. If you are not sure where you are going to print, or if you are going only to the screen, you can use the values in the next step of this exercise.

4 Type **65** in the C (Cyan) text field, **53** in the M (Magenta) text field, **51** in the Y (Yellow) text box, and **95** in the K (Black) text field. Press OK. A warning dialog box appears, asking if you would like to save the target values; press Yes.

It is important to note that your printer may be able to achieve a richer black than the one offered here. If you have a relationship with a printer, ask for their maximum black value and enter it here. Otherwise, use these standard values.

5 Now, select the highlight slider (△), and then hold down Alt (Windows) or Option (Mac OS) and slide it to the right. Notice that the image appears almost posterized: this is the automatic clipping that is visible when you hold down the Alt/Option key. The clipping makes it easier to locate the darkest and lightest areas of an image—an essential task if you are trying to improve an image's tonal values.

6 Drag the highlight slider to the right until you see the most minimal amount of logo on the small boy's shirt, and then release it.

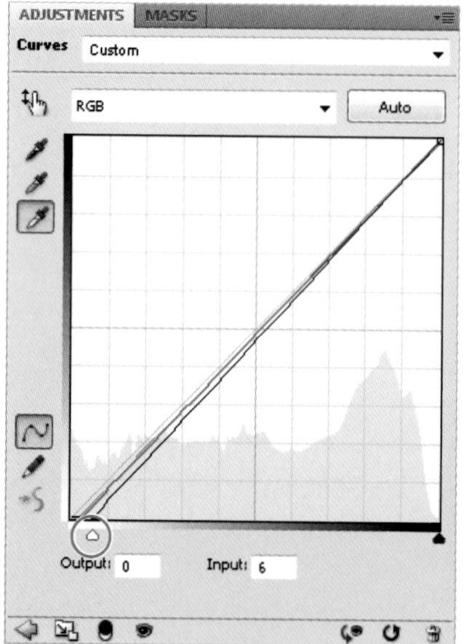

Select the Set White Point button.

Hold down the Alt/Option key while positioning the cursor over the image.

Note that there are some other areas that appear that are considered specular highlights, (the bright sky) and other parts of the image that are not important content. You don't want to set the tone curve of this image by defining the lightest point on the house in the background. The child is the important subject in this image, so you will locate a light and dark point within the child. In the next step, you will simply drop a color sampler on the lightest part of this image. This way, you can refer back to it at a later time.

If you can't see at your current zoom level, release the Alt/Option key and zoom closer into the logo art on the child's sweatshirt, by holding down Ctrl+spacebar (Windows) or Command+spacebar (Mac OS) and clicking. Hold down the spacebar and click and drag to reposition the image, if necessary.

7 With the highlight eyedropper (✐) selected, hover over the image and hold down the Alt/Option key, causing the image to again display in the posterized view.

Here is where it might get tricky: add the Shift key to this configuration, your cursor changes into the Color Sampler too (✐). Click on the light area you can find in the logo art. A color sample appears on the image, but no change has yet been made to the image.

Add a color sample to mark the lightest point in the image.

If necessary, you can reposition the Color Sample by holding down the Shift key and dragging it to a new location.

8 Make sure that the Set White Point eyedropper is still selected, and click on the color sampler you just created on the logo art. This has now defined this area of the image as the lightest point of the tone curve and is adjusted to your newly defined highlight color values.

If this gives you unexpected results, you might have missed the color sampler. You can undo by pressing Ctrl+Z (Windows) or Command+Z (Mac OS), and then try clicking on the white area of the logo art again. Keep in mind that the color sample that you dropped is only a marker; you do not have to move the sampler to change the highlight.

Now you will set the black, or darkest, part of your image.

9 Before you begin, press Ctrl+0 (zero) (Windows) or Command+0 (zero) (Mac OS) to make the image fit in the window.

10 Select the shadow slider (▲) on the Curves Adjustments panel, and hold down the Alt/Option key and drag the slider towards the left.

When dragging the slider (slowly), notice that clipping appears, indicating (with darker colors) the shadow areas of this image. Notice that there are many shadow areas in this image, but we want to focus on the subject matter (the small boy). Slide to the left until you see the shadow areas increase in the folds of the boy's clothing, and then release.

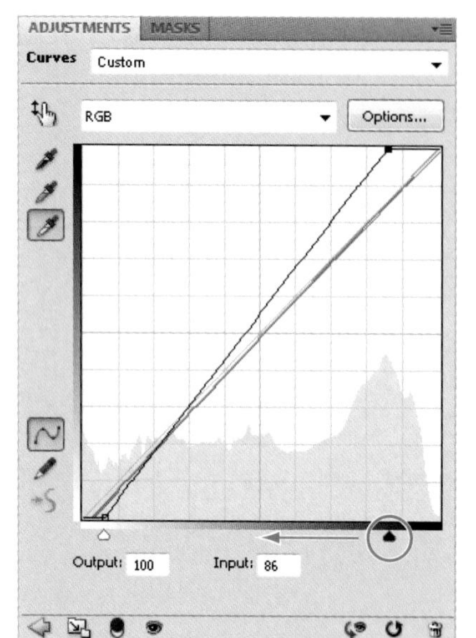

To see the darkest parts of this image, hold down the Alt/Option key and slide the shadow slider to the right.

Depending upon the input device you might have, many areas display as the darkest areas of an image. This is an indication that the input device, whether a scanner or camera, does not have a large dynamic range of tonal values that it can record. You might have to take a logical guess as to what is the darkest part of the image.

11 Make sure that the Set Black Point eyedropper is selected, and then hold down the Alt+Shift (Windows) or Option+Shift (Mac OS) keys and click on the darkest shadow area to leave a color sampler

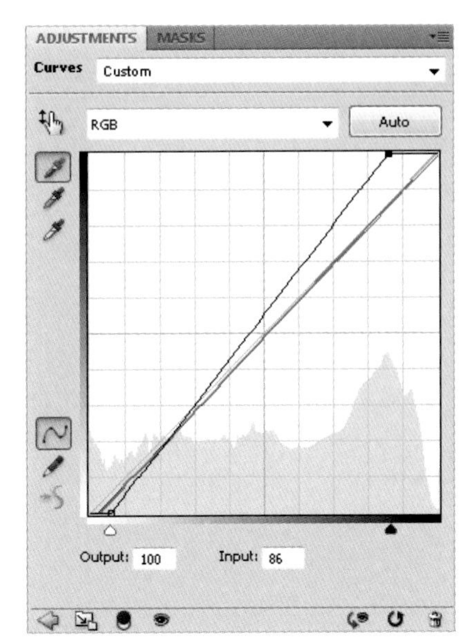

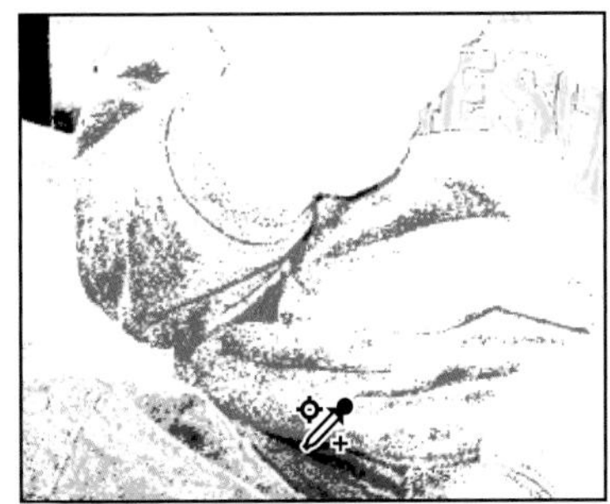

To see the darkest parts of this image, hold down the Alt/Option key and slide the shadow slider to the right.

12 With the Set Black Point eyedropper still selected, click on the color sample that you dropped on the image. This has now been set as the darkest area of the image, using the values you input earlier in this example.

You should already see a difference in the image—a slight color cast has been removed and the colors look a little cleaner—but you are not done yet. The next step involves balancing the midtones (middle values) of the image.

13 Leave the Curves Adjustments panel visible for the next exercise.

Adjusting the midtones

In many cases, you need to lighten the midtones (middle values of an image) in order to make details more apparent in an image.

1 Select the center (midtone area) of the black curve and drag downwards (don't worry about the colored curves, as Photoshop is making an overall change in this window). Move the curve downwards slightly to lighten the image in the midtones. This is the only visual correction that you will make to this image. You want to be careful that you do not adjust too much, as you can lose valuable information.

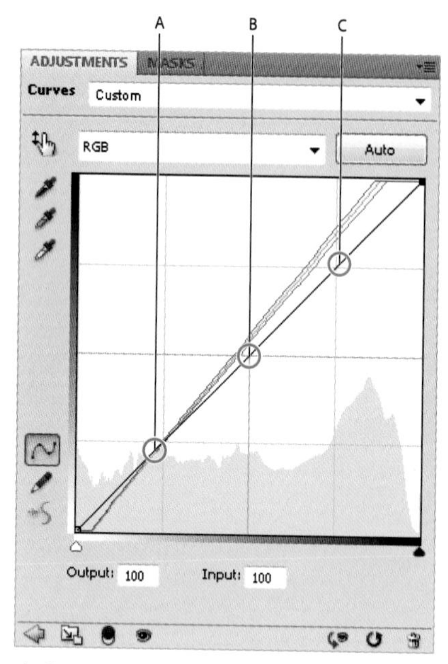

A. Quarter tones. B. Midtones. C. Three-quarter tones.

2 Add a little contrast to your image by clicking on the three-quarter tone area of the black curve line (the area between the middle of the curve and the top, as shown in the figure), then clicking and dragging up slightly. Again, this is a visual correction, so don't make too drastic a change.

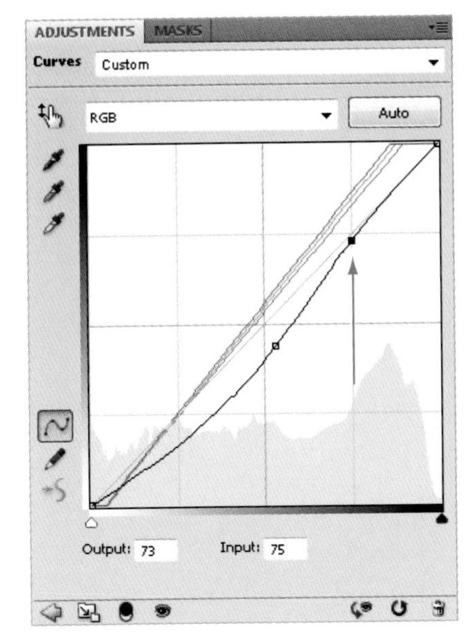

Click and drag the three-quarter tone up slightly to lighten the image.

3 Keep the Curves dialog box open for the next section of this lesson.

You can usually see a color cast by looking at the white and gray areas of an image, but, in some cases, you may not have any gray or white objects in your image. If these are art images, you may not want to neutralize them (for example, orange sunsets on the beach, or nice yellow candlelight images). Use the technique shown in this lesson at your discretion. It helps with a typical image, but it takes practice and experience to correct for every type of image.

Understanding neutral colors

A neutral is essentially anything in the image that is gray: a shade of gray, or even light to dark grays. A gray value is a perfect tool to help you measure color values, as it is composed of equal amounts of red, green, and blue. Knowing this allows you to pick up color inaccuracies by reading values in the Photoshop Info panel, rather than just guessing which colors need to be adjusted.

The first image you see below is definitely not correct, but exactly what is wrong? By looking at the Info panel, you can tell that the RGB values are not equal. In the second image, they are almost exactly equal. By looking at only the RGB values, you can tell that the image on the bottom is much more balanced than the image on the top.

The neutrals in this image are not balanced; you can tell because the RGB values are not equal in value.

The neutrals in this image are balanced; you can tell because the RGB values are equal.

Setting the neutral

In this section, you'll balance the neutrals in the image.

1 With the Curves panel still open, set another Color Sampler marker by Shift+clicking on the gray tree shadows that is visible to the left of the subject. In this image, that is the neutral that you are using as a reference for this example. In your images, you might find a neutral in a shadow on a white shirt, a gray piece of equipment, or a counter top.

Find a neutral gray in the image.

Some photographers like to include a gray card (available at photo supply stores) in their images to help them color-balance their images.

2 If the Info panel is not open, choose Window > Info. The Info panel appears.

In the Info panel, you see general information about RGB and CMYK values, as well as pinpoint information about the three Color Sampler markers you have created. You'll focus only on the #3 marker, as the first two were to indicate highlight and shadow.

Notice that to the right of the #3 marker in the Info panel, there are two values separated by a forward slash. You'll focus only on the set of values to the right of the slash. Depending upon where you clicked in the gray area, you could have different values. The numbers to the left of the forward slash are the values before you started making adjustments in the Curves panel. The numbers to the right of the forward slash are the new values that you are creating with your curve adjustments.

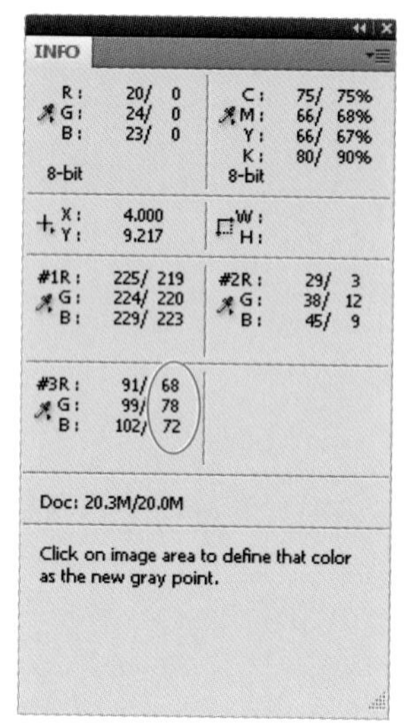

Focus on the values to the right of the forward slash.

3 Select the Set Gray Point button (✐).

4 Click once on the #3 marker you created. The new color values may not be exactly the same, but they come closer to matching each other's values.

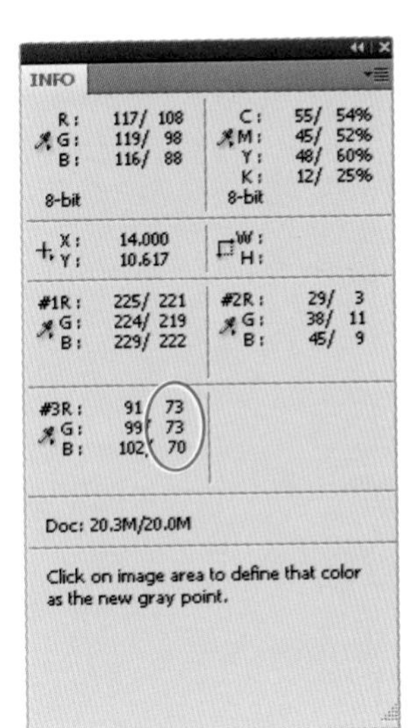

The Info panel after the #3 marker is selected as a gray point.

If you want more advanced correction, you can enter each of the individual color curves and adjust them separately by dragging the curve up or down, while watching the values change in the Info panel.

5 Press Ctrl+S (Windows) or Command+S (Mac OS) to save your work file.

6 If your Layers panel is not visible, choose Window > Layers. On the Layers panel, click on the visibility icon (👁) to the left of the Curves 1 adjustment layer to toggle off and on the curves adjustment you just made. Make sure that the Curves layer's visibility is turned back on before you move on to the next section.

Click on the visibility eye icon to turn off and on the adjustment layer.

7 Choose File > Save. Keep this file open for the next part of this lesson.

Sharpening your image

Now that you have adjusted the tonal values of your image, you'll want to apply some sharpening to the image. In this section, you'll discover how to use unsharp masking. It is a confusing term, but is derived from the traditional (pre-computer) technique used to sharpen images.

To simplify this example, you'll flatten the adjustment layer into the Background layer.

If you are an advanced user, you can avoid flattening by selecting the Background layer, Shift+clicking on the Curves 1 layer, then right-clicking (Windows) or Ctrl+clicking (Mac OS) and choosing Convert to Smart Object. This embeds the selected layers into your Photoshop file, but allows you to view and work with them as one layer. If further editing is needed, you can simply double-click on the Smart Object layer, and the layers open in their own separate document.

1 Choose Flatten Image from the Layers panel menu, as shown in the figure.

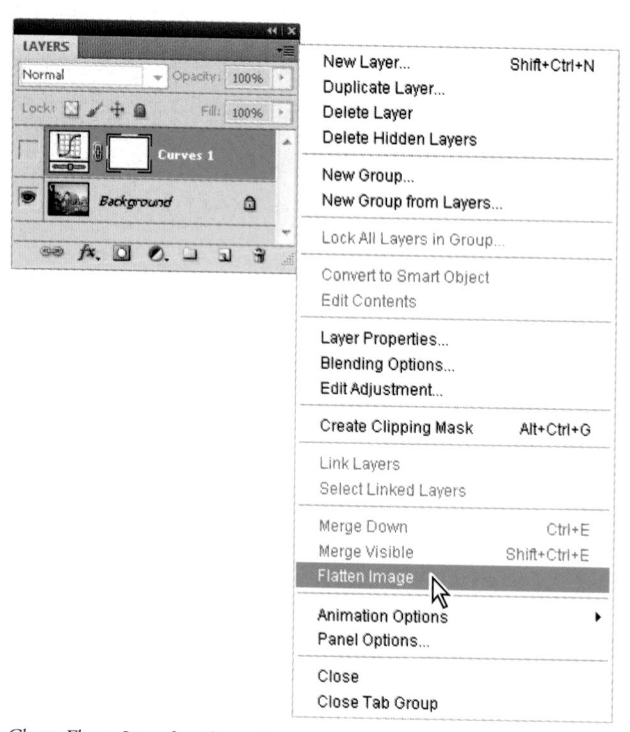

Choose Flatten Image from the panel menu.

2 Choose View > Actual pixels. The image may appear very large; you can pan the image by holding down the spacebar and pushing the image around on the screen. Position the image so that you can see an area with detail, such as one of the eyes. Note that you should be in Actual Pixel view when using most filters, or you may not see accurate results on your screen.

Hold down the spacebar, and click and drag on the image area to adjust the position of the image in the window.

3 Choose Filter > Convert for Smart Filters (this step is unnecessary if you already converted your layers into a Smart Object). If an Adobe Photoshop dialog box appears informing you that the layer is being converted into a Smart Object, press OK. Smart Objects allow you to edit filters more freely. Read more about Smart Objects in Lesson 10, "Get Smart in Photoshop." An icon (▣) appears in the lower-right corner of the layer thumbnail, indicating that this is now a Smart Object.

4 Choose Filter > Sharpen > Unsharp Mask. The Unsharp Mask dialog box appears.

You can click and drag inside the preview pane to change the part of the image that appears there.

Unsharp masking defined

Unsharp masking is a traditional film compositing technique used to sharpen edges in an image. The Unsharp Mask filter corrects blurring in the image, and it compensates for blurring that occurs during the resampling and printing process. Applying the Unsharp Mask filter is recommended whether your final destination is in print or online.

The Unsharp Mask filter assesses the brightness levels of adjacent pixels and increases their relative contrast: it lightens the light pixels that are located next to darker pixels, as it darkens those darker pixels. You set the extent and range of lightening and darkening that occurs, using the sliders in the Unsharp Mask dialog box. When sharpening an image, it's important to understand that the effects of the Unsharp Mask filter are far more pronounced on-screen than they appear in high-resolution output, such as a printed piece.

In the Unsharp Mask dialog box, you have the following options:

Amount determines how much the contrast of pixels is increased. Typically an amount of 150 percent or more is applied, but this amount is very reliant on the subject matter. Overdoing Unsharp Mask on a person's face can be rather harsh, so that value can be set lower (150 percent) as compared to an image of a piece of equipment, where fine detail is important (300 percent+).

Radius determines the number of pixels surrounding the edge pixels that are affected by the sharpening. For high-resolution images, a radius between 1 and 2 is recommended. If you are creating oversized posters and billboards, you might try experimenting with larger values.

Threshold determines how different the brightness values between two pixels must be before they are considered edge pixels and thus are sharpened by the filter. To avoid introducing unwanted noise into your image, a minimum Threshold setting of 10 is recommended.

5 Type **150** into the Amount text box. Because this is an image of a child, you can apply a higher amount of sharpening without bringing out unflattering detail.

Click and hold on the Preview pane to turn the preview off and on as you make changes.

6 Type **1** in the Radius text field and **10** in the Threshold text field, and click OK.

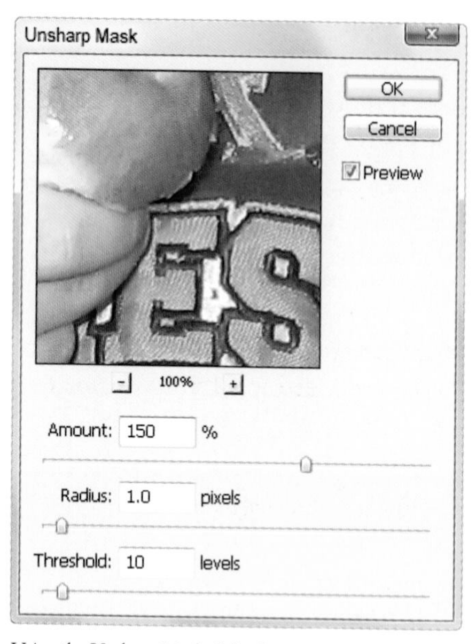

Using the Unsharp Mask dialog box.

7 Choose File > Save. Keep the file open for the next part of this lesson.

Because you used the Smart Filter feature, you can turn the visibility of the filter off and on at any time by clicking on the eye icon to the left of Smart Filters in the Layers panel. You will find out how to apply masks and use other incredible Smart Object features in Lesson 10, "Get Smart in Photoshop."

Comparing your image with the original

You can use the History panel in Adobe Photoshop for many functions. In this section, you'll use the History panel to compare the original image with your finished file.

1 If the History panel is not visible, choose Window > History.

2 Make sure that you have the final step you performed selected. In this case, it should be the Unsharp Mask filter. If you have some extra steps because you were experimenting with the Smart Filter thumbnail, just click on the Unsharp Mask state in the History panel.

3 Click on the Create New Document from Current State button (▤) at the bottom of the History panel. A new file is created.

4 Click back on your original image, ps0701_work.psd, and press Ctrl+0 (zero) (Windows) or Command+0 (zero) (Mac OS) to fit the image on your screen.

5 Click on the original snapshot located at the top of the History panel. This returns you to the original state. Click on the Arrange Documents button in the Application bar and select 2 Up to place the images side by side. Zoom into the area surrounding the small child to see that it appears almost as if a cast of color has been lifted from the image, producing a cleaner, brighter image.

If you are having difficulty viewing the images, choose Window > Arrange > Tile.

Comparing your corrected image with the original image.

6 Choose File > Save, and then File > Close to close your ps0701_work files.

7 Choose File > Close for the unsharp mask file created from your History panel. When asked to save the changes, click Don't Save.

Congratulations! You have finished the color-correction part of this lesson.

Taking care of red eye

Red eye typically occurs when you use a camera with a built-in flash. The light of the flash occurs too fast for the iris of the eye to close the pupil, revealing the blood-rich area alongside the iris. There are many cameras that come with features to help you avoid this phenomenon, and most professional photographers don't experience this, as they typically use a flash that is not directly positioned in front of the subject. Also, there is a solution that is built right into Photoshop.

1 Open the image named ps0702.psd, click and hold down on the Spot Healing Brush tool (✐) and drag down to select the Red Eye tool (+◉).

   Choose File > Save As. The Save As dialog box appears. Navigate to the ps07lessons folder on your hard drive. In the Name text field, type **ps0702_work**, choose Photoshop from the Format drop-down menu, and press Save.

2 Click and drag, creating a marquee around the eye on the left side of the image; when you release the mouse, the red eye is removed. If you missed a section, you can repeat this without damaging the areas that are not part of the red eye.

3 Now, click and drag to surround the other eye, again repeating to add any areas that are not corrected.

4 Choose File > Save, or use the keyboard shortcut Ctrl+S (Windows) or Command+S (Mac OS).

5 Choose File > Close to close this file.

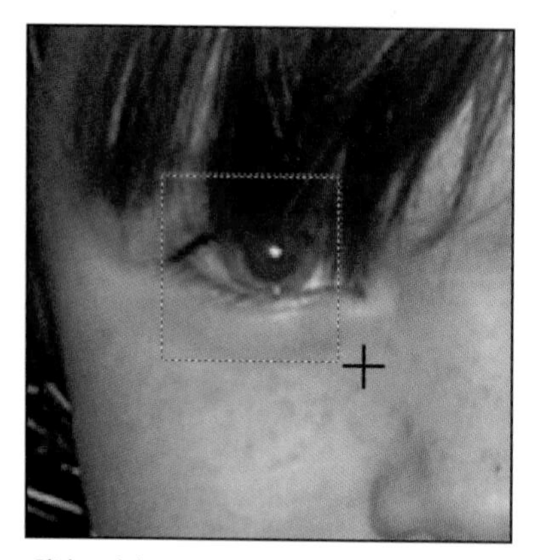

Click and drag, surrounding the iris of an eye, using the Red Eye tool to get rid of the red.

Using the Camera Raw plug-in

In this section, you'll discover how to open and make changes to a Camera Raw file. Camera Raw really deserves more than can be covered in this lesson, but this will give you an introduction, and hopefully get you interested enough to investigate further on your own.

What is a Camera Raw file?

A Camera Raw image file contains the unprocessed data from the image sensor of a digital camera; essentially, it is a digital negative of your image. By working with a Raw file, you have greater control and flexibility, while still maintaining the original image file.

The Raw format is proprietary and differs from one camera manufacturer to another, and sometimes even between cameras made by the same manufacturer. This differentiation can lead to many issues, mostly that you also need the camera's proprietary software to open the Raw file, unless, of course, you are using Photoshop CS5's Camera Raw plug-in. The Camera Raw plug-in supports more than 150 camera manufacturers, and allows you to open other types of files into the Camera Raw plug-in, including TIFFs and JPEGs. If you are not sure whether your camera is supported by the Camera Raw plug-in, go to *adobe.com* and type **Support Camera Raw cameras** in the Search text field.

1 Choose File > Browse in Bridge to launch Adobe Bridge, if it is not already open. You can also select the Launch Bridge button (Br) or Mini Bridge button (MB) in the Application bar to launch Adobe Bridge.

2 Navigate to the ps07lessons folder, inside the pslessons folder on your hard drive. Select the image named ps0702.CR2. This is a Camera Raw file from a Canon Rebel digital camera. Note that each manufacturer has its own extensions; the CR2 extension is unique to Canon cameras.

3 Double-click on the ps0702.cr2 file to automatically launch and open the file in Photoshop's Camera Raw plug-in.

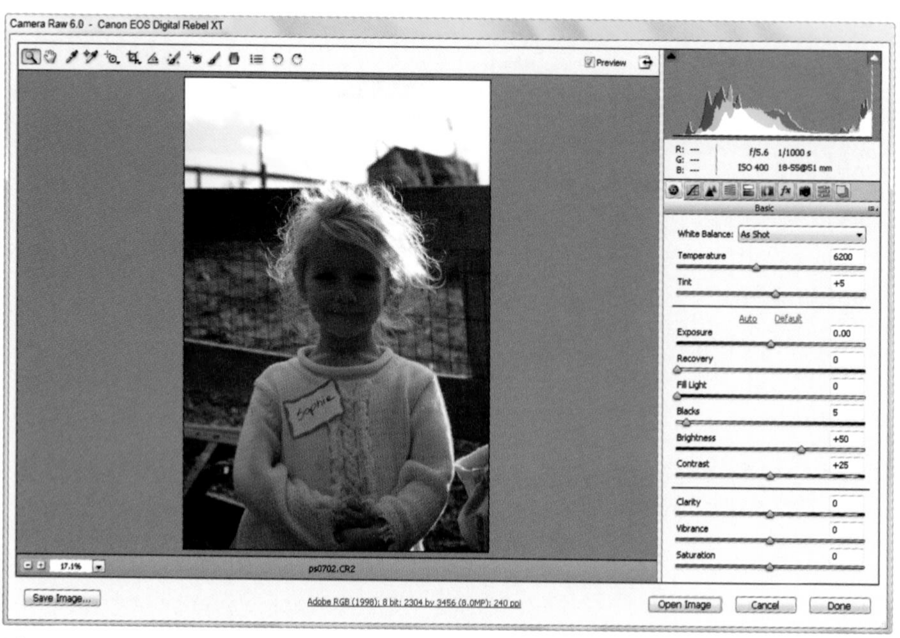

The Camera Raw plug-in automatically launches when a Raw file is opened.

If you attempt to open a Raw file that is not recognized by the Camera Raw plug-in, you may need to update your plug-in. Go to adobe.com *to download the latest version.*

When the Camera Raw plug-in opens, you see a Control panel across the top, as well as additional tabbed panels on the right. See the table for definitions of each button in the Control panel.

ICON	TOOL NAME	USE
	Zoom (Z)	Increases or decreases the magnification level of a Camera Raw preview.
	Hand (H)	Allows you to reposition a Raw image, when magnified, in the preview pane.
	White Balance (I)	Balances colors in a Raw image when you click on a neutral gray area in the image.
	Color Sampler (S)	Reads image data and leave markers on the Raw image.
	Crop (C)	Crops a Raw image right in the preview pane.
	Straighten (A)	Realigns an image.
	Spot Removal (B)	Heals or clones a Raw image in the preview pane.
	Red-Eye Removal (E)	Removes red eye from a Raw image.
	Adjustment Brush (K)	Paints adjustments of color, brightness, contrast, and more.
	Graduated Filter (G)	Replicates the effect of a conventional graduated filter, one that is composed of a single sheet of glass, plastic, or gel that is half color graduating to a half clear section.
	Open preferences dialog box (Ctrl+K, Command+K)	Changes preferences, such as where XMP files are saved.
	Rotate image 90 degrees counterclockwise (L)	Rotates an image 90 degrees counter-clockwise.
	Rotate image 90 degrees clockwise (R)	Rotates an image 90 degrees clockwise.

You'll have an opportunity to use several of these tools in the next lesson. Before starting, have a look at the panels on the right, and learn a bit about how they are used.

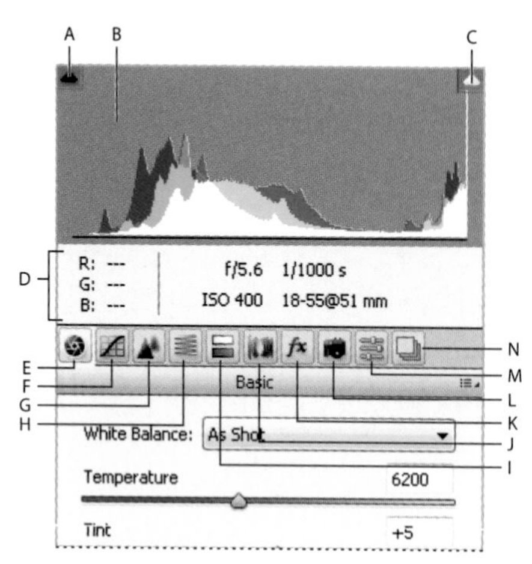

A. Shadow Clipping Warning button. B. Histogram.
C. Highlight Clipping Warning button. D. Info.
E. Basic panel. F. Tone Curve panel. G. Detail.
H. HSL/Grayscale. I. Split Toning. J. Lens Correction.
K. Effects. L. Camera Calibration. M. Presets. N. Snapshots.

A. Shadow Clipping Warning button: Indicates if an image is underexposed, with large areas of shadow being clipped. Clipped shadows appear as a solid dark area if not corrected using the exposure controls.

B. Histogram: Shows you where image data resides on the tone curve.

C. Highlight Clipping Warning button: Indicates if an image is overexposed, with large areas of highlight being clipped. A clipped highlight appears as a solid white area if not corrected using the exposure controls.

D. Info: Displays the RGB readings that enable you to check your colors and balance.

E. Basic panel: Contains the main controls, such as White Balance, Exposure, and Fill Light, among others.

F. Tone Curve panel: Adjusts the tone curve. The Point tab must be brought to the front (by clicking on it) to activate point-by-point controls.

G. Detail: Adjusts Sharpening and Noise Reduction.

H. HSL/Grayscale: Allows you to create grayscale images with total control over individual colors and brightness.

I. Split Toning:
Introduces additional color tones into image highlights and shadows.

J. Lens Correction:
Corrects for lens problems, including fringing and vignetting.

K. Effects:

Applies filters and offers the ability to create post cropping vignetting.

L. Camera Calibration:

With the Camera Calibration tab, you can shoot a Macbeth color reference chart (available from camera suppliers). Then you can set Color Samplers on the reference chart, and use the sliders to balance the RGB values shown in the Info section. Settings can be saved by selecting the Presets tab and clicking on the New Preset button in the lower-right corner, or by choosing Save Settings from the panel menu.

M. Presets:

Stores settings for future use in the Presets tab.

N. Snapshots:

Offers ability to save multiple versions of an image.

Using Camera Raw controls

In this section, you'll use a few of the controls you just reviewed.

1 Make sure that the Camera image is back to its original settings by holding down the Alt (Windows) or Option (Mac OS) key and clicking on Reset, located at the bottom-right corner. The Cancel button becomes Reset when you hold down the Alt or Option key.

2 The first thing you are going to do with this image is balance the color. You can do this with the White Balance controls. In this instance, you'll keep it simple by selecting the White Balance tool (✐) from the Control panel.

A good neutral to balance from is the light gray section of the name tag. With the White Balance tool selected, click on the white part of the name tag. The image is balanced, using that section of the image as a reference.

With the White Balance tool selected, click on the name tag.

You'll now adjust some of the other settings available in the Basic tab, to make the image more colorful while still maintaining good color balance.

The image looks a bit underexposed; the girl's face is somewhat dark. You'll bring out more detail in the girl's face with the Brightness slider. By using a combination of the Brightness and Recovery sliders, you can bring out additional detail without overexposing the highlights.

3 Click on the Exposure slider and drag to the left until you reach the –0.35 mark, or type **–.35** in the Exposure text field.

4 Click on the Brightness slider in the Basic tab and drag to the right to about the +120 mark, or type **120** into the Brightness text field.

5 Recover some of the lost highlights by clicking and dragging the Recovery slider right, to the 60 mark, or by typing **60** in the Recovery text field.

Whenever the original image has a high luminance (brightness) range, a highlight recovery in Camera Raw can help extend the range of the processed image. By adjusting the Exposure down and the Brightness up, you can maintain highlight detail that would otherwise be lost.

6 Increase the contrast in the image by clicking and dragging the contrast slider right, to the 60 mark, or by typing **60** into the Contrast text field.

Increase the richness of color by using the Vibrance slider. Do not increase it too much if you plan on printing the image, as oversaturated, rich colors do not generally convert well to CMYK.

7 Drag the Vibrance slider right, over to the 25 mark, or type **25** into the Vibrance text field.

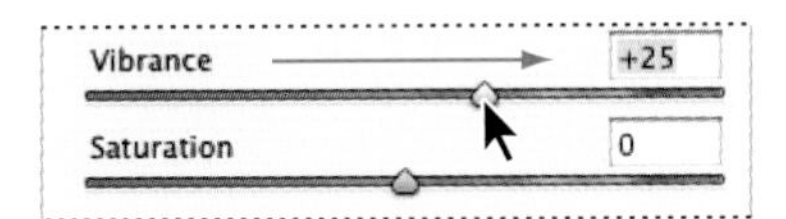

Drag the Vibrance slider to the right.

8 Select the Crop tool (⌗) from the Control panel, and click and drag to select an image area that is a little closer to the girl's face.

Cropping an image in the Camera Raw Plug-in.

Now you'll save your settings.

9 Click on the Presets tab. Press the Save Preset button (⊡) in the lower-right corner of the Presets panel. Type the name **Canon_outdoor** and press OK.

10 Keep the Camera Raw Plug-in window open for the next step.

Saving a DNG file

Next, you will save your image as a DNG file. A DNG file is essentially a digital negative file that maintains all the corrections you have made, in addition to the original unprocessed Raw image.

Adobe created the DNG format to provide a standard for Raw files. As mentioned previously, camera vendors have their own proprietary Raw formats and their own extensions and proprietary software to open and edit them. The DNG format was developed to provide a standard maximum-resolution format that all camera vendors would eventually support directly in their cameras. Right now, DNG provides you with the opportunity to save your original Camera Raw files in a format that you should be able to open for many years to come. Note that you can reopen the DNG over and over again, making additional changes without degrading the original image.

1 Press the Save Image button in the lower-left corner of the Camera Raw dialog box. The Save Options dialog box appears.

2 Leave the Destination set to Save in Same Location, then click on the arrow to the right of the second drop-down menu in the File Naming section and choose 2 Digit Serial Number. This will automatically number your files, starting with the original document name followed by 01.

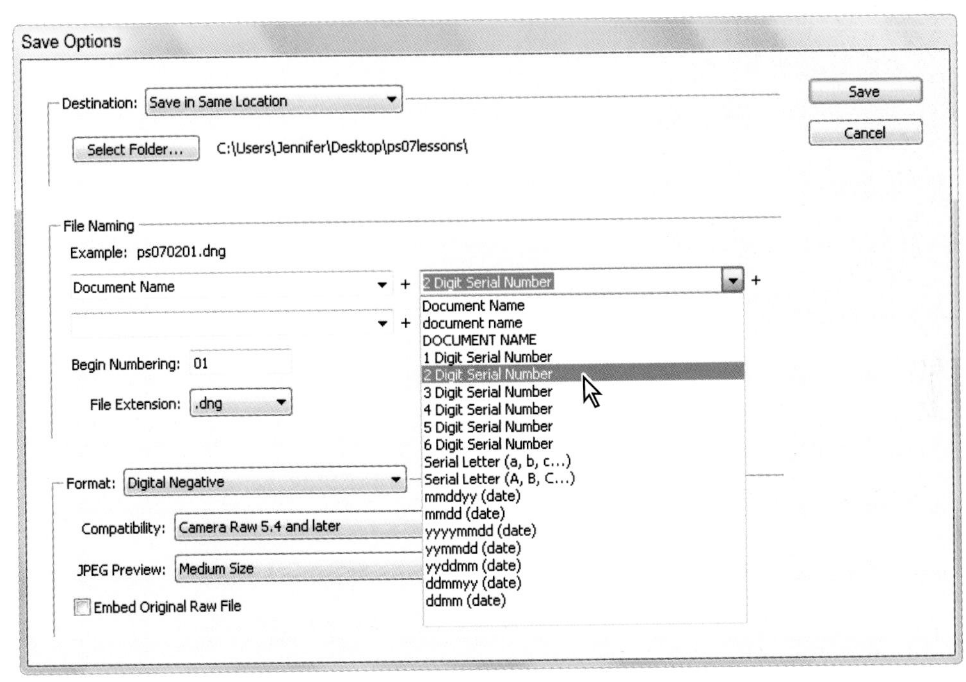

The Camera Raw Save Options dialog box.

3 Press Save. You are returned to the Camera Raw dialog box.

4 Click the Open Image button. The adjusted and cropped image is opened in Photoshop. You can continue working on this file. If you save the file now, you will see the standard Photoshop Save As dialog box. Note that whatever you save is a copy of the original Camera Raw file—your DNG file remains intact.

Reopening a DNG file

You'll now use Bridge to access your saved DNG file.

1 Access Bridge by choosing File > Browse in Bridge, or by selecting the Launch Bridge (Br) or the Mini Bridge button (Mb) in the upper-left corner of the Photoshop window.

2 If you are not still in the ps07lessons folder, navigate to it now. Double-click on the file you have created, ps070201.dng.

Note that the file reopens in the Camera Raw plug-in dialog box and that you can undo and redo settings, as the original has remained intact.

Congratulations! You have completed the lesson on Camera Raw images.

Self study

In this section, you can try this exercise on your own.

In this section, you'll learn how to take advantage of the Smart Objects and Smart Filters features using a technique that includes painting on the Filter effects mask thumbnail.

1 Choose File > Browse and locate the file named ps0703.psd, located in the ps07lessons folder.

2 Alt (Windows) or Option (Mac OS) double-click on the Background layer to turn it into a layer (Layer 0).

3 Select Filter > Convert for Smart Filters, and press OK if a Photoshop dialog box appears. Then choose Filter > Blur > Gaussian Blur. Again, press OK if an Adobe Photoshop dialog box appears. The Gaussian Blur dialog box appears. Use the slider at the bottom of the dialog box to apply a blur to the image. Move the slider until you can easily see the results; there's no exact number that you should set for this exercise, but make sure it is set at an amount high enough that you can see the results easily. Press OK when done. After you apply the Blur filter, a Smart Filter layer appears with a Filter effects mask thumbnail.

4 Select the Filter effects mask to activate it. This is the large white square to the left of Smart Filters in the Layers panel.

5 Choose the Brush tool (🖌) from the Tools panel, and press D on your keyboard. This changes your foreground and background colors to the default colors of black and white.

6 If black is not set as your foreground color, press X to swap the foreground and background colors. Using the Paintbrush tool, paint over the image; note that where you paint with black, the blur disappears. Press X to swap the colors so that white is now the foreground color, then paint over areas where the blur is not visible, to restore it. While painting, try various values: for instance, if you type **5**, you are painting with a 50 percent opacity; if you type **46**, you paint with a 46 percent opacity. Type **0** to return to 100 percent opacity. This is a technique that is worth experimenting with—try other filters on your own to explore painting on Filter effect masks to hide or reveal the effect of each filter.

Review

Questions

1 Name an example of how a color sampler can be used.

2 What color mode is typically used for color-correcting an image?

3 What is a neutral? How can you use it to color-correct an image?

4 How can you tell if an image has been corrected in Adobe Photoshop?

5 What is a DNG file?

Answers

1 It is common for the Color Sampler tool to be used inside the Curves panel, where it can be used to mark white, black, or gray points on the image. Using a Color Sampler makes it much easier to read the data from one particular point of the image from the Info panel.

2 There are many theories as to which color mode is the best working environment for color correction. Unless you are in a color-calibrated environment (using LAB), RGB should be the mode you choose to work in for color correction.

3 A neutral is a gray, or a shade of gray. You can often find a gray area in an image that can be used as a measuring tool to see if your colors are balanced. Some photographers like to introduce their own gray card in order to have a neutral against which to balance. They then crop the gray card out of the image when they are finished correcting the color balance.

4 By viewing the Histogram panel, you can tell if an image's tone curve has been adjusted. Even if you make simple curve adjustments, some degradation will occur in the tonal values of the image.

5 The DNG (Digital Negative) format is a non-proprietary, publicly documented, and widely supported format for storing raw camera data. The DNG format was developed to provide a standard format that all camera vendors would eventually support. You may also use DNG as an intermediate format for storing images that were originally captured using a proprietary camera raw format.

What you'll learn in this lesson:

- Understanding and using layers
- Selecting and moving layers
- Using layer masks
- Creating compositions
- Understanding clipping masks

Getting to Know Layers

Once you discover how to use layers, you can expand your capabilities to create incredible compositions, repair images like never before, and use effects that just aren't available elsewhere.

Starting up

Before starting, make sure that your tools and panels are consistent by resetting your preferences. See "Resetting Adobe Photoshop CS5 preferences" on page 3.

You will work with several files from the ps08lessons folder in this lesson. Make sure that you have loaded the pslessons folder onto your hard drive from the supplied DVD. See "Loading lesson files" on page 5.

See Lesson 8 in action!

Use the accompanying video to gain a better understanding of how to use some of the features shown in this lesson. The video tutorial for this lesson can be found on the included DVD.

Discovering layers

Think of layers as clear pieces of film—each containing its own image data—that can be stacked on top of each other so that you can see through transparent areas of each layer to the layers below. Each layer is independent of the others and can have its contents and opacities changed independently. You can reorder layers to create different stacking orders, and change the blending modes on the layers to create interesting overlays. Once you have mastered layers, you can create composites and repair image data like never before.

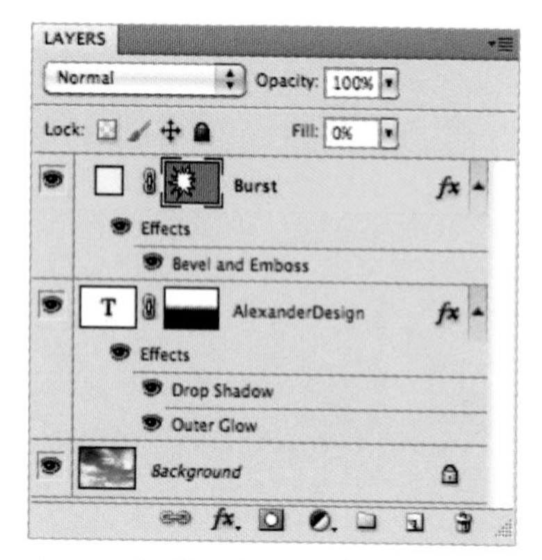

An example of how layers can be used and arranged.

A new image has a single layer. The number of additional layers, layer effects, and layer sets that you can add to an image is limited only by your computer's memory. In this lesson, you'll find out how to take advantage of layers to create interesting composites and make non-destructive changes to your images.

The Layers panel

To help you work with layers, Photoshop provides a panel specific to layers. In addition to showing thumbnail previews of layer content, the Layers panel allows you to select specific layers, turn their visibility on and off, apply special effects, and change the order in which they are stacked.

Getting a handle on layers

In the first part of the lesson, you will work with the most fundamental concepts of using layers. Even if you have already been using layers in Photoshop, it is still a good idea to run through this section. Due to the fast pace of production, many users skip right into more advanced layer features without having the opportunity to learn basic layer features that can save them a lot of time and aggravation.

Creating a new blank file

In this lesson, you'll create a blank file and add layers to it one at a time.

1 Choose File > New. The New dialog box appears.

2 In the New dialog box, choose Default Photoshop Size from the Preset drop-down menu.

3 Choose Transparent from the Background Contents drop-down menu, and press OK.

4 You will now save the file. Choose File > Save As and navigate to the ps08lessons folder. In the Name text field, type **mylayers**. Choose Photoshop from the Format drop-down menu and press Save. If the Photoshop format warning dialog box appears, press OK.

5 If the Layers panel is not visible, choose Window > Layers. Click on the Layers tab and drag it out of the docking area for this lesson so that you can more closely follow the changes you are making.

6 If the Swatches panel is not visible, choose Window > Swatches. Click and drag on the Swatches tab to take it out of the docking area.

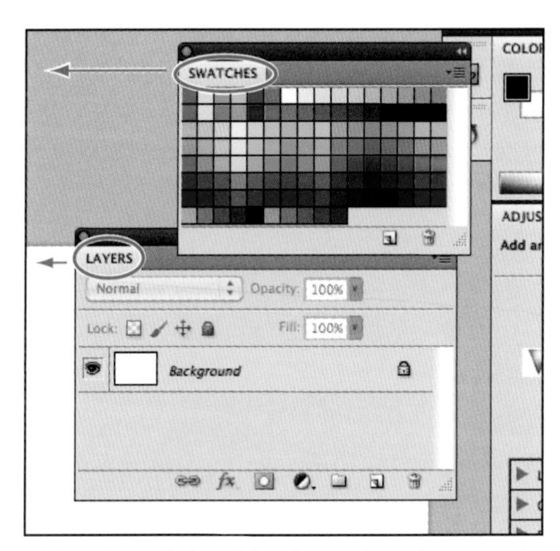

Click on the panel tabs and drag the Swatches and Layers panels out of the docking area.

7 Select the Rectangular Marquee tool (▭) and click and drag; to constrain the marquee selection to a square, hold down the Shift key as you drag. Release the mouse when you have created a large, square marquee. Exact size is not important for this step.

8 Click on any red color in the Swatches panel. In this example, CMYK Red is used.

9 Choose Edit > Fill, or use the keyboard shortcut Shift+Backspace (Windows) or Shift+Delete (Mac OS), to open the Fill dialog box. If Foreground Color is not selected in the Use drop-down menu, select it now. Leave the other settings at their default and press OK.

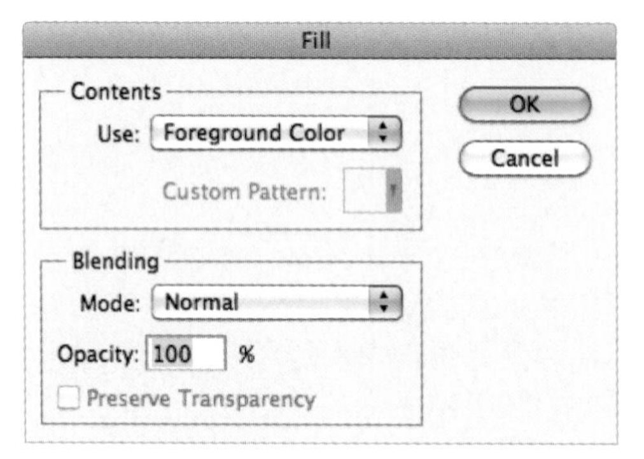

Fill with your foreground color.

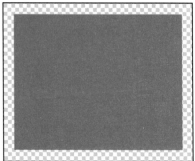

The result.

You can press Alt+Backspace (Windows) or Option+Delete (Mac OS) to automatically fill with your foreground color and not open the Fill dialog box.

10 Choose Select > Deselect to turn off the selection marquee, or use the keyboard shortcut Ctrl+D (Windows) or Command+D (Mac OS).

11 Choose File > Save.

Naming your layer

You will find that as you increase your use of layers, your Photoshop image can become quite complicated and confusing. Layers are limited only by the amount of memory you have in your computer, and so you could find yourself working with 100-layer images. To help you stay organized, and therefore more productive, be sure to name your layers appropriately.

1 Double-click on the layer name, Layer 1. The text becomes highlighted and the insertion cursor appears. You can now type **red square** to provide this layer with a descriptive name.

2 You can also name a layer before you create it. Hold down the Alt (Windows) or Option (Mac OS) key and press the Create a New Layer button (▫) at the bottom of the Layers panel. The New Layer dialog box appears.

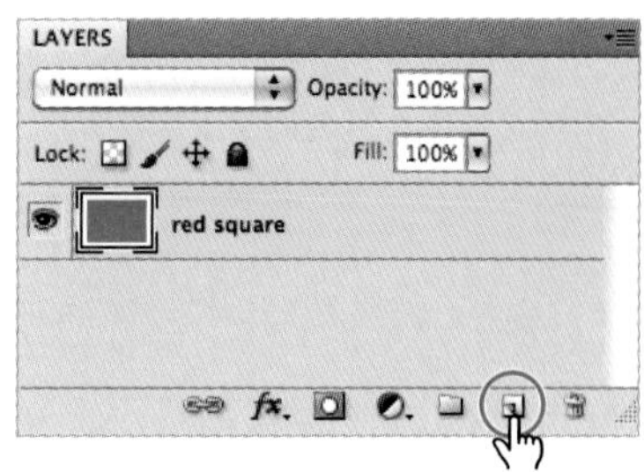

Hold down the Alt/Option key when creating a new layer.

As a default, new layers appear on top of the active layer. Use Ctrl+Alt (Windows) or Command+Option (Mac OS) to open the New Layer dialog box and add the new layer underneath the active layer.

3 In the Name text field, type **yellow circle**, as you are about to create a yellow circle on this layer.

For organizational purposes, you can change the color of the layer in the Layers panel, which can help you locate important layers more quickly.

4 For the sake of being color-coordinated, choose Yellow from the Color drop-down menu and press OK. A new layer named "yellow circle" is created. The layer thumbnail in the Layers panel has a yellow background. This background does not affect the actual contents of your layer.

Now you will put the yellow circle on this layer.

5 Click and hold on the Rectangular Marquee tool (⬚), then choose the hidden Elliptical Marquee tool (◌).

You can also cycle through the marquee selection tools by pressing Shift+M.

6 Click and drag while holding the Shift key down to create a circle selection in your image area.

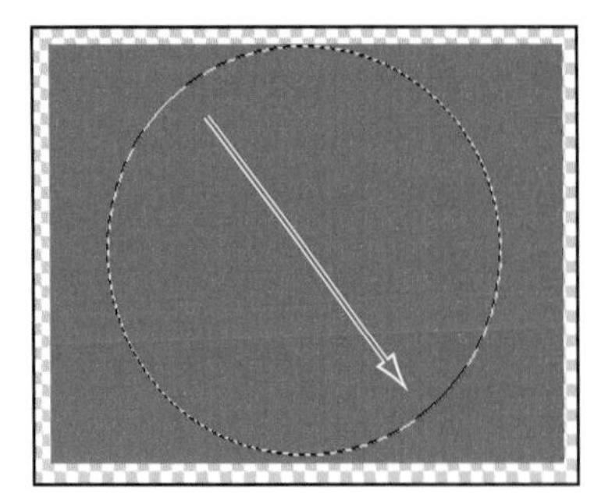

Click and drag while holding the Shift key to create a circle selection.

7 Position your cursor over the Swatches panel and click to choose any yellow color.

In this example, CMYK Yellow is selected.

8 Use the keyboard shortcut Alt+Backspace (Windows) or Option+Delete (Mac OS) to quickly fill the selection with yellow.

9 Choose Select > Deselect, or use the keyboard shortcut Ctrl+D (Windows) or Command+D (Mac OS).

You will now create a third layer for this file. This time, you'll use the Layers panel menu.

10 Click and hold on the Layers panel menu and choose New > Layer. The New Layer dialog box appears.

11 Type **green square** in the Name text field and choose Green from the Color drop-down menu. Press OK. A new layer is created.

If you prefer keyboard shortcuts, you can type Ctrl+Shift+N (Windows) or Command+Shift+N (Mac OS) to create a new layer.

12 Click and hold on the Elliptical Marquee tool to select the hidden Rectangular Marquee tool. Hold down the Shift key, then click and drag a small square selection on your document.

13 Position your cursor over the Swatches panel and click to choose any green color from the panel. In this example, CMYK Green is selected.

14 Use the keyboard shortcut Alt+Delete (Windows) or Option+Delete (Mac OS) to quickly fill the selection with green.

15 Choose Select > Deselect, or use the keyboard shortcut Ctrl+D (Windows) or Command+D (Mac OS).

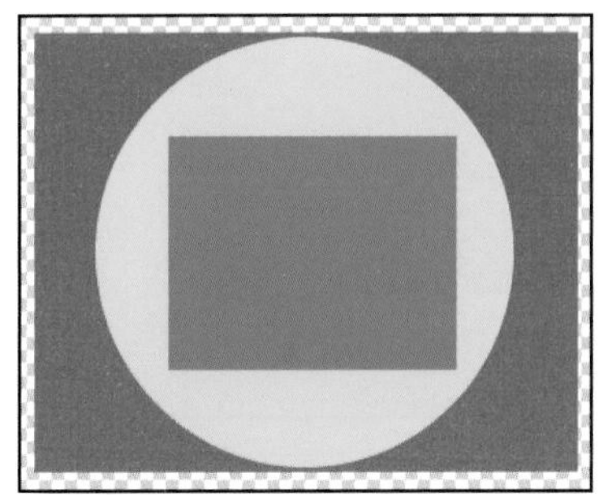

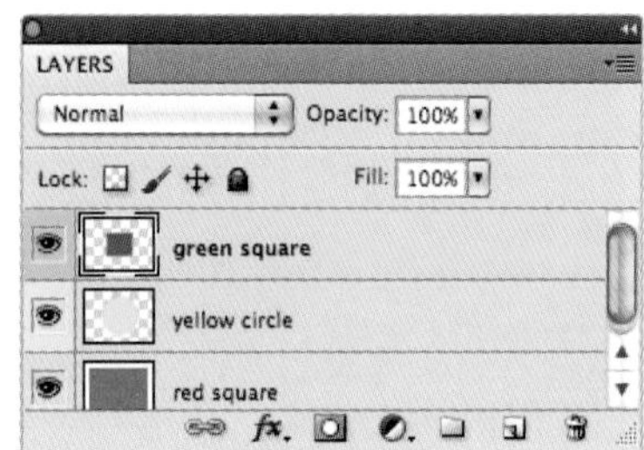

The document now has three layers.

16 Choose File > Save. Keep the mylayers.psd file open for the next part of this lesson.

Selecting layers

As basic as it may seem, selecting the appropriate layer can be difficult. Follow this exercise to see how important it is to be aware of layers by keeping track of which layer is active.

1 You should still have the mylayers.psd file open from the last exercise. If not, access the file in the ps08lessons folder and select the green square layer in the Layers panel.

2 Select the Move tool (▸+) and click and drag to reposition the green square on the green square layer. Note that only the green square moves. This is because layers that are active are the only layers that are affected.

3 With the Move tool still selected, select the yellow circle layer in the Layers panel and then click and drag the yellow circle in your image file. The yellow circle moves.

4 Now, select the red square layer in the Layers panel.

5 Choose Filter > Blur > Gaussian Blur. The Gaussian Blur dialog box appears.

6 In the Gaussian Blur dialog box, type **7** in the Radius text field, then press OK.

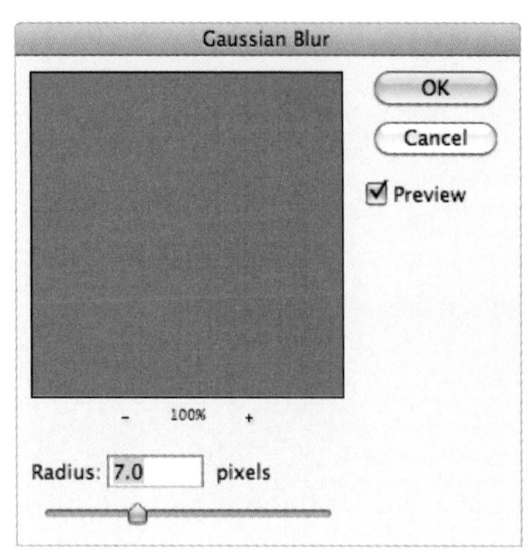

Apply a filter.

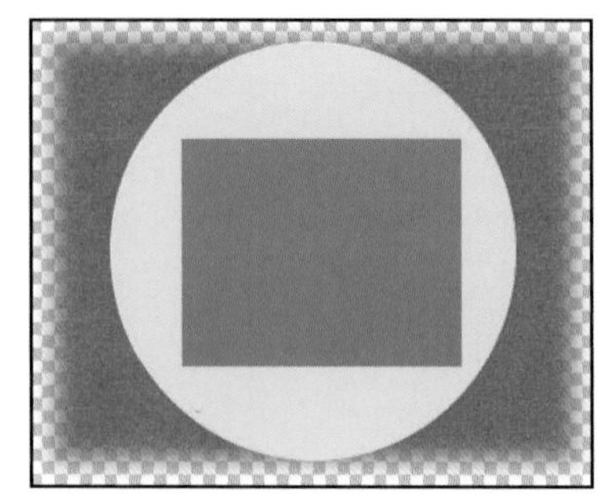

The result.

7 Press Ctrl+Z (Windows) or Command+Z (Mac OS) to undo the Gaussian Blur filter.

8 Choose File > Save. Keep the file open for the next part of the lesson.

Tips for selecting layers

There are several methods you can use to make sure that you are activating certain layers and changing the properties on the specific layer you want to modify.

1 You should still have the mylayers.psd file open from the last exercise. If it is not, access the file in the ps08lessons folder and select the red square layer in the Layers panel.

2 Make sure that the Move tool (▸+) is selected, then hold down the Ctrl (Windows) or Command (Mac OS) key and select the yellow circle in the image file. Notice that the yellow circle layer is automatically selected.

3 Now, hold down the Ctrl (Windows) or Command (Mac OS) key and select the green square in the image file. The green square layer is selected. By holding down the Ctrl or Command key, you turn on an auto-select feature that automatically selects the layer that contains the pixels you have clicked on.

4 Make sure that the Move tool is still selected, and right-click (Windows) or Ctrl+click (Mac OS) on the green square. Note that when you access the contextual tools, overlapping layers appear in a list, providing you with the opportunity to select the layer in the menu that appears. Select the green square layer.

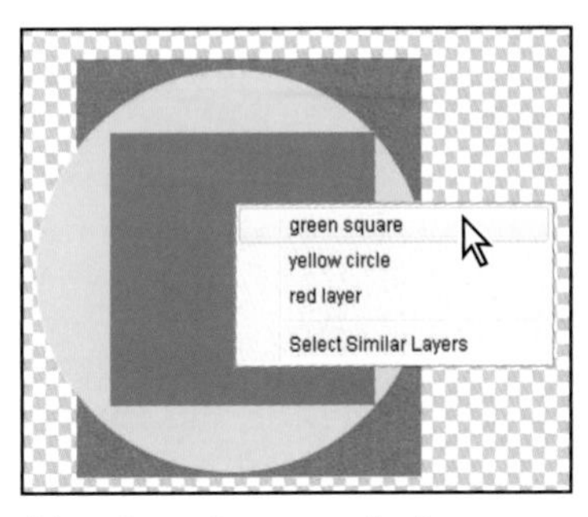

Select a layer using contextual tools.

5 Right-click (Windows) or Ctrl+click (Mac OS) on an area of the image file that contains only the red square pixels to see that only one layer name appears for you to choose from. Choose red square.

Moving layers

Layers appear in the same stacking order in which they appear in the Layers panel. For instance, in the file you have been working on in this lesson, the green square was created last and is at the top of the stacking order, essentially covering up the yellow circle and red square wherever it is positioned.

By moving the position of a layer, you can change the way an image looks, which allows you to experiment with different image compositions.

1 With the mylayers.psd file still open, click and drag the green square layer in the Layers panel below the red square layer. Release the mouse button when you see a dark bar appear underneath the red square layer. The dark line indicates the location of the layer that you are dragging. Notice that the green square may not be visible at this time because it is underneath the red square, and thus hidden.

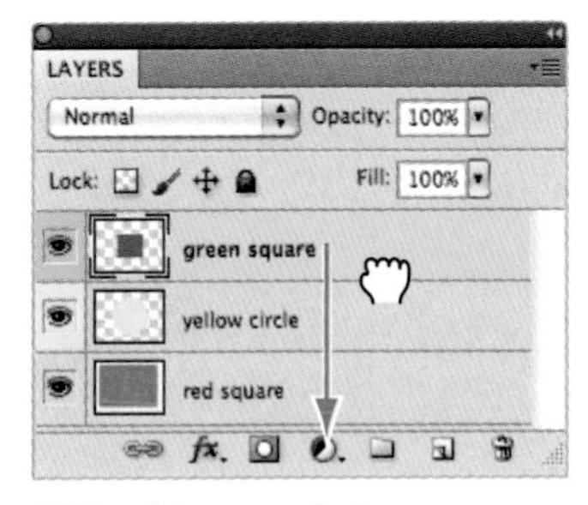

Click and drag to reorder layers.

2 You may find it easier to use keyboard commands to move the layers' positions in the stacking order. Select the green square layer and press Ctrl+] (right bracket) (Windows) or Command+] (right bracket) (Mac OS) to move it up one level in the stacking order. Press this keyboard combination again to move the green square layer back to the top of the stacking order.

3 Select the yellow circle layer and press Ctrl+[(left bracket) (Windows) or Command+[(left bracket) (Mac OS) to put the yellow circle one level down in the stacking order, essentially placing it behind the red square. Press Ctrl+] (right bracket) (Windows) or Command+] (right bracket) (Mac OS) to move it back up one level in the layer stacking order.

The image layers should now be back in the same order as when the image was originally created: red square on the bottom, yellow circle in the middle, and green square on the top.

4 Choose File > Save. Keep the file open for the next part of this lesson.

Changing the visibility of a layer

One of the benefits of using layers is that you can hide the layers that contain pixel data on which you are not currently working. By hiding layers, you can focus on the image editing at hand, keeping distractions to a minimum.

1 With the mylayers.psd file still open, select the visibility icon (👁) to the left of the red square layer. The red square disappears.

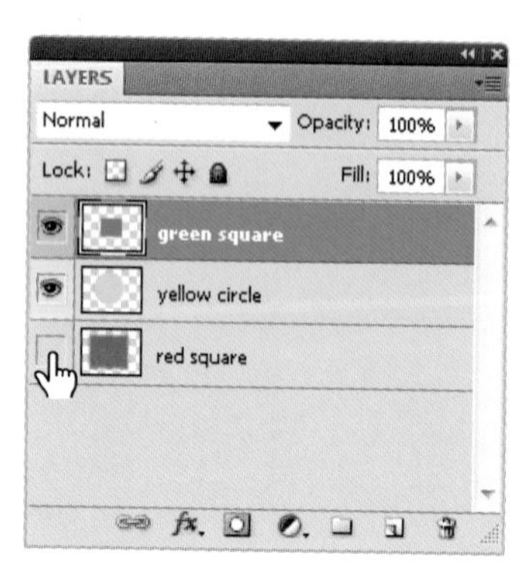

Turn the visibility of a layer off and on by selecting the visibility icon.

2 Click again on the spot where the visibility icon previously appeared. The red square layer is visible again.

3 This time, hold down the Alt (Windows) or Option (Mac OS) key, and click on the same visibility icon. By using the Alt/Option modifier, you can hide all layers except the one you click on.

4 Alt/Option+click on the same visibility icon to make all the layers visible again.

Using masks in a layer

There is one last feature fundamental to understand before you delve further into layers: the layer mask feature. Without the mask feature, making realistic composites or blending one image smoothly into another would be much more difficult.

1 With the mylayers.psd file still open, choose the red square layer in the Layers panel.

2 Press the Add Layer Mask button (◘) at the bottom of the Layers panel. A blank mask is added to the right of the red square layer

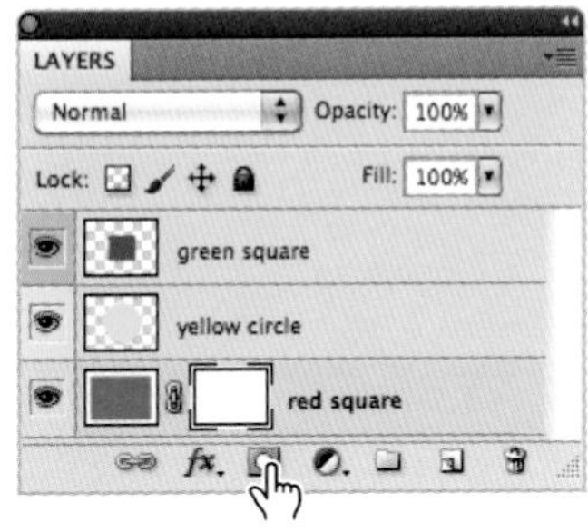

Adding a layer mask.

3 To make sure your foreground and background colors are set to the default black and white, press **D** on your keyboard.

4 Select the Gradient tool (▪) from the Tools panel, and make sure that the Linear Gradient option is selected in the Options bar. Click and drag across the red square in the image from the left side of the square to the right. Note that some of the red square becomes transparent, while some remains visible. Click and drag with the Gradient tool as many times as you like. Note that in the Layers panel, wherever black appears in the mask thumbnail, the red square is transparent, as the mask is essentially hiding the red square from view.

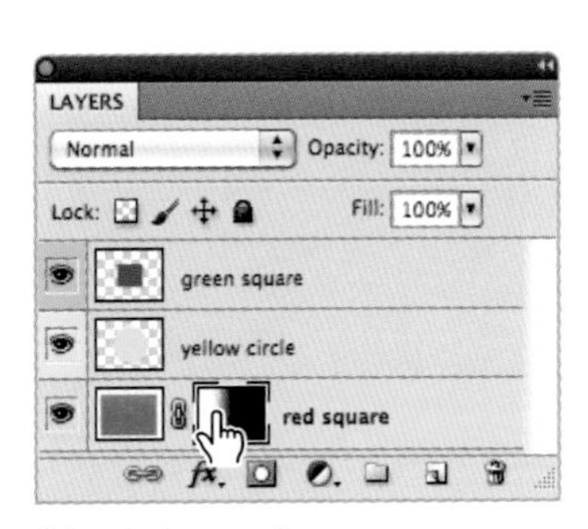

Select the layer mask.

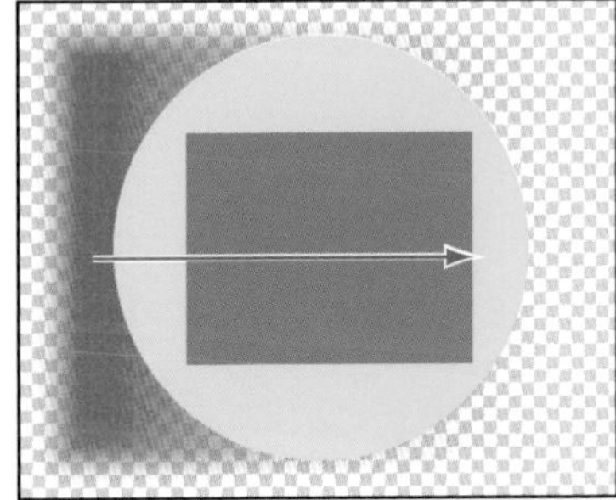

Click and drag using the Gradient tool across the image.

5 Choose File > Save. Keep this file open for the next part of this lesson.

Preserve transparency

The last step in this practice file will be to apply transformations to your layers. Transformations include scaling, rotating, and distorting a layer. To help illustrate how transformations work, you will first duplicate a layer and link it to the original.

1 With the mylayers.psd file still open, select the green square layer.

2 Select the Move tool (), and then hold down the Alt (Windows) or Option (Mac OS) key and position the cursor over the green square in the image. You will see a double-arrow cursor (). While still holding down the Alt/Option key, click and drag the green square to the right. A duplicate of the layer is created; release the mouse to see that a green square copy layer has been added to the Layers panel.

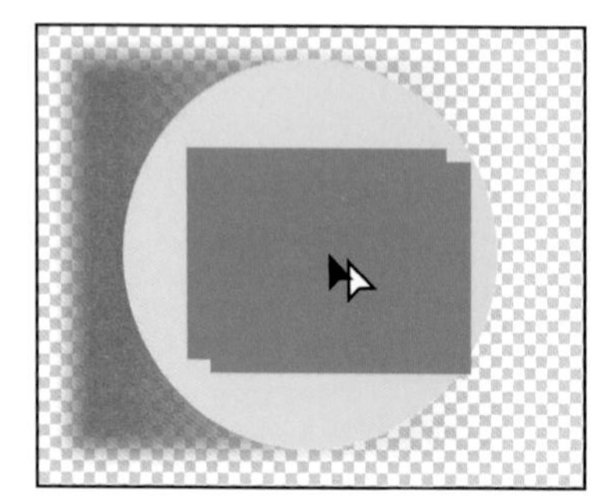

Duplicate a layer using the Alt/Option key.

3 Double-click on the green square layer name; when the text is highlighted, type the name **green square shadow**, then delete "copy" from the green square copy name.

4 Click on the green square shadow layer to select it. You'll now take advantage of a feature that allows you to fill without making a selection. Choose Edit > Fill, or use the keyboard shortcut Shift+Delete. The Fill dialog box appears.

5 In the Fill dialog box, choose Black from the Use drop-down menu. Leave Mode (in the blending section) set to Normal and Opacity set to 100 percent, check Preserve Transparency, and press OK.

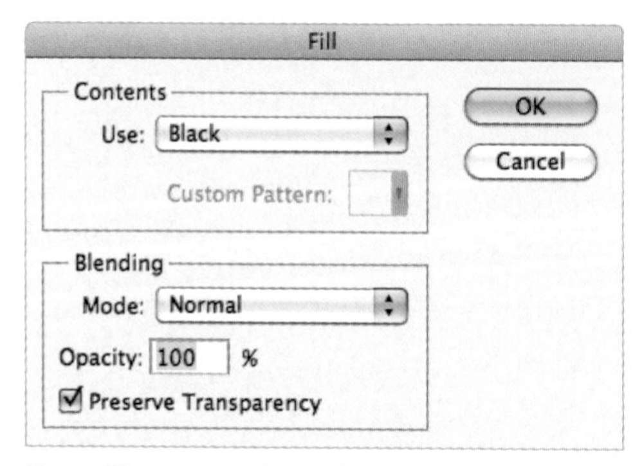

Preserve Transparency maintains the transparent sections of a layer.

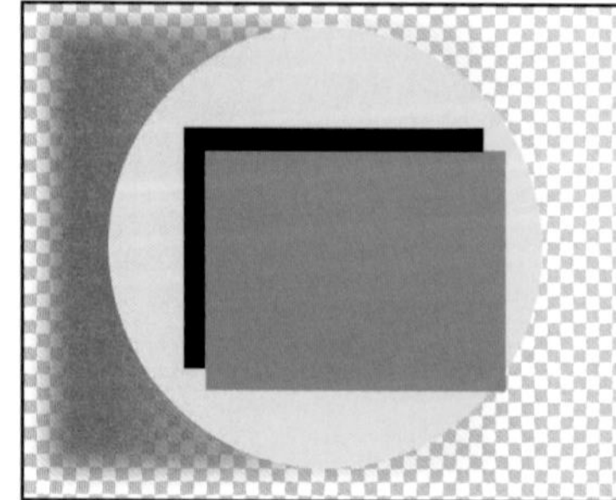

The result.

Notice that because you chose to preserve the transparency, only the green pixels are changed to black and the rest of the layer (the transparent part) remains transparent. You'll use this feature later in this lesson when creating a composition from several images.

6 With the green square shadow layer still active, select Filter > Blur > Gaussian Blur. The Gaussian Blur dialog box appears.

7 In the Gaussian Blur dialog box, type **8** in the Radius text field, and press OK.

8 Using the Move tool (), reposition the green shadow layer so that it appears slightly off to the lower right of the green square layer, creating the look of a shadow.

9 Type **8**. When you have a layer selected, and the Move tool active, you can type a numeric value to instantly change the opacity. By typing 8, you have changed the opacity of the green square shadow to 80 percent.

In this section, you will link the green square layer and green square shadow layer together. This allows you to move them simultaneously and also to apply transformations to both layers at the same time.

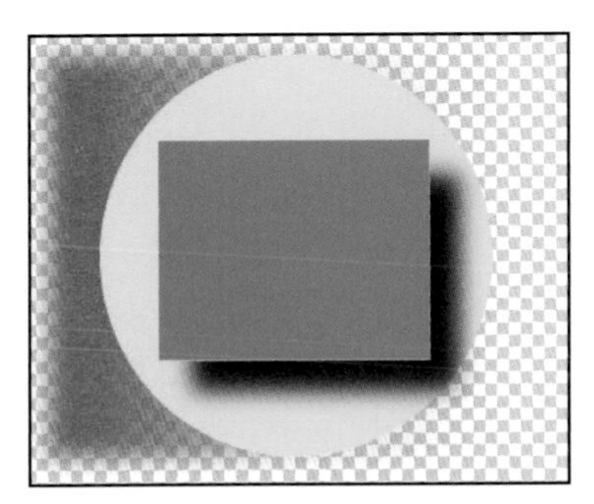

Use the Move tool to reposition the shadow layer.

10 Select the green square layer, then Shift+click on the green square shadow layer. Both are now selected.

11 Select the Link Layers button () at the bottom of the Layers panel. The link icon appears to the right of the layer names, indicating that they are linked to each other.

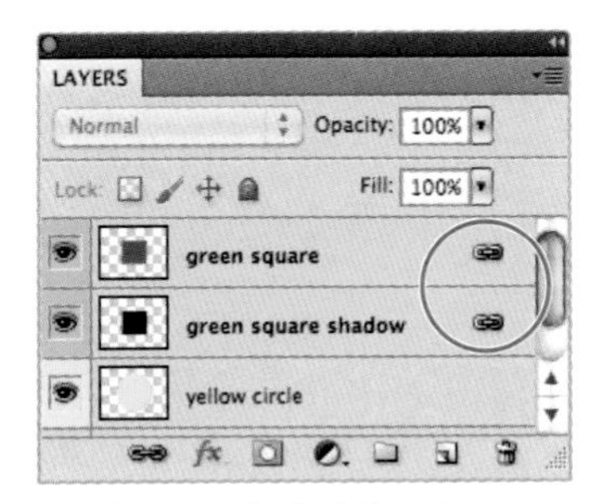

Keep layers together by linking them.

12 Select the Move tool, and click and drag the green square to another location. Notice that the shadow also moves. Move the squares back to the center of the image.

13 Choose Edit > Free Transform, or use the keyboard shortcut Ctrl+T (Windows) or Command+T (Mac OS). A bounding box appears around the green square and its shadow.

14 Click on the lower-right corner handle and drag it to enlarge the squares. Release the mouse when you've resized them to your liking. No particular size is necessary.

Click and drag the bounding box to scale the layer contents.

15 Press the Esc key (in the upper-left corner of your keyboard) to cancel the transformation.

16 Now, choose Edit > Free Transform again, but this time hold down the Shift key while dragging the lower-right corner of the bounding box toward the lower-right corner of your image. Holding down the Shift key keeps the layer contents proportional as you scale. Release the mouse when you're done with the transformation.

17 You can also enter exact scale amounts by using the Options bar. Type **150** in the W (Width) text field and then press the Maintain Aspect Ratio button (). The layer contents are scaled to exactly 150 percent. Select the checkbox in the Options bar to confirm this transformation.

18 Choose File > Save and then File > Close to close this practice file.

Creating a composition

Now you will have the opportunity to put your practice to work by creating a composition with images and type.

1 Choose File > Browse in Bridge to open Adobe Bridge, or select the Launch Bridge (Br) or Mini Bridge button (Mb) in the upper-left corner of the Application bar. Navigate to the ps08lessons folder inside the pslessons folder on your computer.

2 Double-click on the file ps0801_done.psd to see the composition that you will create. You can keep this file open for reference, or choose File > Close.

The completed lesson file.

3 Double-click on ps0801.psd to open it in Photoshop. An image of a blue sky with clouds appears.

4 Choose File > Save As. In the Save As dialog box, navigate to the ps08lessons folder and type **ps0801_work** into the Name text field; leave the format as Photoshop and press Save.

Moving images in from other documents

You'll start this composition by opening another file and dragging it into this file. Be aware that when moving one document into another, an image's resolution plays an important part in how that image appears proportionally in the destination file. For instance, if a 72-ppi image is moved into a 300-ppi image, it becomes relatively smaller, as the 72-ppi image takes up much less pixel space in the 300-ppi image. On the other hand, if you move a 300-ppi image into a 72-ppi image, it takes up a larger space. If you plan to create composites of multiple images, it is best to choose Image > Image Size and adjust the pixel resolutions of the images before combining them. In this section, you will learn how to check the resolution of your images before combining them into one document.

1 With the ps0801_work.psd file open, choose Image > Image Size. The Image Size dialog box appears. Notice that this image's resolution is 300 ppi. Press OK.

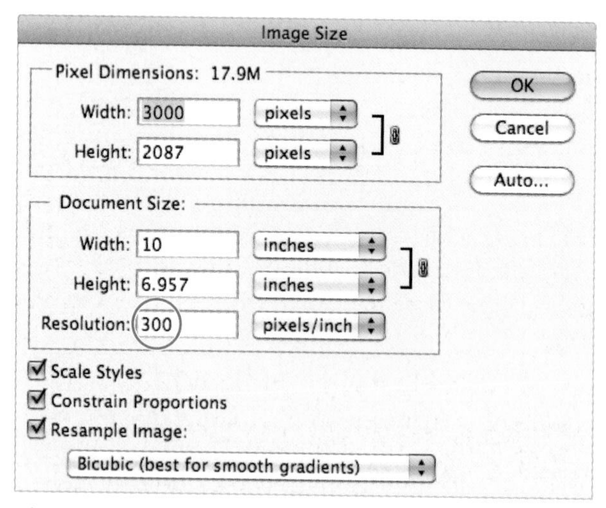

The image resolution of this file is 300 ppi.

2 Choose File > Browse in Bridge to open Adobe Bridge, or select the Launch Bridge (Br) or Mini Bridge button (Mb) in the upper-left area of the Application bar at the top of the workspace. Navigate to the ps08lessons folder inside the pslessons folder on your computer.

3 Double-click on ps0802.psd to open it in Photoshop. An image of a boy jumping appears. For this image, you will check the resolution without opening the Image Size dialog box.

4 Hold down the Alt (Windows) or Option (Mac OS) key, and click and hold on the document size box to see a pop-up window appear, which provides you with dimension and resolution information. Note that this image is also 300 ppi. Release the mouse button to dismiss the pop-up window.

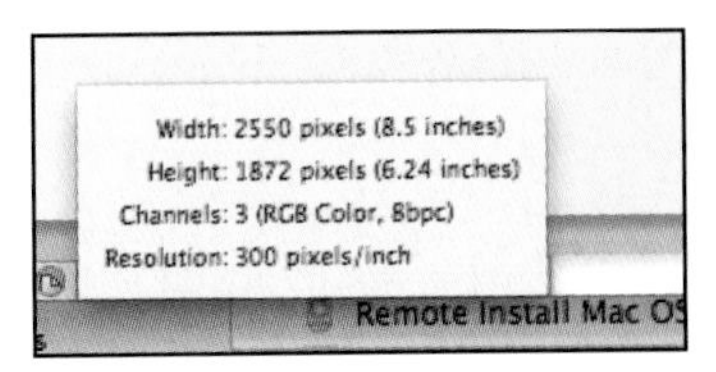

Check the resolution in the document window.

5 Click on the Arrange Documents button (▦) in the Application bar and choose 2 Up. This positions the ps0801_work.psd and ps0802.psd documents so that you can see them both at the same time.

6 Select the Move tool (▸+).

7 Hold down the Shift key, and click and drag the image into ps0801_work.psd. Holding the Shift key assures you that the layer is being placed in the exact center of the document into which it is being dragged. Release the mouse when a border appears around the ps0801_work.psd image.

8 Choose File > Save. Keep the file open for the next part of this lesson.

9 Click on the tab for the ps0802.psd file, and then click the X at the right side of the tab or choose File > Close. You can also use the keyboard shortcut Ctrl+W (Windows) or Command+W (Mac OS) to close the file. If you are asked to save the file, choose No.

Creating a layer mask

You just created the first layer in this document. It is important to keep your layers organized as you work; the Layers panel can become cumbersome when additional layers are created without being properly named.

1 Double-click the word Layer 1 in the Layers panel. When the Layer 1 text becomes highlighted, type **boy**.

   Now you'll select the boy and create a layer mask to cover the background sky.

2 Select the boy layer in the Layers panel to make sure it is the active layer, then select the Quick Selection tool ( ) and start brushing over the image of the boy. A selection is created as you brush. If you accidently select the area around the jumping boy, hold down the Alt (Windows) or Option (Mac OS) key and brush over that area again to delete it from the selection.

   Because you will be turning your selection into a mask, you do not have to be perfectly precise. You can edit the selection later if necessary.

Create a selection using the Quick Selection tool.

3 With the selection still active, select the Add Layer Mask button (◙) at the bottom of the Layers panel. A mask is created, revealing only your selection of the jumping boy.

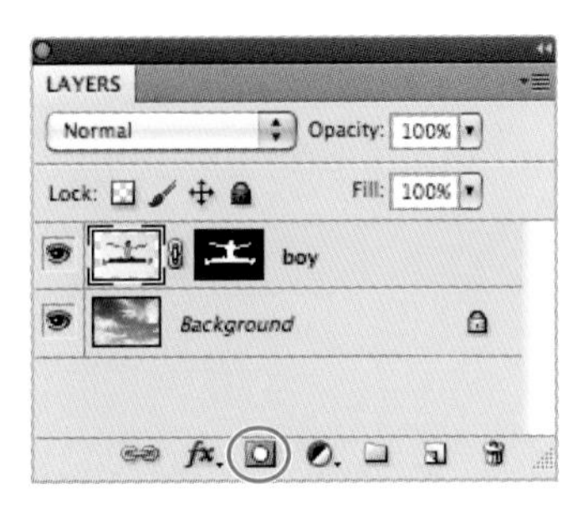

Select the Add Layer Mask button.

The result.

Editing the layer mask

Your mask may not be perfect, but you can easily edit it using your painting tools. In the example shown here, the hand was not correctly selected with the Quick Selection tool and therefore created an inaccurate mask. Zoom into the image and locate a section where your selection may not be precise; it is more than likely this will be around the boy's hands.

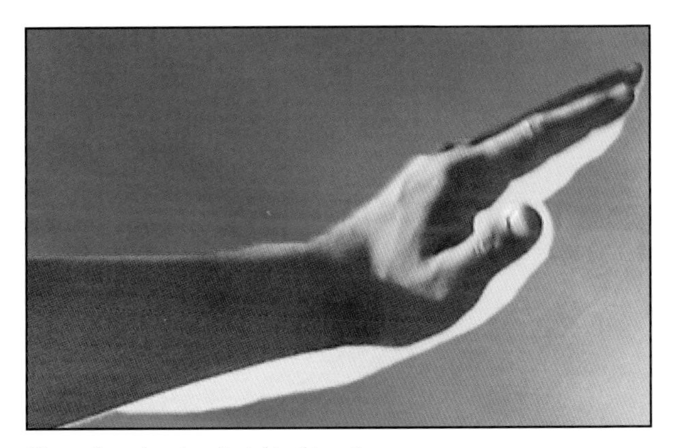
The mask needs to be adjusted in this section.

1 Select the layer mask thumbnail that is to the right of the boy layer's thumbnail in the Layers panel.

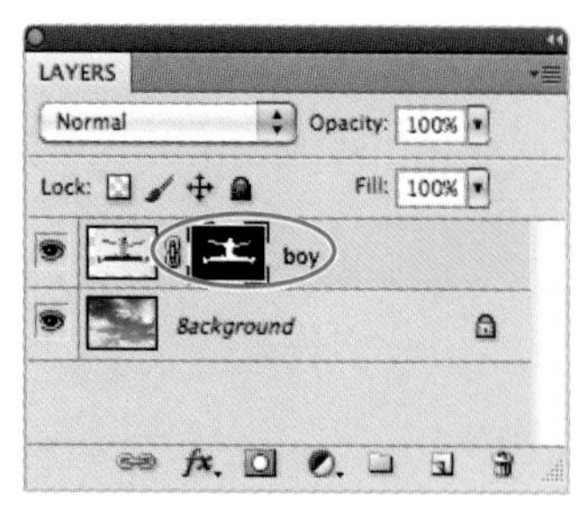

Select the layer mask thumbnail.

2 Press **D** on your keyboard to select the default colors of black and white. Note that when working on a mask, painting with white reveals the image, while painting with black hides it.

3 Press **X** on your keyboard, and note that by pressing X you are swapping the foreground and background colors in the Tools panel. Make sure that black is the foreground color.

4 Select the Brush tool and position the cursor over an area of the image where the mask is a bit inaccurate. You see a circle representing the brush size.

If you have Caps Lock selected, you will not see the brush size preview.

If the brush size is too big or too small for the area of the mask that needs to be retouched, adjust the size before you start painting.

5 Press the] (right bracket) key to make the brush size larger, or the [(left bracket) key to make the brush size smaller.

6 Start painting the areas of the mask that were not accurate; in this case, perhaps where some of the sky on the boy layer still appears. Experiment even further by painting over the entire hand. The hand disappears.

7 Press **X** on your keyboard to bring white to the foreground, and paint over the location where the hand was, to reveal it again. You are essentially fine-tuning your mask by painting directly on it.

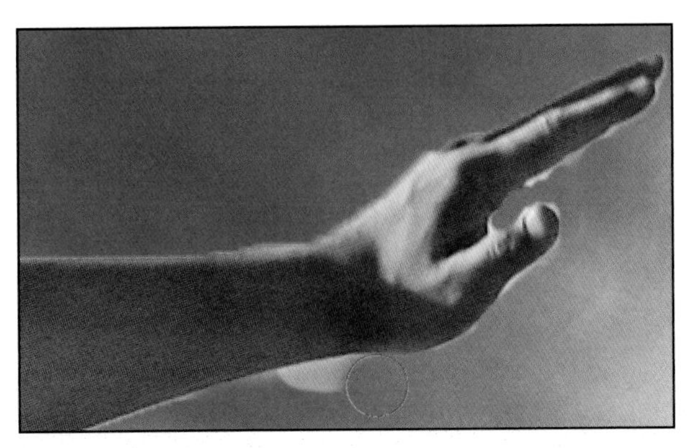

Painting the mask.

8 If you find that your brush should have a harder edge, press Shift+] (right bracket.) For a softer edge press Shift+[(left bracket).

The benefit of working with a layer mask is that you can fine-tune and edit it as many times as you want without permanently altering the image. This gives you a lot of freedom and control, and allows you to make more accurate selections. This type of image editing is referred to as nondestructive.

9 When you are finished editing your selection, press Ctrl+0 (zero) (Windows) or Command+0 (zero) (Mac OS) to return to the Fit in Screen view. Then, to deselect the layer mask thumbnail, select the boy layer thumbnail in the Layers panel.

Cloning layers

You'll now clone (or duplicate) the boy layer two times. You'll then apply filters and adjust the opacity of the new layers.

1 Select the boy layer thumbnail in the Layers panel to ensure that it is the active layer. Select the Move tool (►+) and reposition the boy so that his feet touch the bottom of the image.

Click and drag the boy layer downwards.

2 With the Move tool still selected, click and hold the Alt (Windows) or Option (Mac OS) key while dragging the jumping boy image up toward the middle of the image. By holding down the Alt/Option key, you are cloning the layer. Don't worry about a precise location for the cloned layer, as you'll adjust its position later. Release the mouse before releasing the Alt/Option key.

Clone the layer of the boy jumping.

3 Click and hold down the Alt (Windows) or Option (Mac OS) key once again and drag the newly created layer upwards to clone it. Position this new layer at the top of the image. There are now three layers with the boy jumping.

4 In the Layers panel, double-click on layer name *boy copy.* When the text becomes highlighted, type **boy middle** to change the layer name.

5 Then, double-click on layer name boy copy 2. When the text becomes highlighted, type **boy top** to change the layer name.

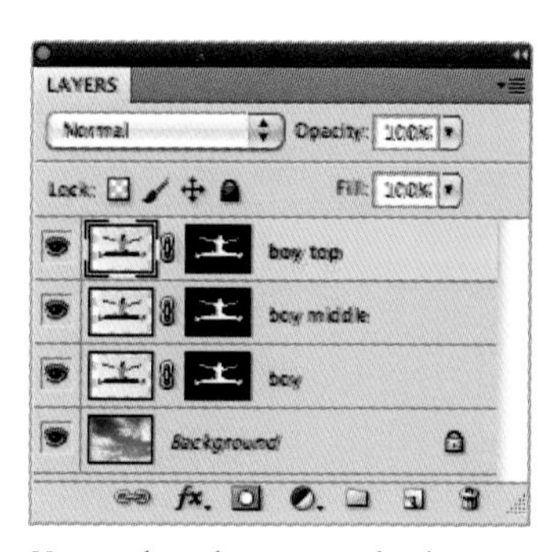

You now have three jumping boy layers.

6 Choose File > Save to save this file. Keep the file open for the next part of this lesson.

Aligning and distributing layers

The layers may not be evenly spaced or aligned with each other. This can be adjusted easily by using the Align and Distribute features in Photoshop.

1 Select the boy layer and then Ctrl+click (Windows) or Command+click (Mac OS) on the boy middle and boy top layers. All three layers become selected.

   Note that when you have two or more layers selected, there are additional options in the Options bar to align and distribute your layers.

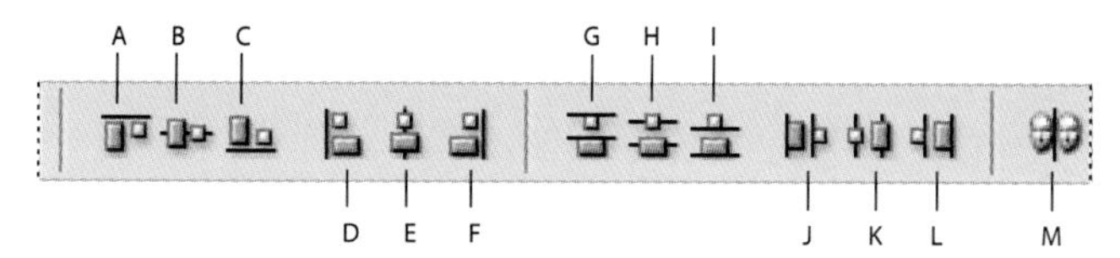

***A.** Align top edges. **B.** Align vertical centers. **C.** Align bottom edges.*
***D.** Align left edges. **E.** Align horizontal centers. **F.** Align right edges.*
***G.** Distribute top edges. **H.** Distribute vertical centers. **I.** Distribute bottom edges.*
***J.** Distribute left edges. **K.** Distribute horizontal centers. **L.** Distribute right edges.*
***M.** Auto-Align layers.*

2 Choose the Align Horizontal Centers button (![icon]) and then the Distribute Vertical Centers button (![icon]). You may or may not see a dramatic adjustment here; it depends on how you positioned the layers when you created them.

3 Choose File > Save. Keep the file open for the next part of this lesson.

Applying filters to layers

Now you'll apply a filter to the boy and boy middle layers and then adjust their opacity.

1 Select the boy middle layer in the Layers panel.

2 Choose Filter > Blur > Motion Blur. The Motion Blur dialog box appears.

3 Type **–90** in the Angle text field, drag the distance slider to 150, then press OK. You have created a blur that makes it look like the boy is jumping up.

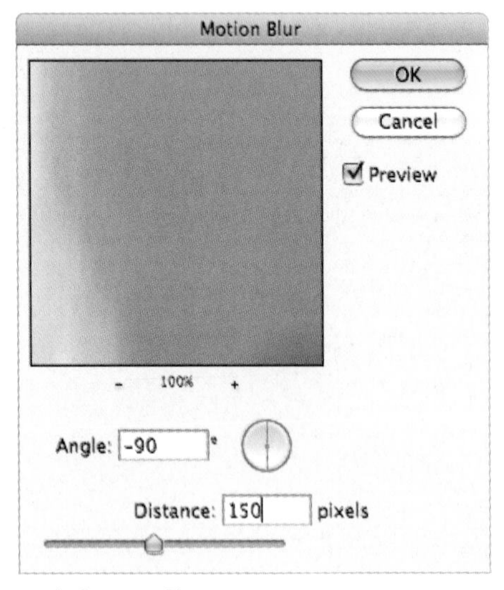

Apply the motion blur.

Result.

4 Choose the boy layer in the Layers panel and press Ctrl+F (Windows) or Command+F (Mac OS). This applies the last-used filter to this layer.

You will now adjust the opacity on these layers.

5 With the boy layer still selected, click on the arrow to the right of Opacity in the Layers panel. A slider appears. Click and drag the slider to the 20 percent mark.

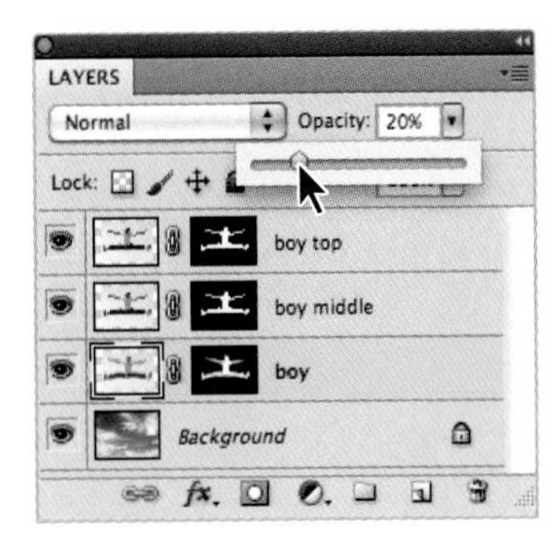

Drag the opacity slider.

6 Make sure that the Move tool (▸+) is active, and select the boy middle layer. This time, you'll change the opacity using a keyboard shortcut. Type **5**; the layer opacity is instantly changed to 50 percent.

The layers after the opacity has been adjusted.

*While the Move tool is active, you can type in any value to set the opacity on a selected layer. For instance, typing **23** would make the layer 23 percent opaque, and **70** would make the layer 70 percent opaque. Type **0** (zero) to return to 100 percent opacity.*

7 Choose File > Save to save this file. Keep the file open for the next part of this lesson.

Creating a type layer

You are now going to add a text layer to this document and apply a warp, as well as a layer style.

1 In the Layers panel, select the boy top layer to make it active. The new type layer will appear directly above the active layer.

2 Select the Type tool (T) and set the following options in the Options bar:

From the font family drop-down menu, choose Myriad Pro. From the font style drop-down menu, choose Black. If you do not have Black, choose Bold.

Type **200** in the font size text field.

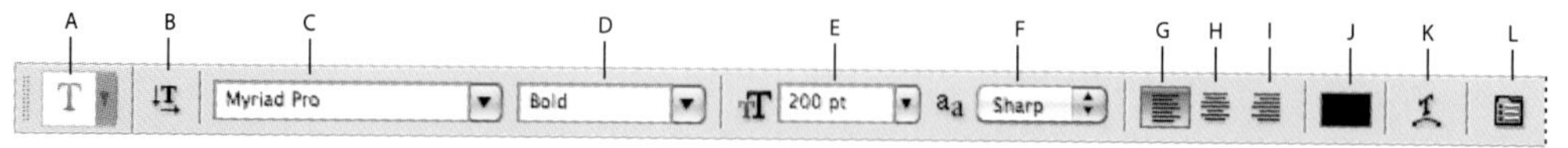

A. Presets. B. Text orientation. C. Font family. D. Font style. E. Font size. F. Anti-aliasing. G. Left-align text. H. Center text. I. Right-align text. J. Text color. K. Warp text. L. Character and Paragraph panels.

3 Now, click once on the Text color box in the Options bar. The Color Picker dialog box appears, with a Select text color pane.

4 You can either enter a color value in this window or click on a color in the color preview pane. In this example, you will click a color. Position your cursor over an area in the image that has light clouds, and click. This samples that color, and applies it to the text. Press OK to close the Color Picker.

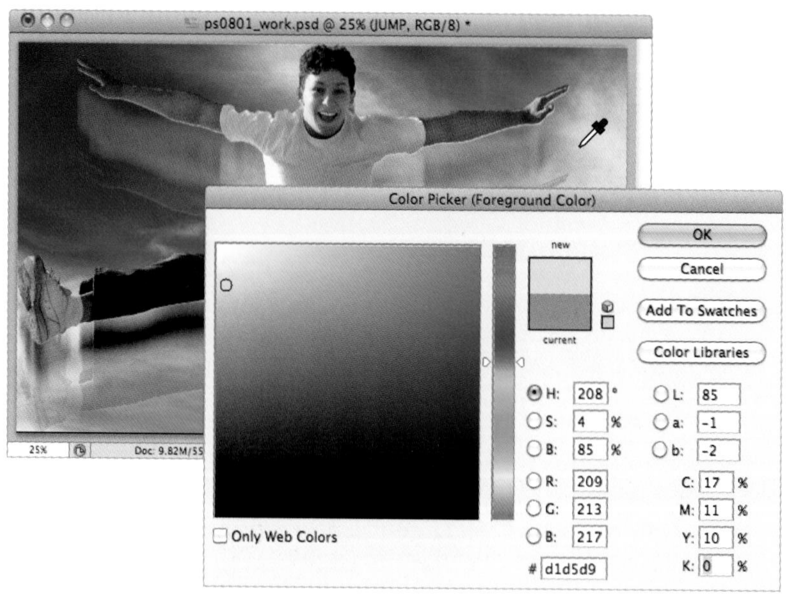

Sample a color from your image.

You are now ready to type.

5 Click once on the image near the boy's sneaker on the left side of the image. Exact position is not important, as it can be adjusted later.

6 Type **JUMP**, then hold down the Ctrl (Windows) or Command (Mac OS) key and drag the word Jump to approximately the bottom center of the image. By holding down the Ctrl/Command key, you do not have to exit the text entry mode to reposition the text.

Reposition the text using the Ctrl or Command key.

7 Select the Create Warped Text button (⌒) in the Options bar. The Warp Text dialog box appears. Select Arc Upper from the Style drop-down menu. If you like, experiment with the other style selections, but return to Arc Upper when finished. Press OK. The text is warped.

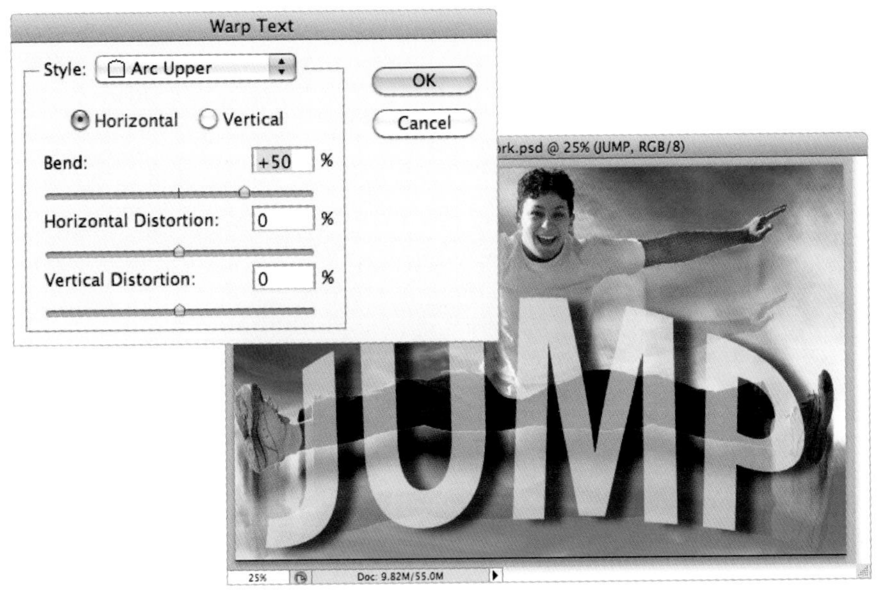

Warping the text. *The result.*

9 Click the check mark (✓) in the Options bar to confirm your text entry.

10 In the Layers panel, click and drag the Opacity slider to about 70 percent, or type **70** into the Opacity text field.

11 Choose File > Save and keep the file open for the next part of this lesson.

Applying a layer style

Layer styles allow you to apply interesting effects to layers, such as drop shadows, embossing, and outer glows, to name a few. In this section, you will add a drop shadow to your text layer.

1 Select the text layer to make sure that the layer is active.

2 Click and hold on the Add a Layer Style button (*fx*) at the bottom of the Layers panel. Choose Drop Shadow from the menu, and the Layer Style dialog box appears.

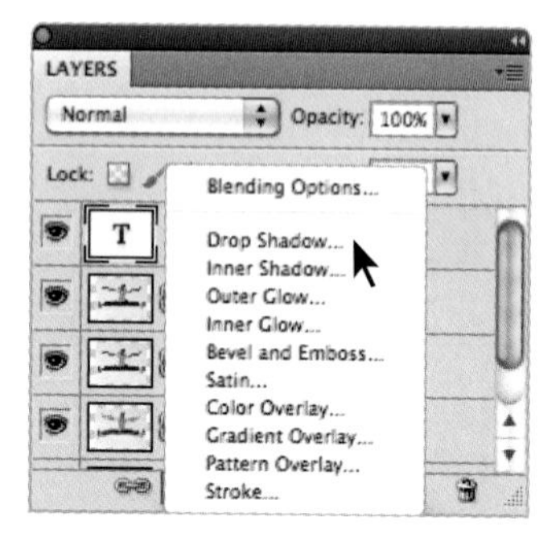

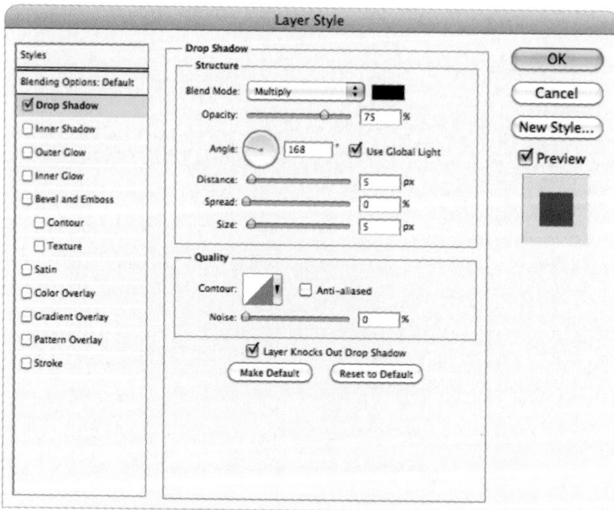

Adding a drop shadow to the text layer.

At some point, you should experiment with all the layer style options listed in the column on the left, but for now you'll work with the drop shadow options.

3 With the Layer Styles dialog box open, click and drag the shadow (in the image window) to reposition it. You can manually enter values. In this example, the shadow is set to an angle of 160, the distance at 70, and the size at 30. Press OK, and the drop shadow is applied.

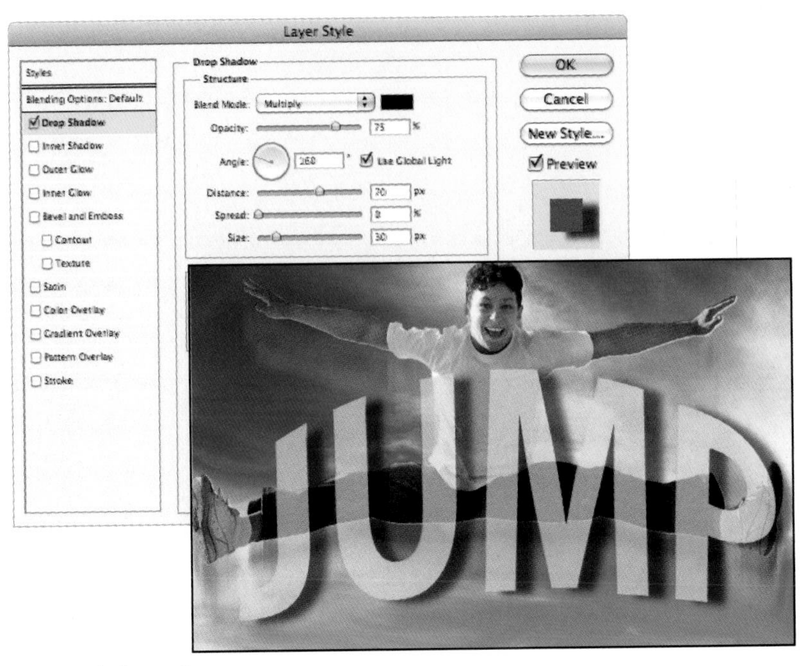

Adjusting the layer style.

Creating a clipping mask

You will now create a clipping mask to complete this image. A clipping mask lets you use the content of one layer to mask the layers above it. In this example, you will create a shape layer and position it under the background layer. You will then clip up through several layers, masking them within that original shape layer. It might sound confusing, but it really isn't once you have seen the clipping mask feature in action.

1 First, you need to convert the Background layer to a regular layer because you cannot position layers underneath the Background layer.

2 Hold down the Alt (Windows) or Option (Mac OS) key and double-click on the Background layer in the Layers panel. It is automatically converted to Layer 0.

3 Double-click on the Layer 0 name, and when the text becomes highlighted, type **sky**.

4 Click and hold on the Shape tool (▭) and select the hidden Rounded Rectangle tool (▭). In the Options bar, make sure that Shape layers is selected, and then type **1 in** (inch) in the Radius text field. This value is for the curved corners of the rounded rectangle you are going to create.

5 Click and drag from the boy's thumb on the left side of the image down to the bottom of the letter P in JUMP. The shape is created; don't worry about the color.

Set the shape options, then click and drag to create the shape layer.

6 In the Layers panel, click and drag the Shape 1 layer so that it is beneath the sky layer.

7 Hold down the Alt (Windows) or Option (Mac OS) key, and position your cursor over the line that separates the Shape 1 layer from the sky layer. When you see the clipping mask icon (↰●) appear, click with the mouse. The sky layer is clipped inside the shape layer.

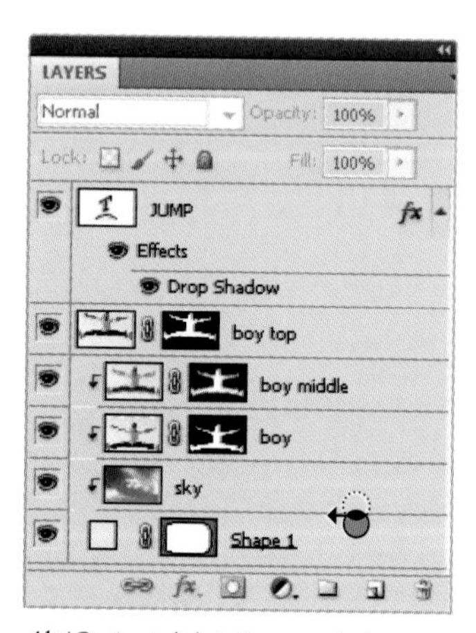

Alt/Option+click in between the layers.

The result.

8 Now, position your cursor on the line separating the sky layer from the boy layer, and Alt/Option+click on the line. The clipping now extends up into the boy layer.

9 Position the cursor on the line separating the boy layer from the boy middle layer, and Alt/Option+click again. The clipping mask is now extended to the boy middle layer.

10 Select the Move tool (▸+) and the Shape 1 layer. Click and drag to reposition the layer to see how the sky, boy, and boy middle layers are clipped inside the shape.

11 If you would prefer not to see the vector path creating an outline around your rounded rectangle shape, click once on the vector mask thumbnail in the Layers panel.

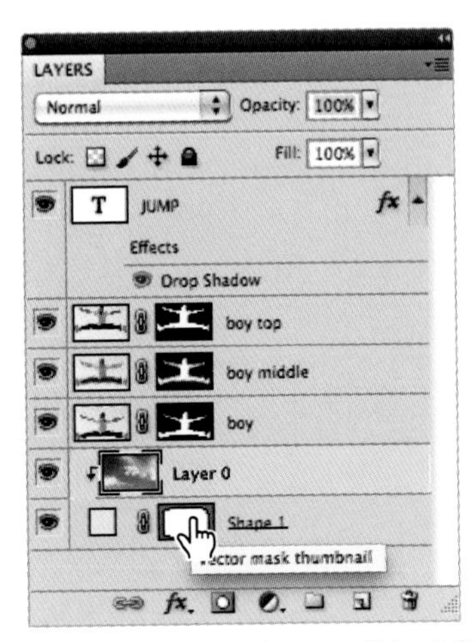

Click on the vector mask to turn off the visibility of the vector path in your image.

You will now trim the layers to eliminate areas you don't need.

12 Choose Image > Trim; the Trim dialog box appears. Leave the settings at the default and press OK. The image is trimmed down to the smallest possible size, without cropping out any image data.

13 Choose File > Save, and then File > Close.

Congratulations! You have finished the lesson on getting to know layers.

Self study

Layers are fun to build and use when creating professional composites. Included in the ps08lessons folder are several images (boyguitar.psd, girlguitar.psd, pianokeys.psd, and sheetmusic.psd) that you can use in any way that you want to create a composite. Experiment with these sample files to create new layers, layer masks, and clipping masks. Take the composition further by adding text and warping it.

Review

Questions

1 List at least three ways that you can create a layer in a document.

2 Why should you be concerned about resolution when compositing several images?

3 What is the difference between the Background layer and a regular layer?

Answers

1 You can create new layers in a document using several methods:

a. Create a new blank layer using the Create a New Layer button (⊡) in the Layers panel. You can also choose Layers > New > Layer or select New Layer from the Layers panel menu.

b. Create a new layer by clicking and dragging content from one image to another.

c. Create a text layer; when you add text, a new text layer is automatically created.

d. Create a shape. If the Shape tool is selected and the Options bar is set to Shape tool, a new Shape layer is automatically created.

2 When combining images from several different sources, it is important for the pixel dimensions or resolutions to be similar, or the images will not be proportional to each other and may not work well as a composite.

3 The Background layer is different from a regular layer in that it does not support layer features. It cannot be moved in the stacking order, repositioned, transformed, or have its blending mode or opacity changed.

What you'll learn in this lesson:

- Making color changes with adjustment layers
- Using the Black and White adjustment layer
- Combining layer styles
- Understanding layer fill and opacity settings

Taking Layers to the Max

Even those who call themselves Photoshop experts can't get enough of layers. Layers provide many creative possibilities, some more evident than others. In this lesson, you will build a layered file, and then you'll take it farther than you ever thought possible, using features such as adjustment layers, layer effects, and clipping groups, among others.

Starting up

Layers, in their simplest form, offer Photoshop users an amazing amount of flexibility to create and modify images. The more advanced features of layers offer even more options, many of which you can exploit in various ways while keeping the original image information intact.

Before starting, make sure that your tools and panels are consistent by resetting your preferences. See "Resetting Adobe Photoshop CS5 preferences" on page 3.

You will work with several files from the ps09lessons folder in this lesson. Make sure that you have loaded the pslessons folder onto your hard drive from the supplied DVD. See "Loading lesson files" on page 5.

See Lesson 9 in action!

Use the accompanying video to gain a better understanding of how to use some of the features shown in this lesson. The video tutorial for this lesson can be found on the included DVD.

Making color changes using adjustment layers

Changing the color of an object in Adobe Photoshop is a pretty common practice, but how do you make it look realistic, and how can you recover the image if you make a mistake? What if you want to see three or four different variations? All these tasks can be completed easily and efficiently, using adjustment layers. In this section, you'll change the color of a jacket on a model, and then, using the same adjustment layer, change it again, multiple times.

1 Choose File > Browse in Bridge to open Adobe Bridge, or select the Launch Bridge (Br) or Mini Bridge button (Mb) in the Application bar that runs across the top of the workspace.

2 Navigate to the ps09lessons folder, inside the pslessons folder you have created on your computer and double-click on ps0901.psd to open it in Photoshop. An image of a girl wearing a blue jacket appears.

   You will take the original jacket and change the colors several times. You will also add a pattern to the jacket, using an adjustment layer.

The original image.

A solid color adjustment.

A pattern adjustment.

3 Choose File > Save As. In the Name text field, type **ps0901_work**, and then navigate to the ps09lessons folder. Choose Photoshop from the format drop-down menu and press Save.

The first thing that you will make is a selection with the Quick Selection tool. What's nice about using an adjustment layer is that you can paint a mask at any point in the process to modify your selection.

4 Select the Quick Selection tool (), then click and drag on the jacket. If you miss some of the jacket, just paint a stroke over it to add it to the selection. If your selection goes too far, hold down the Alt (Windows) or Option (Mac OS) key and click on the part of the selection that you want to deactivate.

You can also increase or decrease your Quick Selection tool size by pressing the [(left bracket) or] (right bracket) keys.

Paint the jacket with the Quick Selection tool to make a selection.

5 If the Layers panel is not visible, choose Window > Layers.

6 Click and hold on the Create New Fill or Adjustment Layer button () at the bottom of the Layers panel.

7 Select Hue/Saturation from the pop-up menu. The Adjustments panel with the Hue/Saturation options becomes active.

Hue refers to the color. By changing the hue, you can essentially change the color of an object without taking away any of the shading properties, which are normally created from the neutral gray value.

8 Check the Colorize checkbox, and click and drag the Hue slider to the right to about the 70 point, or type **70** in the Hue text field.

In the next step, you will bring the saturation down a bit so the green you are creating is less bright.

9 Click and drag the Saturation slider to the left to about the 20 point, or type **20** into the Saturation text field. Press OK.

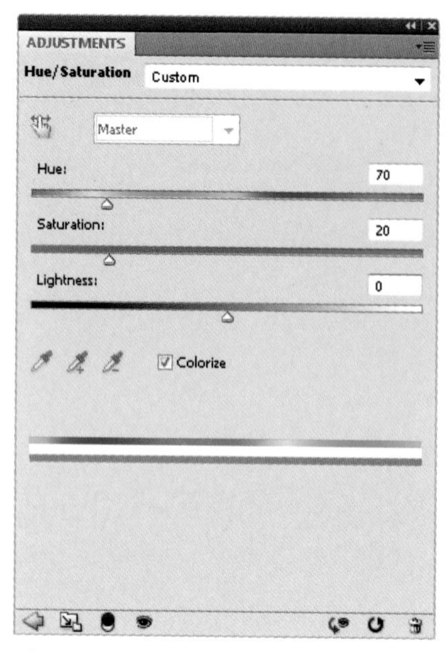

Change the color and saturation using the Hue/Saturation sliders.

The jacket is now green, but your selection might not be as accurate as you would like. In the next section, you will use your painting tools to refine the mask attached to the adjustment layer.

10 Choose File > Save.

If you inadvertently close any images while working on a project, you can quickly reopen them by choosing File > Open Recent, and selecting the file from the drop-down menu.

Refining the adjustment layer mask

If you take a look at the Layers panel you just created, you see a Hue/Saturation adjustment layer that has a mask thumbnail to the right of the layer thumbnail. You can activate this mask separately, and then use painting tools to refine it.

1 Alt+click (Windows) or Option+click (Mac OS) on the adjustment mask thumbnail, to the right of the Hue/Saturation thumbnail in the Layers panel.

   The mask appears. You are not doing anything to the mask at this time, but you should take a look at what the actual mask looks like. Notice that where there is white, the hue and saturation changes take place. Where the mask is black, the changes are not occurring. Using the painting tools in Photoshop, you can edit a mask by painting black and white, and even varying opacities to control the results of the adjustment layer.

Where the mask is white, the Hue/Saturation change is occurring.

2 To return to the normal layer view, click once on the word *Background* in the Layers panel.

You will now make changes to the adjustment mask thumbnail.

3 Click once on the adjustment mask thumbnail (to the right of the Hue/Saturation adjustment layer thumbnail).

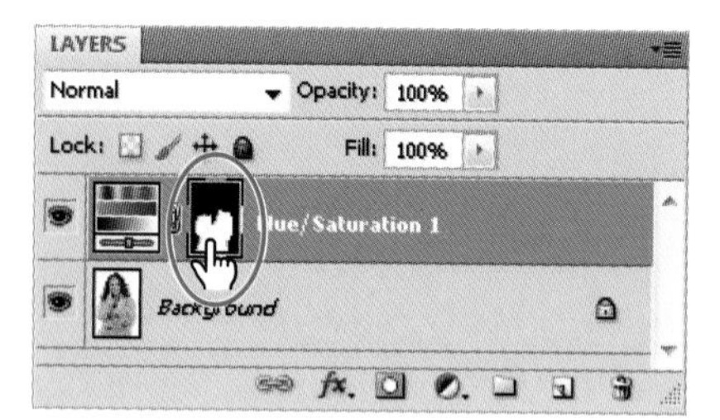

Paint on the adjustment layer's mask to refine your selection.

4 Now, select the Brush tool (), and press **D** on your keyboard to set the colors to the default of black and white. Note that when in a mask, white is the foreground color and black is the background color.

5 Adjust your brush size as needed to paint the areas in the mask that might not have been selected, and thus not affected, when you created the adjustment layer.

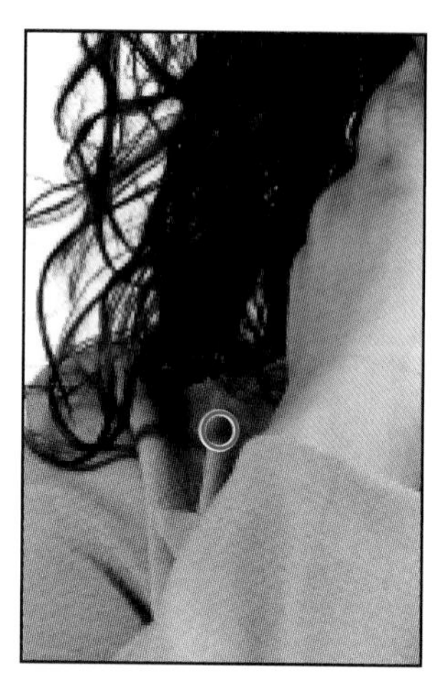

Paint the areas that may have been missed with your original selection.

You can make your brush size larger by pressing the] (right bracket) key and smaller by pressing [(left bracket) key. Make your brush harder by pressing Shift+] and softer by pressing Shift+[.

6 Press **X** on your keyboard to swap the foreground and background colors. Black is now the foreground color.

7 Now, find a section of your image—perhaps the hand tucked in underneath the elbow—that has the Hue/Saturation change applied to it in error.

   You will paint this area with the black paint brush, with the mask active, to block the change from occurring there.

It is very easy to deselect the mask and paint on your actual image. Avoid this by clicking once on the Layer mask thumbnail, just to be sure!

8 Adjust your paint brush to the right size and softness, and paint over the hand to reveal the actual flesh color.

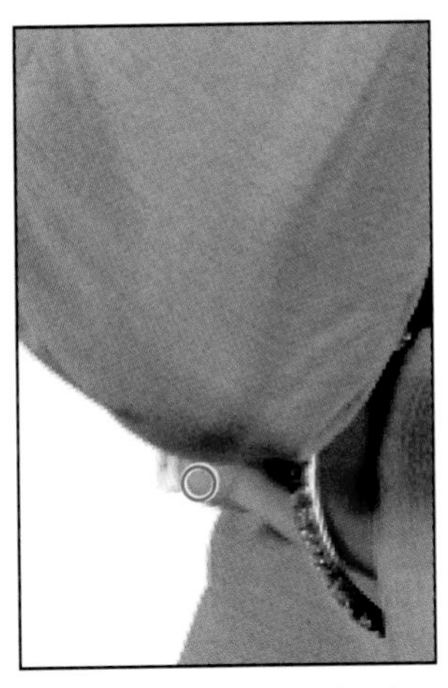

Eliminate the areas that may have been included, in error, in the original selection.

*If you did such an accurate selection that you have no areas to repair, paint an area somewhere on your image anyway, just to see the effects of painting black on the mask. When you are done experimenting, press **X** to swap back to the white foreground color and repair the mask, as necessary.*

Adjusting the Hue/Saturation layer

Now that you have created an accurate mask, the next few steps will be rather simple. Perhaps your client has suggested that you use a more vibrant violet for the blazer. In this section, you will apply more color to the blazer, and also edit the existing hue and saturation.

1 Double-click on the adjustment layer thumbnail to reopen the Hue/Saturation dialog box.

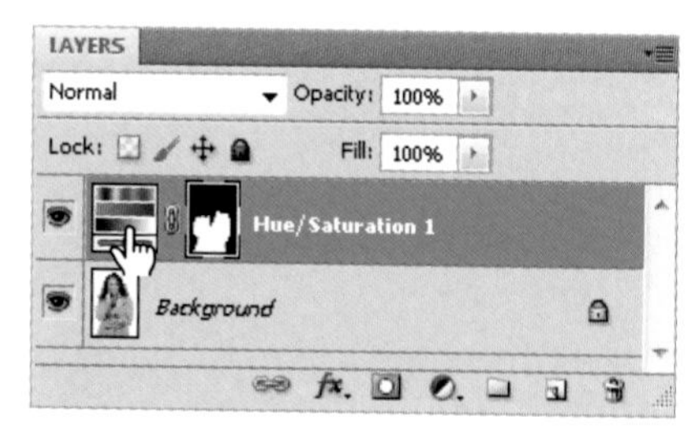

Double-click on the adjustment layer thumbnail to change the settings.

2 Click and drag the Hue slider to the right to about the 260 point, or type **260** into the Hue text field.

3 Click and drag the Saturation slider to the right to about the 40 point, or type **40** into the Saturation text field.

The green is now changed to a violet.

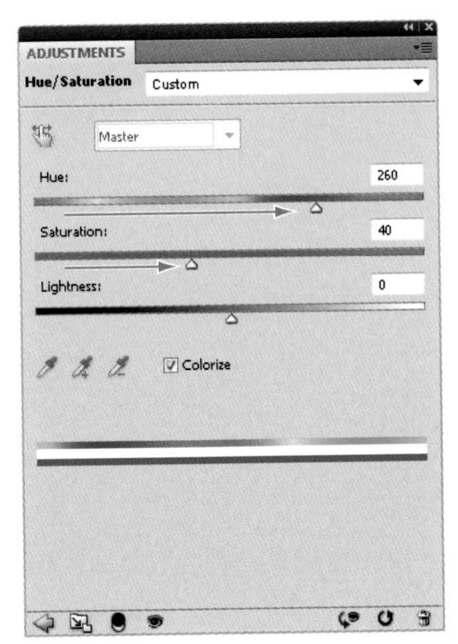

Readjusting the Hue and Saturation.

You can reopen the Hue/Saturation adjustment layer as many times as you like.

4 Choose File > Save, and keep the image open for the next section.

Adding a pattern fill layer

You can add a pattern and apply it to an image using a fill layer. This gives you the ability to scale the pattern, as well as adjust the opacity and blending modes. In this section, you will create a simple pattern that will be scaled and applied to the image, using a new fill layer.

Defining the pattern

You can create a pattern in Photoshop out of any pixel information that you can select with the Rectangular Marquee. In this section, you will use the entire image area as the pattern, but you could also activate a smaller portion of an image and define it as a pattern.

1 Leave the ps0901_work.psd file open, and open an additional image. Choose File > Browse in Bridge to open Adobe Bridge, or select the Launch Bridge (Br) or Mini Bridge button (Mb) in the Application bar.

2 Navigate to the ps09lessons folder, inside the pslessons folder you created on your computer and double-click on the file named ps0902.psd. An image of an ornate pattern appears.

Define a pattern from an entire image, or just a rectangular selection.

Because you are using the entire image to create the pattern, you do not need to select anything.

3 Choose Edit > Define Pattern. The Pattern Name dialog box appears. Type **ornate** in the Name text field, and press OK.

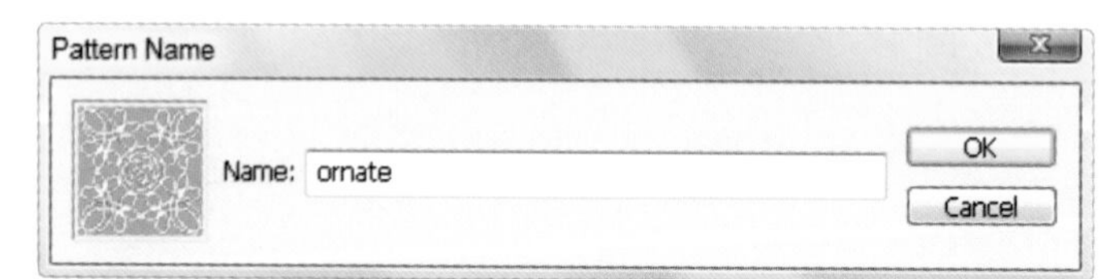

Defining a pattern for future use.

4 Choose File > Close to close the image without making any changes.

Applying the pattern

You will now apply the pattern to the jacket, using a new fill layer.

1 You spent a fair amount of time perfecting your mask, and you certainly don't want to have to do that again. Hold down the Ctrl (Windows) or Command (Mac OS) key and click on the Layer mask thumbnail of your adjustment layer. The mask is activated as a selection.

You can Ctrl/Command+click on any layer or mask to activate its contents as a selection.

2 Now that you have an active selection of the woman's blazer, click and hold on the Create New Fill or Adjustment Layer button (◐) at the bottom of the Layers panel, and choose Pattern. The Pattern Fill dialog box appears.

Your new pattern swatch should be visible. If it is not, click on the downward arrow to the right of the visible swatch to select a different pattern.

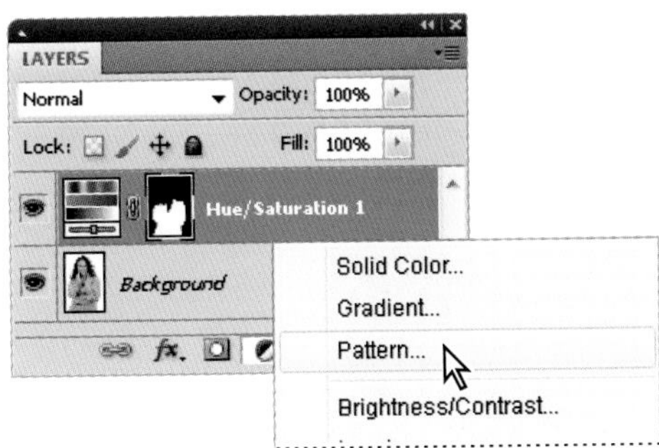

Select the Pattern Fill layer.

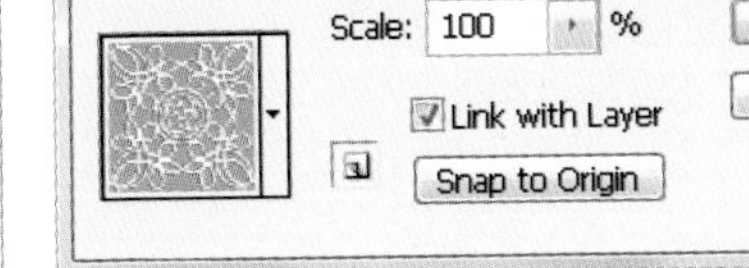

The Pattern Fill dialog box appears.

The result.

The result may be a little unexpected at first, as no scaling or blending mode has been applied to this fill pattern yet.

3 With the Pattern Fill dialog box still open, use the Scale slider to set the scale of the pattern to 25 percent, or type **25** into the Scale text field, and press OK.

4 With your new Fill layer still selected, click and hold on Normal in the blending mode drop-down menu on the Layers panel, and choose Multiply.

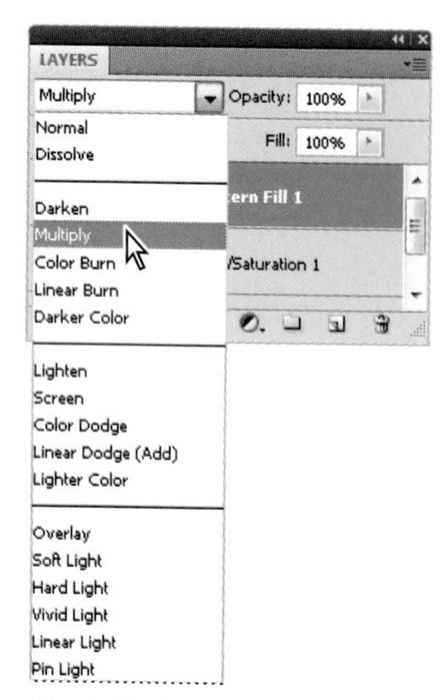

Select the blending mode.

The result.

You can experiment with other blending modes to see how they affect the final rendering of the pattern.

5 Choose File > Save and then File > Close to close this image.

Congratulations! You have finished the adjustment layer section of this lesson.

Using the new Black & White adjustment layer

Changing color images to grayscale is easy—you just switch the color mode using Image > Mode > Grayscale, right? Not if you want to achieve the best possible conversion. In this section, you will learn how to use the new Black & White adjustment layer.

1 Choose File > Browse in Bridge to open Adobe Bridge, or select the Launch Bridge button (Br) or Mini bridge button (Mb) in the Application bar.

2 Navigate to the ps09lessons folder, inside the pslessons folder you created on your computer and double-click on the file named ps0903.psd. A cityscape appears.

You will convert this cityscape image to grayscale.

3 Choose File > Save As; the Save As dialog box appears. Navigate to the ps09lessons folder. In the Name text field, type **ps0903_work** and select Photoshop from the Format drop-down menu. Press Save.

4 Click on the Create New Fill or Adjustment Layer button (◐) at the bottom of the Layers panel and select Black & White. The Black and White settings become active in the Adjustments panel.

This window may appear very confusing at first. Without some assistance, it would be difficult to decipher which color adjustments are going to affect the image and where. Fortunately, Adobe has created some helpful features to make a better conversion easier for users.

5 Click on the pointing finger icon (☝) in the Adjustments panel to make that option active.

6 Click and hold on the sky in the image; a pointing finger with a double arrow (☝) appears. The color that would make changes to that part of the image (the sky) is affected.

7 Continue holding down on the sky image, and drag to the right; notice that you automatically lightened the blues in the sky. Click and drag to the left to make the conversion darker.

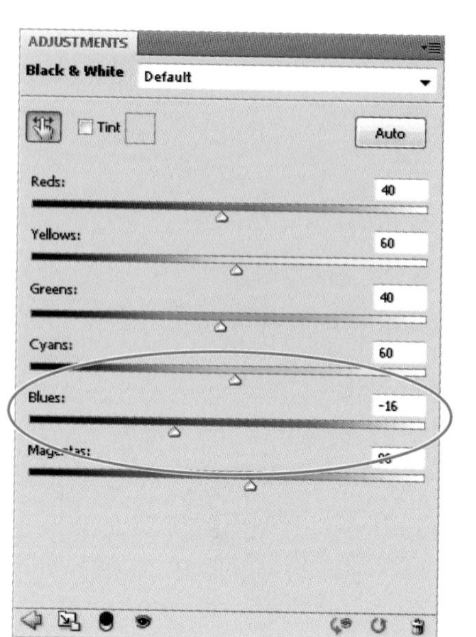

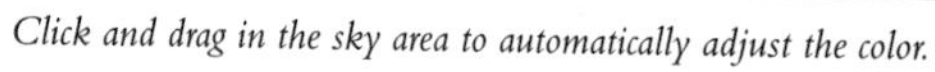
Click and drag in the sky area to automatically adjust the color.

8 Now, click on the darker streaming car lights in the image; the Reds are highlighted. Click and drag to the right to lighten them. You can just make visual adjustments for this image, but if you were concerned about dot values, you would want to have the Window > Info panel open.

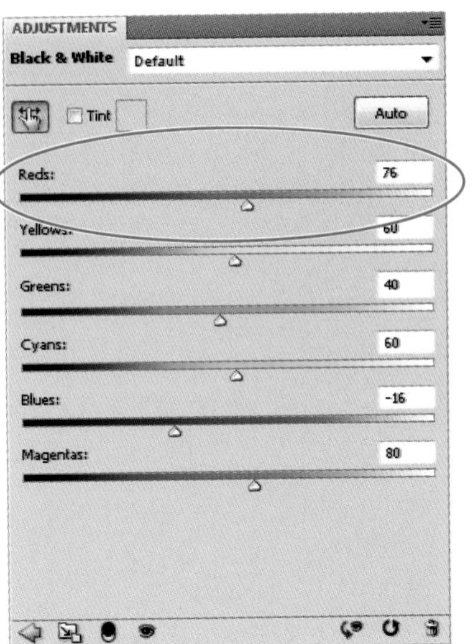

Click and drag on the car lights to lighten the conversion.

9 You can turn the visibility of this adjustment layer off and on by clicking on the visibility icon (👁) to the left of the Black & White 1 adjustment layer.

10 Choose File > Save. Keep the file open for the next section of this lesson.

Adding a tint

In this section, you will add a tint to your image. A tint of color can be added to an RGB image to create a nice effect.

The Black & White adjustment layer is disabled in CMYK mode.

1 Double-click on the Black & White 1 layer thumbnail (◐) icon (to the left of the Black & White 1 name and mask) in the Layer's panel. This activates the Black & White settings in the Adjustments panel.

2 Check the *Tint* checkbox.

You can click on the color box to the right of the *Tint* checkbox to assign a color from the color libraries.

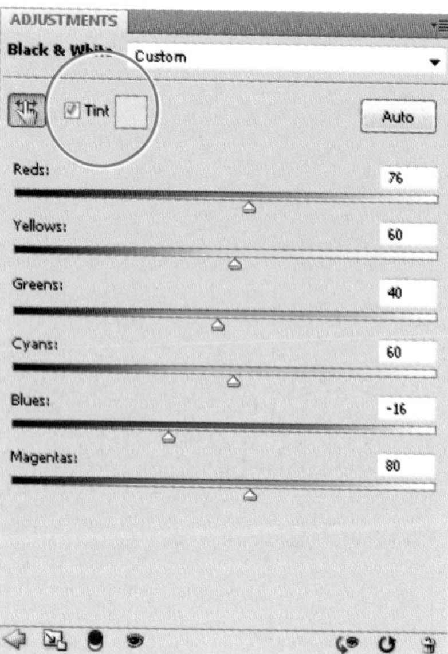

Apply a tint of color in the Black & White adjustment layer.

3 Click once on the Color box to the right of the *Tint* checkbox. The Select Target Color dialog box appears.

4 Press the Color Libraries button; the Color Libraries dialog box appears. From the Book drop-down menu, select Pantone Solid Coated, if it is not already selected.

5 Type **642** quickly, without pausing between typing the numbers. There is no text field in this dialog box, and so, by typing a Pantone number, you can easily locate it in the list of colors. Type too slowly and you could have an inaccurate color selection. You can try it again if Pantone 642 C is not selected. Press OK to close the Color Libraries dialog box. The color tint is assigned Pantone 642 C.

6 Choose File > Save. Leave the file open for the next section of this lesson.

Applying a gradient to the adjustment layer

The next step is a simple one that adds an interesting blending technique for using adjustment layers. By applying a gradient to the mask, you can blend the Black & White effect into a color image.

1 Press **D** on your keyboard to make sure that you are back to the default foreground and background colors of black and white.

2 Click once on the Black & White adjustment layer mask thumbnail to select it.

3 Select the Gradient tool (▣), and type **0**. By typing **0**, you are assigning 100 percent opacity to the gradient.

4 Click and drag from the left side of the image to the right. A gradient is created in the same direction and angle as the line you draw.

When you release the Gradient tool, there is a blend from the black-and-white adjustment to the original color image. If you don't like the angle or transition, you can re-drag the gradient as many times as you want. Click and drag a short line for a shorter gradient transition, or click and drag a longer line for a more gradual transition.

If your colors are opposite to the ones in this example, your foreground and background colors could be reversed. Press **X** to reverse your colors and try again.

Click and drag with the Gradient tool to create a gradient mask.

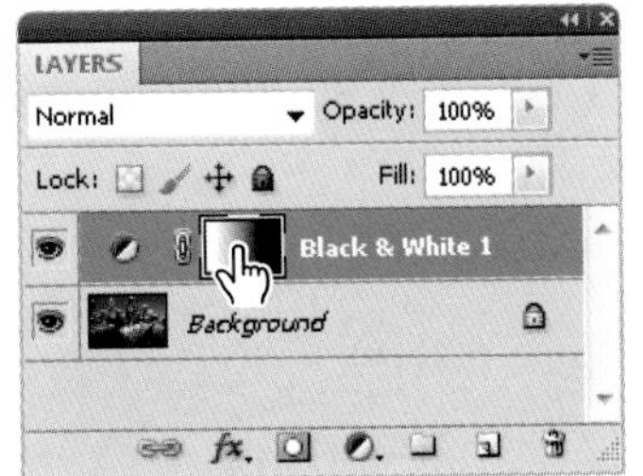

The layer mask.

The Gradient tool can create straight-line, radial, angle, reflected, and diamond blends. Select the type of gradient from the Options bar across the top of the Photoshop work area. If you want to drag a straight gradient line, hold down the Shift key while dragging to constrain the gradient to a 0-degree, 45-degree, or 90-degree angle.

5 Choose File > Save. Keep the file open for the next part of this lesson.

Congratulations! You have completed the Black & White adjustment layer section of this lesson.

Layer styles

By using layer styles, such as shadows, glows, and bevels, you can change the appearance of images on layers. Layer styles are linked to the layer that is selected when the style is applied, but they can also be copied and pasted to other layers. Combinations of styles can also be saved as a custom style to be applied to other layers.

Creating the text layer

In this section, you will create a text layer and apply a combination of effects to it. Then you will save the combined effects as a new style to apply to another layer. You should still have the file ps0903_work.psd open from the last lesson.

1 Select the Type tool (T) and click anywhere on the image. Type **CITY LIGHTS**.

2 Press Ctrl+A (Windows) or Command+A (Mac OS) to select all the text. Alternatively, you can choose Select > All from the menu bar.

Get ready for a three-key command. It may seem awkward if you haven't used this combination before, but it is used in most other Creative Suite applications to resize text visually, and is a huge time-saver.

3 Hold down Ctrl+Shift+> (Greater Than) (Windows) or Command+Shift+> (Mac OS), and repeatedly press the > key. The text enlarges. You can change the combination to include the < (Lesser Than) key to reduce the size of the text. No particular size is needed; you can choose a size that you prefer.

If you would rather not use the key command, type **85** in the font size text field in the Options bar at the top of the Photoshop workspace.

Next, you will find a typeface that you want to use. Again, no particular typeface is required for this exercise. Pick one that you like, but make sure that it is heavy enough to show bevel (edge) effects. The font in the example is Optima Extra Black, but you can choose any available font from your font list.

4 Make sure the Type tool is still active and the text is selected, by pressing Ctrl+A (Windows) or Command+A (Mac OS), or by choosing All from the Select menu.

5 Now, highlight the font family name in the Type tool Options bar at the top of the Photoshop workspace, and press the up- or down-arrow key to scroll through your list of font families.

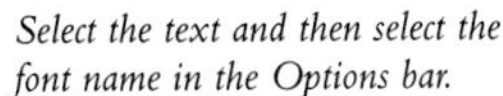

Select the text and then select the font name in the Options bar.

Press the down or up arrows to change the font selection. Your font selection may differ from this example.

If you would rather not use the font shortcut, you can select the font you want from the Font family drop-down menu in the Options bar.

If your Swatches panel is not visible, choose Window > Swatches to bring it forward.

6 With the text still selected, choose White from the Swatches panel. Press the Commit check mark (✓) in the far right of the Options bar to commit your type changes.

Do not leave the Type tool to select the Move tool and reposition the text. If you want to reposition your text, keep the Type tool selected and simply hold down the Ctrl (Windows) or Command (Mac OS) key while dragging.

Applying the Outer Glow layer style

Now you will apply a combination of layer effects to the text layer you just created.

1 Click on the text layer name CITY LIGHTS, which is to the right of the Text layer indicator in the Layers panel, to make sure the layer is active.

2 Click on the Add a Layer Style button (*fx*) at the bottom of the Layers panel, and select Outer Glow from the pop-up menu. The Layer Style dialog box appears. The default settings may be too subtle, so you will make some changes.

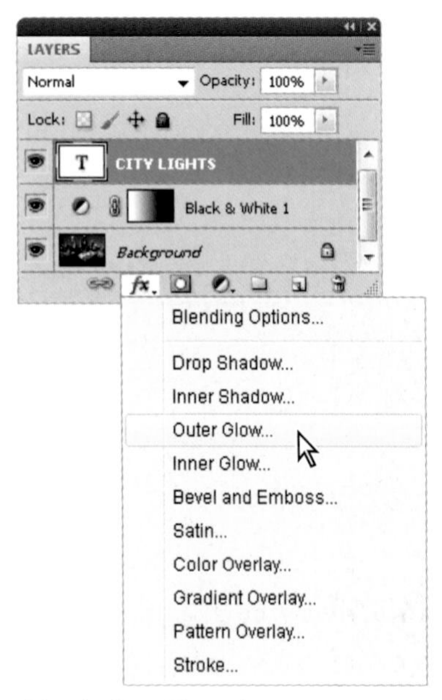

Select the Outer Glow style.

There are many options available for each layer style. As a default, certain blending modes and opacities, as well as spread size and contours (edges), are already determined. In the next step, you will change the contour and the size of the outer glow.

What is a layer style contour?

When you create custom styles, you can use contours to create unique edge effects and transitions. As you can see in the examples shown here, the same style can look very different:

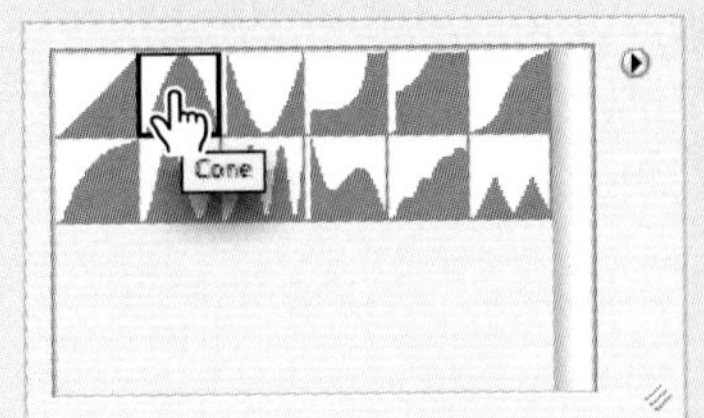

The Cone contour.

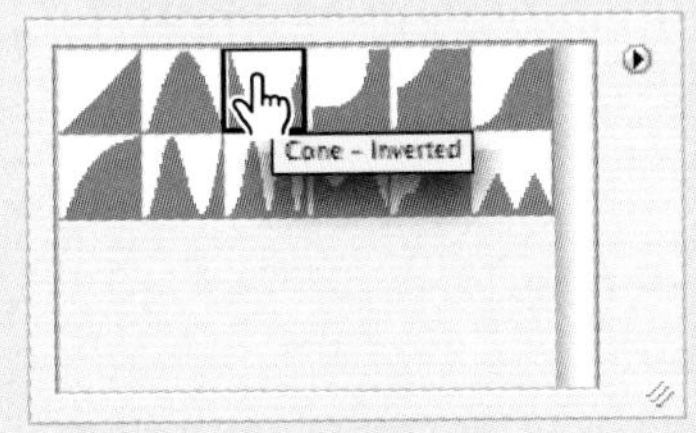

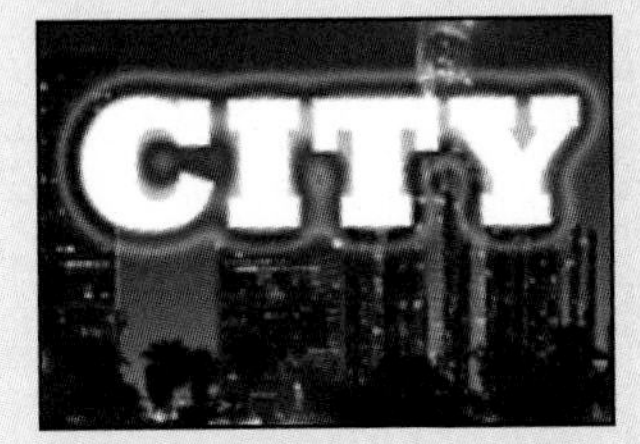

The Cone-Inverted contour.

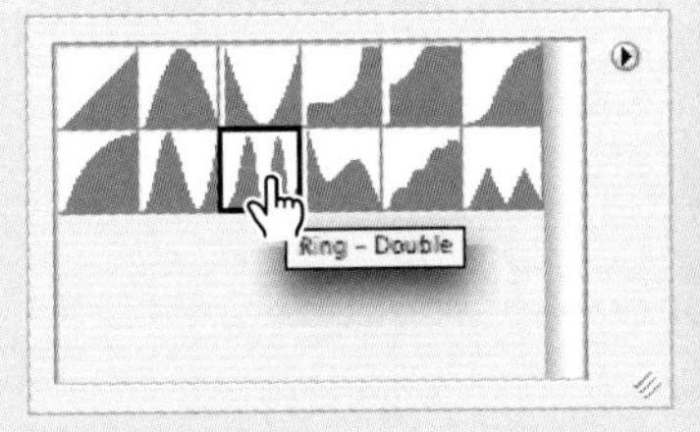

The Ring-Double contour.

3 Select the arrow to the right of the Contour thumbnail in the Quality section of the Layer Style dialog box. The Contour Presets dialog box appears. Click on the Half Round contour. Double-click on the Half Round contour to close the dialog box.

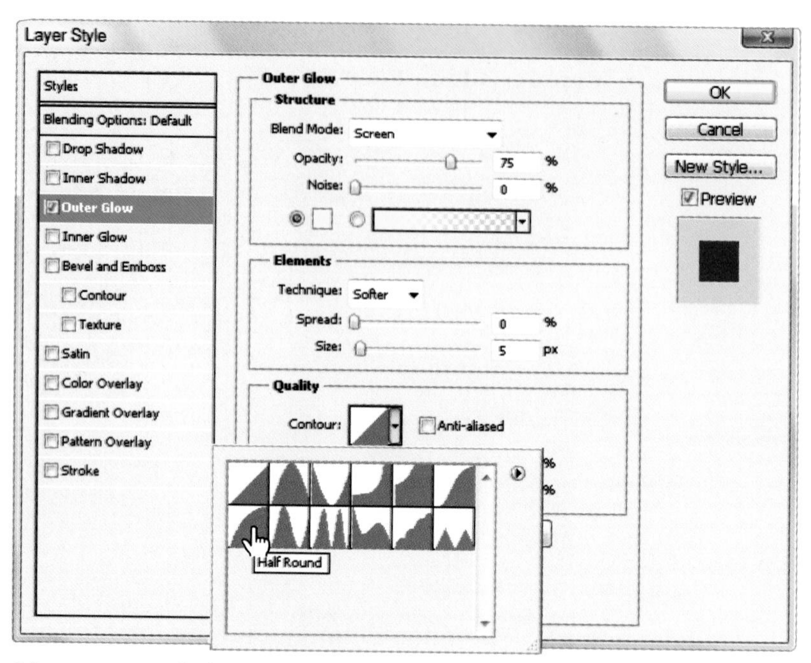

Select a preset contour for the Outer Glow style.

You can open the Contour Editor and create your own custom contours by clicking on the Contour thumbnail instead of selecting the arrow to the right of the thumbnail.

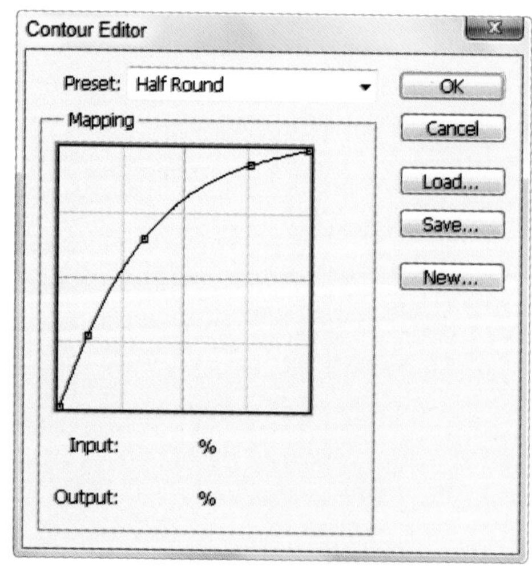

Editing a contour.

Now you will change the size of the outer glow.

4 In the Elements section of the Layer Style dialog box, drag the Size slider to the number 60, or type **60** into the Size text field. The glow becomes more apparent.

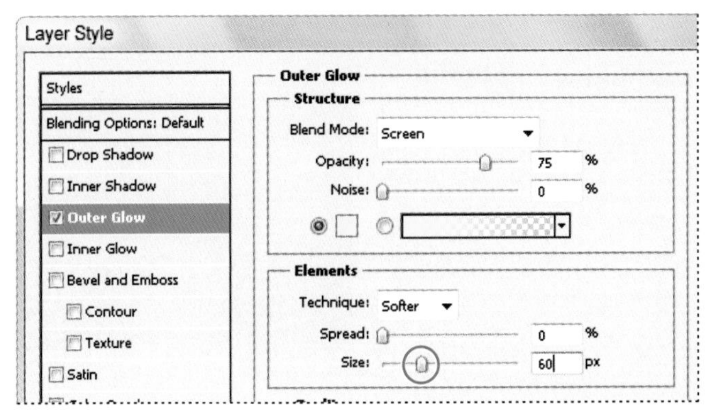

Drag the size slider to 60.

The result.

5 Keep the Layer Style dialog box open for the next step.

Applying the Bevel and Emboss layer style

You will now apply a second style. The Layer Style dialog box should still be open. If it is not, you can double-click on the word Effects in the Layers panel. This reopens the Layer Styles dialog box.

1 Click on Bevel and Emboss in the Styles list on the left side of the Layer Style dialog box. The Bevel and Emboss effect is applied, and the options appear on the right.

If you check a style, the options do not appear on the right. You must click on a style name for its options to appear.

2 From the Style drop-down menu in the Structure section of the Layer Style dialog box, choose Emboss.

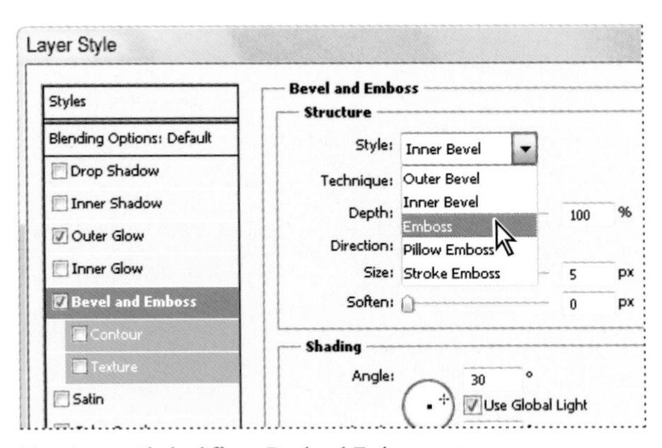

Experiment with the different Bevel and Emboss structures.

The result.

You can experiment with many bevel and embossing styles. You can change the Technique to be Smooth, Chisel Hard, or Chisel Soft, or even direct the embossing to go down or up, using the Direction radio buttons. Experiment with these options; no particular settings are needed for this exercise.

Changing the shading

You will now change the shading. In the Shading section of the Bevel and Emboss Layer Style dialog box, there are several choices that relate to light, including the Angle, Gloss Contour (as discussed earlier), or Highlight and Shadow colors. In this section, you will change the angle of the light and the highlight color.

1 In the Shading section to the right of Angle, there is a Direction of light source slider. You can change the current light angle by clicking and dragging the marker indicating the current light angle. Click and drag the marker to see how it affects the embossing style.

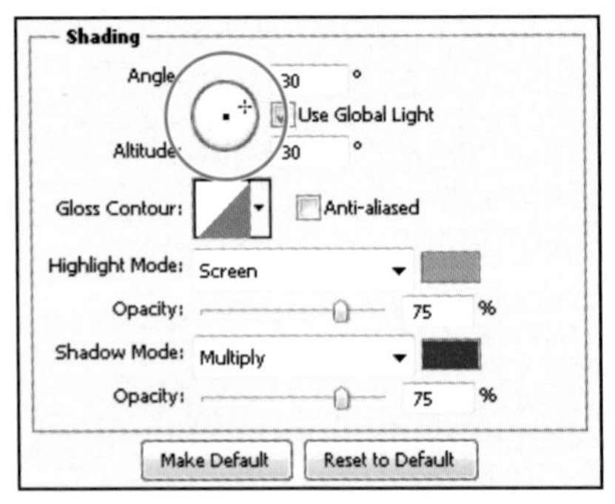

Click and drag inside the circle to change the direction of the light source.

Global light is checked as a default. This assures you that all other effects that rely on a light source use the same angle that you determine for this style.

2 Click and hold to select Normal from the Highlight Mode blending drop-down menu.

3 Now, click on the white box to the right of Highlight Mode. This opens the Select highlight color picker and allows you to sample a color from your image, or create your own highlight color using the Color Picker. Choose any yellow-gold color; in this example, an RGB value of R: 215, G: 155, B: 12 is used. Press OK.

4 Click on the Shadow color box, to the right of Shadow Mode, and change the color to blue. In this example, an RGB value of R: 30, G: 15, B: 176 is used.

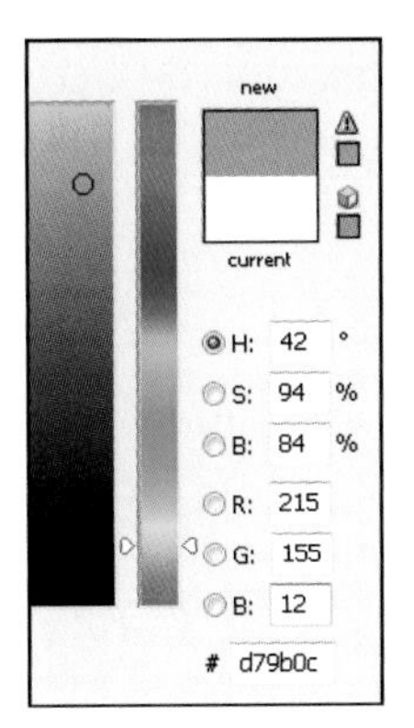

Set a highlight color.

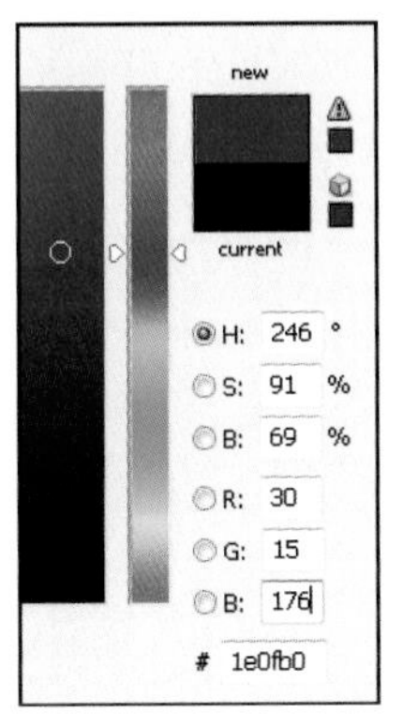

Set a shadow color.

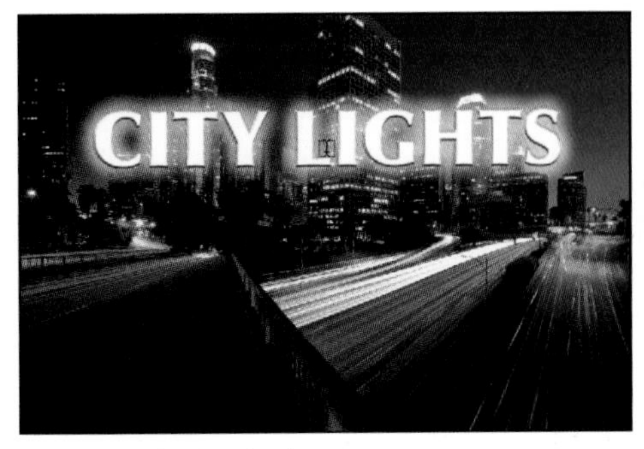

The resulting bevel and emboss.

5 Press OK to close the Color Picker. Keep the Layer Style dialog box open for the final step in this project.

Changing the fill opacity

In addition to setting opacity, which affects layer styles as well as the contents of the layer, you can adjust the fill opacity. The fill opacity affects only the contents of the layer, keeping the opacity of any layer styles that have been applied at the original opacity. This is a very easy method to use to make text look like it is embossed on paper or engraved in stone.

1 Select the Blending Options: Default. This is the top-most item underneath the Styles panel.

2 Click and drag the Fill Opacity slider to the left. In the example, it is dragged to the 20 percent point and click OK. Keep the Layer Style dialog box open for the next part of the lesson.

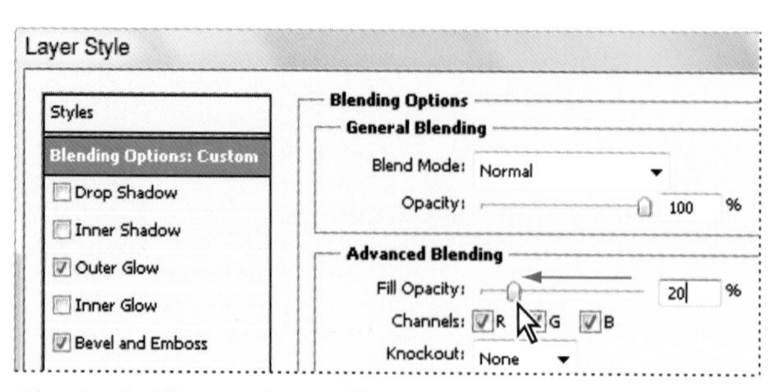

Changing the fill opacity does not affect the layer style opacity.

The result as semi-transparent text.

Saving the style

Now you will save the style you created.

1 With the Layer Styles dialog box still open, click on the New Style button, on the right side of the window. The New Style dialog box appears.

2 Type **my glow** in the Name text field, and press OK.

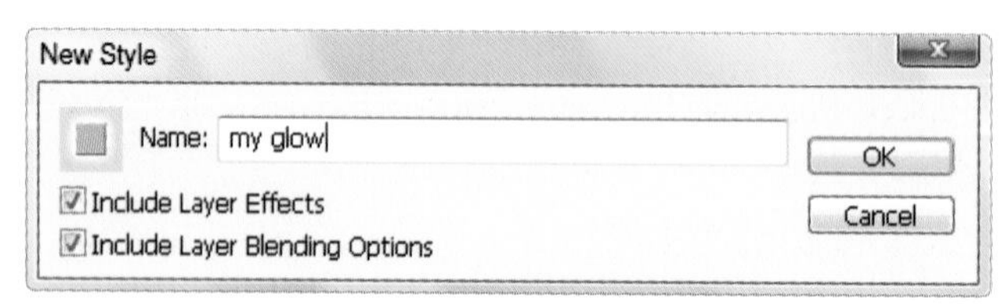

Saving a style from combined styles.

3 Press OK in the Layer Styles dialog box. The style is now added to the Styles panel.

Accessing the style

Now you will create a new shape layer and apply the saved my glow style to it.

1 Click and hold on the Rectangle tool (▭) to select the hidden Custom Shape tool (✱).

2 Make sure that Shape layers is selected in the Options bar at the top of the Photoshop workspace.

3 Click on the arrow to the right of the Custom Shape preview in the Options bar, and double-click on the Light Bulb 2 shape.

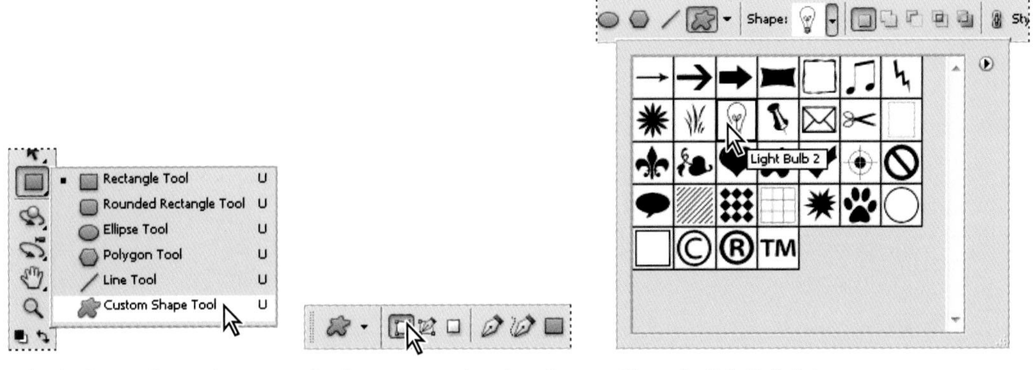

Select the Custom Shape tool. *Confirm you are creating a layer shape.* *Choose the Light Bulb 2 shape.*

4 Press **D** on your keyboard to make sure you are back to the default black-and-white foreground and background colors.

5 Hold down the Shift key (to keep proportions correct), and click and drag in the image area to create the light bulb shape layer.

6 If any effects were automatically applied, delete them by clicking on the Effects sublayer and dragging it to the Delete button (🗑) in the lower-right corner of the Layers panel.

7 If the Styles panel is not visible, choose Window > Styles. The Styles panel appears. It is easier to find your saved style if you view the panel as a list, rather than a thumbnail. You can change the view by selecting the panel menu and choosing Small List.

8 Scroll down if necessary, and then choose my glow.

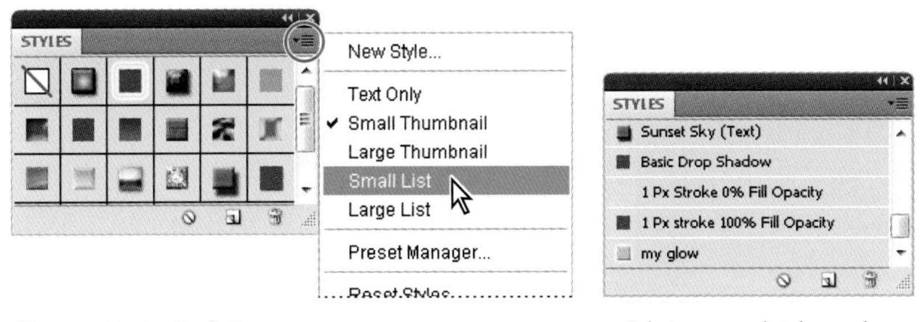

Choose to view by Small List. *Select your saved style, my glow.*

The same style is applied to the light bulb shape. Note that you may be viewing a path outline of the light bulb. Click once on the thumbnail (on the right) of the light bulb layer.

9 Choose File > Save.

Congratulations! You have finished the lesson on maximizing your layers.

Self study

Adjustment layers only affect the layers beneath them, leaving any layers on top of them in the Layers panel unaffected.

1 To experiment with this concept, open the file named ps0905.psd.

2 Select the sky layer and create a Hue/Saturation adjustment layer for it.

3 Drag the Saturation slider all the way to the left, effectively creating an RGB grayscale image. Press OK.

4 Click and drag the adjustment layer up through the layers in the Layers panel to see how the position of the adjustment layer affects the layers beneath.

Review

Questions

1 Name three reasons why you should use an adjustment layer to change color in Photoshop.

2 What can you do to make a pattern fill layer blend in more naturally with the image underneath?

3 What does Global Lighting mean?

Answers

1 **a**. By using an adjustment layer, you keep the original image data intact.

b. Using the Color Picker and a Color adjustment layer, you can choose a specific hue, which you can then change again repeatedly until you get the color you want.

c. You can easily update or change the color by double-clicking on the adjustment layer thumbnail.

2 You can experiment with several blending modes to create a more natural blend with a pattern fill layer. In the example in this lesson, Multiply was selected, but other modes, such as Darken and Lighten, can create interesting results as well.

3 Global Lighting helps to keep the light source consistent between layer styles. This way, the light source for a shadow is the same as for the bevel and emboss, helping the image lighting effects look more realistic.

What you'll learn in this lesson:

- Opening an image as a Smart Object
- Converting a layer to a Smart Object
- Placing and editing a Smart Object
- Replacing the contents of a Smart Object layer

Getting Smart in Photoshop

Using Smart Objects adds more capabilities to Photoshop's non-destructive workflow. In the simplest form, you can use them to retain an image's original information, even after a filter has been applied. You can also place graphics as Smart Objects, convert them to Smart Objects right in Photoshop, and even combine Smart Objects for greater flexibility and creativity.

Starting up

Smart Objects allow you to transform pixel-based layers in new ways: you can scale, transform, and warp images without permanently destroying the original image data. In addition, Smart Objects create a link to their source files, which means that when you make changes to the source files, the Smart Objects are automatically updated with those changes.

Knowledge of Smart Objects will change the way you work with layers. In this lesson, you will find out how to open new images as Smart Objects, in addition to how to convert existing layers into Smart Objects. Throughout this lesson, you will also have the opportunity to place and edit Smart Objects.

Before starting, make sure that your tools and panels are consistent by resetting your preferences. See "Resetting Adobe Photoshop CS5 preferences" on page 3.

You will work with several files from the ps10lessons folder in this lesson. Make sure that you have loaded the pslessons folder onto your hard drive from the supplied DVD. See "Loading lesson files" on page 5.

See Lesson 10 in action!

Use the accompanying video to gain a better understanding of how to use some of the features shown in this lesson. The video tutorial for this lesson can be found on the included DVD.

Creating a composition using Smart Objects

1 Choose File > Browse in Bridge to open Adobe Bridge, or select the Launch Bridge (Br) or Mini Bridge button (Mb) in the Application bar. Navigate to the ps10lessons folder, then double-click on the image named ps1001.psd to open it in Photoshop. Alternatively, you can choose to right-click (Windows) or Ctrl+click (Mac OS) and select Open with Photoshop CS5.

2 Choose File > Save As; the Save As dialog box appears. Navigate to the ps10lessons folder. In the Name text field, type **ps1001_work**, leave the format as Photoshop (PSD), and select Save. Keep the image open for the next section.

3 Open ps1001_done.psd to view the compilation you will create. You can keep this file open for reference, or choose File > Close. If asked, don't save changes.

The starting lesson file.

Opening an image as a Smart Object

In this lesson, you'll compile many images of rainforest animals to create a photo illustration that could be used for a travel advertisement.

One of the defining characteristics of Smart Objects is the ability for layers to be transformed multiple times without the traditional resampling that occurs by default with Photoshop. In this section, you will go through an exercise to help you understand the main difference between a standard Photoshop layer and a Smart Object.

1 Click on the visibility icon (👁) to the left of the type layer named Visit the Rainforests of Palenque. This layer has been locked so that you can't accidentally move it, and it will remain hidden for most of this lesson.

2 Select the Butterfly layer and then select the Move tool (▸+). Choose Edit > Free Transform to scale this layer. Alternatively, you can use the keyboard shortcut Ctrl+T (Windows) or Command+T (Mac OS).

3 Hold the Shift key, and then click and hold the bottom-right corner of the transform box. Drag toward the center of the box to make the box smaller. Holding the Shift key ensures that the width and height are constrained proportionally. In the Options bar at the top of the screen, note that as you scale down, the percentage values begin to decrease. Scale the butterfly until the horizontal values are approximately 25 percent. Press Enter (Windows) or Return (Mac OS) to commit the transformation (you can also press the Commit check mark (✓) on the right side of the Options bar).

You can view the scale percentage in the Options bar.

You have reduced the width and height of this layer by 75 percent. This also means that the original pixel data has been lost through the scaling process (also called downsampling). This creates problems if you decide at some point to make the image on this layer larger.

4 Choose Edit > Free Transform, or use the keyboard shortcut Ctrl+T (Windows) or Command+T (Mac OS), to turn the transform bounding box on again. Press the Shift key, and then click and drag the bottom-right corner of the transform box diagonally downward and to the right to scale the image to approximately 400 percent. Remember to watch the percentage as it changes in the options W (Width) and H (Height) text fields. Press Enter (Windows) or Return (Mac OS) to commit the scale transform.

The butterfly layer after rescaling.

The image is fuzzy and pixelated because you have now enlarged the layer information, forcing Photoshop to fill in pixel information. This is called destructive editing because the original layer lost its detail through the resampling process.

You will now open the same image as a Smart Object so that you can see the benefit of non-destructive editing.

5 Click on the visibility icon (👁) next to the Butterfly layer to turn the layer's visibility off. You will turn it back on shortly so that you can compare the two layers.

6 Choose File > Open As a Smart Object. Navigate to the ps10lessons folder and choose the ps1002.psd file. Press Open to open the image in a new document window. In the Layers panel, note that the thumbnail for the layer is now a Smart Object thumbnail. All Smart Objects have a Smart Object icon in the lower-right corner of the layer thumbnail to help you distinguish them from standard layers.

The image is opened as a Smart Object.

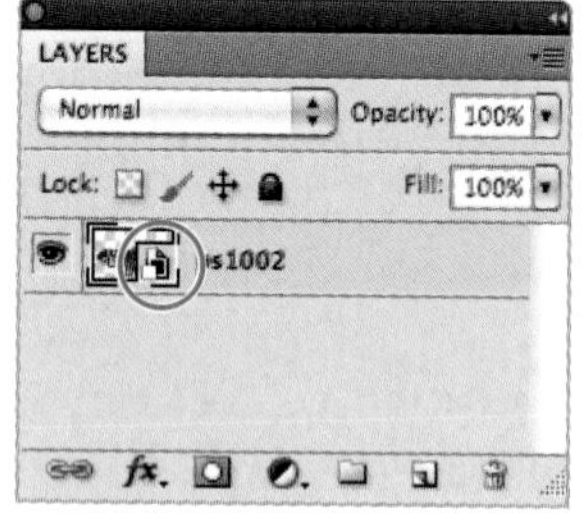

Smart Object icon.

7 Click and hold on the Arrange Documents button on the Application bar, and choose Tile All Vertically from the drop-down menu. This repositions the image windows so that you can see both the ps1001_work.psd and the ps1002.psd images.

8 Select the Move tool (▸+). Click and drag the butterfly image from ps1002.psd into your ps1001_work.psd image, using the Move tool to reposition the new layer at the bottom of the screen. The bottom of the butterfly wings should be touching the bottom of the image.

9 In the Layers panel, double-click directly on the layer name, ps1002. When the layer name becomes highlighted, type **Butterfly 2** and press Enter (Windows) or Return (Mac OS) to commit the change.

10 Click on the tab for the ps1002.psd image to make it active, and choose File > Close. When prompted to save the file, choose to not save the file.

11 In the ps1001_work file, choose Edit > Free Transform or use the keyboard shortcut Ctrl+T (Windows) or Command+T (Mac OS).

12 Press the Shift key, click and hold the top-right corner of the transform box, and drag toward the center of the box. Scale the butterfly down in size until the horizontal value is approximately 25 percent. Press Enter (Windows) or Return (Mac OS) to commit the transformation.

13 Use the keyboard shortcut Ctrl+T (Windows) or Command+T (Mac OS). Press the Shift key, and then click and drag the top-right corner of the transform box away from the center to scale the image up to 100 percent. Press Enter (Windows) or Return (Mac OS) to commit the change.

When scaling Smart Objects, they "remember" their original size in the scale text boxes for Width and Height in the Options panel. This makes it easy for you to control the sizing and not dramatically stretch the image beyond its original size.

14 In the Layers panel, click on the eye icon (👁) to the left of the Butterfly thumbnail. Readjust the layers as needed to compare the two images. Notice that the detail has not been lost, because Smart Objects maintain their original pixel data even if they are scaled and resized.

***A**. Standard layer, scaled and resized. **B**. Smart Object layer, scaled and resized.*

Converting a layer to a Smart Object

In the last exercise, you created a Smart Object by using the Open as Smart Object feature. However, this is not always ideal. For example, perhaps you have a document in which you have already added several layers, and then you realize that you will be performing operations that require the use of Smart Objects. Rather than opening the original images again as Smart Objects, you can convert existing layers to Smart Objects.

1 Drag the Butterfly layer to the Delete button (🗑) at the bottom of the Layers panel. The Butterfly layer is deleted.

2 Select the Butterfly 2 layer in the Layers panel. Choose Edit > Free Transform, or press Ctrl+T (Windows) or Command+T (Mac OS).

3 You will now enter an exact value into the Width and Height text fields in the Options panel. Type **35** into the W (width) text field, and press the Maintain aspect ratio icon (🔗) in between the W and H text fields. Press Enter (Windows) or Return (Mac OS) to commit the transformation. The layer is scaled to 35 percent. Reposition the butterfly to the upper-left corner.

4 In the Layers panel, select the Toucan layer and then click on the visibility icon (👁) next to the left of the Toucan layer thumbnail; the layer is now visible. You will now convert this layer to a Smart Object.

5 Choose Layer > Smart Objects > Convert to Smart Object.

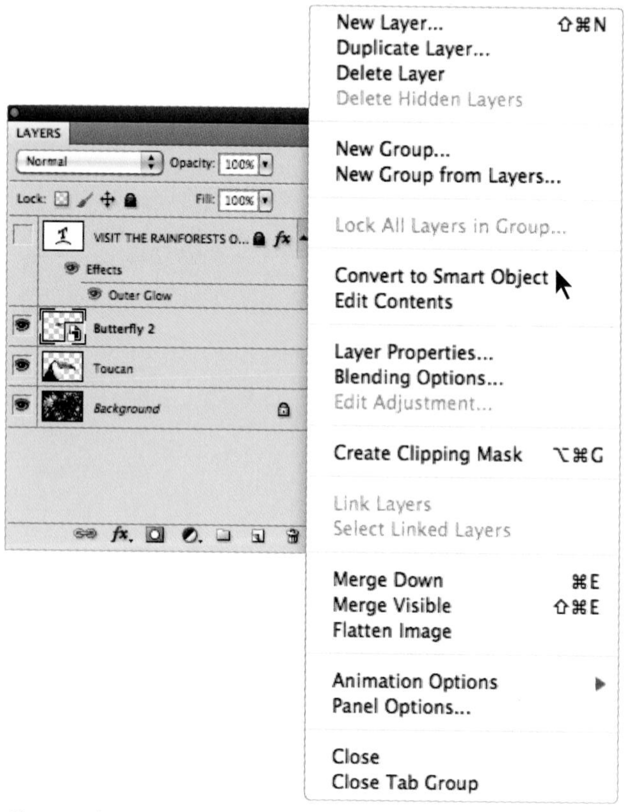

Changing a layer to a Smart Object.

There is no visible change in the image, but the Smart Object icon (▣) in the Toucan layer now appears in the lower-right corner, indicating that it is now a Smart Object.

6 Choose Edit > Free Transform, or use the keyboard shortcut Ctrl+T (Windows) or Command+T (Mac OS) to transform the toucan image. Grab the top-right corner of the bounding box, and, while holding the Shift key, click and drag a corner point to scale it to about three-quarters its current size (75 percent). If necessary, reposition the image in the lower-left corner. Press Enter (Windows) or Return (Mac OS) to commit the change.

Placing a Smart Object

In addition to opening new documents as Smart Objects, and converting existing layers to Smart Objects, you can also use the Place feature to import an image as a Smart Objects

1 Choose File > Place; the Place dialog box appears. Navigate to the ps10lessons folder, select the ps1004.psd file, and press Place. This places the parrot image into your ps1001_work.psd file.

   When documents are placed, they become Smart Objects by default. Note the large X on the layer; this is a bounding box that allows you to transform the Smart Object before confirming the placement.

2 Click and drag the parrot image until the bottom-right corner snaps against the bottom-right corner of your work file. Hold the Shift key, and then click on the top-left anchor point of the transform bounding box. With the Shift key still pressed, click and drag toward the center to scale the image down in size. Scale the parrot until the top is approximately even with the top of the toucan image.

Scale the parrot so that it is approximately the same size as the toucan.

3 Select the Commit check mark (✓) in the Options bar, or press Enter (Windows) or Return (Mac OS) to commit the change. Remember that because this is a Smart Object by default, you can scale it back to its original size and still retain the original detail.

4 In the Layers panel, double-click the layer name, ps1004. When the layer name becomes highlighted, type the name **Parrot**.

Editing a Smart Object

There are additional benefits to Smart Objects besides their ability to be resized without loss of detail. To fully understand these benefits, you should know a little bit about how Smart Objects work. When a layer is a Smart Object, Photoshop preserves the original content of the source file by embedding it into the current file. In this exercise, you will learn how to edit the contents of Smart Objects. You will also find out how multiple Smart Object layers can be modified at the same time, how to replace the source for Smart Objects, and even how to export the contents of a Smart Object.

1 Choose File > Open As Smart Object. Navigate to the ps10lessons folder, select the ps1005.psd file, and press Open to open the image in a new window. Notice that the title bar of the window reads ps1005 as Smart Object-1. This is not the original file, but rather a copy of the original file.

An image opened as a Smart Object.

2 Click on the Arrange Documents button (▦) on the Application bar, and choose Tile All Vertically from the drop-down menu.

3 Select the Move tool (▸+), then click and drag the butterfly image into your ps1001_work.psd image. Note that the layer is named ps1005 and has the Smart Object thumbnail.

4 In the Layers panel, double-click on the layer name, ps1005. When the text becomes highlighted, type **Butterfly 3**. Press Enter (Windows) or Return (Mac OS).

5 Select the ps1005.psd image, and choose File > Close, or select the Close button in the document window. When prompted to save the file, choose to not save the file. The Smart Object file is separate from the original and is essentially embedded inside the ps1001_work.psd file.

6 In your ps1001_work.psd file, select the Butterfly 3 layer and, using the Move tool (✥), drag it to the center of the image window. Choose Edit > Free Transform, or use the keyboard shortcut Ctrl+T (Windows) or Command+T (Mac OS). Click and hold the Shift key while dragging any corner anchor point. Scale the butterfly to approximately 20 percent. Press Enter (Windows) or Return (Mac OS) to commit the change. Reposition the butterfly to the upper-right corner.

This is a large image. If you cannot see the edges of the Butterfly 3 smart object, type ***20*** *into the W and H text boxes in the Options panel at the top of the workspace.*

7 Choose Image > Adjustments. Note that virtually all the options are grayed out. This is because image adjustments such as Levels and Curves are destructive by nature. Release the mouse without making a choice.

8 Click on the Brush tool (🖌). Position your cursor over the image. Don't click, but notice that the non-editable icon (⊘) appears. You cannot paint on this layer because that would be destructive.

So, what if you need to modify the layer? Perhaps you want to selectively dodge and burn parts of the image or use image adjustment commands. You have two choices when working with Smart Objects:

- Edit the original in its own separate window.
- Rasterize the Smart Object layer before using common editing tools.
- For this example, you will rasterize the Smart Object. Using the term *rasterize* is actually confusing in this instance. The image is already a raster image (composed of pixels), but the term refers to the step of *unsmarting* your image and putting the original pixels back into the ps1001_work.psd image.

You can apply any changes made in the Adjustments panel to a Smart Object without having to edit the original, or rasterize the image.

9 Select the Blur tool (💧) from the Tools panel. Click anywhere on the butterfly; a warning dialog box appears, informing you that the layer will be rasterized. Press OK to rasterize the image.

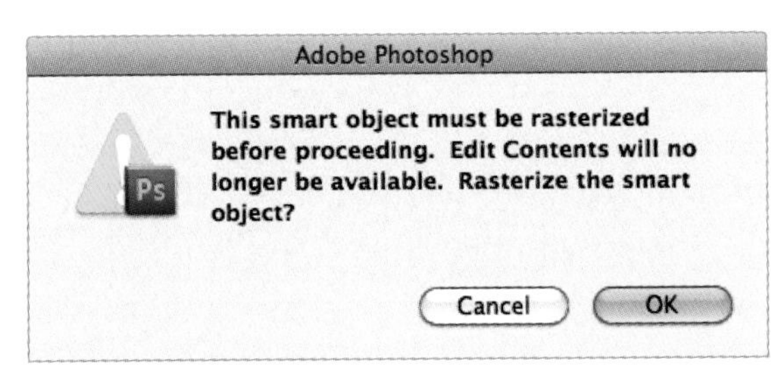

Press OK to rasterize the layer.

10 Using the Zoom tool (🔍), zoom in closer to the butterfly, and click and drag the Blur tool several times over the edges of the butterfly to see the blur effect. You are now able to edit the image because it has been converted to pixels. However, it has also lost its Smart Object status.

All the editing tools, such as Dodge, Burn, Clone Stamp, and Eraser, are destructive and therefore not usable when a Smart Object layer is active.

11 Press Ctrl+0 (Windows) or Command+0 (Mac OS) to zoom make the image window fit your screen.

12 Choose Edit > Free Transform, or use the keyboard shortcut Ctrl+T (Windows) or Command+T (Mac OS). While holding the Shift key, click and drag any corner anchor point to make the layer larger. Scale until you see approximately 300 percent in the W (width) and H (height) text fields in the Options bar. Press Enter (Windows) or Return (Mac OS) to commit the transformation. The butterfly is slightly blurry now because the standard rules of resampling apply.

13 Drag the Butterfly 3 layer to the Delete icon (🗑) in the Layers panel. You will be adding the layer again in the next exercise.

Editing the contents of a Smart Object

In the last exercise, you saw how you could modify a Smart Object by rasterizing the layer. The problem with this method is that rasterizing the layer removes the unique characteristics of the Smart Object layer. Using the method shown, you will edit the contents of the embedded Smart Object without changing its Smart Object status.

1 Choose File > Place, and navigate to the ps10lessons folder. Select the ps1005.psd file and click Place. The butterfly image appears in your screen.

2 Holding the Shift key, click and drag any corner anchor point towards the center until you see an amount close to 25 percent in the W and H text fields in the Options bar, or type **25** into the W and H text boxes. Reposition the butterfly to the upper-right corner of the image. Press Enter (Windows) or Return (Mac OS) to commit the change.

3 In the Layers panel, double-click on the layer name, ps1005, to highlight the text name. Type **Butterfly 4** and press Enter (Windows) or Return (Mac OS).

4 Now, double-click the Butterfly 4 layer thumbnail in the Layers panel (do not click on the layer name or the layer itself, but specifically on the Smart Object thumbnail). A dialog box appears, reminding you that you need to save the document after you edit the contents. Press OK. The ps1005.psd file is now open on your screen.

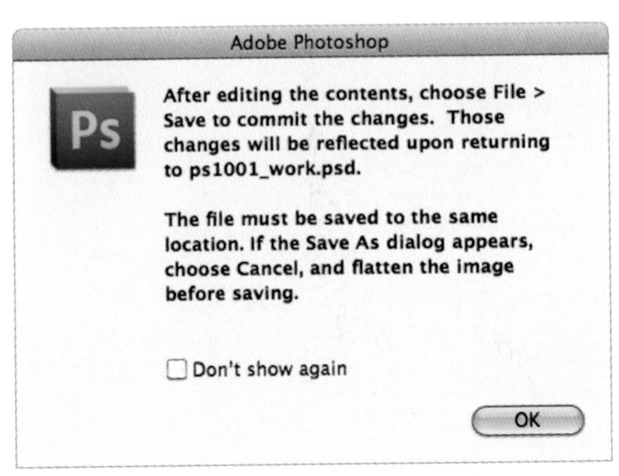

A warning dialog box appears when you edit a Smart Object.

By double-clicking on the Smart Object layer, you open the original file as a separate document. You'll now make some adjustments to the original image. In this case, you will be adjusting the hue and saturation.

5 Press the Create New Fill or Adjustment Layer button (◐) at the bottom of the Layers panel, and choose Hue/Saturation from the menu.

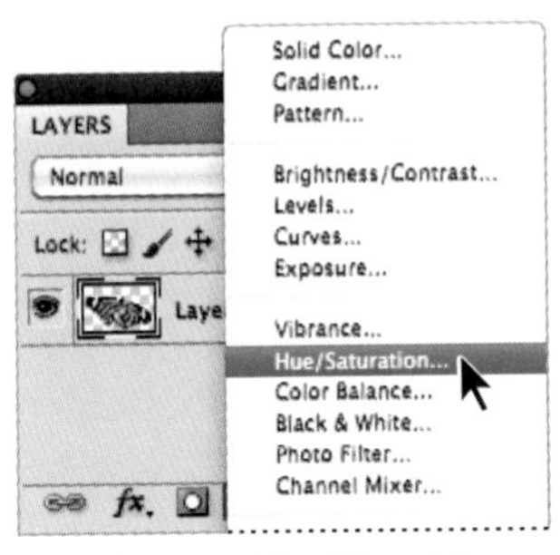

Select the Create New Fill or Adjustment Layer button.

The Adjustments panel appears with the Hue/Saturation settings visible. Using an adjustment layer ensures that your original pixel data remains untouched.

6 Drag the Hue slider to the left to approximately the -180 mark, or type **-180** in the Hue text box. This adjusts the color of the butterfly to blue.

7 Choose File > Save. This is the crucial step. As noted in the dialog box in step 4, you must save the current document without renaming it. Choose File > Close to close the image.

8 In the ps1001_work.psd file, notice that the blue butterfly has been updated. This is because Butterfly 4 is a Smart Object layer connected, or linked, to the original file, which is now embedded inside the ps1001_work.psd file.

9 Double-click on the Butterfly 4 layer thumbnail to reopen the source file. The warning dialog box you saw previously appears. Press OK.

This dialog box can be turned off by clicking the Don't Show Again *checkbox in the lower-left corner.*

10 If necessary, click the adjustment layer icon on the Hue/Saturation layer (in the Layers panel) to reopen the Adjustments panel with the Hue/Saturation options visible.

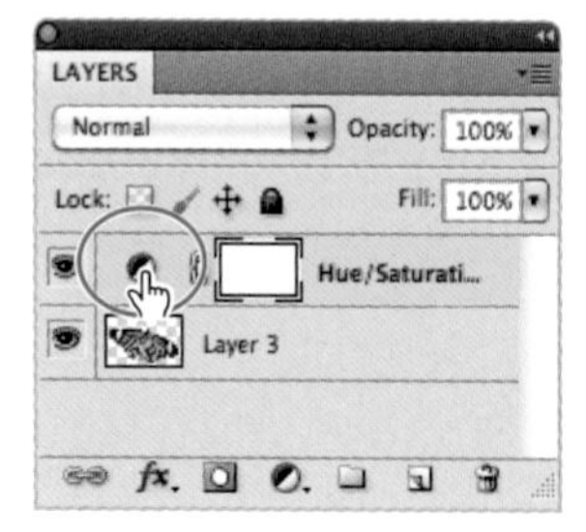

Select to make a edit an existing adjustment.

11 Click and drag the Saturation slider to –60, or type **–60** in the Saturation text field. This tones down the bright blue.

12 Choose File > Save, and then File > Close to close the file.

Using this combination of adjustment layers and Smart Objects allows you to have a tremendous amount of flexibility with your layers. Adjustment layers and Smart Objects encourage you to experiment without fear of destroying the integrity of the original image. As you will see in the next exercise, this ability to edit the contents of a Smart Object has even more power when you have multiple Smart Objects.

Modifying multiple Smart Object layers

Another benefit of Smart Object layers is that multiple layers can be modified at the same time.

1 In the main composition, ps1001_work.psd, click and drag the Butterfly 4 layer down to the Create a New Layer button (◻) in the Layers panel to duplicate it. Select the Move tool (▸+), then click and drag the copy to the far left, next to the yellow butterfly.

Duplicate the Butterfly 4 layer.

You can also duplicate layers by choosing Layer > Smart Objects > New Smart Objects Via Copy.

2 In the Layers panel, double-click the layer name, Butterfly 4 Copy. When the layer name becomes highlighted, type **Butterfly 5** to rename the layer.

3 Double-click on the Butterfly 5 layer thumbnail in the Layers panel to open the original ps1005.psd image. Press OK to dismiss the Save dialog box if necessary. You will now add a Curves adjustment layer to increase the contrast of both butterflies.

4 Press the Create New Fill or Adjustment Layer button (◐) at the bottom of the Layers panel, and choose Curves from the menu. The Curves adjustment appears.

5 Position your cursor in the middle of the curves graph, then click and drag the line upward and to the left to increase the brightness and contrast. If you would like to match the image in this example, type an Input value of **105** and an Output value of **138**.

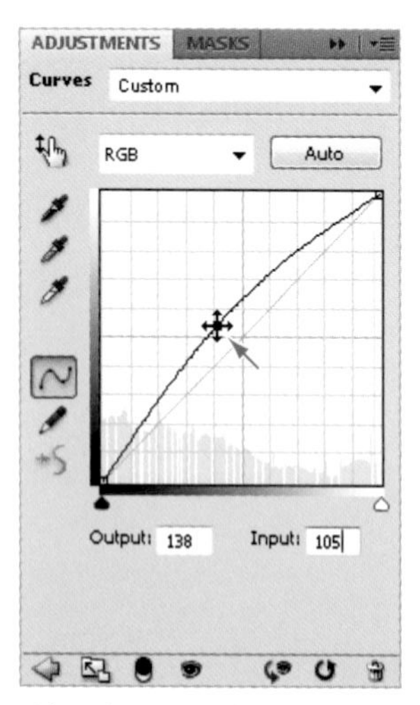

Adjust the curve in the Adjustments panel.

6 Choose File > Save, and then File > Close to close the file. Both butterflies are now brighter. Multiple Smart Object layers can be linked to the same source file. When the source file is changed in some way, all the linked files also change.

Replacing the contents of a Smart Object layer

Because multiple Smart Object layers can be controlled by the original file, you will now take it a step further and change the source file of the two Smart Object layers. To understand the usefulness of this exercise, imagine that you have created several butterflies and rotated, resized, and warped them in different ways. A replacement image is found, and instead of having to delete the existing layers and repeat the same steps, you can simply replace the existing butterfly image with a new one, and all the transformations will stay the same.

1 In your ps1001_work.psd image, click on Butterfly 5 in the Layers panel. Then select Edit > Free Transform, or use the keyboard shortcut Ctrl+T (Windows) or Command+T (Mac OS), to transform the first butterfly in the left corner. Hold the Shift key, click the top-left anchor point of the transform bounding box, and drag downward and to the right, scaling the image down to approximately 15 percent.

2 Position your cursor slightly above and to the right of the top-right corner anchor point. A cursor with a rounded arrow appears. Click and drag to the left to rotate the image approximately –45 degrees. Reposition the image slightly to the right of the yellow butterfly. Press Enter (Windows) or Return (Mac OS) to commit the transformation.

Both the scaling and rotating are tracked in the Options panel.

3 Select the Butterfly 4 layer in the Layers panel. Press Ctrl+T (Windows) or Command+T (Mac OS) to transform the layer. You will now use Photoshop's Warp feature to simulate the butterfly moving through the air.

4 Choose Edit > Transform > Warp. Feel free to create your own warping effect; for this effect, you would click and drag the top-left corner down and to the right until the wing begins to curl.

Clicking and dragging the warp handles to warp the image.

5 Press Enter (Windows) or Return (Mac OS) when you are satisfied with the effect.

Now you will replace the two butterflies with a new image, while maintaining the transformations you created.

6 With the Butterfly 4 layer still selected, choose Layer > Smart Objects > Replace Contents. Locate the ps10lessons folder, select ps1006.psd, and press Place. Both the images update automatically, while retaining their individual transformations.

Replacing Smart Objects.

This technique can be extremely helpful, because it saves you from having to repeat similar steps.

Working with Smart Filters

Now that you have a good foundation for Smart Objects, the concept of Smart Filters shouldn't be too hard to follow. A Smart Filter is simply one of the Photoshop filters applied to a Smart Object layer. Filters are usually destructive—that is, any effect applied to a layer becomes more difficult to remove. When you use a Smart Filter, any filter you apply is not permanent. Effects can be toggled off and on, combined, or deleted. As you will see in this exercise, you can work with the built-in mask of a filter effect to customize your filter effects in ways that were previously not possible in Photoshop.

In this exercise, you will be applying a combination of two filters to create an effect of motion, then you will use the layer mask to refine the effect with the Brush tool.

1 Select the Butterfly 4 layer, and choose Filter > Sharpen > Smart Sharpen. The Smart Sharpen dialog box appears. Change the Amount value to 200 percent and the Radius to 1.0; then press OK. A dramatic sharpen effect is applied; the butterfly should now show more detail.

2 In the Layers panel, below the Butterfly 4 layer, there is a Smart Filter listed with a white thumbnail to the left. Immediately below that is the Smart Sharpen filter effect. These two lines were automatically added when you applied the filter. You will now examine how they work.

3 Click on the visibility icon (👁) next to the Smart Sharpen filter effect. This turns the Smart Sharpen filter off and allows you to view the original image. Click in the now-empty space to toggle the filter back on.

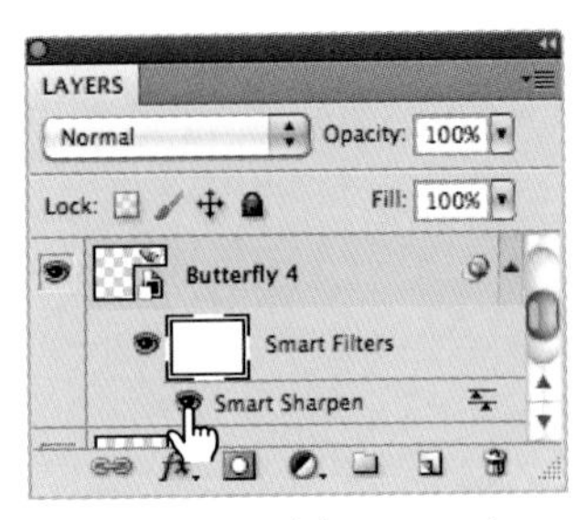

Clicking on the visibility icon toggles a filter effect on and off.

You will now add a Blur filter in addition to the Smart Sharpen filter.

4 Choose Filter > Blur > Motion Blur. You may have to click and drag down and to the left inside the filter preview window to see the image. In the Motion Blur window, type **50** in the Distance text field. This creates a blur of 50 pixels in both directions. Now you will change the angle of the blur.

5 Click on the right side of the angle dial, and then click and drag counter-clockwise until the angle value is approximately –65 degrees; then press OK. Don't worry about how the effect looks; you will be editing it shortly. The Motion Blur effect is now above the Smart Sharpen effect.

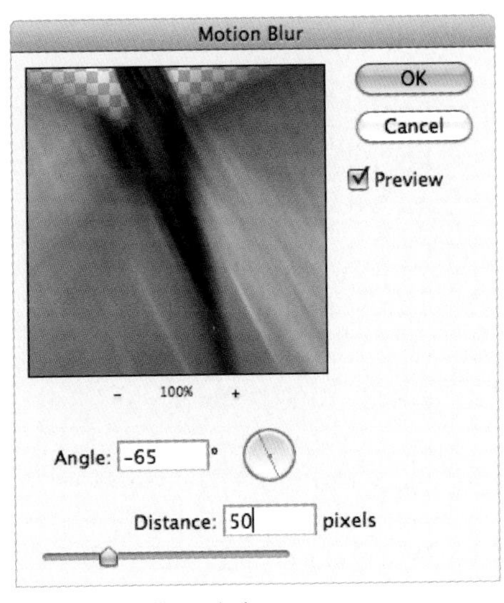

Apply a motion blur to the layer.

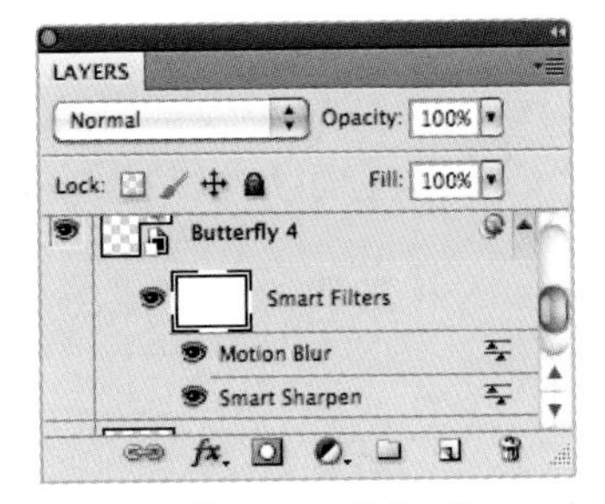

Two smart filters are applied to the same layer.

6 Click on the eye icon to the left of the Motion Blur effect. The Smart Sharpen effect is still active; it is just hidden by the blur. Click the eye icon in the Motion Blur line to bring the Motion Blur effect back.

This feature of Smart Filters is great, but what if you want only part of the filter to be applied to the layer? In this example, combining Sharpen and Blur filters doesn't make much sense. However, with a bit of masking, you can allow certain areas to remain sharp, while other areas are blurred.

7 Select the white thumbnail in the line marked Smart Filters, immediately above the two filter effects. This is the default layer mask that is created whenever you add a Smart Filter. It will allow you to mask out the areas where you don't want the filter effects to appear, while leaving the areas you do want filtered alone.

8 Select the Brush tool (✓) and click and hold on the arrow to the right of the Brush Preset picker in the Options bar. Select the Soft Round brush preset, and use the slider to change the Size value to approximately 45. Click on the Options bar to make the Brush Preset picker disappear.

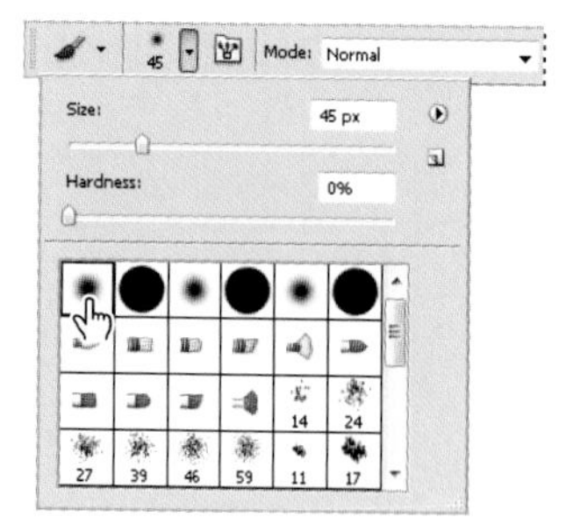

Select the Soft Round brush and change the size to 45.

For more information about working with Photoshop brushes, please review Chapter 6, "Painting and Retouching."

9 Press **D** on your keyboard to revert the foreground and background colors back to the default of black and white. Press **X** on your keyboard to swap the foreground and background colors. Black is now the foreground color and white is the background color.

10 Place your brush at the top of the butterfly, and begin painting from left to right and then downward. As you paint, the filter effects are concealed by the layer mask you are adding.

For an in-depth look at layer masks, please review Chapters 8, "Getting to Know Layers."

11 Continue painting downward until the bottom half of the butterfly is blurred. Press the letter **X** on your keyboard to swap the foreground color to white. Now, paint over the top half again, and notice how the effect is revealed again. By toggling between white and black, and painting on the Smart Filter mask, you can reveal or conceal the filter effects.

Paint on the butterfly.

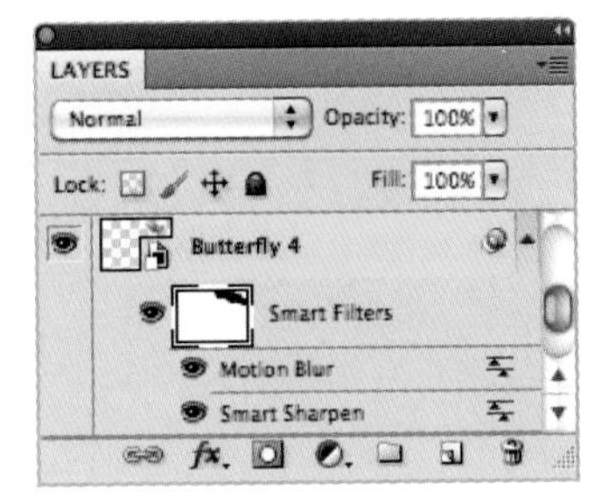

The resulting mask.

12 Press **X** on your keyboard to set black as the foreground color, and then paint the mask to hide virtually all the filter effect at the top part of the image. There are also areas at the bottom that you will want to hide. You want your Butterfly 4 layer to look approximately the same as the example shown here. The effect is still not exactly what you desire, but, in the next section, you will fine-tune the motion blur effect.

The Butterfly 4 layer at this point.

Modifying a Smart Filter

Once you add a Smart Filter, you can go back and modify the effect, even if you've added a mask, as in this case.

1 In the Butterfly 4 layer, double-click on the Motion Blur effect; the Motion Blur dialog box appears. You may have to click and drag down and to the left inside the filter preview window to see the image. Change the angle to 87 degrees by clicking and dragging the dial to the right. Press OK when you are done.

   Changing the angle of the motion blur now requires you to go back with the paintbrush and modify the mask.

2 Click on the layer mask thumbnail to the left of Smart Filters to activate it. Then begin to paint from the top down, leaving just a blur at the bottom of the butterfly. If you mask out too much of the effect, you can press X to switch to white as the foreground color to restore the effect in the desired areas.

3 Click on the eye icon (👁) next to the Smart Filter mask. This turns the mask off completely, and can help identify areas affected by a filter that you may have missed. Click to turn the mask back on and clean up any areas where you don't want the filter applied.

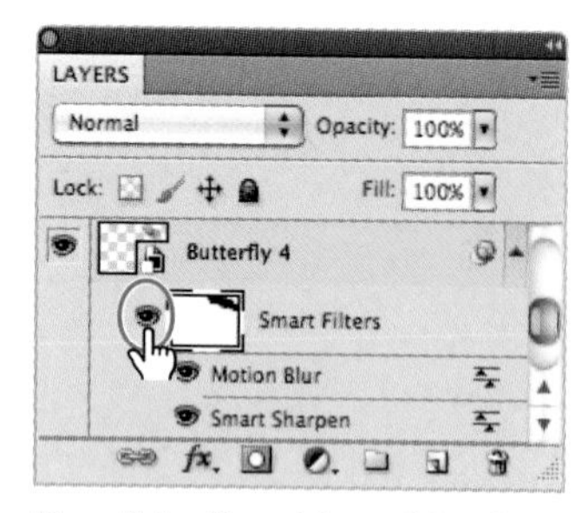

Turn off the effects of the mask by selecting the eye icon.

4 In the Layers panel, click on the eye icon to the left of the Visit the Rainforests type layer on the top. Select the Move tool, and then click and drag to reposition the layers as needed.

5 Choose File > Save. Congratulations! You have finished this part of the lesson.

The completed lesson file.

Self study

In this section, you can complete some exercises on your own. Use adjustment layers to adjust the brightness, contrast, hue, and saturation of the lesson files.

Currently, the individual butterfly and bird images do not blend as well into the background as they could. Using the techniques laid out in "Editing the contents of a Smart Object," add adjustment layers to the objects in the photo-illustration, and fine-tune the appearance of the individual objects. Try to make the individual layers match each other as much as possible to create a cohesive photo illustration.

Creating multiple Smart Objects

In this lesson, you learned how to work with Smart Objects in their various forms. Create additional copies of the butterfly or bird images, and experiment with creating a collage. Apply filters to your existing Smart Objects. For different effects, try applying a black-to-white gradient on a Smart Filter mask to achieve a smooth transition that would be difficult to achieve using just the Brush tool alone.

Working with Illustrator files

If you have Adobe Illustrator, you can also place .ai files into Photoshop files as Smart Object layers. They work in similar ways. Create an image in Illustrator, and place it into Photoshop. Create multiple copies of the Illustrator layer, and then modify the original .ai file to see the changes applied to the layers in the Photoshop file.

Review

Questions

1 What are three ways that you can create a Smart Object layer?

2 Why would you convert a standard layer to a Smart Object layer?

3 How do you replace the contents of a Smart Object layer? When would you do so?

4 What are Smart Filters, and what are the benefits of using them?

Answers

1 You can bring an image into an existing file as a Smart Object by choosing File > Open as Smart Object and selecting the file, choosing File > Place, or, when using Adobe Bridge, selecting the file and choosing File > Place > Into Photoshop. If an image is currently inside a document and you would like to convert it to a Smart Object, select the layer in the Layers panel and choose Layer > Smart Objects > Convert to Smart Objects.

2 A Smart Object layer can be resized indefinitely without losing resolution due to resampling.

3 You can replace the contents of a Smart Object layer by choosing Layer > Smart Objects > Replace Contents. You might use this technique if you wanted to replace one image with another without losing any scaling, rotating or warping you had created for the image.

4 Any filter applied to a Smart Object is a Smart Filter. Smart Filters appear in the Layers panel below the Smart Object layer to which they are applied. Because you can adjust, remove, or hide Smart Filters, they are non-destructive.

What you'll learn in this lesson:

- Working with filters
- Fading filter effects
- Using the Filter Gallery
- Taking advantage of Smart Filters
- Using Vanishing Point

Using Adobe Photoshop Filters

Filters allow you to apply artistic effects to your images. You can make images look as though they were sketched with chalk, drawn with a graphic pen, or even add perspective to them. In this lesson, you will learn how to use filters to apply interesting effects to your images.

Starting up

Before starting, make sure that your tools and panels are consistent by resetting your preferences. See "Resetting Adobe Photoshop CS5 preferences" on page 3.

You will work with several files from the ps11lessons folder in this lesson. Make sure that you have loaded the pslessons folder onto your hard drive from the supplied DVD. See "Loading lesson files" on page 5.

See Lesson 11 in action!

Use the accompanying video to gain a better understanding of how to use some of the features shown in this lesson. The video tutorial for this lesson can be found on the included DVD.

Filter basics

Filters are accessed using the Filter menu. When you select certain filters, the Filter Gallery opens. Other filters, when selected, open their own dedicated dialog box. Some, like the Clouds filter, don't even have a dialog box.

Filters are always applied to the layer you currently have selected and cannot be applied to Bitmap mode or indexed color images. Note that some filters, such as Brush Strokes and Sketch, work only in the RGB mode and are not available when working in the CMYK mode.

Starting to use filters

Before starting, you may want to view the file that you are going to create.

1 Choose File > Browse in Bridge, or select the Launch Bridge (Br) or the Mini Bridge button (Mb) in the Application bar, to open Adobe Bridge. Navigate to the ps11lessons folder and open the file ps1101_done.psd.

A file including several monsters and a package design appears.

The completed lesson file.

2 You can keep this file open for reference, or choose File > Close to close it.

Using the Clouds filter

In this lesson, you will use the Clouds filter to build a smoke-like background. The Clouds filter generates a cloud pattern, using random values from the selected foreground and background colors.

1 Choose File > Browse in Bridge, or select the Launch Bridge (Br) or the Mini Bridge button (Mb) in the Application bar, to open Adobe Bridge. Navigate to the ps11lessons folder and open the file ps1101.psd.

2 Choose File > Save As. In the Save As dialog box, navigate to the ps11lessons folder and type **ps1101_work** in the File name text field. Choose Photoshop from the format drop-down menu and click Save.

3 If the Layers panel is not visible, select Window > Layers. Click on the layer named *sky background* to activate this layer.

4 Many filters in Photoshop render differently, depending on your current foreground and background colors. Press **D** on your keyboard to return to the default colors of black and white.

Select the sky background layer

5 At the bottom of the Tools panel, click the foreground color, black. The Color Picker opens.

6 In the RGB text fields, type the values, R: **55**, G: **71**, B: **92**. Then press OK. Your foreground color has been changed. You are now ready to apply the Clouds filter.

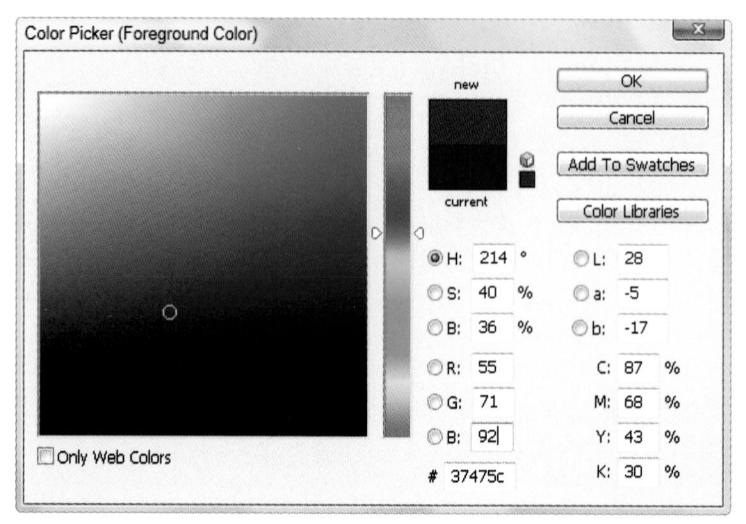

Enter custom values in the Color Picker.

7 Choose Filter > Render > Clouds.

A cloud pattern is generated, using random values of the foreground and background colors. Do not save your file, continue to the next part of this lesson.

To achieve a more high-contrast effect, press the Alt then Shift keys (Windows) or the Option key (Mac OS) while selecting the Clouds filter.

Fading your filter

Now that you have made some clouds, you'll fade the effect of the Cloud filter. The Fade command gives you the opportunity to change the opacity and blending mode of a filter effect immediately after you have applied it. Fade also works with the erasing, painting, and color adjustment tools.

1 Choose Edit > Fade Clouds. The Fade dialog box appears. Check the *Preview* option to preview the effect if it is not already checked.

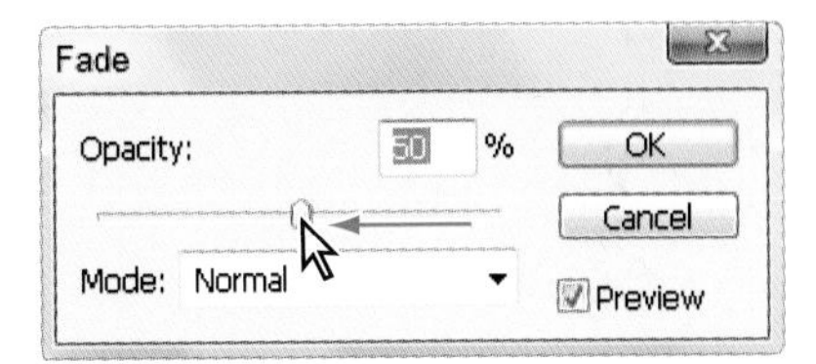

The Fade dialog box.

If Fade Clouds is not available, you did something else with the file after using the Clouds filter. Use the Window > History panel to select the Clouds state, then select Edit > Fade Clouds again.

2 Drag the slider to the left to adjust the opacity from 100 percent down to 50 percent. Leave the Mode drop-down menu set to Normal, then press OK. Keep this file open for the next part of this lesson.

Fading the effect of the Cloud filter.

Using the Filter Gallery

The Filter Gallery allows you to apply more than one filter to an image at a time, and rearrange the order in which the filters are applied.

Note that not all filters are available in the Filter Gallery, and that the Filter Gallery is not available in CMYK, Lab, or Bitmap mode.

1 With ps1101_work.psd open, click the visibility icon (👁) next to the layer group named monsters. Three monsters appear.

2 Expand the layer group by clicking on the triangle immediately to the left of the monsters layer group. This displays the monster1, monster2, and monster3 layers that are included in this group.

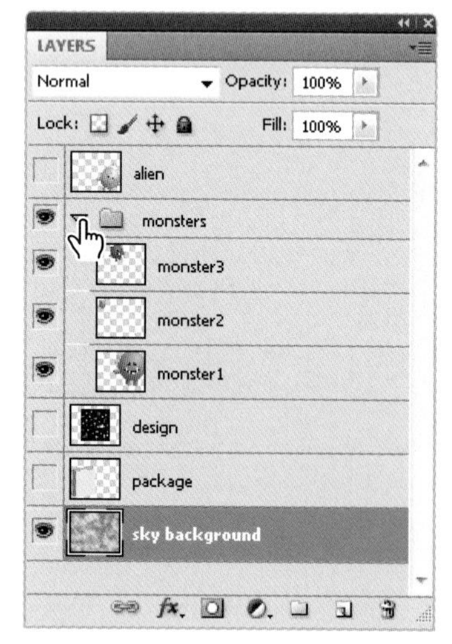

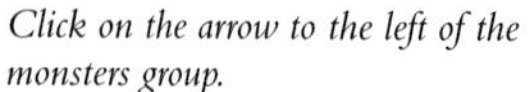
Click on the arrow to the left of the monsters group.

The individual monster layers are revealed.

3 Select the monster1 layer.

4 Press **D** on your keyboard to return to the default foreground and background colors of black and white.

5 Choose Filter > Filter Gallery. The Filter Gallery dialog box appears.

6 Press Ctrl+- (minus sign) (Windows) or Command+- (minus sign) (Mac OS) four times to zoom to 25%.

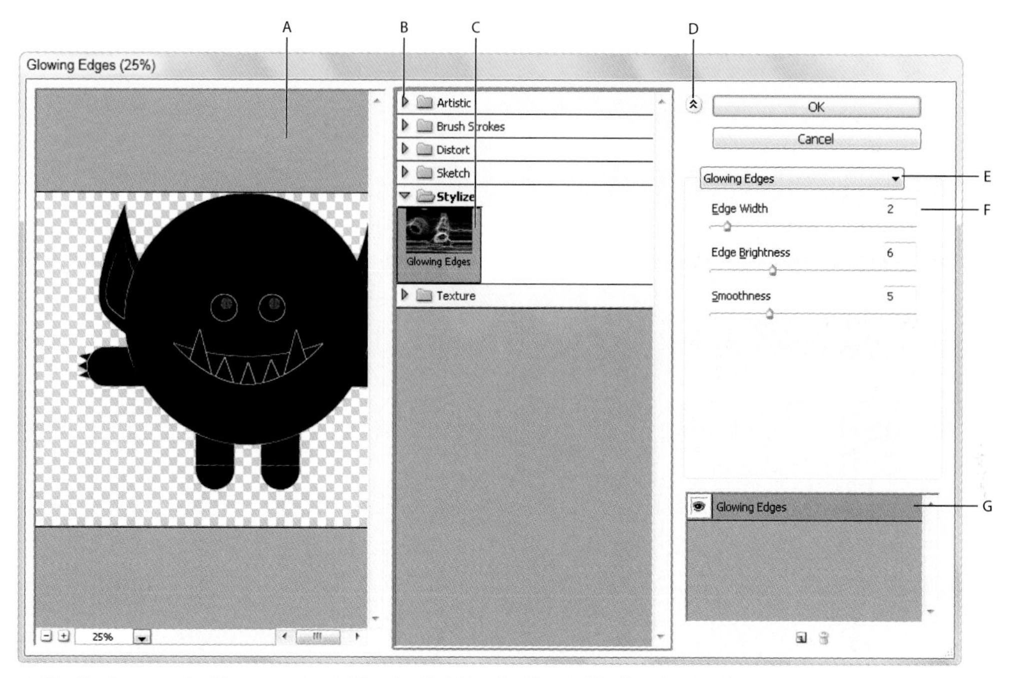

A. The Preview pane. B. Filter categories. C. Thumbnail of filter. D. Show/Hide filter thumbnails. E. Filters drop-down menu. F. Options for the selected filter. G. List of filter effects.

Applying filters in the Gallery

You'll now apply several filters to create different versions of the monster image. When you apply a filter from the filter categories, located in the center portion of the window, a preview of the image with the filter applied is displayed in the Preview pane. Along the right side of the window, options for the selected filter are displayed.

1 In the filter categories section, expand the triangle next to the Stylize folder to reveal the Glowing Edges filter.

2 Click the Glowing Edges thumbnail to add a glow to the edges of areas with color; the monster now has bright neon, glowing edges. Press OK to apply the filter.

The monster with the Glowing Edges filter applied.

3 To make the monster slightly transparent click and drag the Opacity slider in the Layers panel until you reach 50%.

You'll now apply additional filters to the other monster layers.

4 Select the monster2 layer in the Layers panel.

5 Choose Filter > Filter Gallery to apply a filter to this layer. Do not select the Filter Gallery menu item that appears first under the Filter menu. That is where your last-used filter appears, and it does not allow you to change options. Choose the Filter Gallery menu item that appears further down in the menu.

6 Click on the triangle to the left of Artistic to expand and show the artistic filters, and then click on the Fresco thumbnail. The Fresco filter is applied to the image in the Preview pane.

Fresco is an Italian term for a mural painting done on a wet, freshly plastered wall. It creates an interesting abstract effect. The Fresco filter adds a good deal of black to the image in the process of abstracting it, so you will tone it down a bit with another filter.

7 In the Fresco filter options pane make sure the Brush size is set to **2**, the Brush Detail to **10**, and the Texture to **1**. Do not press OK, as you will add another filter.

Applying the Fresco filter effect.

Now you'll apply a second filter to this layer.

8 Click the New Effect Layer button (⊡) located at the bottom of the filter effects area. This adds a new filter instance above the previous filter effect. There are now two instances of the Fresco filter applied.

9 Click the triangle to the left of Artistic to close that filter category, and then click the triangle to the left of Texture to expand that category.

10 In the filter categories section, select Craquelure. Craquelure is a term used for the network of fine cracks that can appear on a painting, either over the whole painting or just in parts. You will use the Craquelure filter to add some texture to the monster.

11 In the Craquelure filter options pane use the sliders to change the Crack Spacing to **6**, the Crack Depth to **2** and the Crack Brightness to **2**. Press OK to apply the filter.

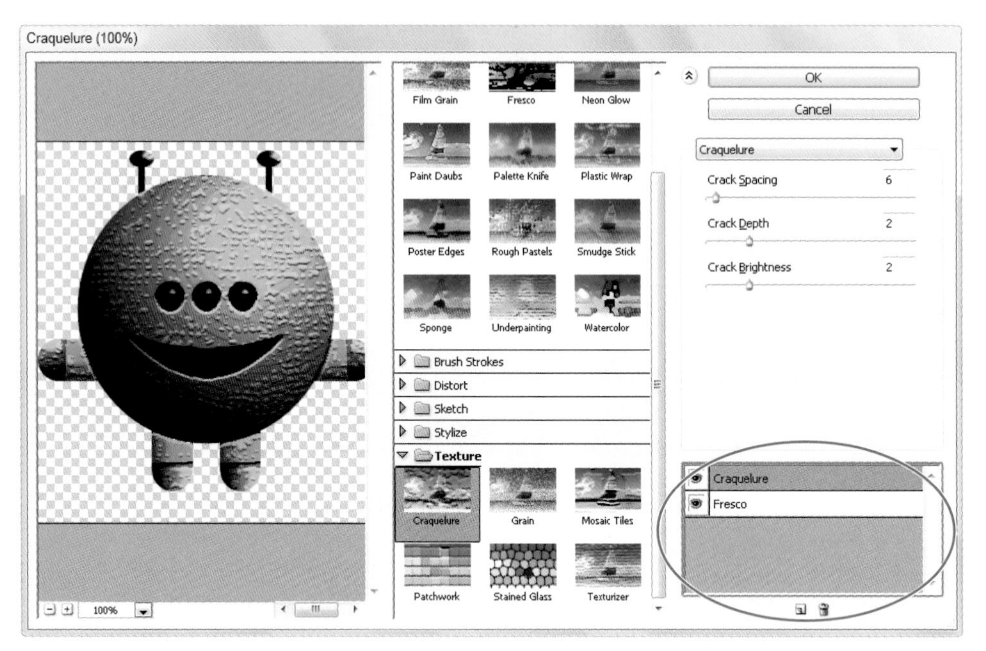

Click and drag the effects to change the primary effect.

12 Choose File > Save. Keep this file open.

You can add more effect layers and experiment with different orders to produce new effects. You can also show and hide the visibility of each filter effect by clicking on the visibility icon next to each effect.

Taking advantage of Smart Filters

The filters you applied in the last section were destructive, meaning that any changes you made using these filters affected your original image data. As you discovered in Lesson 10, "Getting Smart in Photoshop," Smart Filters are a non-destructive way to apply filters to an image. In this lesson, you will practice applying filters using the Smart Filter feature.

Applying a Smart Filter

1 Select the monster3 layer in the Layers panel.

2 Choose Filter > Convert for Smart Filters. A warning dialog box may appear, advising you that the layer will be made into a Smart Object. Press OK.

A Smart Object icon appears in the lower-right corner of the monster 3 layer thumbnail. This indicates that this layer is now converted for use with Smart Filters. Next, you will apply some filters in the Filter Gallery, and then update and change the way the filters are applied to the image.

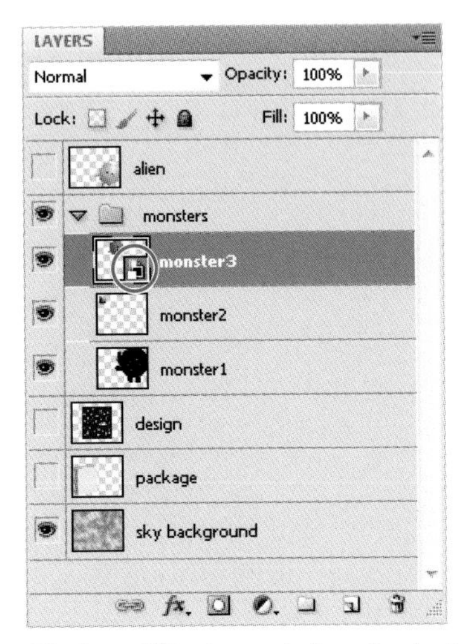

The Smart Object icon on the layer thumbnail.

3 Make sure that the monster3 layer is still selected, and then choose Filter > Filter Gallery. Make sure you do not select the Filter Gallery listed first in the Filter menu.

Note that the last filters you used are applied to the layer by default, although these can be changed.

4 Click on Craquelure filter effect in the list of filter effects in the lower-right side of the Filter Gallery dialog box.

5 In the filter categories section, expand the Artistic category and select Plastic Wrap. The Plastic Wrap filter replaces the Craquelure filter.

6 Click on the Fresco filter effect and then select the Sponge filter effect from the Artistic category. The Sponge effect replaces the Fresco effect.

7 Using the sliders, in the filter effects options, change the Brush size to 0, the Definition to 6 and the Smoothness to 2. Press OK.

A thumbnail appears underneath your monster3 layer named Smart Filters.

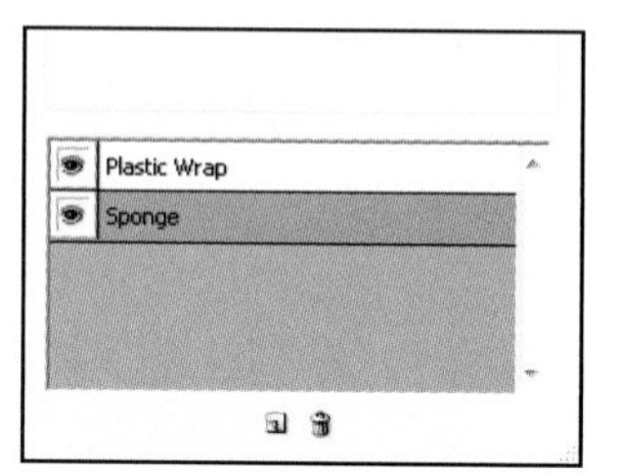

The image now has texture applied. Two filters have been applied.

You have just applied filters from the Filter Gallery to the monster3 layer, much the same way you applied filters to the monster1 and monster2 layers. The difference is that you converted monster3 to a smart object before applying the filters. This offers you the opportunity to make changes, or even delete the filters at a later time.

8 In the Layers panel, double-click on Filter Gallery located underneath the monster3 layer. The Filter Gallery dialog box opens again.

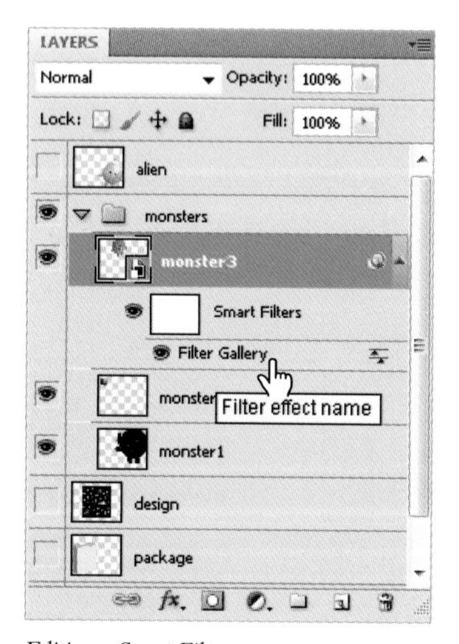

Editing a Smart Filter.

9 In the filter effects area, select Plastic Wrap from the list of applied filters.

10 Using the sliders in the Plastic Wrap effect options, change the Highlight Strength to **20**, the Detail to **1** and the Smoothness to **1**.

11 In the filter effects area of the Filter Gallery, drag Plastic Wrap below Sponge. This changes the filter order, and creates a different effect. Press OK.

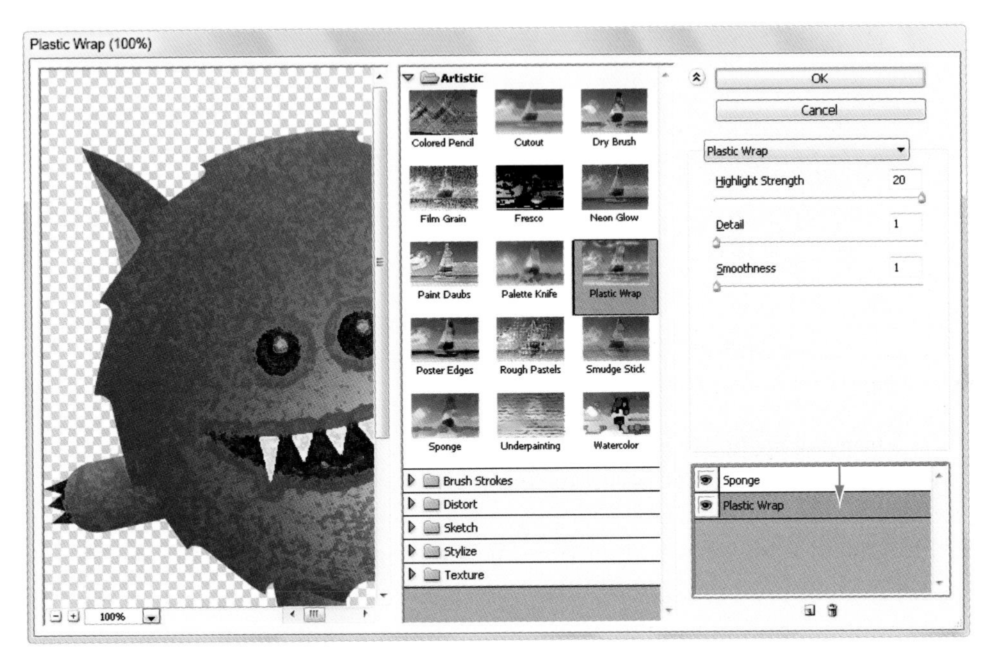

Changing the order of the filters.

12 Choose File > Save.

Smart Filter options

Next, you will explore additional filter options. You'll start by fading the filters and by editing the Smart Filter Blending Options. You will then discover how to disable a filter and how to take advantage of the Filter effects mask thumbnail.

1 In the Layers panel, right-click (Windows) or Ctrl+click (Mac OS) on Filter Gallery, located under the monster3 layer Smart Filter. Select Edit Smart Filter Blending Options from the contextual menu.

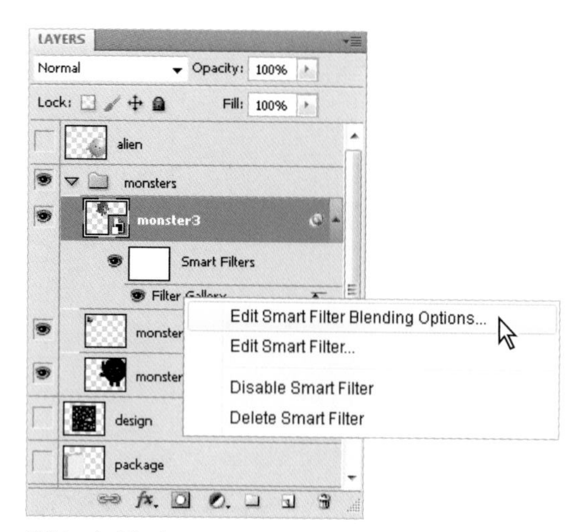

Editing the Blending options.

Like the Fade option used earlier in this lesson, the Smart Filter blending options allow you to control the intensity of a filter. However, this method is non-destructive. You can change the Fade settings multiple times and not impact the original image. You can also access the Blending Options at any time, unlike the Fade dialog box, which had to be accessed immediately after applying a filter to a regular (non-smart) layer.

2 In the Blending Options dialog box, click and drag the opacity slider to the left, lowering the opacity to 60 percent. Click the *Preview* checkbox on, and then off, to see the change that has been applied to the image, then press OK.

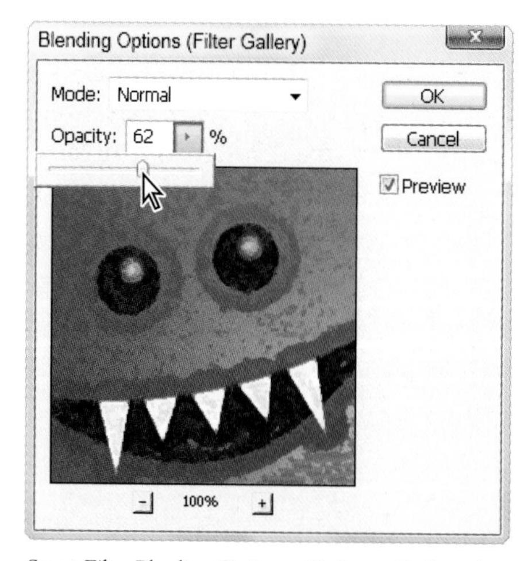

Smart Filter Blending Options with the specified opacity.

3 Choose File > Save.

Enabling and disabling effects

Because you used a Smart Filter, you can turn the filter on or off.

1 In the Layers panel, right-click (Windows) or Ctrl+click (Mac OS) on the Filter Gallery filter under Smart Filters, and choose Disable Smart Filter to hide the filter's effect.

   You can also turn off the visibility of the filter by clicking the visibility icon (👁) to the left of the filter name in the Layers panel; click again on the eye icon to make the filter visible. Make sure the Filter Gallery filter is visible for the monster3 layer.

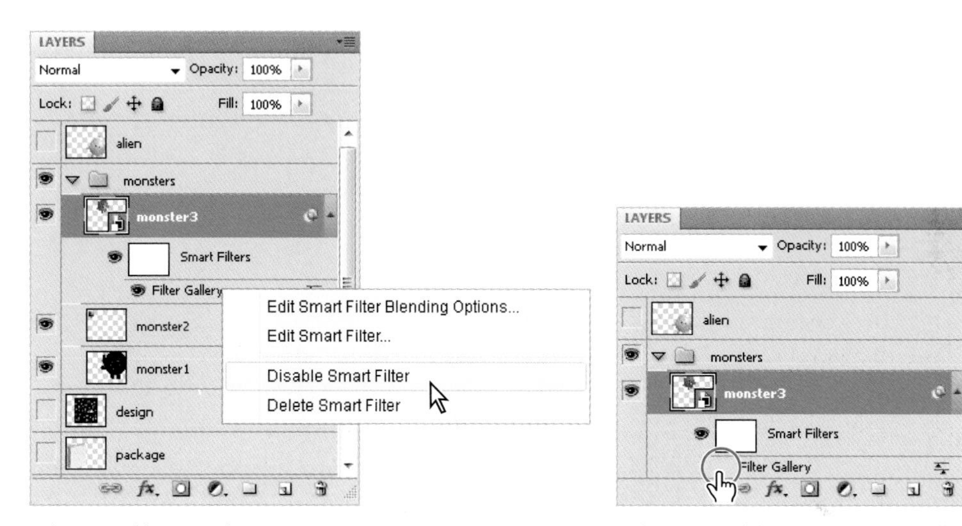

Selecting Disable Smart Filter.

The visibility of the Smart Filter turned off.

Using a filter effects mask

When you apply a filter to a layer that has been converted for Smart Filters, a mask, called the Filter effects mask thumbnail, is created. This provides the ability to selectively modify a filter effect. The thumbnail appears on the smart object layer as a white box labeled Smart Filters. You can click on the mask to activate it, and then paint with shades of black or white to hide or show the filter's effect on the layer. You'll now convert a layer for Smart Filters, apply a few filters, reduce the opacity of those filter effects, and then mask the effects to appear on only portions of the image.

1 To give you more room to work in the Layers panel, click the triangle next to the monsters layer group to collapse the monster layers into the folder.

2 Click the eye icon next to the alien layer to show the alien image, and then click on the alien layer to select it.

3 Select Filter > Convert for Smart Filters; if a warning dialog box appears, press OK.

You will now apply a motion blur to this layer. It may appear drastic at first, but you will customize the application of the filter using the Filter effects mask thumbnail.

4 Choose Filter > Blur > Motion Blur. The Motion Blur dialog box appears. Type **65** into the Angle text field, and then use the slider to set the distance for approximately 300 pixels. Press OK.

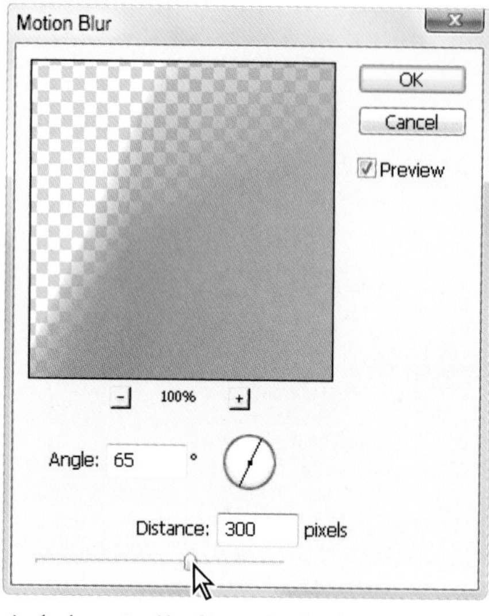

Apply the motion blur filter to the alien layer.

5 Click on the white thumbnail that appears to the left of Smart Filters in the Layers panel. This is the Filter effects mask thumbnail.

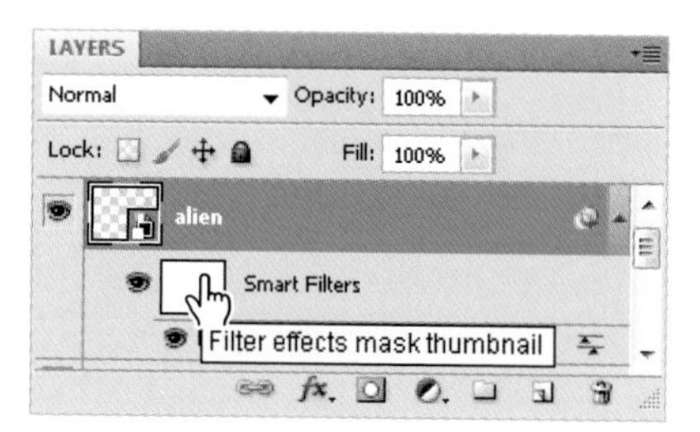

Click on the Filter effects mask thumbnail.

6 Select the Gradient tool from the Tools panel and press **D** to reset the foreground and background colors back to the default of black and white.

7 With the Gradient tool selected, review the settings in the Options bar to make sure that Linear gradient is selected, the Blending mode is Normal, and the Opacity is 100%.

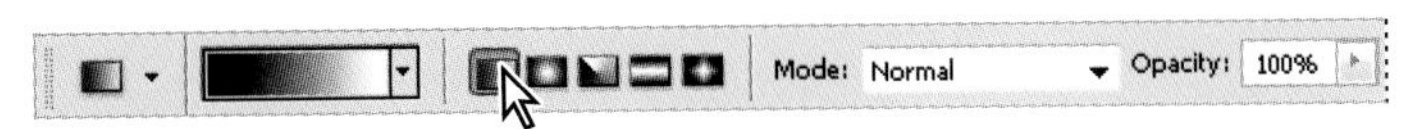

Verify the Gradient tool settings.

8 Click and drag across the alien image. Notice that the motion blur filter now fades into the original image. Click and drag multiple times to see the different results you achieve by selecting new start and end points.

Notice how the dark to light gradient on the Filter effects mask affects the application of the filter. Where it is dark, the filter is less visible. Where it is light, the filter is more visible.

9 When you are finished experimenting, press **X** on the keyboard to switch the Foreground and Background colors so that black is the Foreground. With the Gradient tool active, click beneath the eyes and drag downward toward the alien's feet and then release. The motion blur is now only occurring at the bottom of the alien.

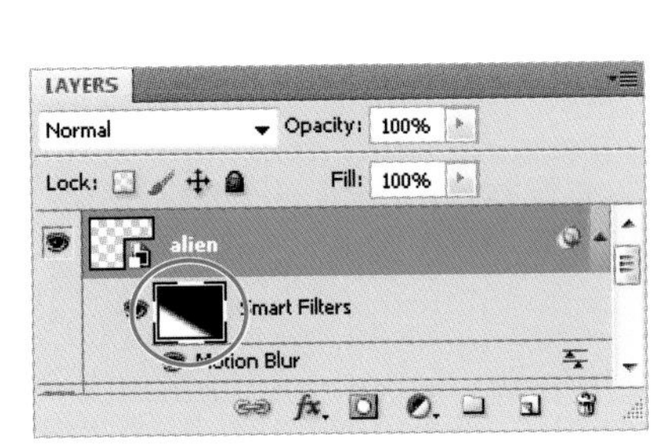

Selecting the Smart Filters mask thumbnail.

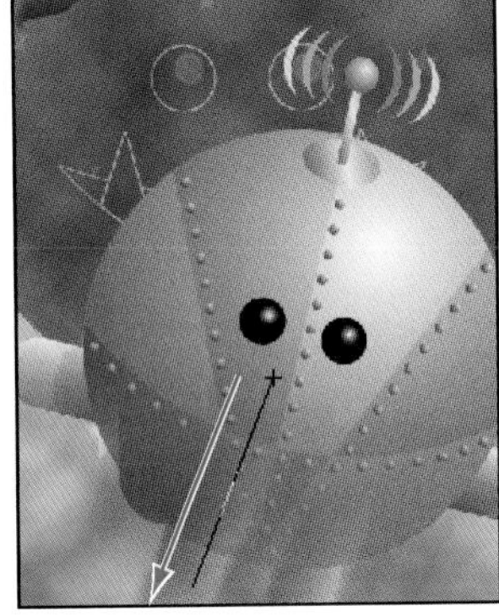

Click and drag with the Gradient tool.

You will now use painting tools to control the mask more precisely.

10 Select the Brush tool (🖌).

11 With the Brush tool selected, right-click anywhere in your image area to open the Brush Preset picker. Type **150** into the Size text field and **0** (zero) into the Hardness text field. Press Enter (Windows) or Return (Mac OS) to close the Brush Preset Picker.

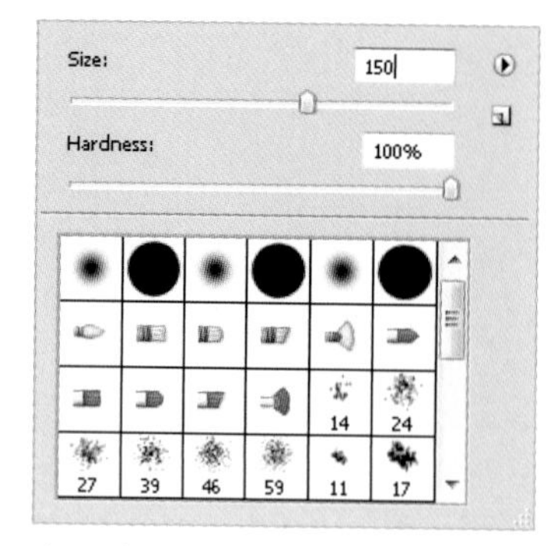

Access the Brush Preset picker contextually.

12 Press **D** on the keyboard to make sure you are at the default colors of black and white.

13 Press **X** on the keyboard to switch the foreground and background colors. Your foreground color should be black.

14 Using the Brush tool paint directly on the image at the bottom of the alien's body, notice that as you paint on a region affected by the filter that the filter is not applied. Continue experimenting with painting out the filter effect on the alien's body, leaving the effect on the legs.

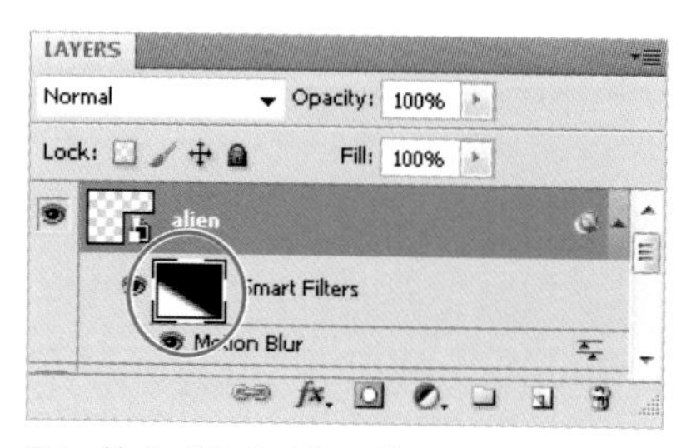

Paint black while the Filter effects mask is active.

The filter is not applied in those regions.

15 Press **X** to switch to white as a foreground color. Paint over some of the areas where the filter effect is not occurring. Notice that the effect is again revealed.

Experiment with this technique, pressing X to switch between painting the effect and covering it up, also experiment with changing the Brush tool's opacity (in the Options bar) to create more subtle effects.

16 Choose File > Save. Keep this file open for the next part of this lesson.

Using the Vanishing Point filter

The Vanishing Point filter simplifies the task of editing images that are in perspective, such as the sides of a box. With the Vanishing Point filter, you can easily add additional elements to any type of artwork that is composed of flat planes. With this filter, you first define the planes in an image, and then apply edits by painting, cloning, copying, pasting, and transforming your image. The planes you define control the perspective of the edits you make, giving your image a realistic perspective effect.

In this exercise, you'll map a pre-made design to a box so that three sides of the box are showing.

1 Turn on the eye icon (👁) next to the design and package layers to make them visible. Using the Layers panel, turn off the visibility of both the monsters layer group and the alien layer.

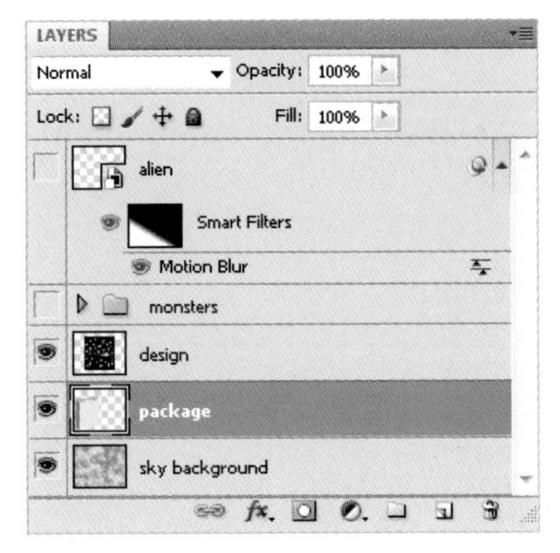

Showing the design and package layers.

You will now cut the image on the design layer so that it can be pasted into the Vanishing Point dialog box.

2 Hold down the Ctrl (Windows) or the Command (Mac OS) key, and click on the design layer thumbnail in the Layers panel. A selection is now visible around the package design.

3 Click on the design layer to make sure it is the active layer, then choose Edit > Cut. The package design is now on your clipboard.

Before using the Vanishing Point filter you will want to create a blank layer. By creating a blank layer, you can have the effects of the vanishing point separated from the rest of your image, allowing you to turn off or on the results of the filter.

4 Click on the package layer and then Alt+click (Windows) or Option+click (Mac OS) on the Create a New Layer icon (◻) in the Layers panel. The New Layer dialog box appears.

5 Type **package wrap** into the Name text field and press OK. Make sure that the package wrap layer is active.

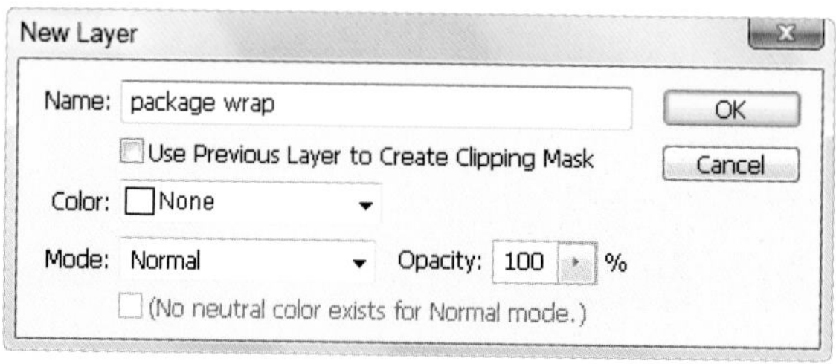

Create a new layer for the Vanishing Point results.

6 Choose Filter > Vanishing Point. The Vanishing Point dialog box appears. In the first part of this exercise, the perspective planes are made for you. You will create one yourself later.

This file has a pre-built perspective plane.

7 With the Vanishing Point dialog box open, press Ctrl+V (Windows) or Command+V (Mac OS) to paste the package design you cut in step 3. When you paste, the tool changes to the Marquee selection tool.

8 Click and drag the pasted design over the perspective plane. The design artwork maps to the perspective plane. Keep the Vanishing Point dialog box open for the next part.

Click and drag the pasted artwork on the plane.

Building your own perspective planes

A grid defines the four corner points of a perspective plane. When building a perspective plane, it helps to have objects in your image that can define your plane. In this example, the package itself offers a good source from which you can create your perspective plane.

Now that you know the capabilities of the Vanishing Point filter, you'll delete the existing plane and create your own.

1 Press and hold down the Alt (Windows) or Option (Mac OS) key. This turns the Cancel button into a Reset button. Click Reset.

2 Select the Edit Plane tool (), then click on the existing planes and press the Delete key. The perspective planes are deleted.

3 Select the Create Plane tool (). You'll now create a new plane by defining each corner of the plane.

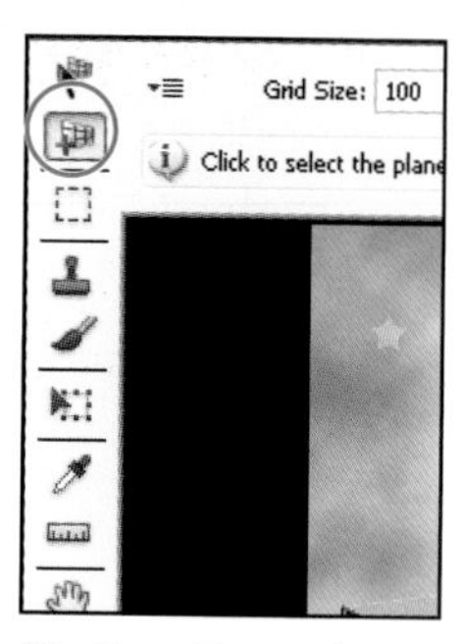

The Create Plane tool.

4 Click on the top left of the front of the box, then on the top right, then on the bottom right, and once more on the bottom left. Notice that a blue grid indicates a valid plane. If your plane is red or yellow, it is invalid; use your Edit Plane tool to readjust your corners until the grid is blue.

When drawing a plane, you can temporarily hold down the X key on your keyboard to magnify an area for more precise drawing of the plane.

For a plane to be valid, two sides of the plane should be parallel, while the other two sides show the perspective.

Building an attached plane

You can control the angle of a plane, and you are not restricted to 90 degree angles.

1 Make sure that the Create Plane Tool is selected. Press and hold down the Ctrl (Windows) or Command (Mac OS) key, and drag the left-middle edge node toward back edge of the box. This creates a perpendicular plane that will be used for the left side of the box. Don't worry if it is not aligning at the exact angle. You will fix that in the next step.

Ctrl/Command+click.

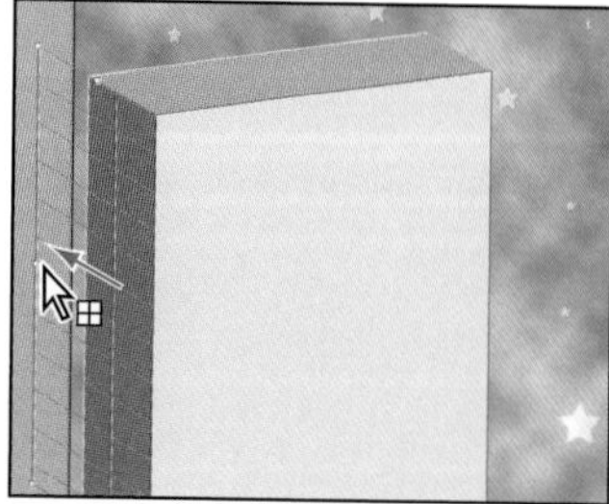

Drag out a new perpendicular plane.

2 Press and hold the Alt (Windows) or Option (Mac OS) key, and position your cursor over the left-middle edge node; a double-headed curved cursor appears. Click and drag either up or down to adjust the angle of the plane. You may need to zoom in to get this just right. Press **X** on the keyboard to temporarily zoom in for a better view. If you are on a Macintosh, it might be easier to hold down the Option key and drag the upper-left corner into place, and then Option drag the lower-left corner into place.

You are adjusting the plane so that it follows the left side of the box. As you adjust the plane, you may find that you need to release the Alt/Option key and adjust the middle edge node so that it is not extending beyond the left edge of the box.

Alt/Option+click and drag to change the angle of a plane.

3 Choose Edit > Paste to paste the package design in the Vanishing Point dialog box, or use the keyboard shortcut Ctrl+V (Windows) or Command+V (Mac OS).

4 Click and drag the design over the box. As it appears over the grid, the sides of the design conform to the sides of the grid. Notice how the image automatically adjusts itself to the contours of the perspective planes.

5 Make sure the image is exactly where you want it positioned on the plane, then press OK.

6 Make the monsters layer group visible by clicking to the left of the monsters folder in the Layers panel. The visibility icon appears, and you see the contents of the group. Then click to the left of the alien layer to reveal the entire design.

7 Choose File > Save. Congratulations! You have finished this lesson.

Self study

Using ps1102.psd, in your pslessons folder, convert various layers to smart objects and then stylize the monster layers.

Note that you can take multiple layers and convert them into one smart object to apply a filter to many layers at a time. If you want to experiment with this feature, Right-click (Windows) or Ctrl+click (Mac OS) on the layers you wish to convert to a smart object and choose Convert to Smart Object, then apply filters as you normally would.

You can double-click on the smart object layer to open the original (separated layers) at any time.

Review

Questions

1 When is the Fade option available for a filter that you have applied?

2 If you want to apply a filter in a non-destructive way, what is your best option?

3 How do you add a new perpendicular plane to an existing perspective plane and then control the angle of a new plane in the Vanishing Point dialog box?

Answers

1 Unless you are using the Smart Filter feature, you must apply the Fade feature as the next step after applying a filter, or right-click on the filter listed under Smart Filters in the Layers panel. If you are using a Smart Filter, you can right-click (Windows) or Ctrl+click (Mac OS) on the applied Smart Filter (listed in the Layers panel) and select Edit Smart Filter Blending Options to access the same fade options.

2 Convert the layer for Smart Filters, then apply the filter.

3 To create a perpendicular plane from an existing perspective plane, click and hold down the Ctrl (Windows) or Command (Mac OS) key on an edge node (not a corner node) and drag out a new plane. You can control the angle of the plane by holding the Alt (Windows) or Option (Mac OS) key and dragging an edge node (not a corner node) until the new plane is at the correct angle.

What you'll learn in this lesson:

- Creating web and video presets
- Saving a still image for use on the Web
- Saving a still image with transparency for video
- Building animation for web and video

Creating Images for Web and Video

Photoshop's flexibility and range of features have allowed it to gain acceptance in nearly every sector of the computer graphics industry. A very common use for Photoshop is creating imagery for web and video production.

Starting up

In this lesson, you'll create a group of projects for both web and video production. You'll work with still and animated graphics for each medium.

Before starting, make sure that your tools and panels are consistent by resetting your preferences. See "Resetting Adobe Photoshop CS5 preferences" on page 3.

You will work with several files from the ps12lessons folder in this lesson. Make sure that you have loaded the pslessons folder onto your hard drive from the supplied DVD. See "Loading lesson files" on page 5.

In order to work with video in Photoshop, you must have the Extended version and the QuickTime player plug-in installed on your computer. While pre-installed with the Mac OS operating system, for Windows users, the QuickTime player is available as a free download from the Apple web site, *apple.com/quicktime*.

See Lesson 12 in action!

Use the accompanying video to gain a better understanding of how to use some of the features shown in this lesson. The video tutorial for this lesson can be found on the included DVD.

Using Photoshop for Silverlight and Flash design

Adobe Photoshop can serve as the starting point for your interactive designs. If you want to create a Silverlight application, such as a video player, you can mock-up the design in Photoshop, and then import your layered Photoshop file into the Silverlight design tool, Expression Blend. Expression Blend lets you convert things like buttons and sliders in your static mock-up into live working controls. It is available for Windows computers and you can explore these programs through the Website Spark program run by Microsoft, which provides the Expression tools for creating Silverlight content at no cost to small businesses and independent designers: *www.microsoft.com/web/websitespark/*.

If you want to design for Flash, you can import your Photoshop files into Flash CS5. The Flash CS5 program is part of the suite if you purchased Photoshop as part of the Creative Suite Design Premium collection. If you purchased Photoshop separately, you can download a free trial version from the Adobe website at *www.adobe.com*. You can learn more about integrating Photoshop work into Flash in the companion to this book, the *Flash CS5 Digital Classroom*, available from your favorite bookseller.

Viewing the completed file

Before starting this lesson, you'll use your browser to view the completed page with navigational links that you will create in this part of the lesson. This might be used as a starting point for a web page, or for comping a wireframe for client approval.

1 Open your web browser—you can use any browser for this lesson (Firefox, Safari, Opera, or Internet Explorer, to name a few).

2 Choose File > Open, or Open File. The exact menu selection may vary, depending upon the type and version of your browser, but the menu item for opening a page in your browser should be under the File menu.

This page is created using CSS, you can export pages built from tables of CSS out of Photoshop's Save for Web and Devices feature. Find out more about CSS (Cascading Styles Sheets) at w3.org/Style/CSS/.

3 In the Open dialog box, navigate to the ps12lessons folder on your hard drive and open the file named ps1201_done.html. An image created to help viewers navigate a web site appears.

The completed web page in a web browser.

4 Click on the Sales, Service, About and Contact text links to see that you are directed to generic pages with related titles.

You will create this web page from start to finish, including adding the links, and export the page using CSS technology.

5 You can keep the finished web page open in the browser for reference, or choose File > Close.

6 Return to Photoshop CS5.

Determining image size for the Web

This figure represents a typical monitor that is set at a screen resolution of 800 x 600. Many viewers will use a higher resolution, but this is the typical resolution that most web designers build images to fit.

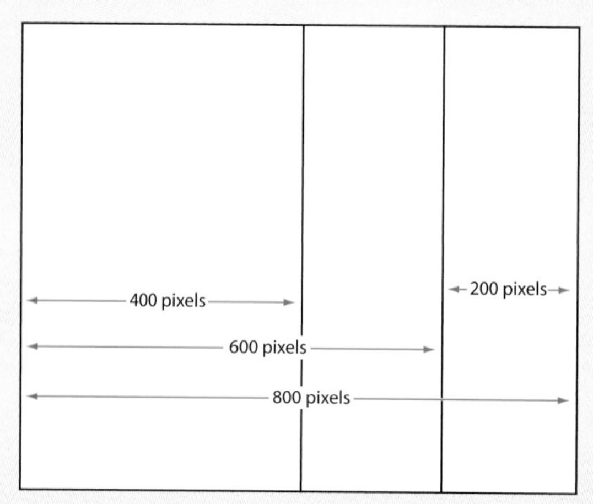

A typical screen display broken into quarters.

To determine how wide a web image should be, break down the total number of screen pixels into sections. Instead of thinking about how many pixels wide an image should be, think about what percentage of the screen you want the image to occupy. In other words, if you want the image to occupy half of the screen (typically estimated at 800 pixels for browser windows), type **400** into the Width text field in the Pixel Dimension section of the Image Size dialog box. For one quarter of the screen, type **200**, and so on. It is a different way of thinking, especially for those from the print design environment. It should also be noted that a pixel is a pixel, no matter what the ppi resolution of your image is. So, 200 pixels in a 300 ppi image takes up the same amount of disk space as 200 pixels in a 72 ppi image.

Changing your units of measurement

Before starting the web project, verify that your measurements are set in the pixel unit. You make that change in your Photoshop Preferences.

1 Choose Edit > Preferences > Units & Rulers (Windows) or Photoshop > Preferences > Units & Rulers (Mac OS). The Preferences dialog box appears, with Units & Rulers already selected.

2 From the Units section of the Preferences dialog box, choose pixels from the Rulers drop-down menu. Leave all the other settings at their default. Press OK.

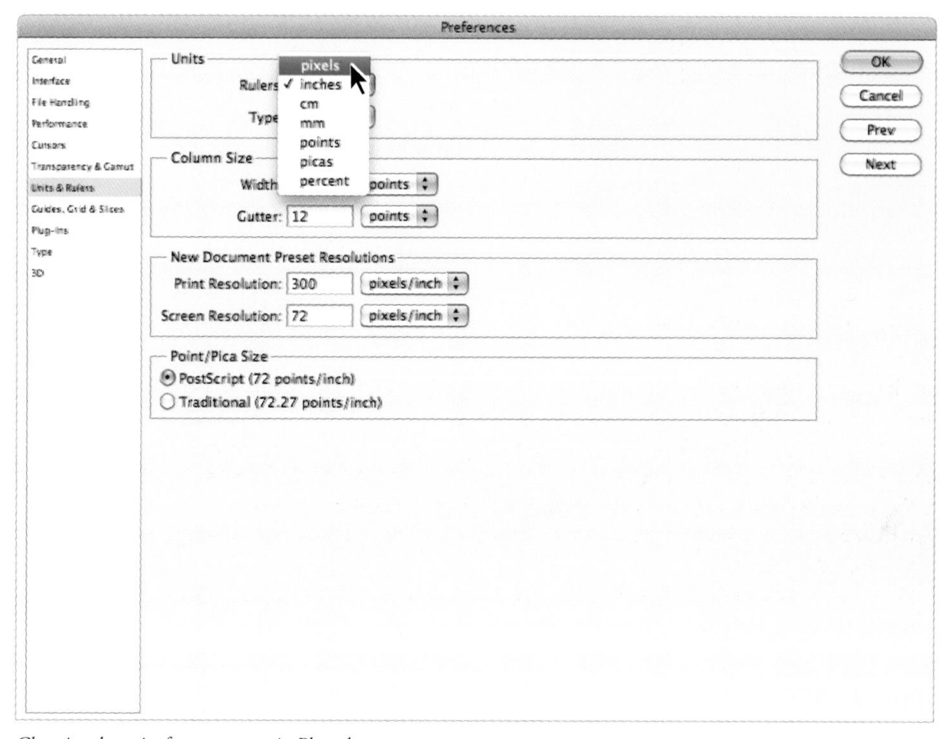

Changing the unit of measurement in Photoshop.

Creating the web page

In this part of the lesson you will open the start file and get right to work adding content, links and slices.

1 From Photoshop choose File > Browse in Bridge, or click on Launch Bridge (Br) or Mini Bridge buttons (Mb) in the Application bar. When Adobe Bridge appears, navigate to the ps12lessons folder and double-click to open the file named ps1201.psd. An image of a man on a beach with a kite appears.

The ps1201.psd image.

The first step you will take with this file is save it as a work file, then flip the image so that man is on the left side rather than the right.

2 Choose File > Save As. When the Save As dialog box appears navigate to the ps12lessons folder and type ps1201_work.psd into the Name text field. Choose Photoshop from the Format drop-down menu and press Save.

3 Choose Image > Image Rotation and select Flip Canvas Horizontal. The image flips so that the man is now on the left. Press Ctrl+S (Windows) or Command+S (Mac OS) to save the file.

Adding the Text

You will now add the header text, in the upper-left of the image, and the text that will serve as links in the final page.

1 Select the Type tool (T) and click anywhere in the upper left of the image, the text cursor appears. In the Options bar, select Myriad Pro from the Font family drop-down menu, Bold from the Font style drop-down menu, and 60 from the Font size drop-down menu.

2 Press the Center text button (≡) in the Options bar, then click once on the Text color swatch in the Options bar and choose white from the Color Picker dialog box that appears, press OK.

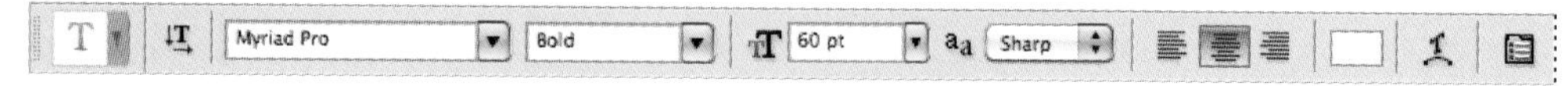

The Options bar as it appears after step 1 and 2.

3 Now that the text options are set, type the following with returns as shown:

Go

Fly

a Kite

If you need to reposition your text, and do not wish to exit the type options, hold down the Ctrl (Windows) or Command (Mac OS) key, then click and drag to reposition the text layer.

You will now fine-tune the text by adjusting the leading (space between the lines of text) and the kerning (space between the letters).

4 With the text area still active press Ctrl+A (Windows) or Command+A (Mac OS) to select all the text, then press Alt+Arrow Up key (Windows) or Option+Arrow Up key to reduce the space between the letters. If the space is reduced too much, press Alt+Arrow Down key (Windows) or Option+Arrow Down key (Mac OS) to move the lines of text further apart from each other. Try to set the leading so that the text is almost on top of the next line.

5 Reduce the spacing between the word *a* and *kite* by clicking to insert the cursor anywhere between those letters, then hold down the Alt+Left Arrow key (Windows) or Option+Left Arrow key (Mac OS) and press repeatedly until the space is smaller, you can determine the amount of space. In our example, the Alt/Option+Left Arrow key was pressed approximately 15 times.

Alternately, you could have left no space between the words a *and* kite*, kern out the space between by repeatedly pressing the Alt/Option+Right Arrow key.*

6 While the text is still active, click on the Create warped text button (⌶) in the Options bar. The Warp Text dialog box appears. You can warp text to create all sorts of effects, in this example the text is being distorted to add a little dimension.

7 In the Warp Text dialog box, select Rise from the Style drop-down menu, and make sure that the Horizontal radio button is active.

8 Click and drag the Bend slider to the left to change the value to +10, or type +10 into the Bend text field.

9 Verify that the Horizontal Distortion is set to 0 (zero), then click and drag the Vertical Distortion slider to the right to about the value of 25, or type **25** into the Vertical Distortion text field. Press OK. The warp is applied to the text.

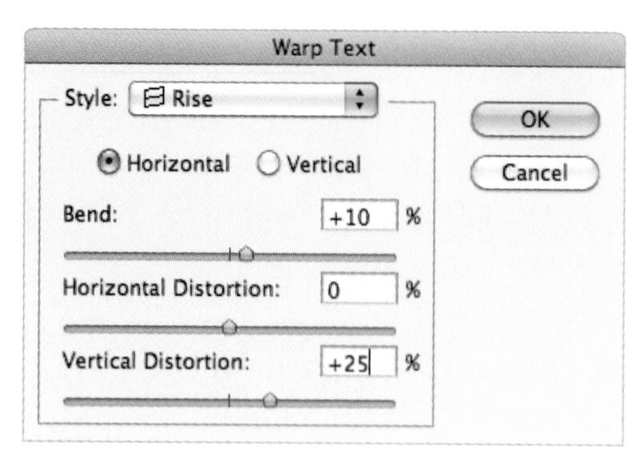

Applying the Rise warp.

Result.

10 Click on the Commit checkbox (✓) on the right side of the Options bar to confirm your text edits. If necessary choose the Move tool (►+) and click and drag to reposition the text so that it is visible in the upper-left corner of the image.

Adding Style to the text

Now that you have your header text created, you will add a layer style to it.

1 With the Go Fly a Kite text layer still selected, click the Add a layer style button (*fx*) at the bottom of the Layers panel. Select Outer Glow from the layer style drop-down menu. The Layer Style dialog box appears with Outer Glow settings visible.

2 From the Blend Mode drop-down menu choose Normal.

3 In the Structure section, click once on the Set color of glow swatch, the Color Picker appears. Click and drag the slider, on the right of the color pane, until you see blue colors in the color pane. Click on a navy blue and press OK.

4 Click and drag the Size slider to the right until you reach the value of 25, or enter **25** into the Size text field. Press OK to close the dialog box.

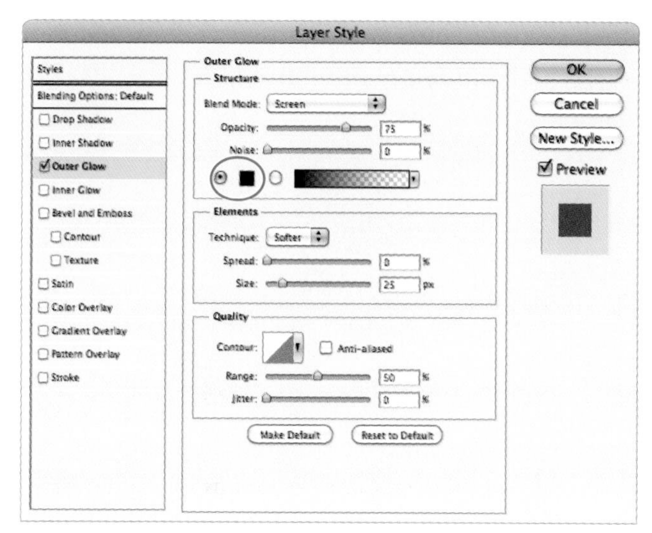

Change the options for the Outer Glow style.

Result.

Creating the text for the links

Now that you have the header text completed, you will create the individual text layers that will serve as links.

1 Select the Type tool (T) and click somewhere to the top right of the large kite the man is holding in the image, the text cursor appears.

The Type tool remembers the last settings, such as font and size. Before typing you need to change the text size and orientation.

2 Choose 30 from the Font size drop-down menu, then click on the Left align text button (≡) in the Options bar.

3 Type **Sales**, then press Ctrl+Enter (Windows) or Command+Return (Mac OS) to commit the text entry and exit the type options.

Pressing Ctrl/Command+Enter or Return is the same as pressing the Commit (✓) checkbox in the Options bar.

4 Position your cursor under the Sales text and click to create a new text entry. Exact position is not important as you will reposition the text later. Type **Service**, then press Ctrl+Enter (Windows) or Command+Return (Mac OS) to commit the text entry and exit the type options.

5 Position your cursor under the word Service and click and type **About**, then press Ctrl+Enter (Windows) or Command+Return (Mac OS) to commit the text entry and exit the type options.

6 Position your cursor under the word About, to make the last text entry, and click. Type the word **Contact**, then press Ctrl+Return (Windows) or Command+Enter (Mac OS) to commit the text entry and exit the type options.

7 Choose File > Save, or press Ctrl+S (Windows) or Command+S (Mac OS) to save the file. Keep this file open for the next part of this lesson.

Positioning and distribution of text

In this part of the lesson, you will use the Move tool to reposition the text and then distribute the vertical space between them evenly.

1 Select the Move tool (▸+) and Ctrl+Click (Windows) or Command+Click (Mac OS) on the word Sales (in the image). By holding down the Ctrl/Command key you have turned on the auto-select feature. You can easily activate layers without having to go to the Layers panel.

   With the Sales layer selected, click and drag the text so that it is off to the right of the curved edge of the kite.

2 Hold down the Ctrl/Command key and click on the other three text layers and position them off to the right of the kite, following the curve of the kite image.

3 Make sure that the Layers panel is visible and select the Sales text layer. Then Ctrl+Shift+click (Windows) or Command+Shift+Click (Mac OS) on the Service, About, and Contact text layers (in the Layers panel).

   Note that when you select three or more layers, the Align and Distribute options become visible in the Options bar. Align becomes visible with two layers selected.

4 Choose Distribute vertical centers (≛) from the Options bar. The text layers are distributed evenly.

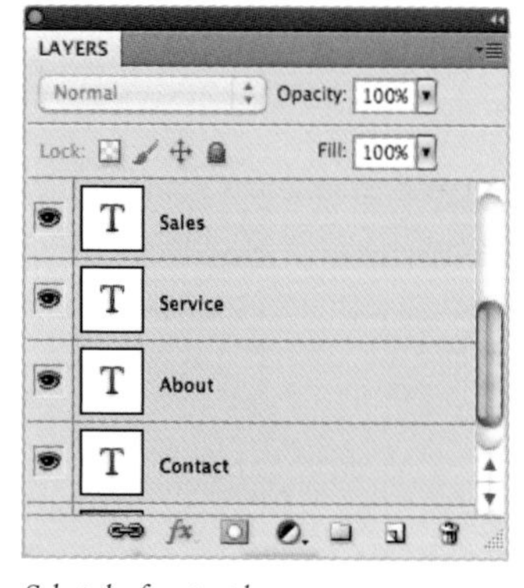

Select the four text layers.

Distribute the text layers vertically.

Creating slices

A slice is a part of an image that is cut from a larger image. Think of a slice as a piece of a puzzle that, when placed alongside other related pieces, creates an entire image. What holds the pieces together is either an HTML table or CSS. In this example, you will use Cascading styles to create the final HTML page.

An example of a sliced image.

Slices can be beneficial when images are large in size, as downloading smaller packets of information on the Web is faster than downloading one large packet, and also better when you need to save parts of an image in different formats. In this exercise, you will create guides that will then determine where the slicing of your image occurs.

1 If rulers are not already displayed, choose View > Rulers to show the rulers on the top and left side of the document window.

2 Choose View > Snap to turn off the snapping features for the rest of this lesson. The snapping features sometimes force the cursor to align with elements in your images such as the edges of the text layers.

   Using the rulers, you will create guides on your document that will later define where you want to slice your image.

3 Click directly on the top (horizontal) ruler and then click and drag to pull a guide from the ruler. Continue dragging the guide; release it when the guide is just above the Sales text layer.

4 Now, click and drag another guide from the top ruler and release it when it is between the word *Sales* and the word *Service* in the image area.

Click and drag horizontal guides to separate the text.

5 Click and drag another guide from the top ruler and release it between the Service and About text on the image, and another between the About and Contact text.

6 Finally, click and drag a guide from the top ruler and release it underneath the Contact text. You should have a total of five horizontal guides. You will now create the vertical guides.

7 Click on the ruler on the left side of the image window and drag out a guide; release the guide when you reach the left side of the Sales, Service, About, Contact text on the image.

8 Click again on the ruler on the left, and drag out a guide; release it when it is on the right side of the Sales, Service, About, Contact text on the image.

The guides are completed, the image with guides should look similar to our example.

The image with the guides in place.

If necessary, you can use the Move tool (▸+) to click and drag existing guides.

Slicing it up

No slicing has occurred at this point. In this part of the lesson, you will use options that are available when using the Slice tool to easily create your slices.

1 Click and hold down on the Crop tool to select the hidden Slice tool (). Note that the options change in the Options bar.

2 Click on the Slices From Guides button in the Options bar. Your image is automatically sliced into several smaller images, based upon the location of your guides. The image is not actually sliced in Photoshop, but will be when you save the file in the Save for Web & Devices section of this lesson.

The slices created from the position of the guides.

Selecting and combining slices

In this section, you will select several slices and combine them into one slice. You can combine and divide slices easily using contextual tools in Photoshop. You will first remove the guides since you no longer need them.

1 Choose View > Clear Guides. The guides are cleared, but the slices remain.

2 Click and hold on the Slice tool () to choose the hidden Slice Select tool (). Using this tool, you can click to activate and adjust your slices.

You will now select all the slices that are not going to be hyperlinks, and combine them.

3 Using the Slice Select tool, click on the large slice in the lower-left corner of the image. Then Shift+click on each one of the slices above. This adds each slice to the selection.

4 When you have all the slices on the left side selected, right-click (Windows) or Ctrl+Click (Mac OS) and select Combine slices from the contextual menu. The slices are combined into one slice.

Select all slices on the left.

Combine into one.

5 Now use the Slice Select tool to select the slice directly above the Sales text slice, then hold down the Shift key and select the slice to the right. Right-click (Windows) or Ctrl+Click (Mac OS) and select Combine slices from the contextual menu. The slices are combined into one slice.

6 Select the large slice in the lower right of the image and select it with the Slice Select tool. Shift+click on the slices above it, excluding the top slice, which you have already combined. Right-click (Windows) or Ctrl+Click (Mac OS) and select Combine slices from the contextual menu. The slices are combined into one slice.

The task of combining slices is finished.

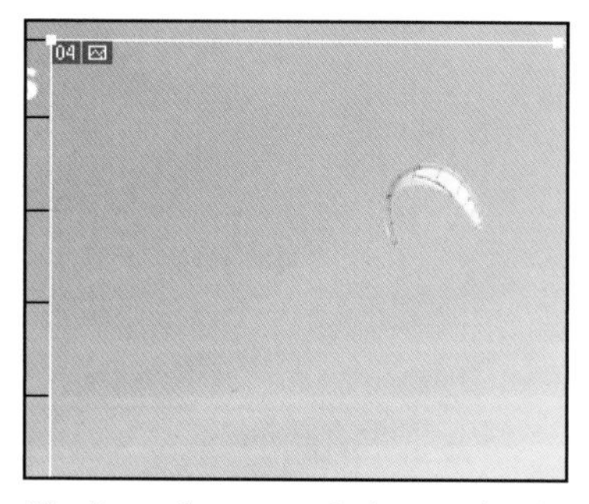

The slices as they appear after being combined.

In this example, you are combining slices manually, but you can also select slices across columns and rows and let Photoshop determine which slice combination works best.

7 Choose File > Save to save this file. Keep the image open for the next part of this lesson.

Applying attributes to your slices

Now that you have defined your slices, you will apply attributes to them. The attributes that you will apply in this lesson are URL and Alt Tags. By defining a URL, a link is made from that slice to a location or file on the Web. By defining an Alt Tag, you allow viewers to read a text description of an image. This is helpful if a viewer is visually impaired or has turned off the option for viewing graphics. An Alt Tag also helps search engines find more relevant content on your page.

1 With the ps1201_work.psd file still open and the Slice Select tool (↗) still selected, select the slice containing the Sales text.

2 Click on the Set options for the current slice button (▤) in the Options bar. The Slice Options dialog box appears.

   You will be supplied with a link to a file in your lessons folder to test your links.

3 Type **sales.html** into the URL text field.

4 Type **Sales** into the Alt Tag text field and press OK.

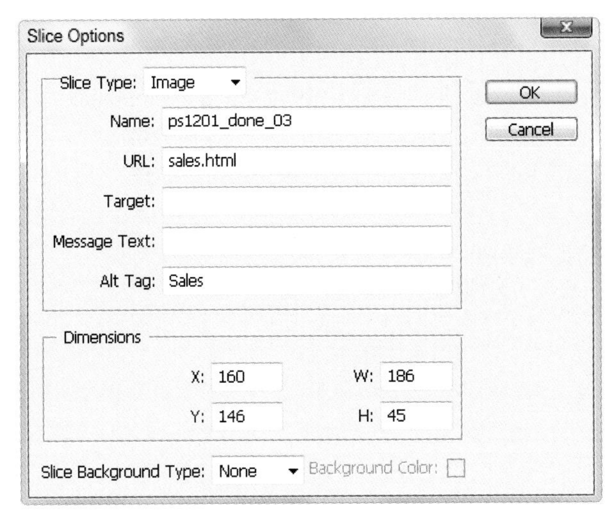

Enter the URL and Alt Tag information.

Your HTML file must be saved inside the ps12lessons folder in order to have a working link.

5 Now, select the slice containing the text Service, and choose the Set options for the current slice button in the Options bar. The Slice Options dialog box appears.

6 Type **service.html** into the URL text field and **Service** in the Alt Tag text field. Press OK.

7 Select the slice containing the text About, and choose the Set options for the current slice button in the Options bar. The Slice Options dialog box appears.

8 Type **about.html** into the URL text field and **About Us** in the Alt Tag text field. Press OK.

9 Select the slice containing the text Contact, and choose the Set options for the current slice button in the Options bar. The Slice Options dialog box appears.

10 Type **contact.html** into the URL text field and **Contact Us** in the Alt Tag text field. Press OK.

11 Choose File > Save. Keep the document open for the next part of the lesson.

For this lesson, you do not put an alt tag on each slice, but it is recommended that you assign a descriptive alt tag to each slice when producing images for the Web.

Using Save For Web & Devices

The process of making an image look as good as possible at the smallest file size is called optimizing. This is important for all images that are to be used on the Web, as most viewers don't want to wait long for information to appear.

In this part of the lesson, you'll use the Save For Web & Devices feature to optimize your navigational banner.

1 With the ps1201_work.psd file still open, choose File > Save For Web & Devices. The Save For Web & Devices dialog box appears.

2 Select the 2-up tab to view your original image on the top and your optimized image on the bottom. Note that the window may display the original on the left side and the optimized image on the right.

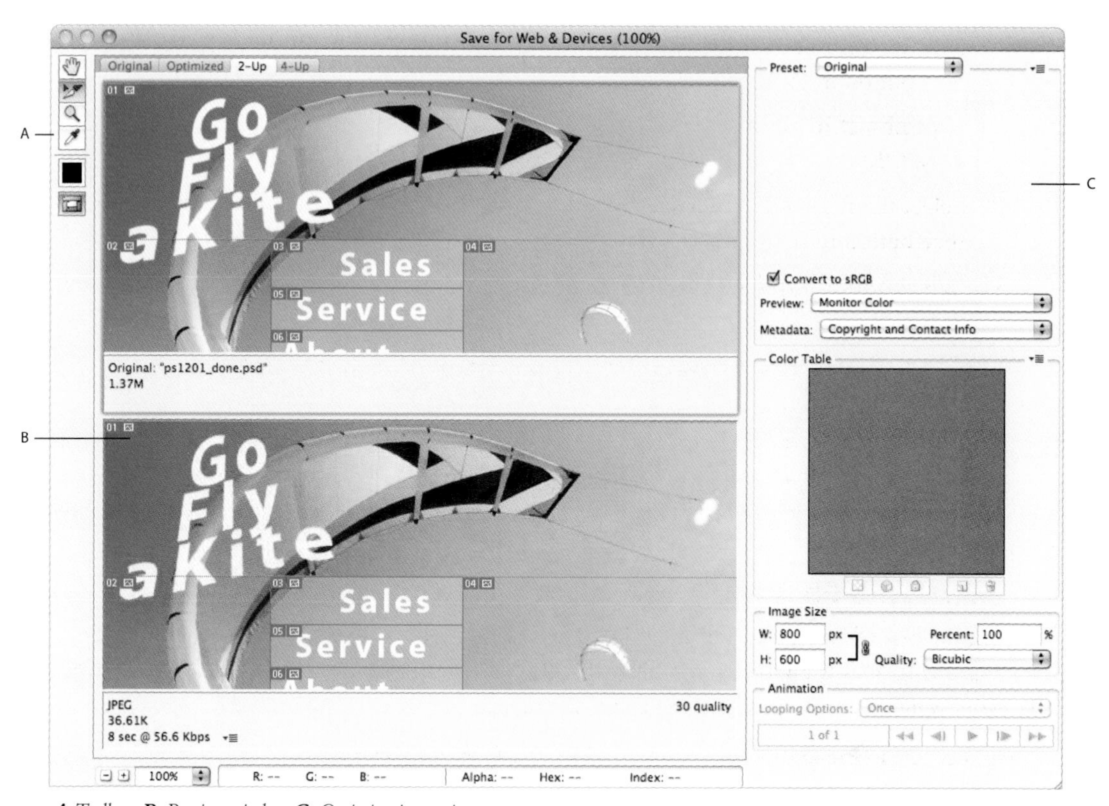

A. Toolbox. B. Preview window. C. Optimization settings.

3 Select the Hand tool (✋) and click and drag directly on the image in either window to reposition the image so that you can see the four slices containing text.

The Save For Web & Devices window is broken into three main areas:

Toolbox: The Toolbox provides you with tools for panning and zooming in your image, selecting slices, and sampling color.

Preview window: In addition to having the ability to view both the original and optimized images individually, you can also preview the original and optimized images side-by-side in 2-up view or with up to three variations in the 4-up view.

Optimization settings: The Optimization settings allow you to specify the format and settings of your optimized file.

How to choose web image formats

When you want to optimize an image for the Web, what format should you choose? Based upon the image you have in front of you, choose the format best suited for that type of image.

GIF: An acronym for Graphic Interchange File, the GIF format is usually used on the Web to display simple colored logos, motifs, and other limited-tone imagery. The GIF format supports a maximum of 256 colors, as well as transparency. GIF is the only one of the four formats here that supports built-in animation.

JPEG: An acronym for Joint Photographic Experts Group, the JPEG file format has found wide acceptance on the Web as the main format for displaying photographs and other continuous-tone imagery. The JPEG format supports a range of millions of colors, allowing for the accurate display of a wide range of artwork.

PNG: An acronym for Portable Network Graphics. PNG was intended to blend the best of both the GIF and JPEG formats. PNG files come in two different varieties: like GIF, PNG-8 can support up to 256 colors, while the PNG-24 variety can support millions of colors, similar to the JPEG format. Both PNG varieties support transparency and, as an improvement on GIF's all-or-nothing transparency function, a PNG file supports varying amounts of transparency so that you can actually see through an image to your web page contents. Note that not all browsers support the PNG format.

WBMP: A standard format for optimizing images for mobile devices, WBMP files are 1-bit, meaning they contain only black and white pixels.

4 Using the Slice Select tool (), click on the Sales slice, then Shift+click on the Service, About, and the Contact slices. Now they are all active.

Make sure that you are selecting the text slices in the Optimize preview, not the Original preview window.

Now you will use a preset to optimize this text for the web. Typically, artwork with lots of solid colors and text are saved as GIF or PNG-8, but images, like photographs fare better in size and final appearance when saved in the JPEG, or PNG-24 format. In this example you will save just the text as GIF slices, and the rest of the image slices as JPEG.

5 In the Optimize panel, on the right, choose GIF 64 No Dither from the Preset drop-down menu. The options are loaded in the optimize settings below the Preset drop-down, but can be further edited, and customized if necessary.

This is why you selected this preset:

- The GIF format was selected because the text contains a solid white color. GIF compresses images with solid colors to the smallest possible file size.
- 64 represents the number of colors that are retained when the file is saved in GIF format. GIF files utilize a color table model that allows up to 256 colors in an image. The fewer the number of colors, the smaller the file size. You can see the color table in the Color Table panel on the right side of the Save for Web & Devices dialog box.
- No Dither indicates that you do not want Photoshop to use dithering, or pixelation, to create colors that are not included in the 64-color panel you have specified.

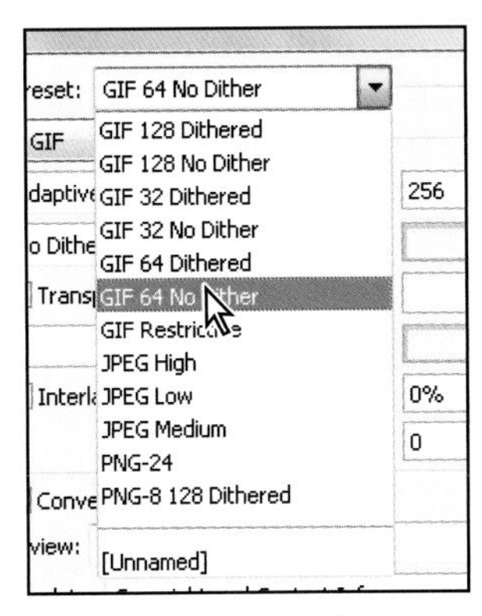

Select GIF 64 No Dither format for the slices containing text.

6 If it is not already selected, choose Adaptive from the Color reduction algorithm drop-down menu, which is directly underneath the Optimized file format drop-down menu.

Note that the file size of the optimized image, based upon your current settings, is displayed at the bottom of the optimized image preview.

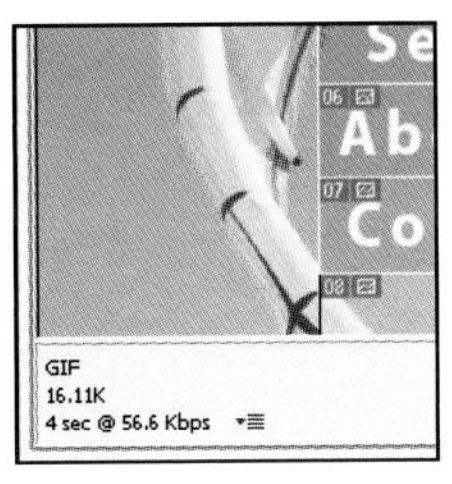

The file size of the optimized image.

Understanding Color Algorithms

GIFs can be reduced in size by reducing the amount of colors that create the image. This is referred to as the Color Algorithm. The color Algorithm helps to specify the color palette that will create the final image. There are four main choices from which you can select:

Perceptual: a perceptual rendering is one where the goal is to produce a pleasing reproduction of an original. This a good choice for illustrative graphics where color consistency or integrity is less important.

Selective: creates a color table similar to the Perceptual color table, but favoring broad areas of color and the preservation of web colors. If color integrity is important, this would be a good selection. Selective is the default option.

Adaptive: creates a custom color table by sampling colors from the predominant spectrum in the image. For example, if an image has many shades of red, the sampled colors are created from colors in the red spectrum, providing a better range of important colors.

Web: uses the standard 216-color color table common to the Windows and Mac OS 8-bit (256-color) palettes. This option ensures that no browser dither is applied to colors when the image is displayed using 8-bit color. Using the web palette can create larger files, and is becoming less of an issue as viewers increase their monitor capabilities.

Optimizing the image slices

Now that you optimized the text slices you will optimize the remaining image slices using a different format. Though this isn't always recommended, it can work well for some images. You can optimize images even more by saving varying levels of the same format, for instance select JPEG for all the slices but vary the quality level, depending upon the importance or location of the slice.

1 Switch to show only the Optimized view, and open up the image preview window, by clicking on the Optimized tab.

2 Using the Slice Select tool (), click on the slice in the upper left side of the image, then Shift+click on each of the other three (non-text) slices. There should be a total of four slices selected.

3 From the Preset drop-down menu in the Optimized panel choose JPEG Medium.

   You can test your file in a web browser directly from the Save For Web & Devices dialog box.

4 Select the Preview in default browser button at the bottom of the Save For Web & Devices dialog box. If you have a default browser installed, your image is opened on a browser page. You can also define a browser using the Preview the optimized image drop-down menu.

Notice that the slices are not apparent and that the code is visible in your preview.

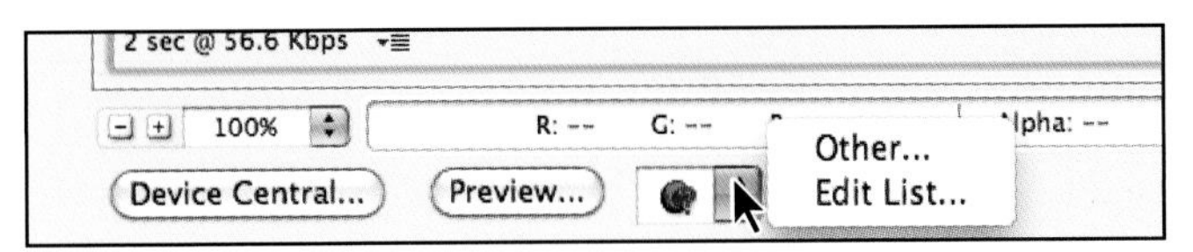

Preview the optimized image in a browser.

5 Click on the slices that you designated as having URLs. You should be connected to the assigned URLs. Use the Back button in your browser to return to your sliced image. Close the browser window when you are finished testing the image. The Save For Web & Devices Dialog box is still open.

6 Choose Save, and the Save Optimized As dialog box appears. Browse to the ps12lessons folder and choose HTML and Images from the Save as type (Windows) or Format (Mac OS) drop-down menu. Press Save.

An HTML page, along with the sliced images, is saved in your ps12lessons folder. You can now open the file in Dreamweaver, or any other web editing program, and continue building the page, or copy and paste the table to another page.

7 Choose File > Save to save your original image. Choose File > Close to close the file.

Saving files for video

If you are saving into Adobe applications such as After Effects, Premiere, or Flash, you do not need to take extra steps to maintain transparency. In fact, you can simply browse, search, and organize native .psd images directly in Adobe Bridge from the other Adobe Creative Suite applications.

When importing into a non-Adobe video application, you need to consider transparency. Each video application has its own set of importable formats. For this lesson, you will open a pre-built file and save it as a TIFF with an alpha channel. Video editing applications recognize alpha channels when defining transparent areas on an image.

1 Open the file ps1202.psd. The image that appears is intended to overlay a video file.

An image with transparency applied to it.

2 If the Layers panel is not visible, choose Window > Layers to open the Layers panel.

3 Position your cursor over the vector mask on the Shape 1 layer. Hold down the Ctrl (Windows) or Command (Mac OS) key and click on the vector thumbnail for the Rectangle Shape layer. This selects everything on that layer that is not transparent.

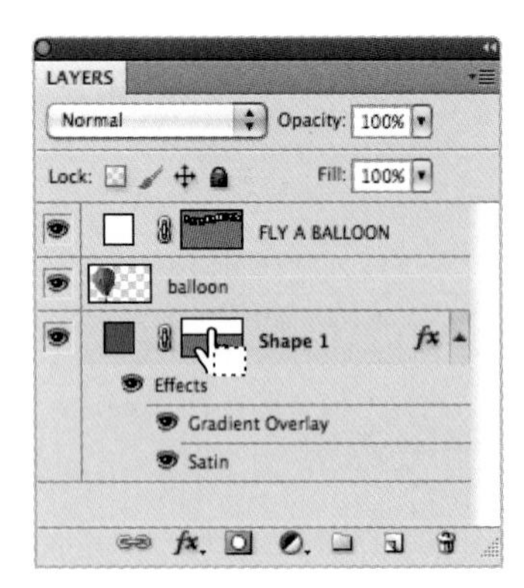

Ctrl/Command+click to make a selection from a layer's contents.

4 Click and hold the Ctrl+Shift (Windows) or Command+Shift (Mac OS) keys, and click on the layer thumbnail for the layer named balloon. This adds the balloon layer to the selection.

5 If the Channels panel is not visible, choose Window > Channels to open the Channels panel.

6 Press the Save Selection as channel button (◙) at the bottom of the Channels panel. This creates an alpha channel from the active selection.

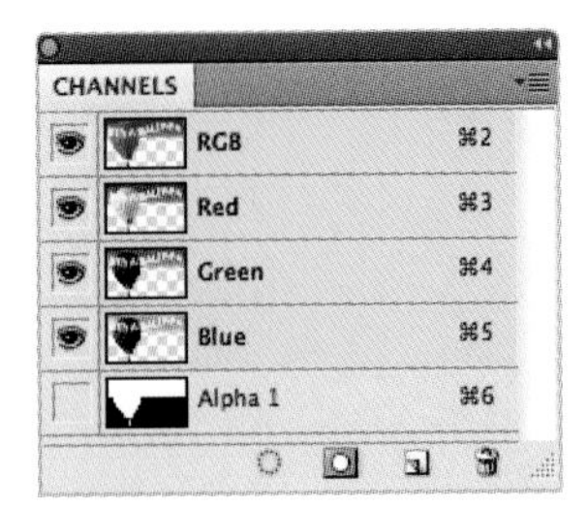

Create an alpha channel from the selection.

In your alpha channel, the areas that are black are fully transparent, the areas that are white are fully opaque, and any areas that are gray will be varying degrees of transparency. This is the standard way that video editing applications treat alpha channels.

7 Choose File > Save As. When the Save As dialog box appears, navigate to the ps12lessons folder and type **ps1202_work.psd** into the Name text field. Select TIFF from the Format drop-down menu.

8 In the Save Options field, make sure that Layers is not checked and Alpha Channels is checked. A warning stating that this image needs to be saved as a copy appears, which means that your original file will keep layers intact. Press Save. The TIFF Options dialog box appears.

9 In the TIFF Options dialog box, make sure that None is selected in the Image Compression section and leave other settings at their default settings. Select OK in the TIFF Options window. You have saved a TIFF file with an area that will appear transparent in your video editing application.

10 Close the original Photoshop document by choosing File > Close. If asked if you would like to save the changes, choose Don't Save.

Creating animation

In this lesson, you will create an animation using the default animation panel. If you have Photoshop CS5 Extended, you can take the lesson further and use the Advanced timeline in the video lesson that follows.

Working in Frame mode

Working in the Frame mode of the animation panel is much like creating an animation using a flip book. When played, each frame is converted into a final animation. Using the Frame animation panel, you can also build individual frames and then have Photoshop automatically create transitions between the frames for you. This process is called tweening. For this part of the lesson, you will add a floating hot air balloon to the image of the lake.

1 Choose File > Browse in Bridge and navigate to the ps12lessons folder. Select the images named ps1203.psd and ps1204.psd, then Right-click (Windows) or Ctrl+click (Mac OS) and select Open from the contextual menu. An image of a lake and an image of a red hot air balloon open in separate document window tabs.

2 Click on the arrow to the right of the Arrange Documents (▣) icon in the Application bar at the top of the workspace and choose 2 Up from the drop-down menu.

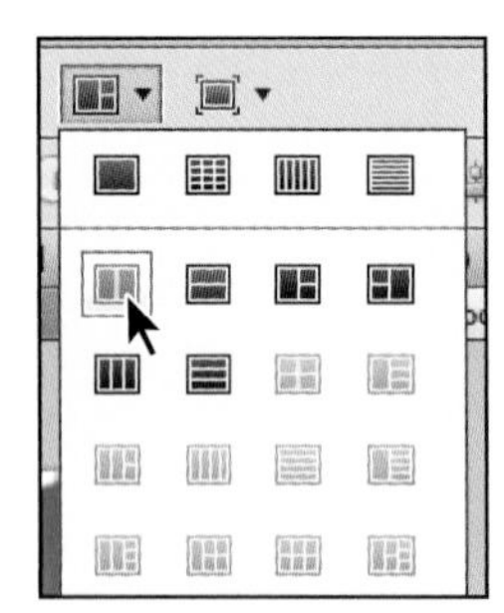

Choose to show your two images, side by side.

3 Select the Move tool (▸+) and click and drag the balloon image (ps1204.psd) over to the image of the lake (ps1203.psd). Release the mouse when you see the border appear around the document window of the ps1203.psd image.

4 Click on the ps1204.psd image to make it active, and choose File > Close.

5 Choose Window > Animation to open the Photoshop Animation panel. As a default, the Animation panel displays as a frame animation panel. If you see the Animation Timeline, choose Convert to Frame Animation from the panel menu in the upper-right corner or click on the Convert to Frame Animation button in the bottom-right corner of the Animation panel.

Using the Frame Animation panel, you will create two different key frames and have Photoshop automatically build the additional frames for you.

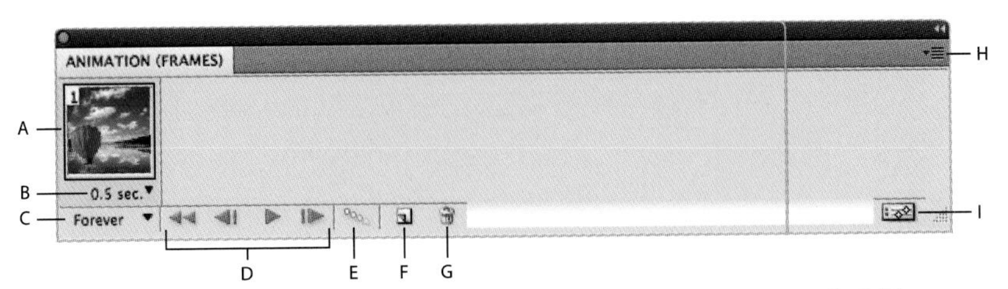

A. Key frame. B. Selects frame delay time. C. Selects looping options. D. Player controls. E. Tween. F. Duplicates selected frames. G. Delete selected frames. H. Panel menu. I. Convert to timeline animation.

6 If the Layers panel is not visible, choose Window > Layers. Select the balloon layer to make sure that it is the active layer, then, using the Move tool, click and drag the balloon so that it is in the lower left corner of the lake image.

Position the balloon to be in the lower left corner.

7 Type **15** to change the layer to a 15% opacity.

8 Click on the Duplicate selected frames button (⧉) at the bottom of the Animation panel. A second frame is added to the right of the original.

9 Verify that you still have the balloon layer selected, then, using the Move tool (►+), click and drag the balloon to the upper right corner of the lake image. Then type **0** (zero) to set the layer opacity at 100%.

10 Click the Add a layer style button (*fx*) at the bottom of the Layers panel, and choose Outer Glow from the list of styles. The Layer Style dialog box appears with Outer Glow selected.

11 In the Elements section of the Layer Styles dialog box, click and drag the Size slider to the right until you reach approximately 70, or type **70** into the Size text field. Press OK. A glow has been applied to the balloon layer.

12 From the Animation panel menu, select Tween or click on the Tween button (⁂) at the bottom of the Animation panel.

13 On the Tween menu, press OK to add five frames to your animation. Your former frame 2 now becomes the seventh and last frame in your animation.

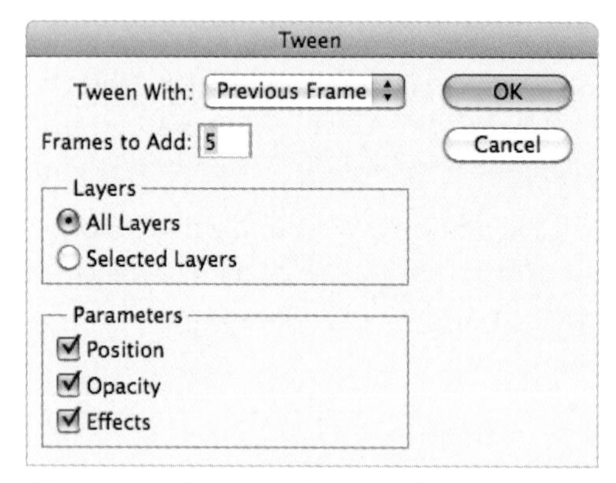

Choose to insert five frames in between the frames.

In addition to the number of frames to add to the animation, the Tween menu gives you the ability to choose which layers to include in your frames and which parameters to animate. As the default, all layers and parameters are included.

14 Select all the frames of your animation by clicking on the first frame, holding down the Shift key, and clicking on the last frame.

15 With all your frames selected, click on the value for Selects frame delay at the bottom of any frame and select 0.5. Because all the frames are highlighted, the delay time of all your frames is adjusted. Press the Play button (▶) at the bottom of the Animation panel to preview your animation. If your animation continues to loop, press the Stop animation button (■) (same location as the Play button) to stop the animation.

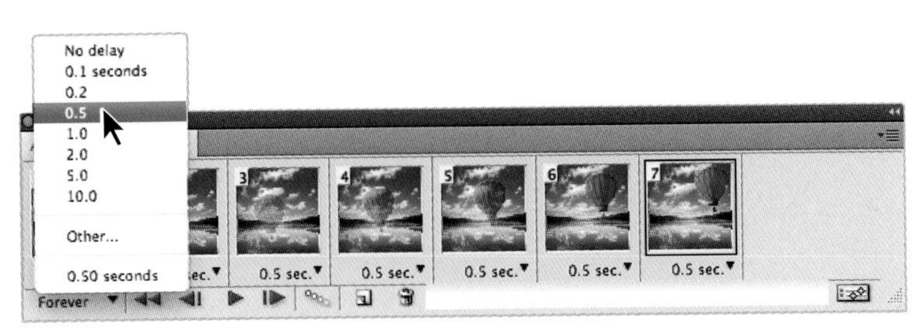

Select 0.5 as the frame delay time.

As a default, your animation is set to replay over and over again. If you prefer to set the number of times your animation plays, click and hold on the text, Forever, *that appears in the lower left corner of the animation panel and select Once, or choose Other to input a custom value.*

16 Choose File > Save As. The Save As dialog box appears. Navigate to the ps12lessons folder and then type **animation_done** in the Name text field. Choose Photoshop (PSD) from the Format drop-down menu and press Save. Keep the file open for the next part of this lesson.

Saving an animated GIF

Now you will save the animation in a format that will recognize the frames and can be posted to the Web.

1 Choose File > Save For Web & Devices. The Save For Web & Devices dialog box appears.

2 Choose 2-up from the display tabs at the top of the dialog box. This allows you to see the original image next to a preview of the optimized image.

3 Choose GIF 128 Dithered from the Preset drop-down menu. This is a good preset to use for an animation with multiple colors. It creates a good balance between file size and image quality.

4 Press the Save button to save your file as a GIF animation. Navigate to the ps12lesson folder and type **animation_done.gif** in the File name text field.

5 In the Format drop-down menu, choose Images Only and press Save.

6 Choose File > Save to save your file, then choose File > Close to close your Photoshop document.

7 If you would like to test your file, open any browser application and choose File > Open File, and then browse to locate your .gif and open it directly into your browser window.

Creating animation for video

For this part of the lesson, you will create a type of on-screen graphic called a lower third. Usually seen on television and in documentary-style films, a lower third is the text and graphics that usually appear on screen to introduce a speaker. They take their name from the fact that they take up the lower third of the frame. To create the lower third, you'll bring a graphic into a blank document and animate its opacity parameter so that it fades in. Then you'll render the video file so that it can be imported into a video editing application.

IMPORTANT! Photoshop CS5 Extended is required for the following part of this lesson.

Working in Timeline mode

The Timeline mode of the Animation panel functions differently from the Frame mode. In the Timeline mode, each layer has parameters for position, opacity, and effects that can each have key frames assigned to them individually.

1 Choose File > New and choose Film & Video from the Preset drop-down menu. Leave the size at the default, NTSC DV. Choose Transparent from the Background Contents drop-down menu. Press OK.

   A warning dialog box appears, telling you that the pixel aspect ratio is for previewing purposes only. Press OK.

2 Choose View > New Guide. While the presets include guidelines to define the Action and Title safe areas of the video frame, there is nothing to indicate where your lower third should end.

3 In the New Guide dialog box, select the Horizontal radio button and type **66%** in the Position text field, and press OK. This creates a new guideline 66% from the top of your document and marks the lower third of the video frame.

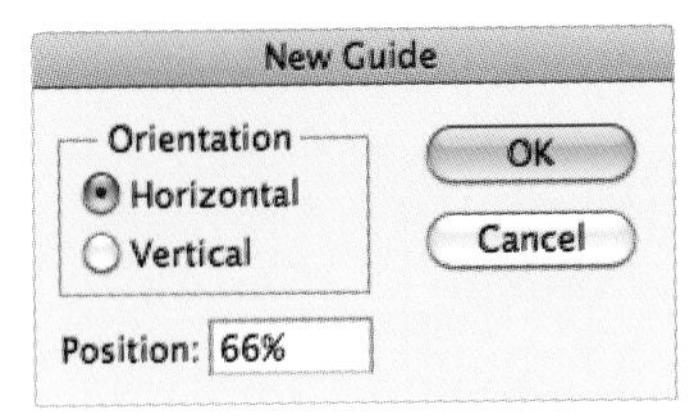

Create a guide indicating the lower third.

4 Choose File > Open and open ps1205.psd from the ps12lessons folder. When the pixel aspect ratio warning box appears, press OK.

5 Click on the arrow to the right of the Arrange Documents (▣) icon in the Application bar at the top of the workspace and choose 2 Up from the drop-down menu

6 Using the Move tool (▸+), drag and drop the contents of ps1205.psd into your empty document. You can close the ps1205.psd file after you drag over the contents.

7 Position the graphic so that it is below the lower third guide.

Position the graphic so that it is below the lower third.

8 If the Layers panel is not open, choose Window > Layers. Layer 1 was created automatically when you created your document and you don't need it, so delete it by highlighting it in the Layers panel and dragging it to the Delete layer button (🗑) at the bottom of the panel.

9 If the Animation panel is not open, choose Window > Animation. If it is not already in Timeline mode, select Convert to Timeline from the Animation panel menu or clicking on the Convert to Timeline Animation button (▭) in the bottom right of the Animation panel. Note that the Timeline appears only in Photoshop CS5 Extended.

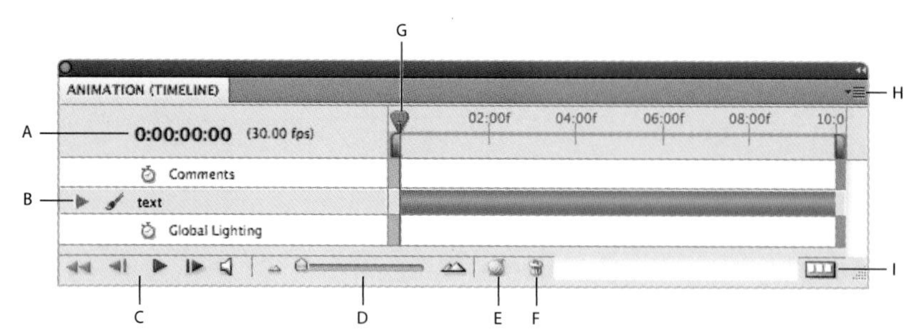

A. Current Time. B. Layers. C. Player controls. D. Zoom Slider. E. Toggle Onion Skins. F. Delete Keyframes. G. Current Time Indicator. H. Panel menu. I. Convert to Frame Animation.

10 In the Animation panel, click the triangle to the left of the layer name to reveal its animatible parameters.

What are animatible properties?

When you edit a layer's properties over time, the computer builds an animation by interpreting the change. In Adobe Photoshop, animation information is stored in keyframes. Keyframes represent extremes of animatible properties. For example, if you wanted to have a circle move from left to right, you would need to create two keyframes, one with the circle on the left and the other with it on the right. You would then have the computer analyze the change and build the rest of the animation for you.

11 Click the stopwatch (⏱) next to the Opacity parameter to enable animation. A keyframe is created at the beginning of the Timeline.

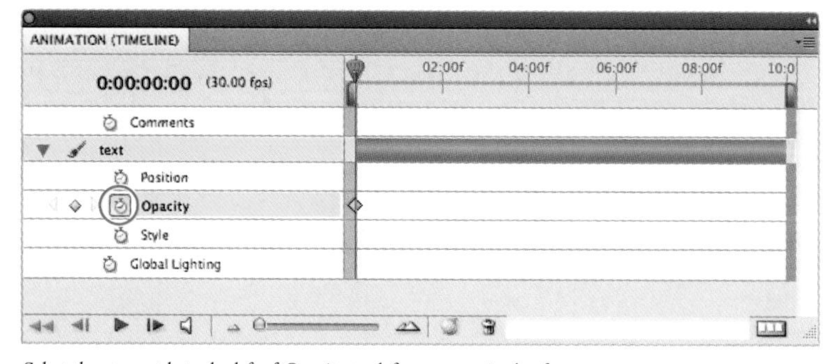

Select the stopwatch to the left of Opacity to define an opacity keyframe.

The stopwatch enables animation when it is clicked on. If clicked off, it disables animation. A by-product of disabling the animation of a property is that all the keyframes for that property are deleted.

12 In the Layers panel, type **0** in the Opacity text field and press the Enter or Return key.

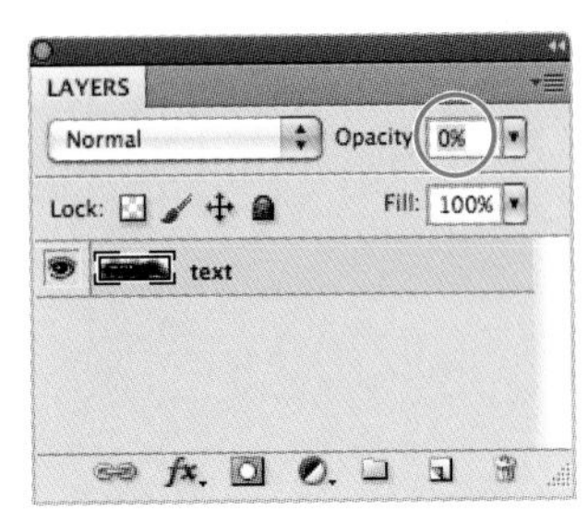

Adjust the opacity so the text layer is not visible.

13 Double-click on the Current Time field (top left of Animation panel). The Set Current Time dialog box appears. Type **3:00** and press OK. This moves your Current Time Indicator to the three-second mark on the Timeline. The Current Time Indicator (the blue wedge at the top of the Timeline) indicates your animation's current time.

14 In the Layers panel, type **100** in the Opacity text field, and press Enter/Return. This creates a new keyframe where your Current Time Indicator is located.

This is the nature of timeline-based animation in Photoshop. If animation is enabled for a parameter, any change made to that parameter will create a new keyframe at the location of the Current Time Indicator.

15 Return the Current Time Indicator back to the starting point by clicking on the 0.0 at the beginning of the Timeline.

16 Press the Play button (▶) at the bottom of the Animation panel to preview the animation. The text fades in over three seconds. You can press the Stop button (■) when you are finished viewing the animation.

17 Choose File > Save As. The Save As dialog box appears. Navigate to the ps12lessons folder and type **ps1205_animation.psd** into the File name text field. Select Photoshop from the Format drop-down menu and press Save. Keep the file open for the next part of this lesson.

Rendering a video file

1 Select File > Export > Render Video. This opens the Render Video window.

Note that the Render Video Window is divided into four areas: Location, File Options, Range, and Render Options.

Location: Allows you to specify a name for the file that you are going to export and a location to save that file.

File Options: Controls the type of file you want to create from your animation. QuickTime export will create video files in a wide variety of common formats for mobile, video, and web distributions, while the Image Sequence option renders video as a series of sequential still images. This area also allows you to specify the exported files' dimensions.

Range: Controls the amount of the animation to export. By default, it will export the entire animation timeline, but you can limit the export range to lesser parts of the Timeline.

Render Options: Controls whether an alpha channel is included in the output file along with the file's frame rate. Some exportable formats will not allow you to include an alpha channel.

2 In the Location section, type **ps1205** into the Name text field, click the Select Folder button, and navigate to the ps12lessons folder, then press OK or Choose.

3 In the File Options section, make sure that QuickTime Export radio button is selected and QuickTime Movie is selected from the drop-down menu on the right. The Size drop-down menu at the bottom of the File Options field should be set to Document Size. The default setting used here produces a QuickTime movie optimized for playback on a computer, as well as a variety of mobile devices.

The settings button to the right of the drop-down menu can be used to format a QuickTime movie for other media such as TV and video.

4 In the Range section, make sure that the radio button next to All Frames is clicked on.

5 In the Render Options section, select *Premultiplied with White* from the Alpha Channel drop-down menu and also make sure that the Frame Rate drop-down menu is set to Document Frame Rate.

6 Press the Render button to create your video file. The rendering time will vary, depending on your computer hardware.

7 Choose File > Close. You can return to the native Photoshop file to make edits at a later point, if necessary. You can test your file by navigating to the ps12lessons folder and selecting your ps1205 file. It should open the QuickTime Player, and you can view your work in action.

The default settings rendering video are designed to produce a high-quality video file with an alpha channel that can be imported into a video editing or motion graphics program. Areas of your animation that are transparent will become transparent when you import them into these applications; however, they will not appear transparent when you view them in the QuickTime player.

Self study

1 Using the Standard Frame Animation panel, create a text layer and experiment with animating its position so that it moves around your document.

2 Using the Advanced Timeline Animation panel, experiment with animating the effects on a layer. Animate a drop shadow so that it moves over time.

Review

Questions

1 What is more important to note in an image size to be used on a web page, pixel dimensions or resolution?

2 When would you need to save a video file with an alpha channel?

3 Name four web image formats and provide an example of when to use each one.

Answers

1 It is more important to have the pixel dimensions of an image accurate, rather than the resolution. As a web and video creator, you would only use the top section of the Image Size dialog box.

2 While other Adobe applications can read native PSD files with transparent areas, non-Adobe applications cannot. The alpha channel is the only way for these applications to understand which parts of your graphic are transparent and which are opaque.

3 **a.** The JPEG format is used for saving photographs and other continuous-tone imagery.

b. The GIF format is used for saving limited-tone imagery (images with lots of solid color) such as logos and other graphics. GIF supports transparency and animation.

c. The PNG format is used for saving either photographic imagery or images with a lot of solid color. It can also support transparency in varying amounts.

d. The WMBP format is used for saving images for mobile content devices like cell phones.

What you'll learn in this lesson:

- Discovering 3D
- Wrapping an image around an object
- Adjusting the light
- Rendering an image

Introducing 3D

For many Photoshop users, 3D will be a brave new world to explore. For those of you who have been straddling the world of 3D applications and digital imaging, Photoshop CS5 offers some solutions that will save hours of work. In this lesson, you are introduced to the basics of working with the new and improved 3D Features.

Starting up

Before starting, make sure that your tools and panels are consistent by resetting your preferences. See "Resetting Adobe Photoshop CS5 preferences" on page 3. If you want to complete the video portion of this lesson make sure that you have QuickTime Player installed. You can download a free copy of Quicktime at *apple.com/quicktime*.

You will work with several files from the ps13lessons folder in this lesson. Make sure that you have loaded your pslessons folder onto your hard drive from the supplied DVD. See "Loading lesson files" on page 5. Now, let's take a look at what's new in Photoshop CS5.

See Lesson 13 in action!

Use the accompanying video to gain a better understanding of how to use some of the features shown in this lesson. The video tutorial for this lesson can be found on the included DVD.

Creating a 3D object

Creating a 3D object can be as simple or as complicated as you want. For the scope of this lesson, the process will be introduced assuming that you are not typically editing in a 3D environment. In this lesson, you will use the 3D features in Photoshop CS5 to open an image and wrap it around a cylinder. Along the way, you will discover some features to help create more flexible textures and artwork, as well as find out how to export your 3D artwork, to be used as 2D or 3D art in its final form.

Getting an image ready for 3D

You will now start the 3D project by opening a file that contains many layers, layer masks, and text layers. In order to create a 3D object, these need to be converted into one layer. You could do this by flattening the image, but that leaves you with a file in which the layers can no longer be individually edited. This would make it difficult to change the name of the product, or replace one of the layers. To keep this composition in editable form, you will select the layers and convert them to a Smart Object.

1 Choose File > Browse in Bridge, or click on the Launch Bridge button (Br) in the Application bar.

2 Navigate to the ps13lessons folder and double-click to open the file named ps1301.psd. A comp for the label of a soda can is visible.

3 If the Layers panel is not visible, choose Window > Layers.

4 Choose the Move tool, and then click on the texture layer in the Layers panel to select it. Then hold down the Ctrl (Windows) or Command (Mac OS) key and click on each layer until you have reached the top text layer, named FizzyPop! All the layers are activated.

You could also click on the texture layer and then Shift+click on the FizzyPop! text layer to select all layers in between.

5 Click on the Layers panel menu and choose Convert to Smart Object from the panel drop-down menu. The layers appear to flatten into one layer. Fortunately, you can double-click on this layer at any time to reopen the composition in its original (non-flattened) form.

6 Choose File > Save As. In the Save As dialog box, navigate to the ps13lessons folder, then type **ps1301_work.psd** into the Name text field. Choose Photoshop from the Format drop-down menu and press Save.

Wrapping the image around a soda can

Now that you have consolidated the composition to one layer, you can easily wrap, or map, this image to a 3D shape. Photoshop provides you with default shapes that you can select from the 3D menu item. Once this image has been wrapped around the shape, it is considered a texture for the object.

1 Choose 3D > New Shape From Layer, and then choose Soda Can from the drop-down menu. If your video card does not support hardware-accelerated 3D rendering, you will receive a warning dialog box. Press OK to render with software only. The image is converted into a 3D soda can shape, and the FizzyPop! layer is now a 3D layer.

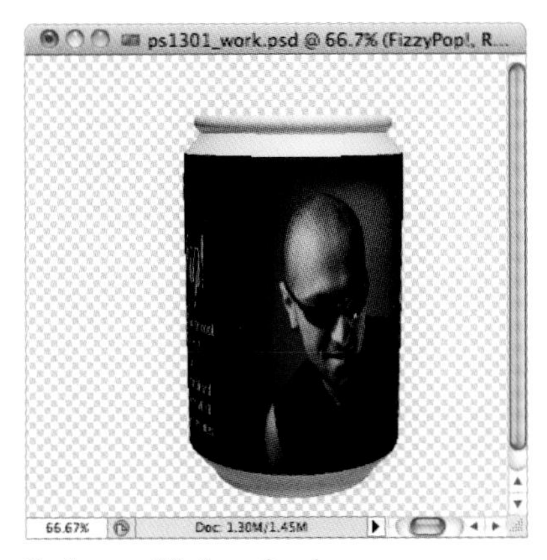

Easily create 3D shapes from layers.

Getting 3D images in and out of Photoshop CS5

Photoshop provides you with many preconfigured 3D shapes from which you can choose, but it also enables you to import existing files from 3D applications. Formats that you can import include:

- **.dae** (Collada)—the recommended format for interchange.
- **.3ds**—3D Studio.
- **.obj**—Wavefront.
- **.u3d**
- **.kmz**—Google Earth's format. This is the same as a zipped Collada file.

Rendering your 3D image

You can choose to export a 3D layer from Photoshop to a format that can be imported into 3D applications. Choose 3D > Export 3D Layer, and when the Save As dialog box appears, choose from one of these formats:

- Collada (DAE)
- Google Earth 4 (KMZ)
- U3D (U3D), which you can import into Acrobat 8 and 9 files.
- Wavefront|Obj (OBJ)

You will now rotate the object to make the text on the texture (the layer you wrapped around the can) visible using the Object Rotate tool.

2 Click on the Object Rotate tool (◎) and drag the can to rotate the 3D image. You may have to release and click and drag several times to get the can in a position where the text is visible.

You can also use Photoshop CS5's 3D Axis widget which is visible by default. This tool allows you to work with 3D objects directly within your image rather than having to switch tools.

Place your cursor over each of the three handles in the 3D Axis widget and note that they will light up yellow as you hover over them. Each of these handles represent a 3D axis and will allow you to control various properties of the object.

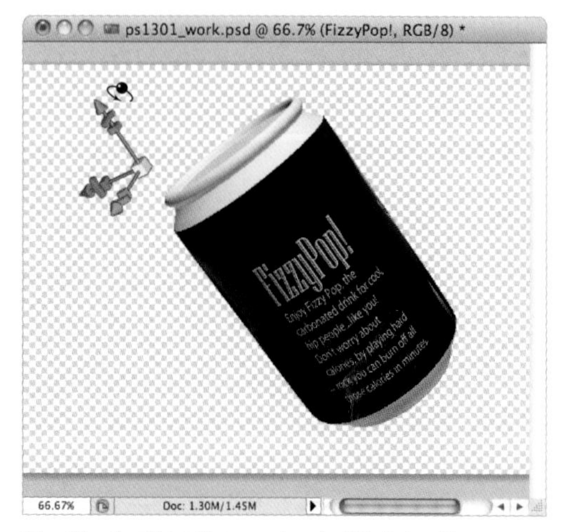

Use either the Object Rotate tool or the 3D Axis widget to reposition the can.

You will now reposition the image texture on the can.

3 Double-click on the FizzyPop! layer thumbnail; the 3D {Scene} panel opens. You will use this panel to change the properties of the 3D layer.

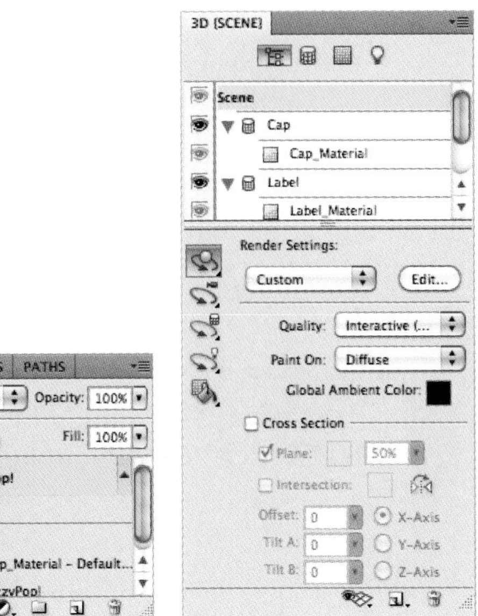

Double-click on the 3D layer thumbnail in the Layers panel.

The 3D {Scene} panel opens.

4 If the Label category in the 3D panel is not open, click on the arrow to the left to show Label_Material, and then click on Label_Material to make its options visible.

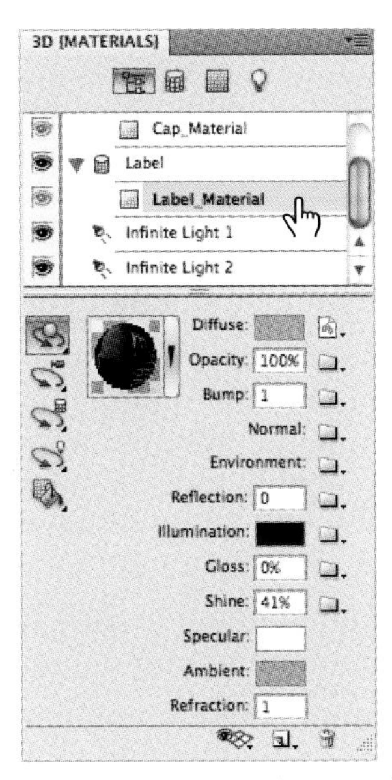

Select Label_Material in the 3D panel to make changes to the texture.

The FizzyPop! layer is considered a texture that has been applied to this 3D object. Click in the Opacity text field for the 3D Materials and type **50%**. Press Enter (Windows) or Return (Mac OS) to see the label reduced to 50% opacity. Press Ctrl+Z (Windows) or Command+Z (Mac OS) to undo and return the opacity to 100%.

5 Press Ctrl+S (Windows) or Command+S (Mac OS) to save this file.

Adjusting the lighting

When working with 3D objects in Photoshop, you can control the lighting, and add additional light sources, or change the position and direction of the default lighting. In this part of the lesson, you will adjust the lighting to be more intense, thereby improving the readability of the text on the can.

1 With the ps1301_work file still open, and the 3D panel still open, scroll down to the first Infinite Light 2 and click on it.

2 In the options below, use the slider to change the intensity to a value of 2. The light source for the entire can now becomes much brighter.

Select Infinite Light 2, then increase the light intensity.

You can experiment with the placement of the light by using the Light Rotate button () in the 3D panel. In this part of the lesson, you simply select the Light Rotate button and randomly reposition the light; no specific coordinates are necessary.

3 Click on the Light Rotate button in the 3D panel, and click and drag the light source directly on the 3D image to rotate the light source around the 3D image.

As mentioned earlier, no specific coordinates are required for this; simply find a location that you feel works well for the image.

4 Press Ctrl+S (Windows) or Command+S (Mac OS) to save the file. Keep the ps1301_work file open for the next part of the lesson.

Animating the soda can

You touched on some animation techniques in Lesson 12; now you will have the opportunity to make your can go for a spin.

1 You can switch tools directly within the 3D panel. Click on the Object Rotate tool and then click and drag your can until the man's face is visible.

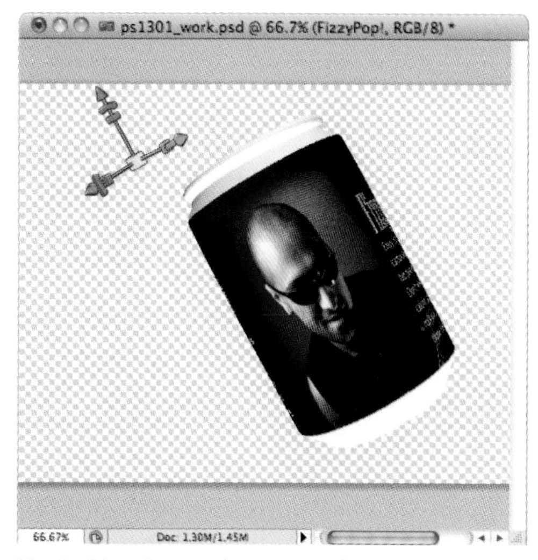

Use the Object Rotate tool to reposition the can.

2 Choose Window > Animation. If the Animation window does not say ANIMATION (TIMELINE) on the tab, click and hold down on the Animation's panel menu and choose Convert to Timeline from the drop-down menu.

3 Click on the arrow to the left of FizzyPop! to view all the properties that you can animate. Then click on the stopwatch icon (⏱) to the left of the 3D Object Position. This adds a keyframe and defines the present position as being the starting point for the animation.

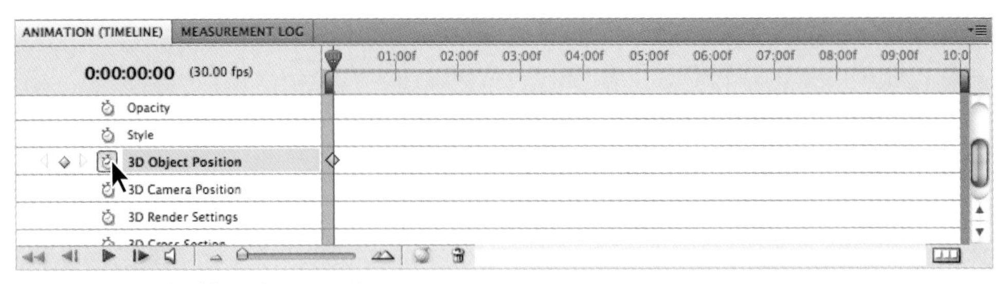

Start the animation by defining the starting object position.

4 Now click and drag the Current Time Marker (CTM) over to 3:00 in the Timeline.

5 Using the 3D Rotate tool, click and drag the 3D object until the text is visible. A keyframe is automatically entered on the Timeline, indicating that there is a change in the position.

6 Using the 3D Roll tool (located under the 3D Rotate tool), click and drag to tilt the can in a different direction. No exact adjustment is necessary.

You have already created an animation, but you will now copy your first keyframe and paste it later in the Timeline so that the can returns to the same position.

7 Right+click (Windows) or Ctrl+click (Mac OS) on the keyframe at the start of the Timeline, and choose Copy Keyframes from the contextual menu.

8 Click and drag the CTM to 6:00, and from the Animation panel menu, choose Paste Keyframe(s). The keyframe is pasted at the 6:00 point in the Timeline.

Testing your animation

You will now test your animation, and export it as a QuickTime movie.

1 Click and drag the CTM back to the beginning of the Timeline in the Animation panel.

2 Press the Play button (▶) in the Timeline panel to see your animation in action. When you are finished viewing, press the Stop button (■).

3 Choose File > Export > Render Video. Understand that this is a basic introduction to the possibilities of using 3D and video, so you will leave the settings in the Render Video at their defaults. If you are a video professional, you will find many of the features that you need to output a quality video in this dialog box (based on the speed of your system, this render make take a few minutes, you may want to return to this step at the end of the lesson).

4 Type **ps1301_work.mov** into the Name text field, if it is not there already. Then click on the Select Folder button to navigate to your ps13lessons folder.

5 In the File Options category, choose QuickTime Movie from the QuickTime Export drop-down menu.

Notice the additional file formats that you can select in the drop-down menu. By using the Settings button, you can customize each one of these file formats for an optimal export.

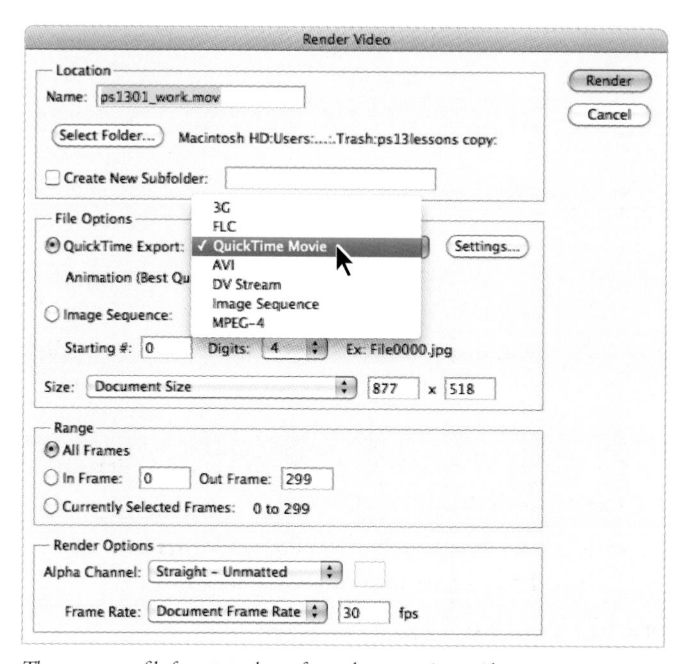

There are many file formats to choose from when exporting a video.

6 Press Render.

You have now created a working 3D video. To test this movie, launch the QuickTime Player, and choose File > Open File. If you do not have the QuickTime Player, you can download it at *apple.com/downloads*.

7 When you are finished viewing the video return to Photoshop and Choose File > Save to Save your file, then choose File > Close.

Using the Repoussé feature to create 3D Text

Photoshop's new Repoussé feature allows you to convert 2D objects into 3D objects which you can then style in different ways using the 3D features. The term repoussé refers to a metalworking technique in which patterns are created by hammering or pressing a metal object from the reverse side. Photoshop CS5 accomplishes a virtual version of this technique by converting 2d paths to 3D meshes. You can apply the Repoussé effect to paths, selections, layer masks and text layers. Potential uses include font design, stroke design, photo enhancement, and free-form 3D shape design.

1 Open the file ps1302.psd and choose File > Save As. In the Save As dialog box, navigate to the ps13lessons folder, then type **ps1302_work.psd** into the Name text field. Choose Photoshop from the Format drop-down menu and press Save. This file is has a text layer set in Myriad Pro.

2 Select the 3D text layer in the Layers panel, then choose 3D > Repoussé. The only option available will be text layer although you can also apply the effect to layer masks, paths and selections. Choose the text layer option. You will be prompted to rasterize the text, click Yes. The Repoussé dialog box appears and your text now has the default 3D effect applied.

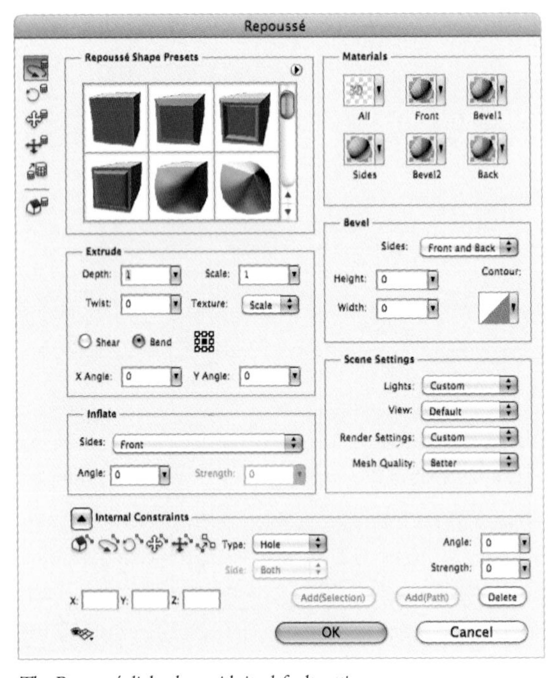

The Repoussé dialog box with its default settings.

To understand some of the capabilities of the effect you can choose from the built-in shape presets.

3 Click the panel menu on the right side of the Repoussé Shape Presets section and select Small List from the drop-down menu. This way you can see the presets listed by name.

4 In the Repoussé Shape Presets section, scroll down and locate the Bend preset. To identify the names of presets, you can hover over a thumbnail to see the label. Once you locate the Bend preset, click on it to apply. You will see the 3D effect apply to your text.

This effect is actually based on a 3D mesh which you have the ability to control in order to simulate effects such as depth and volume.

5 In the Extrude section, change the depth value to **4** to extend the length of your mesh. In the Inflate section, change the angle to **80**. This creates a smooth mesh effect which appears as if it is being inflated or pushed from behind.

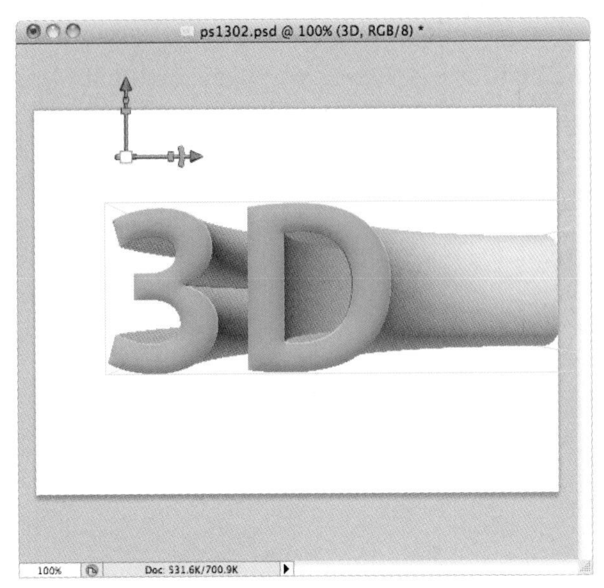

Text with the Bend preset plus Extrude and Inflate applied.

Another feature of the Repoussé effect is the ability to apply materials to the 3D mesh. You can choose to apply the same material to all sides, or apply different materials to different sides.

6 Click on the All menu in the Materials section and scroll down, if necessary, to locate the Organic Orangepeel material. Click on it to apply (be sure to be patient when you apply a material, the 3D rendering takes time).

At any point you can readjust the position of your mesh directly within the Repoussé dialog box. You have the ability to Rotate, Roll, Pan, Slide, and Scale your mesh by choosing these tools in the upper left corner of the dialog box.

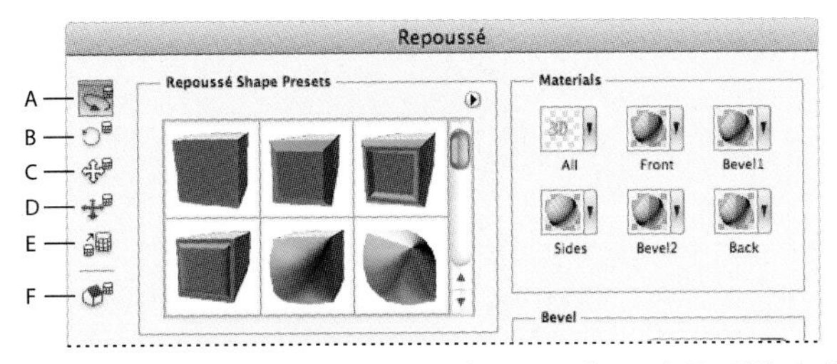

***A**. Rotate the Mesh. **B**. Roll the Mesh. **C**. Pan the Mesh. **D**. Slide the Mesh. **E**. Scale the Mesh. **F**. Return to initial mesh position.*

7 Click on the Rotate the Mesh tool and change the position of your mesh. No particular angle is needed here, experiment until you find an angle you are happy with. Click OK when finished.

Photoshop CS5 Extended has an updated version of a feature called Adobe Ray Tracer which offers powerful behind-the-scenes improvements for the rendering of 3D objects. 3D effects such as shadows, lighting and textures have all been significantly improved.

8 In the 3D panel, click on the Scene layer, if necessary. In the Render Settings section, click on the Quality menu and choose Ray Traced Final. Photoshop's feedback tiling feature will start running on your screen.

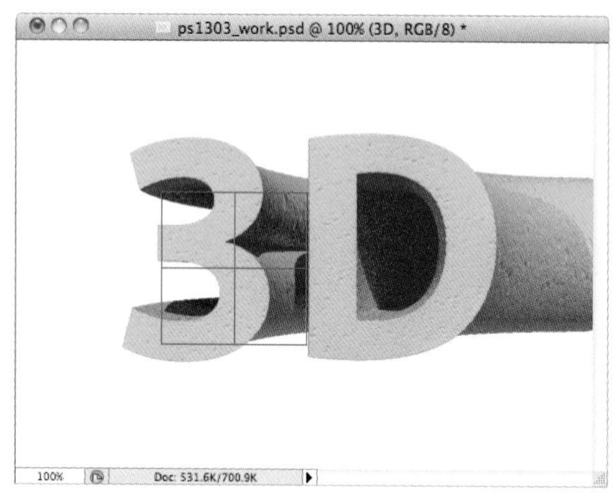

Rendering your 3D object.

This feature is a real-time preview of the different sections of your image as they are being rendered. When the tiles stop appearing this means your rendering is complete.

Based on your system's video card and other factors, even small files may take a while to render. You may pause the process at any point by clicking anywhere within your image.

To resume a render you can choose 3D > Resume Progressive Rendering. You can also choose a small area to render by making a selection on the 3D layer and choosing 3D > Progressive Render Selection.

9 Choose File > Save but keep this file open for the next exercise.

Rasterizing your 3D images

When you save a file in either the PSD, PDF or TIFF formats you preserve the 3D model information such as the lighting and 3D layers. Occasionally you may want to flatten your image or export your image for other uses. You can do this by rasterizing your image, just be aware that once a 3D image is rasterized there is no going back, so you should always keep a master 3D backup.

1 Choose File > Save As. In the Save As dialog box, navigate to the ps13lessons folder, then type **ps1303_rasterized.psd** into the Name text field. Choose Photoshop from the Format drop-down menu and press Save.

2 Make sure your 3D layer is selected in the Layers panel and then choose 3D > Rasterize. Your image is now a standard bitmapped image and you can do everything you would with any other image such as make selections, apply filters and so on.

   Using this layer as an element in a composite is now simple.

3 Click on the background layer in the Layers panel and then click on the Gradient tool in the Tools panel.

4 Click and drag the Gradient tool across the screen. You are not going for any particular effect here, this is simply a way to illustrate the composite features of your rasterized 3D layer.

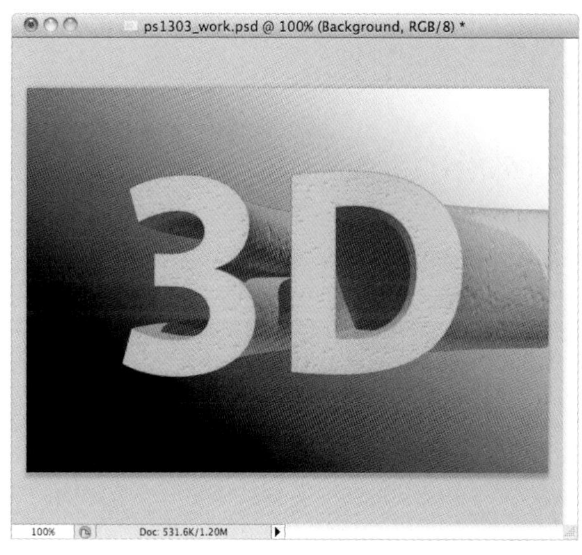

Create a gradient effect behind the 3D rendered text.

5 Save your file. Congratulations! You have completed Lesson 13, "Introducing 3D."

Self study

In this lesson, you barely touched the surface of what you can accomplish using 3D in Photoshop CS5. With normal 2D images, you can now create more dynamic images. Try creating a simple 3D postcard, and then painting on the 3D object.

1 Open any 2D image. An extra one is provided for you in the ps13lessons folder, named ps1303.psd.

2 Choose 3D > New 3D Postcard From Layer.

3 Choose the 3D Rotate tool, and click and drag to see that you have turned your 2D image into a 3D postcard.

4 To experiment further, you can choose a unique brush and change its blending mode. In this example, Flowing Stars was selected from the Brushes panel, and its Master Dimension was changed to over 600 pixels; the blending mode was changed to Vivid Light.

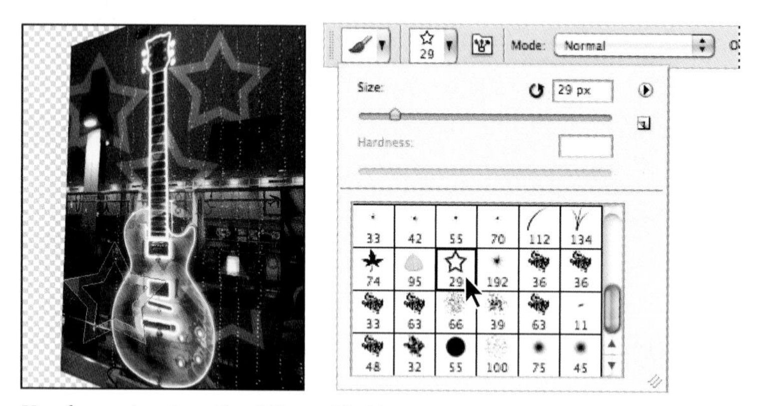

Have fun experimenting with painting on 3D objects.

Experiment with gradients and all your brush tools, including the Clone Stamp tool (). Just make sure that you change blending modes to create realistic painting effects on your image.

Review

Questions

1 What type of file do you need to have open to create a 3D object?

2 What steps can you take to reposition a texture on a 3D object?

3 What file formats can you export your 3D layer to and still maintain the 3D Object?

Answers

1 You do not need to have any particular file type open in order to create a 3D object. If it opens in Photoshop, and you are in RGB mode, it will work.

2 To reposition a texture on a 3D object, follow these steps:

a. Double-click on the 3D layer; the 3D panel appears.

b. In the 3D panel, choose the layer name, Label or Cap, that the texture is applied to.

c. Click on the Edit the Diffuse Texture button to the right of Diffuse, and choose Edit Texture.

d. In the Texture Properties dialog box, enter new values for the U Offset and/or V Offset, and then click OK.

3 You can choose 3D > Export 3D layer and choose to export using any one of these formats:

a. Collada (DAE)

b. Google Earth 4 (KMZ)

c. U3D (U3D), which you can import into Acrobat 8 and 9 files.

d. Wavefront|Obj (OBJ)

What you'll learn in this lesson:

- The Mini Bridge panel
- New Puppet Warp Feature
- Adobe Repoussé
- Content Awareness Retouching

Adobe Photoshop CS5 New Features

In this section, you discover some of the new features of Photoshop. The features that are covered are broad and include improvements that affect print, web, 3D, and multimedia designers. The features are summarized in this chapter so that you can quickly find out what's new. Don't worry about comprehending all the new features, as many of these features, as well as other workflow improvements are incorporated into the lessons.

Mini Bridge

For those of you who love the power of Adobe Bridge, but don't like to exit Photoshop, you can now take advantage of Mini Bridge. Mini Bridge is essentially a scaled down version of Adobe Bridge. Much of the same functionality is in Mini Bridge, in fact you can not only organize your files, but perform other tasks such as batch actions and more.

You can access Mini Bridge by clicking on the Mini Bridge button (Mb) in the Application Bar, or choosing File > Browse in Mini Bridge, you can easily view and organize your files without exiting Photoshop. Some of the other tasks that you can take advantage of in Mini Bridge are as follows:

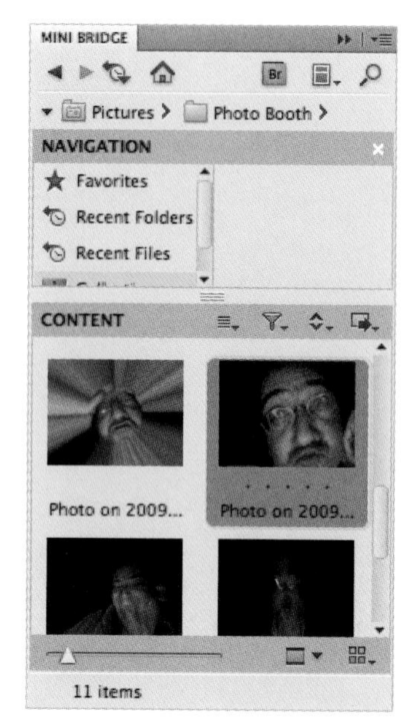

Use many of the features from Adobe Bridge, right in Photoshop with the new Mini Bridge.

By simply clicking on Search (⌕) in the upper-right of the Mini Bridge panel, you can take advantage of the Spotlight Search icon. Once you initiate the search you can change the search criteria from the Search drop-down menu.

Mini Bridge includes search capabilities.

Sort and rate items in the Content window by using the icons directly above the Content pane.

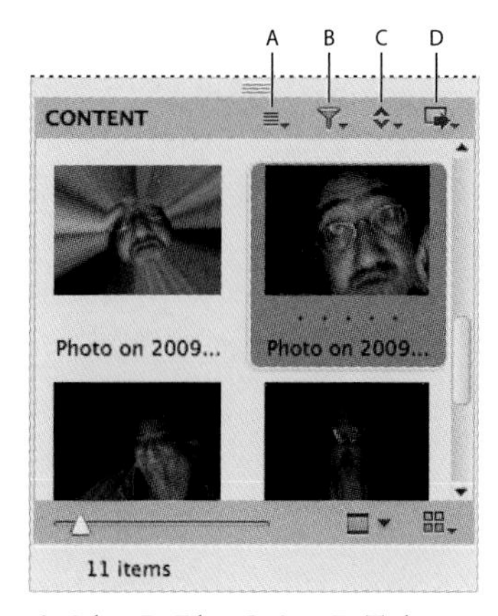

***A**. Select. **B**. Filter. **C**. Sort. **D**. Tools.*

Place files directly into Photoshop, or use other tools, such as Batch Actions.

Place files, or run batch actions on them in Mini Bridge.

In addition to taking advantage of the typical Adobe Bridge capabilities such as viewing recent files, and previewing, you can easily hop to the full version of Adobe Bridge by clicking on the Launch Bridge button (Br) in the upper right of the Mini Bridge panel. Find out more about the Mini Bridge in Lesson 3, "Using Adobe Bridge."

Puppet Warp

The Puppet Warp feature allows artists to warp objects using a skeleton that can have pins applied that can act as joints in the warp. You can use the Puppet warp feature for moving parts of an image, like adjusting an arm or leg, or creating interesting abstract effects by applying multiply warp points to one image and adjusting them individually. The Puppet Warp feature can be applied to layers that include, text, and vector layers; smart objects; and layer and vector masks. Find out more about the Puppet Warp feature in Lesson 1, "Exploring Photoshop."

Place pins in a mesh to control individual warp locations.

Turn 2D objects into 3D using Repoussé

Adobe Repoussé is a tool for turning 2D paths into 3D meshes. The term Repoussé is derived from the art creating a shaped metal piece by hammering from the reverse side. You can use the Repoussé feature to take a layer and add dimension.

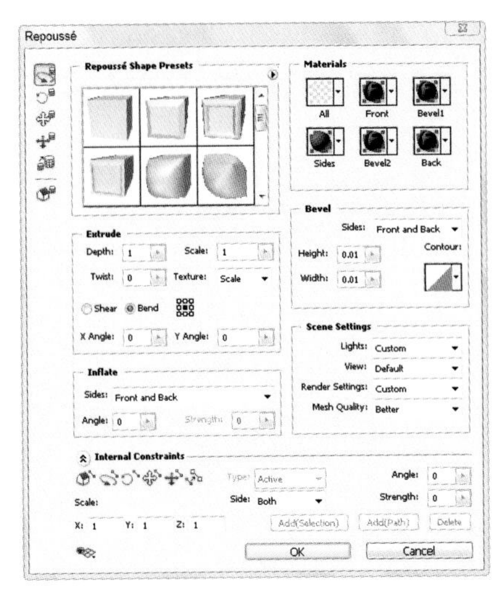

Apply 3D effects to 2D images by using Repoussé.

By selecting a text layer, or layer mask, work path or current selection, you can convert a 2D area in your image into a 3D mesh, offering you the ability to work with 3D features such as bevels, embosses, this is especially useful for creating 3D text effects.

Once in the Repoussé dialog box, you can apply a 3D preset to your object, or customize your own using the Materials, Extrude, Bevel, Inflate, Scent and Internal Constraints settings.

Content-Aware retouching

In Photoshop CS5, you can retouch complex images in just a stroke. The Content-Aware filling feature is not always perfect, but it does offer surprisingly accurate results when used to retouch images. You can use the new Content-Aware retouching feature by checking the Content-Aware radio box in the options of the Spot Healing Brush tool ().

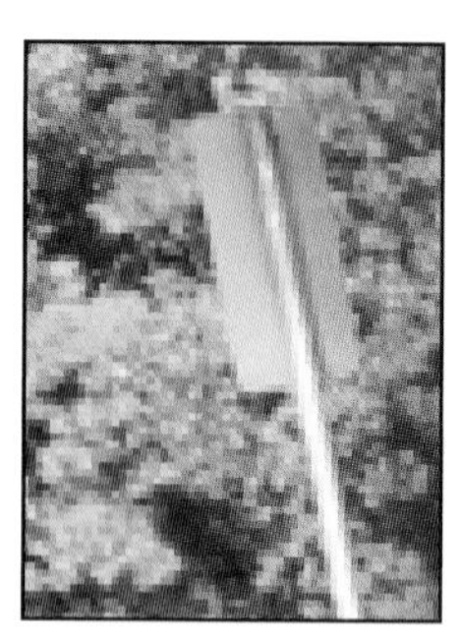

Using the Content-Aware feature you can quickly, and fairly accurately remove objects from your image.

Selections made easier

Select like a pro using the new and improved Refine Edge feature. Using the refine edge feature you can adjust a selection radius and even customize your selection further by taking advantage of the Refine Radius tool (). This can be especially helpful when creating selections of fur or hair. Find out more about the Refine Radius feature in Lesson 5, "Making the Best Selections."

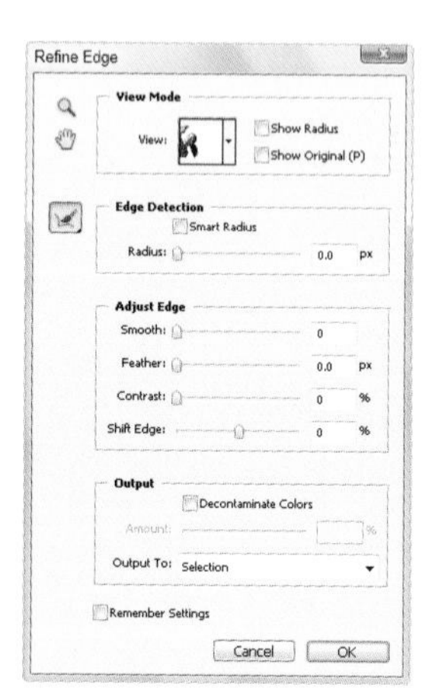

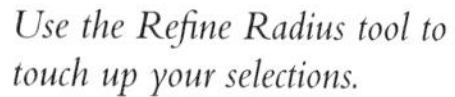

Use the Refine Radius tool to touch up your selections.

Brushing over edges builds a better selection.

Hopefully these features have inspired you to dive right into Photoshop CS5. As you progress through the lessons you will find additional enhancements, that have been added to Photoshop CS5. These enhancements will make your job of creating a stunning image a more streamlined and exciting process.

Index

Numerics

A

B

C

D

G

H

I

N

O

S

V

W

Y

Z

Wiley Publishing, Inc.
End-User License Agreement

READ THIS. You should carefully read these terms and conditions before opening the software packet(s) included with this book "Book". This is a license agreement "Agreement" between you and Wiley Publishing, Inc. "WPI". By opening the accompanying software packet(s), you acknowledge that you have read and accept the following terms and conditions. If you do not agree and do not want to be bound by such terms and conditions, promptly return the Book and the unopened software packet(s) to the place you obtained them for a full refund.

1. **License Grant.** WPI grants to you (either an individual or entity) a nonexclusive license to use one copy of the enclosed software program(s) (collectively, the "Software") solely for your own personal or business purposes on a single computer (whether a standard computer or a workstation component of a multi-user network). The Software is in use on a computer when it is loaded into temporary memory (RAM) or installed into permanent memory (hard disk, CD-ROM, or other storage device). WPI reserves all rights not expressly granted herein.
2. **Ownership.** WPI is the owner of all right, title, and interest, including copyright, in and to the compilation of the Software recorded on the physical packet included with this Book "Software Media". Copyright to the individual programs recorded on the Software Media is owned by the author or other authorized copyright owner of each program. Ownership of the Software and all proprietary rights relating thereto remain with WPI and its licensers.
3. **Restrictions on Use and Transfer.**

   (a) You may only (i) make one copy of the Software for backup or archival purposes, or (ii) transfer the Software to a single hard disk, provided that you keep the original for backup or archival purposes. You may not (i) rent or lease the Software, (ii) copy or reproduce the Software through a LAN or other network system or through any computer subscriber system or bulletin-board system, or (iii) modify, adapt, or create derivative works based on the Software.

   (b) You may not reverse engineer, decompile, or disassemble the Software. You may transfer the Software and user documentation on a permanent basis, provided that the transferee agrees to accept the terms and conditions of this Agreement and you retain no copies. If the Software is an update or has been updated, any transfer must include the most recent update and all prior versions.
4. **Restrictions on Use of Individual Programs.** You must follow the individual requirements and restrictions detailed for each individual program in the "About the CD" appendix of this Book or on the Software Media. These limitations are also contained in the individual license agreements recorded on the Software Media. These limitations may include a requirement that after using the program for a specified period of time, the user must pay a registration fee or discontinue use. By opening the Software packet(s), you agree to abide by the licenses and restrictions for these individual programs that are detailed in the "About the CD" appendix and/or on the Software Media. None of the material on this Software Media or listed in this Book may ever be redistributed, in original or modified form, for commercial purposes.
5. **Limited Warranty.**

   (a) WPI warrants that the Software and Software Media are free from defects in materials and workmanship under normal use for a period of sixty (60) days from the date of purchase of this Book. If WPI receives notification within the warranty period of defects in materials or workmanship, WPI will replace the defective Software Media.

(b) WPI AND THE AUTHOR(S) OF THE BOOK DISCLAIM ALL OTHER WARRANTIES, EXPRESS OR IMPLIED, INCLUDING WITHOUT LIMITATION IMPLIED WARRANTIES OF MERCHANTABILITY AND FITNESS FOR A PARTICULAR PURPOSE, WITH RESPECT TO THE SOFTWARE, THE PROGRAMS, THE SOURCE CODE CONTAINED THEREIN, AND/OR THE TECHNIQUES DESCRIBED IN THIS BOOK. WPI DOES NOT WARRANT THAT THE FUNCTIONS CONTAINED IN THE SOFTWARE WILL MEET YOUR REQUIREMENTS OR THAT THE OPERATION OF THE SOFTWARE WILL BE ERROR FREE.

(c) This limited warranty gives you specific legal rights, and you may have other rights that vary from jurisdiction to jurisdiction.

6. **Remedies.**

(a) WPI's entire liability and your exclusive remedy for defects in materials and workmanship shall be limited to replacement of the Software Media, which may be returned to WPI with a copy of your receipt at the following address: Software Media Fulfillment Department, Attn.: *Adobe Photoshop CS5 Digital Classroom*, Wiley Publishing, Inc., 10475 Crosspoint Blvd., Indianapolis, IN 46256, or call 1-800-762-2974. Please allow four to six weeks for delivery. This Limited Warranty is void if failure of the Software Media has resulted from accident, abuse, or misapplication. Any replacement Software Media will be warranted for the remainder of the original warranty period or thirty (30) days, whichever is longer.

(b) In no event shall WPI or the author be liable for any damages whatsoever (including without limitation damages for loss of business profits, business interruption, loss of business information, or any other pecuniary loss) arising from the use of or inability to use the Book or the Software, even if WPI has been advised of the possibility of such damages.

(c) Because some jurisdictions do not allow the exclusion or limitation of liability for consequential or incidental damages, the above limitation or exclusion may not apply to you.

7. **U.S. Government Restricted Rights.** Use, duplication, or disclosure of the Software for or on behalf of the United States of America, its agencies and/or instrumentalities "U.S. Government" is subject to restrictions as stated in paragraph (c)(1)(ii) of the Rights in Technical Data and Computer Software clause of DFARS 252.227-7013, or subparagraphs (c) (1) and (2) of the Commercial Computer Software - Restricted Rights clause at FAR 52.227-19, and in similar clauses in the NASA FAR supplement, as applicable.

8. **General.** This Agreement constitutes the entire understanding of the parties and revokes and supersedes all prior agreements, oral or written, between them and may not be modified or amended except in a writing signed by both parties hereto that specifically refers to this Agreement. This Agreement shall take precedence over any other documents that may be in conflict herewith. If any one or more provisions contained in this Agreement are held by any court or tribunal to be invalid, illegal, or otherwise unenforceable, each and every other provision shall remain in full force and effect.